Lifting the Veil

Also by Janet Farrar, Stewart Farrar, and Gavin Bone:

The Inner Mysteries
The Healing Craft
The Pagan Path
The Complete Dictionary of European Gods and Goddesses (with Glenn Tyler)

Also by Janet Farrar and Stewart Farrar:

A Witches' Bible: The Complete Witches' Handbook
The Witches' God
The Witches' Goddess
The Witches' Way
Eight Sabbats for Witches
Spells and How They Work
The Life and Times of a Modern Witch

Lifting the Veil

A WITCHES' GUIDE TO TRANCE-PROPHECY, DRAWING DOWN THE MOON, AND ECSTATIC RITUAL

Janet Farrar & Gavin Bone

Foreword by M. Macha NightMare

Acorn Guild Press
Portland, Oregon

About the Authors

Janet Farrar is one of the world's leading experts on the subject of Wicca. She is best known for her pioneering work with her late husband, journalist and author Stewart Farrar. Together, they produced some of the classics of modern Witchcraft, including *Eight Sabbats for Witches* and the best-selling *A Witches' Bible: The Complete Witches' Handbook*. Janet was initiated into Wicca in 1970 by Alex and Maxine Sanders, the founders of the Alexandrian Tradition.

Gavin Bone is the coauthor of *The Healing Craft, The Pagan Path,* and *The Complete Dictionary of European Gods and Goddesses* with his partner, Janet Farrar, and Stewart. A registered nurse, Bone is a natural spiritual (empathic) healer. He was initiated in 1985 into Raymond Buckland's Seax-Wica tradition. With Janet, he travels extensively, speaking and leading experiential workshops to sold-out audiences in the US, Europe, and Australia.

Published by Acorn Guild Press
4207 SE Woodstock Blvd # 168
Portland, OR 97206-6267
USA
http://www.acornguild.com/

Orders and review copies: (800) 888-4741

ISBN 978-1-936863-85-3

Cover art by John Collier, "Priestess of Delphi" (1891)
Figures and illustrations by Marc Potts, Tommy Lindeman, and Gavin Bone
Photo page 275 © 2016 Michel De Groot

Library of Congress Cataloging-in-Publication Data pending

Dedicated to the memory of Maureen Wheeler ("Aunty Bunty," 1938–2015), "a witch from the day she was born."

Contents

Appendices

Photographs and Illustrations

Photographs

Illustrations

foreword

Back in the days when most Witches and Pagans lived in the shadows of the broom closet, we had little contact with one another. There was mistrust. Because of the necessity for discretion—dare I say secrecy?—few practitioners of the Craft knew each other. Most of us feared being revealed. These fears were, in fact, well grounded. There was real danger of persecution or, at the very least, misappropriation. Today we're more visible, and in some segments of society accepted, although sometimes reluctantly.

Due to this wariness, opportunities for us to discuss and compare experiences and techniques were rare. As a result, there was little uniformity in the ways certain techniques, which I call "sacred technologies," were taught.

Nor did we have a commonly understood vocabulary for these various phenomena. I think there's a lot of confusion among terminologies. Add to that cultural differences and you don't have much cohesion; you lack a mutual language and understanding. The glossary in *Lifting the Veil* helps immensely, as does the entire book.

We know that 'mediumship' is not 'prophecy,' for instance; nor is 'Drawing Down' parallel to being 'ridden' by a *loa*. Thanks to the glossary provided herein, we have a vocabulary, if not necessarily universally agreed upon, that facilitates discussion about the material in this book.

In addition to lacking any corpus of proven practices, many individual practitioners achieved successful deity contact due to inherent talent rather than through a broader knowledge, and subsequent practice, of the particular sacred technology. This fact led to the mistaken conclusion that only certain gifted persons were capable of what we then called "Drawing Down."

My own knowledge lacked a solid foundation in Drawing Down and aspecting because at that time my primary teacher (who today is well known) was still developing her own teaching skills. As a result, at the first informal class I attended, when I was eight months pregnant, the teacher drew down the Goddess into my body, except that I had no clue and no preparation. So I stood there, receptive and listening, but hardly achieving a different state of consciousness.

From that class on, the teacher began invoking, or directing everyone present to invoke, deity into everyone present. I cannot attest that I felt it was especially moving, although I did, for the most part, love the words.

Following closely upon that practice, the pro forma practice became one priest/ess speaking words intended to imbue everyone in the circle with the presence of the particular deity being invoked.

It's always bugged me when I see individuals using the opportunity to 'carry' a deity for self-aggrandizement and ego. I'm sure readers have encountered similar situations. I'm sure you recognise when someone is faking it. Now it's understandable that a technique for manifesting the divine within a particular individual just doesn't work every time. And we Witches do have The Charge of the Goddess as a backup, as the authors discuss.

Once I attended an event put on by a local "psychic institute" that purports to teach such things as trance mediumship. Well, I have strong streak of skepticism, which I happen to think is beneficial when exploring spirito-magical worlds. So I view these events with something of a jaundiced eye. And what I witnessed earned my leeriness.

The "channelers" or "trance mediums," as they were called, sat in a row of chairs on an elevated stage, where alleged adepts stood behind them and waved their arms over the heads of each medium, perhaps spoke into their ears, and voila! a deity was assumed. I didn't see much change in visage. It was when these channelers (media?) began to speak, however, that my suspicions were confirmed. The language they used—I especially remember the channeling of ever-popular "Aphrodite"—was psychobabble, pretentious pseudo-psychological gibberish. It doesn't take an adept to spot a phony in such a scene.

I've also seen people speak authoritatively about something they deem must be done, being bossy and pushy and insisting it's the god making those demands. Such people avoid taking responsibility for their actions by blaming their bad behavior on the deity. Those present who are new to such activities tend to be more credulous, allowing such scammers to con them into believing what they see. But alas, the world is full of flim-flamming ego-trippers. It's best to avoid them.

On the other hand, when I've witnessed what I identify as genuine deity assumption, the human begins to move differently from her everyday way of walking, to speak in a different voice, to use language differently, and to display a change of visage. Often the person's "tender" or partner in the work needs to work hard to restore the person to a normal state of consciousness.

The effects upon a person ridden by a loa can be even more dramatic, and can require greater efforts on the part of those maintaining a normal state of consciousness to ease the 'horse' back to normalcy when the loa departs. In such cases, there is a tradition within the group; there is a community familiar with the phenomena and prepared to accept the change as well as to assist in reintegration.

The authors repeatedly remind the reader that humility is essential in order for anyone to genuinely achieve one of these nonordinary states. They emphasize the importance of mutual trust and understanding within a given group. Deity assumption and related states of consciousness are not, in my view, performance art. They require the surrender of individual consciousness, stepping aside from one's own personality, an ability to let go of personal masks. In other words, these techniques cannot be successful if they are ego-driven.

Asserting that ecstatic techniques of shamanism evolved and became incorporated into religions, Witchcraft in particular, the authors have explored mediumship, channeling, aspecting, Drawing Down, prophecy, and these many similar, related, and overlapping phenomena. They've provided useful information from around the world, from different historical times, in different locations (for some, such as oracles, are place-centered), in different ethnicities and religions, showing readers the universality of these different names for different but related phenomena and sacred technologies. This reminds us that religious traditions and their dogmas are human-made.

Also of great help to our understanding is the inclusion of reference to Nietzsche's theory of Apollonian and Dionysian approaches promulgated in his book *The Birth of Tragedy*. Although Nietzsche offered this theory to explain the dramatic arts, I find it's very useful in helping us—well, me, at least—understand different styles of religious practice and different approaches to teaching. The former tends to be more orthopraxic, the latter more ecstatic. Orthopraxy tends to be more predictable.

An Apollonian view tends toward distance and objectivity. Dionysian ecstatic practices, on the other hand, open participants to the unexpected, the extreme, to untamed wildness. The Dionysian does not invite analysis or quantification.

Generally, Witchcraft, if not other expressions of Paganism, tends to be orthopraxic: you perform certain specific acts, using prescribed language, and you achieve what you achieve—or not. Not every participant in a ritual will necessarily have the same experience as anyone else in the circle. The specific meanings and experiences of these rites are personal. This method eliminates the need for dogma.

The authors explore various approaches to achieving other-than-human states of consciousness, how to foster them, how to aide the changed-consciousness individual, how to restore one to normal consciousness (reground), how to evaluate the success, although what constitutes "success" is indeterminate and subjective. I am happy to see this book is a valuable addition to a growing corpus of work by many practitioners and thinkers about what our Pagan religions are all about.

M. Macha NightMare (Aline O'Brien)
Witch at large, activist, and ritualist
San Rafael, California
Midsummer 2015

Preface

"For mine is the ecstasy of the spirit ..."
—The Charge

In recent years, there has been an upsurge of interest in the subject of trance-prophecy within the neo-Pagan movement. It is perhaps important to first define what we mean by trance-prophecy, as undoubtedly there will be some reading this book who are unfamiliar with its modern practice. We use the term trance-prophecy to define a collection of methods found in many different traditions, ancient and contemporary. They embrace trance to connect to the divine in its different forms, the purpose of which is to communicate with divinity and ask for guidance. This can take the form of simple visualization exercises, such as pathworkings, all the way to full possession by the deity's spirit. It can also include ecstatic states on a personal level and as a group experience brought on by trance and ecstatic ritual. This is found in ancient traditions, such as the Dionysian practises of Greece and in contemporary traditions such as Vodoun, where the participant may be "ridden" by a *loa* (also spelled *lwa* or *lwha*, and pronounced "low-ha"), a deity or ancestral spirit. As we are writing this book primarily for Western neo-Pagans, we decided to title it *Lifting the Veil: A Witches' Guide to Trance-Prophecy, Drawing Down the Moon, and Ecstatic Ritual* for several reasons. We decided on *Lifting the Veil* as it refers to the red veil of the sibyl and seeresses of ancient times, particularly the Oracle at Delphi, while also being a secondary reference to "The Leviter Veslis"—the piece of prose originating from Gerald Gardner, which was the basis of Doreen Valiente's "Charge of the Goddess." We are, of course, not the first to use this as a title. Diane Champigny, one of the contributors to chapter 4, used it as the title of her contribution to the book *Priestesses, Pythonesses, Sibyls* (edited by Sorita d'Este. See Bibliography). We, therefore, believe that in all fairness we must give Diane credit to this title as much as ourselves. Of course, the "lifting" in the title suggests the intention of this book—to show the face of the sibyl, the face of the mystery of oracular work. While it is our intention to do this throughout the whole of this book, nothing sums up this statement more than chapter 4 where several practitioners of trance techniques "lift their own veils" and share their personal experiences with trance.

Initially we thought about titling this book *Diana's* or even "Hekate's Children." At first this may seem odd, but Diana, as Aradia, was present from the moment Gardner (and Valiente) conceived Wicca and gave it birth. Like all good organic works, it evolved beyond its initial working title. This is mainly because trance-prophecy goes beyond any one tradition of neo-Paganism. Our emphasis in this book is on Witchcraft and Wicca because it was the first neo-Pagan tradition,* excluding of course, contemporary traditions such as Vodoun, which has a trance technique built within its ritual structure.

Modern Witchcraft has had several 'aunts' and 'uncles' who have assisted its growth. From the aforementioned Gardner and Valiente, through to its rather eccentric Uncle Alex (Sanders), the esteemed Uncle Buckland, and on to the many competent teachers who did not just teach those entering into the Craft but have also guided its development and evolution. What was once Gardnerian and Alexandrian Wicca has evolved into other traditions of Witchcraft. Some have been more willing to explore and push the boundaries, which includes the areas of trance states. Diana, as Aradia, can be seen as the "Fairy-Goddess Mother" of this evolution. She acted as its inspiration, as well as the spiritual teacher who whispered words of guidance into the ears of her high priestesses during trance. Her inclusion in Wicca was very much due to the fact that the only truly traditional Witchcraft source material existent in the early days was from Leland's *Aradia*, which was first published in 1899 (although we accept that some still debate its origin and authenticity). Of course, as time went on, those within Wicca have realised that Diana was one of many goddesses of witchcraft. By the 1990s her job was done; now other deities were being embraced, not just those of the Western world, including Isis, Freya, Hekate, and Cerridwen, to name a few, but also those from other cultures: the

---

* We tend to use the terms Wicca and Witchcraft interchangeably throughout the book. This was common practice within our generation.

Durga of India, Kwan Yin of Buddhism, and the loa of Vodou, and orisha of Santeria. After all, spirituality knows no boundaries, and when our beloved Stewart (Farrar) described the world as "a global village" in the early '90s, he was not just talking about the social and material world but also spiritual. This has, of course, created a dilemma for those who are more comfortable embracing the Judeo-Christian paradigm of "boxing" and labelling the magical traditions of the West. What happens when a priestess of Isis channels an orisha such as Oshun? Should she say, "Sorry, you are not part of my tradition, go away!" or should she recognise that spirit and accept its validity? Some would say, "Well, that doesn't happen, does it?" But our experience, as well as that of others, is that this does occur. This is an important point to realise for anyone who is planning to study trance-prophecy seriously—it is a tradition of experience rather than one of academia or the human need to apply rules to the higher realms. What happens when the deity has other ideas? Who is right and who is wrong? Our view is that the deity-spirits make the choice, not many, and that traditions should change according to the experience of their practitioners. This is the divine nature of spiritual evolution.

A book based on experience will always have a subjective element to it. To use this book, it is necessary to discuss how we embarked on this strange journey, which, of course, gave us some advantages in understanding the subject. Janet's journey started from an early age when she began to get spirit manifestations in her garden in Leyton in the late 1950s. For Gavin, it was when he first entered a Spiritualist temple in the early 1980s to learn about healing. We shall go into more detail on this in the next paragraph, but for us, it has been a journey related to what we have believed to be at the core of Witchcraft: the experience of divinity, of God and Goddess; the union, both personal and divine, with the Ultimate, the Divine Spirit, which manifests around the world as the many faces of the divine: the gods and goddesses who gave birth to the cosmos. We independently made a connection with Freya, the Northern European Goddess more commonly known as a goddess of love and beauty. In her older form as Freya-Vanadis, she was the goddess of trance and prophecy, and much of what we know about Norse cosmology comes from one of her *valas* or seeresses. In fact, we would have little knowledge of Yggdrassil and its nine worlds if it was not for the one seeress whose words were put to paper as the Voluspa ("Song of the Seeress") in The Poetic Edda. We are dedicated as priestess and priest of Freya, acting as her servants and performing her wishes; and one of her wishes has been to speak and to allow the other deities to speak. She has not been the only one we have made connections with, although she remains our patroness. Hekate, Brid, and several others including those of Hindu and African origin have made their presence felt and made it clear to us that the old gods are "awakening" and want to communicate with us. This has very much become the focus of our work over the last decade: teaching that the deities of ancient paganism are real and wish to have their say in the world again after a gap of over one thousand years. With this connection comes the ecstatic experience hinted about in the title, an experience more often associated with shamanism. We are not the only ones, though, who have come to realise the importance of this work in the evolution of neo-Paganism: Diana Paxson, Jenny Blain, and Ivo Dominguez are all advancing neo-Pagan boundaries and encouraging reconnection with the divine.

As we mentioned, we feel it is important for the reader to understand our origins and the experiences we have had in dealing with spirituality. As most readers are aware, Janet was originally initiated into Wicca by Alex Sanders in the early 1970s. What most may not be aware of is that she was born a natural medium, although for years she had no idea that this was a gift. Her mother, Ivy, probably had "the sight," too, but as she died when her daughter was very young, Janet can only go by what her family has told her over the last ten years. It does seem that while she was in her mother's womb, her mother had an encounter with the spirit of a Druid, who pointed at the Ivy's pregnant belly and in the process nearly scared her half to death! Such was the furore this incident caused, that the police were called in to hunt for the strange intruder. It is surprising that Ivy wasn't incarcerated for the remainder of her pregnancy—well, you try telling the police about a bearded man wearing plaid and brandishing a sickle! It is interesting that her mother's ancestry was Southern Irish and her father was Welsh, traceable back to Owen Glyndwr, the Welsh Prince. Owen was a Druid and, if we are to believe the statement in Shakespeare's *Henry IV,* also a magician: "I can conjure devils from the vastly deep" was supposed to be one of his most famous statements. It is known that many of Janet's ancient ancestors died on the Isle of Anglesey attempting to protect the druidical stronghold against the Roman Governor Suetonius Paulinius in 60 CE. Even today, many modern Druids will spit at the mention of this Roman's name. Janet's father, Ron, a devout Christian, also had a little of the sight into the spirit world. When he encountered his first member of the *sídhe*, the Celtic otherworld people, his reaction was a mixture of delighted surprise and Christian blessings. "Well," he said, "they are God's children, too!" From the age of five through puberty, Janet saw many of the spirit forms we mention in this book including the Fey, departed human souls, and what at the time she believed to be angels. Initially this was clairvoyance; she experienced it in visions. Later she also heard them, developing clairaudience after many years. The first deceased human spirit who spoke to her was her next-door neighbour, Kathy, with whom she was very close. The week following her death, she materialised beside Janet's bed, kissed her on the cheek, and thanked her for the requiem she had cowritten with Stewart. (That same requiem appeared later in the book *A Witches' Bible*.) It is not surprising, therefore, that Janet took her abilities with her into Wicca. In fact, it was her innate mediumship abilities that attracted several occultists to Janet, as well as her ability to easily invoke specific goddesses into herself during the process of Drawing Down the Moon, which she had been taught in Alex and Maxine Sander's coven.

Gavin is not a natural medium, although he was born empathic and is energy sensitive, making him an effective spiritual healer. This is reflected in this book's sections on energy work, as the same gifts related to his healing also have worked to his advantage when acting as a *psychopompos*—a guide for those entering trance and descending into the underworld (see chapter 6). Although he had been attending Spiritualist Temple for some time, where he had been learning about spiritual healing, Gavin's first introduction to spirits came about after the first group ritual he was ever involved in. It was the mistakes of this group of would-be Witches, none over the age of twenty-four, with little knowledge of what they were doing, which started Gavin on his path in Wicca and in the realms of the spirits. It started with a mutual friend holding a dinner party, and resulted in a Samhain ritual on the south coast of England in the wind and pouring rain. When it was over, everyone was fine except for Gavin. He felt uneasy for a while afterwards, but he didn't know why. The group came together a couple of times after this to discuss the ritual. Someone pointed out that no circle was cast and that it seemed customary in most rituals to cast one. Gavin had walked away with company of a spirit nature; it was nothing serious, but it did prompt him to seek advice as the uneasiness grew. Your average person would not have had this problem, but Gavin was empathic, giving off energy that attracted such entities. It was easily cured by removing the lower-form entity through spiritual healing. On the positive side, this resulted in Gavin's introduction to his first magical group at the shop where he sought advice and healing. It was an interesting group of people. There were several spiritualist mediums, at least one of them being a Sufi practitioner, and a Cabalistic ritual magician. Gavin was the youngest member. For several months, Gavin worked with the group at every full moon. He got a real understanding of the importance of spirits in magical work. He discovered that it was not possible to separate working with spirits from magical practise. Mediums had always been incorporated into the Western Tradition of magic, although this was not Gavin's path in the long term. When he trained and qualified as a registered nurse, he realized he was, in fact, "sensitive" to spirits. This came about from his exposure to death on a regular basis; he quickly found himself assisting many of his dying patients to pass spiritually over to the other side, particularly those who had died suddenly without warning and were at risk of becoming trapped between worlds. This is a subject we felt was very necessary to cover in this book, as anyone sensitive to the gods and goddesses as spirit forms will also be sensitive to other spirit forms.

It became very apparent to us when writing this book that it was necessary to cover many overlapping subjects, which anyone embarking on an exploration of trance would inevitably have to study. Obviously, our emphasis comes from our Wiccan backgrounds, which means we naturally put an emphasis on Drawing Down the Moon, although in recent years we have moved away from more orthodox Wiccan practices, and embraced and experimented with other Pagan traditions to get to the root of the trance experience. In a subject so vast, it is easily possible to write several books on the topic of oracular work. We leave this to such accomplished writers on the subject as Diana Paxson (see chapter 3), and have decided instead to create a guide for Witches and neo-Pagans who are encountering the subject for the first time. It should not be considered a definitive study by any means. This book also indirectly asks one of the most important questions facing the growing neo-Pagan community today: What is the ultimate purpose of spirituality and religion? For most people who decide to walk the spiritual path, this question is answered by their desire to connect with the divine, which manifests in Paganism as the myriad forms of gods and goddesses, past and present, found in the ancient and modern cultures around the world. It is the reason we came into Witchcraft, not for spells or magic, but to attain that connection, that feeling of union with a higher purpose—union with the Ultimate. The reality is that some will have the ability to connect more than others. Such people became the seers of the ancient religion of paganism, the priesthood. Their role was to connect for their communities, and relay messages from the spirits to their tribe or village.

The roots of the techniques, methods, and training systems we describe in this book started as a series of workshops in 2002 (the Inner Mysteries intensives), which quickly developed into full-on teaching of trance-prophecy in extended workshops, with amazing results. We discovered an untapped wealth of talent within the neo-Pagan community, and had experiences that few would believe, unless of course, you were there! Initially, the focus was on the Wiccan rite of Drawing Down the Moon, but as time went on, it became something more. The focus of these workshops taught four main things: working with magical energy, spiritual cosmology, the nature of deity, and the application of trance states in Drawing Down the Moon. While the first two—energy and cosmology—were originally used to give an underlying frame to ritual practise, it became very obvious that these subjects were applicable to the understanding and practise of trance-prophecy. As our experiences grew, it quickly became about applying an underlying system that could be used to teach anyone from any neo-Pagan background how to trance-prophesy. From all four core teachings, developed what we now call the *Four Keys to Trance-Prophecy* (outlined in chapters 7, 8, 9, and 10). We would like to point out that although many elements are of ancient origin, it is a modern system we have developed ourselves over the years. Apart from teaching a core system of trance that underlies most traditions, it was also important to teach it in a safe, controllable way. Quite simply put, if you aren't ready for the experience and are in danger in any way by doing it, it won't happen, as the techniques taught in the Four Keys have built-in safety mechanisms. Do the work, and what we teach here in this book will work for you in a safe manner. The same is true of the other method that we developed originally for teaching Drawing Down the Moon: the Underworld Descent Technique (chapter 11). Depending on your level of competency, this either works as a pathworking or as a method of trance induction. It is at the core of our training in trance and deity-connection techniques and, like the Four Keys, will only work on a higher level for you if you are ready to experience it. But when you are ready, the training you have learnt through these systems will enhance the experience and make it more controllable. This is important, as the subject of trance has always invoked strong emotions in many people; we are brought up in a society that teaches us to be in control rather than to "let go."

Western culture has either encouraged us to dismiss the spirit world as fantasy or, if we are accepting of it, to be terrified of contact with it. It is something many neo-Pagans find themselves wresting with when they first become involved in trance-prophecy practises. It may seem strange to say this, but subconsciously we have been programmed to see communication with this realm as losing control of reality. For many, this is the realm of "maya," of illusion. It means when first encountering someone who has the ability to talk to spirits in trance, we do one of two things: either dismiss the seer out of hand as needing possible counselling for psychiatric problems or, if we come into direct spirit contact, our reaction is one of fear, influenced more often than not by our monotheistic upbringing. We enter a state of fear and paranoia from a belief that we are possessed by an undesirable entity or 'demon.' This happens because our modern culture generally fails to recognise or accept that we humans have been surrounded by elemental forms, the dead, the gods, and many other perfectly joyous but invisible life-forms from the day we are born. We can honestly say that in all the years we have practised the magical arts, we have only once ever had to deal with a genuinely malevolent force. This was generated by a young alcoholic Witch with an axe to grind; this force being nothing more than an extension of his negative emotional state.

We do feel it important to point out that some of the traditional methods employed in native shamanistic techniques, particularly the use of hallucinogens, are fraught with dangers. While we are in no way prejudiced against the methods used in these aboriginal cultures, we do feel the use of herbal and fungal preparations, such as psilocybin mushrooms or ayahuasca, apart from their obvious illegality in some states, can have negative effects on the physical, mental, and psychic well-being of the Western practitioner of magic. We, therefore, cannot condone their use in any way. Any reference to them to them is purely for academic and anthropological reasons.

Regardless of your background, whether you are on an eclectic path or practising a specific tradition, whether you are a beginner or have been practising for many years, our hope is that even if you do not practise trance-prophecy, this book will be enlightening purely for its historical and magical aspects. And, of course, we hope that it will inspire you, the reader, to engage in the exercises we have outlined in this book in a safe way, therefore advancing the evolution of neo-Pagan practise.

No introduction would be complete without thanking all those who have contributed to the book. There are many. Courtney Weber, Tamirha Richardson, Gayleen Jacobs, Gede Parma, Susi Auth, Jaimie Plasiance, Diane Champigny, and Lora O'Brien, plus those not mentioned who are quoted throughout the book. Special thanks goes to those who took the time to read and check our work: Monte Plaisance for his help with the Greek language; Mary Caliendo for her help with the tantric aspects; our beloved Miriam, who did the first read through; and Macha NightMare for writing the foreword. Our thanks goes to all. Blessed be.

April 2016   Janet Farrar and Gavin Bone
                                              Hernes Cottage
                                              KELLS
                                              Co Meath
                                              Ireland

Part I

The History of Trance in Ancient and Contemporary Pagan Spiritual Tradition

Chapter 1

Sibyls and Shamans: Ecstasy and Trance in Ancient Times

On the east coast of Ireland, the green rolling hills and the agriculture that has gone on for centuries form a valley less than thirty minutes from where we live. At the bottom of the valley flows the mighty River Boyne. Her rushing torrent flows through many of the counties in Ireland, finally entering in to the Irish Sea at the estuary, just past the town of Drogheda. This river was sacred; it was sacred before the English came; it was sacred before the Normans and the Vikings came; and it was sacred before the Sons of Mil, the *Keltoi* or Celts, came. As you stand on the south side of the River Boyne, you see a sight that isn't seen anywhere else in the world: a white wall of rain-polished quartz reflecting the sunlight back at you. This great wall is the face of *Brugh na Boyne*, or as it is more commonly known today, New-grange. There is a predominant myth about Newgrange: it was the palace of Boann, the goddess of cattle and fecundity, which the Dagda, the Good God, gave to her. Eventually, Aengus Og, the god of wisdom and youth, wrestled it from her, but it remains named after her even today, and the area is still sacred.

Newgrange is a passage tomb that was constructed of quite a few hundred tons of rock over several generations. This burial mound nestles in the heart of Boyne Valley, where it broods expectantly, waiting for the sun to rise every winter solstice, its phallic rays piercing the vulva of the stone-mantled entrance, guaranteeing fertility of the cattle and crops of the ancient peoples who built it and lived in the Boyne Valley. At least once a year, or possibly more, the spirit-man or woman of the tribe would enter the cruciform chamber. But who were these peoples? Where did

3

they come from? Nobody really knows, but they were travellers from the
east, not the red- and blonde-headed Irish Celts that we see today. Rather, they were swarthy, dark Eurasians, possibly even relatives of today's
Saami-Lappish, Siberian, and Tunguska tribes. It was from them that the
first spiritual and magical practises came to Ireland, as well as the rest
of Europe. This was the cult of ecstasy and trance that is now commonly
called "shamanism."

But Newgrange is more than a tomb. To quote Stewart Farrar, in
his sometimes gruff voice: "To call Newgrange a 'tomb' would be to
call Westminster Abbey a family crypt." It is a place where two worlds
meet, where spirit touches the mundane world of man; where man can
communicate with the world of the ancestors. Back in the mists of time,
this journey began with a boat ride across the sacred river, what is now
known as the River Boyne. This reflected in Greek myth of Charon ferry-
ing the dead across the river Acheron. Then there was the climbing of the
great stone, decorated in spirals and diamonds, which marks the passing
into the transitory realm between life and death. Finally, there was the
journey down the passage into the very heart of the dark, cold structure;
a path which weaves like a serpent, narrowing as it descends into the
central chamber. Carved on the stones on either side of this path are the
patterns of journeying, the same spirals and diamonds found on the great
entry stone, but also others more sublime.

Upon entering the chamber, the spirit-man found himself looking up
at the great corbelled roof made of spiralling slabs. A roof that even today is jokingly referred to as "the driest in Ireland." On both sides and
straight ahead were the alcoves, where the remains of the ancestors were
laid. These remains had been burnt, and powdered before being sorted
into the stone basins found in each alcove. The skulls had been fractured
at the back by a small marble hammer so that the spirit could leave, for
this place was a place of the spirits; a place where the spirit-man could
commune with them for the benefit of the tribe. This is where he could
ask for their advice or assistance by entering a state of trance induced
by chanting, wafting incense, and possibly by the use of hallucinogenic mushrooms, which grow abundantly in the valley around the River
Boyne.

We do not know if the spirit-man returned to the world possessed by
one of the spirits that he communed with, but it is a possibility, as we
know that these same people were responsible for spreading shamanistic
practises of prehistory. They were the shamans who dressed as deer, with

skin and antlers, as we can see in the cave painting of Les Trois Frères in France, or of which we have accounts of from the Russian Steppes. Here the shaman was believed to be possessed by the spirit of the animal; the animal god, the Horned God, so that he could hunt his prey successfully. By doing so, he became both the hunter and the hunted, as he danced feverishly and ecstatically around the fire, while the men of the tribe symbolically killed him as part of the rites. During that time, he was the God who uttered predictions not only for the hunt, but also for the tribe in general, as the God-Spirit relayed messages to him in his ecstatic trance state. As time went on, the adorning of the animal skins and antlers would be used not just for the hunting rites, but also for magical practises such as healing when the power of the God-Spirit was needed. Although these were powerful experiences for the men of the tribe, they could not rival the effect the Goddess-Spirit of the Moon was having on the women folk of his tribe. The women seemed to enter such trance states more easily without the help of the mushroom spirits, which the men sometimes used to aid them.

The moon has always had a fascination for a man, and more importantly for a woman. It governs the flow of water, the tides of the sea, and the rising of the rivers. It was not long before a woman realised that there was a relationship between this heavenly body of the night and her monthly cycle of fertility and menstruation. She also realised that there were times when she was more intuitive and more psychic due to its influence; an effect that was lost on her father, her brothers, and her lovers. At its fullest, this Goddess of the heavens could induce some women to trance; to see visions more clearly than even the most accomplished shaman of the tribe. Sometimes they even became possessed by this dark Goddess-Spirit of the Moon and night, uttering prophecies and warnings, which even the most foolhardy would be stupid to ignore; those women become oracles. These oracles gained fame for their abilities, and were often visited from far and wide, which was customary around the Mediterranean. Of course, some oracles also travelled. This was the case in Northern Europe, where travelling was more limited due to geography and weather conditions. It was here that *seidr* or *seith* developed and continued to be practised for several centuries among what are known today as Germanic peoples. Undoubtedly a similar cult developed among the Celts, but little is known of these practises since not much was recorded. The early practises of German peoples were recorded by the Romans, most notably by Julius Caesar himself:

When Caesar inquired of his prisoners, wherefore Ariovistus did not come to an engagement, he discovered this to be the reason — that among the Germans it was the custom for their matrons to pronounce from lots and divination whether it were expedient that the battle should be engaged in or not; that they had said, 'that it was not the will of heaven that the Germans should conquer, if they engaged in battle before the new moon.' (*Commentarii de Bello Gallico*, Book 1, paragraph 50)

The Roman historian Tacitus describes a possible cult center in his work *Germania*, connected to the goddess Nerthus. Such centers were rare and not as common as the oracle centers of Greece and the classical world. The Northern oracles suffered at the hands of the Romans, as well as Christianity. The Northern European *völva* or *vala*, as she was known, was more likely to have travelled from village to village with her entourage during the seasonal cycles, rather than remaining in one place. On arrival at a settlement, she would often be perched on a high hill or on a platform specially built for her, where she would enter trance and answer questions prophetically, giving guidance on everything from planting crops to birth. This practise continued up until the early medieval period, with the last recorded vala practising in Iceland in the thirteen century.

The late demise of seidr practises among the Viking settlers of Iceland is pertinent for anyone studying trance-prophecy. And while there is some recorded history on these techniques, it does not come anywhere near the wealth of information we can obtain from the practises of Greece and the classical world. Even for modern seidr practitioners, those practises remain an important source of information on techniques and methods.

Alexander the Great and Siwah:
The Oracles and Their Rise to Power

During the time of Alexander the Great (356 BCE to 323 BCE), it was said that there were ten known oracles in the world, which at that time stretched from the Western Mediterranean to the Black Sea. These were

- the Libyan sibyl at Siwah, Libya;
- the Delphic oracle at Mount Parnassus, Greece;
- the Cumaean sibyl on the Bay of Naples, Italy;
- the Samian sibyl on the Island of Samos, Greece;
- the Cimmerian sibyl, Crimea;
- the Erythraean sibyl, North East Africa;

- the Tiburtine sibyl, Rome;
- the Hellespontian sibyl at Marpessus, Greece;
- the Phrygian sibyl, Anatolia; and
- the Persian sibyls.

At these oracular centers, the prophetesses of the old religion of paganism plied their trade with the common persons, as well as the rulers of kingdoms. Empires and kings rose and fell according to the oracles' prophecies, and the known world waited with baited breath at what their next words would be. Of course, there were some who doubted the prophecies, but few of them were willing to put these doubts into words in case they angered the gods, as each oracular prophet was a priestess or priest of one of the gods.

When Alexander the Great was young, his father, King Philip II of Macedonia, visited the Oracle at Delphi. It was predicted to him that his son, Alexander would one day rise to greatness and become one of the greatest rulers the world has ever known. In 332 BCE, Alexander, stirred by this prediction, visited the oasis of Siwah. His purpose was to consult the oracle of Ammon, and ask for guidance on how to defeat the all-powerful Persian army. This was one of the oldest-known oracles in the ancient world, having origins with one of the oldest-known seeresses, the wife of Ammon, or "God's Wife." This role in Egyptian society can be traced back as far as the Tenth Dynasty, 1470 BCE, and was always held by women of non-noble birth who served the gods Min, Amun, or Ptah. In the later kingdom, this position was changed, and it was then held by the wife or mother of the king. Going forward, there seems to be no evidence of oracular function, but this doesn't necessarily mean that it didn't take place. By the Twenty-Fifth Dynasty (747 BCE) there certainly is evidence of an oracle performing a prophetic role, but it was still primarily a political office and was often combined with that of the chief priestess of Amun. The oracular function was no doubt used to maintain the established political order, as any political decisions were always confirmed by the oracle through prophesies. As a child, Alexander had been brought up on the myth that both Heracles (Hercules) and Perseus had consulted this oracle before achieving greatness. His journey to the oracle was not uneventful: according to Ptolemy, Alexander and his entourage were escorted by two snakes which led them to the oracle, a place which was not easy to find among the shifting sands of the desert. Another account by Aristobulus states that they were escorted by two crows. Regardless, these signs and the subsequent prophecy from the oracle were seen as being divine intervention, which was to herald his conquering of the Persian army and led to him ruling one of the greatest empires of the ancient world.

The oracles gained such power and prestige due to the power of the human mind and the spiritual will of the individual. Many of the techniques used in classical times can still be found today in cultures we call shamanistic or magically trance-orientated: the Saami-Lappish, Native-American, the peoples of the South-American Rainforest, and the African diaspora religions of Vodoun and Santeria. This is because the oracles themselves originally derived from a time before the classical religions of Greece, Rome, or Persia appeared. The core of this practise was a belief in spirits of plants and animals, a belief in animism; that the world itself is alive, every stone and every object, animate or inanimate. From this simple belief developed the idea that it was possible to communicate with spirits, to ask them for help and guidance. Initially, the oracles were simple village people, prophesying for the tribe by communicating with the ancestors, the spirits of the dead, and with the many spirits of nature. As the belief in the classical gods and goddesses developed, they began to communicate with these "greater spirits" and convey their messages and their will to the people. The prophets passed their techniques down to their students, and news spread of their abilities far and wide. Soon they were not just divining for their people, but also for visitors and foreign dignitaries. The time of the great oracles had been born, and what was once a simple village, became a thriving temple of stone dedicated to the god or goddess of the oracle. Still at this time, the deities of trance were the goddesses of the earth—chthonic underworld deities, such as Gaea and Hekate. This was to change with the coming of the new gods and goddesses of order and light, such as the Olympian Apollo, whose priesthood suppressed the Dionysian rites of the old oracular goddesses.

Delphi and the Sibyls: From Dionysos to Apollo

The Oracle at Delphi remains one of the most famous and written about of the ten oracles in Greece and the ancient world. It is for this reason the oracle of Delphi is one of the most important ones to study when embarking on the practise of trance-prophecy. Delphi, positioned in lower central Greece, was neither the oldest, nor was it originally the most senior oracular site. It became important simply because of geography; its position was central to the major city-states of ancient Greece, which made it easily accessible to everyone. The oracle and the associated temples that surrounded it can still be found on the side of Mount Parnassus and in the Valley of Phocis, close to the Gulf of Corinth. From about 1400 BCE different peoples settled in the area, including the Minoans. This helped infuse the area with different cultures, which by 1000 BCE created a unique ecstatic tradition. Apart from the central figure of a seeress and the use of trance, the rites had little in common with what most classical writers wrote about after the eighth century. It was originally the site of a Dionysian cult, the memory of which was to continue in local myth: Apollo ruled the summer months, and Dionysos ruled the hillsides during the winter months. Originally the oracle was situated in a cave at Lykorei, some miles up the mountain from the valley. This is a common pattern in the spiritual cosmology of Europe, with entrances to the underworld commonly found on the side of mountains in the form of a cave. Where such caves were not present, as in the British Isles, passage tombs were constructed to perform the same role.

The Temple to Apollo was built in 650 BCE, with other buildings and structures slowly being added to the temple complex (see Photograph 1). It was destroyed by an earthquake in 373 BCE and rebuilt forty-three years later. It was built in the same style as a Doric hexastyle temple, with the classic thirty columns in two rows on the three-step platform, or *crepidoma*. It was by climbing these that you reached the inner *hestia*, or hearth, where the eternal flame to Apollo burnt. Here was where the lower central chamber was situated—the *adyton*, where the seeress, the sibyl, sat, making her the central focus of the structure. The adyton measured only nine-by-twelve feet, and was reserved for the sibyl, the priesthood, acolytes of the oracle and, of course, those who had come to ask their questions. The oldest part of the complex was the *omphalos stone,* which represented "the navel of the earth." It was kept in its original place, even though it dated to the pre-Apollonian period. In 586 BCE, a hippodrome, a gymnasium, baths, and accommodations were added for the athletes taking part in the Pythian Games. The Amphictyony League, a political and religious confederation of Greek states, added more treasuries. The most impressive was the Athenian Treasury, which was built to commemorate the Athenian victory at the Naval Battle of Salamis against the Persians in 480 BCE.* Even though zealous Christians destroyed much of the temple complex in the fourth century, the foundations of many buildings remain. Many were excavated from the eighteen century onwards.

---

* According to the historian Pausanias, the oracle told the Athenians to put their faith in the "wooden walls," which was interpreted to mean their naval ships. Although they were heavily outnumbered, they heeded this advice and destroyed the Persian navy.

Photograph 1: The Temple of Apollo in Delphi, Greece
(Courtesy www.dreamstime.com)

Most writers on the classical period state that Delphi was a site of worship of "the Earth Goddess,"[1] although only a few have given her a name. The site therefore links these practises to those in Northern Europe where Earth goddesses, such as Nerthus are also linked with prophecy. This suggests a common connection between earth goddesses and prophecy throughout Europe. She has been conflated with the Titan goddess Gaea or Rhea, even though there is plenty of evidence linking the oracle to the earlier cult of the Cybelean Siburi. The title *Siburi* means "cave dweller," a term originating from Sumeria. A Siburi led Gilgamesh into the underworld, just as Medea later led Jason to recover the Golden Fleece in the classic story. Medea is clearly a *sibyllae* or *sibyl*; a prophetic priestess of Hekate. The term *sibyl*, in fact, derives from the word Siburi,* who were priestesses of the ecstatic cult of Inanna in ancient Sumeria (4000 BCE). Over the centuries, the Goddess Cybele was to emerge out of this cult, taking on many of its aspects. The cults of Hekate and Cybele were later to merge. Both goddesses

---

* *Siburi* later became the word *siburu*. Over time this became *sybelle* and finally the Greek word *sibyllae*. This also shows a clear link with the Goddess name Cybele.

hold Innana's keys to the three worlds. The links with Dionysus and the maenads through this cult of ecstasy suggest that priestesses of Delphi were originally dedicated to Cybele's service. A Boeotian plate found at Delphi dating from the middle of the fifth century supports this theory. The plate shows the Earth Goddess seated on her throne in front of the famous omphalos stone. She holds poppy heads, ears of wheat and, most importantly, a flaming torch. The poppy heads are clearly linked to ecstatic narcotic states, while the ears of wheat may be connected with the fertility nature of the Earth Goddess and the goddess Demeter. It is this last item, the torch, which is of importance. It is associated with Persephone, the daughter of Demeter, descending in to the underworld, as an aspect of Hekate and the earlier Cybele.[2] In support of this, from about 550 BCE, the site became associated with Artemis of Eleusis, who had also merged with Hekate "to hold power equally in heaven and under the earth. Men paid honour to her both in association with her musician brother Apollo at the famous cult centers of Delos and Delphi and in combination with Hekate at crossroads as lunar and infernal deity. Above all else, however, Artemis was the divine symbol of chastity and its guardian."[3]

The chaste nature of Artemis, no doubt, appealed to the patriarchal priesthood of Apollo. This association creates an interesting link between the modern Wiccan practise of Drawing Down the Moon (see chapter 12) and the Oracle at Delphi, as Artemis is, of course, the Etruscan Diana. Her association with Hekate, the Goddess of the three realms of heaven, the underworld, and the sea, were to further link the oracle with the earlier ecstatic period of the site. Eventually the cults of Cybele, Hekate, Persephone, and Artemis were all to be absorbed by the cult of Isis as the Great Mother Goddess during the Roman period. During the early years of the first millennium, Isis finally took over from Artemis in Delphi, Eleusis and Delos. Regardless of which name the Goddess took at Delphi, she was an ancient underworld goddess of ecstatic trance, whose chosen priestesses were, like the Suburi of Sumeria, young women who had just reached sexual maturity. Although goddess names may have changed, up until 800 BCE, there was clearly a continuing cult at Delphi which centered on an underworld goddess, whose symbolism changed very little over the centuries. The history of Delphi before the coming of the priesthood of Apollo is therefore essential to anyone analyzing the origins of trance-prophecy. Historically, it was a feminine ecstatic cult, and to use Nietzche's term, a *Dionysian* one. The psychologist Nietzche used this term to define ecstatic ritual and ceremony in the form of theatre, just as he defined organised structured theatre as *Apollonian.*

By the seventh century, Delphi had become the most famous and most powerful oracular site in the known world, with visitors coming from everywhere, seeking the wisdom of the seeresses who prophesised there. Political changes resulted in Delphi being declared independent from the Phocians, who ruled it previously. The seat of the Amphictynoy League was transferred to Delphi. It was at this time that the patriarchal Apollonian priesthood finally had the opportunity to completely usurp the ecstatic feminine cult. The oracle center moved from the Lykorei cave, where it had once been situated, into the temple itself, which had carefully been built over the same system of volcanic fissures as the original cave. By shifting the oracle into a temple, they were able to reorganise and take over the internal workings of the oracle. These changes were rationalised in several myths, designed to explain the god Apollo's right to be in charge of the oracle. According to the primary myth, found in the Homeric *Hymn to Apollo,* he took control of the area around Mount Parnassus when "the Gods of the sky vanquished the Gods of the earth," symbolised in the myth by the infant Apollo killing the python, the dragon snake, who clearly represented the original ecstatic Earth Goddess, Gaea. This is important, because according to the myth, after Apollo's victory, a dolphin swam out to a passing boat and chose its crew as his new priesthood for the oracle. Apollo represented the new patriarchal order of self-control and reason, which saw the excesses of the past as a threat to established order. The priesthood had never approved of the sexual excess which took place, or the lack of priestly control. Apollo was, after all, a god of moderation in all things. The older nature of the oracle could not be subdued completely; it was said that when Apollo wasn't present, Pan played in the woods around the shrine, and the seeresses retained for some time their older title of pythia or pythoness.

It is said that after Apollo had slayed the python, its body fell into the volcanic fissure that the oracle was built around. Its decaying body created the fumes, which put the seeresses into trance. Symbolically, we see within the myth the descent of the seeress into the underworld (Jung's realm of *Shadow*), with Apollo and his priesthood controlling the process (the ego), as opposed to the previously frenzied ecstatic practises. Prior to Apollo's arrival, the priestesses were young, just having reached sexual maturity. Their duties included sexual rites, as part of the fertility cult which existed there. Under the new Apollonian rule, this was changed.

The pythoness was chosen from "virtuous" local women over the age of fifty, known to have had a blameless life, and according to Herodotus, "thus insuring that oracle would be inspired by Apollo and not by a woman's love." The name was also changed from Pytho to Delphi after Apollo's transformation into a dolphin (Greek: *delphis*),* and the term *pythoness* was slowly replaced over time with the term *sibyllae*.

Another myth cited to justify these changes was the myth of Apollo and Daphne, the daughter of the poet Teiresisa. In the myth, Apollo falls in unrequited love with Daphne and grants her the gift of prophecy, thus making her one of the sibyls at Delphi. Her father's long life inspired Daphne to ask Apollo for eternal life. Apollo grants her wish "for as many years of life as she has grains of dust in her hand." While she believed that she fooled the love-struck god, Apollo refused to grant her the accompanying gift of eternal youth, as his love for her had been rejected. She slowly withered away until there was so little left of her that she could be hung upside down in a bottle. When asked what she wished for, all she would say was that she wished to die. In this way, the Apollonian priesthood could justify their changes in age of the seeresses and their right to control their activities.

When seekers arrived at the Apollonian Delphi,† they paid a fee to the priesthood before purifying themselves at the Castalian spring, which emerged from the nearby rock face. They then continued on their journey along the sacred way, which led up to the hill. As they followed the zigzagging path, their eyes were drawn to the shrines, statues, and offerings that lined the way up to the oracle. Dignitaries of cities presented most of these offerings as a thank you for advice obtained from the sibyl, which proved to be fruitful. Upon reaching the Temple of Apollo, pilgrims would make sacrificial offerings of sheep or goats, close to the omphalos stone. The priests of Apollo who were present would then perform augury; divination on the entrails of the offered animals to see if there were any omen present. One by one, the travellers were allowed to enter the oracular temple to ask the sibyl their questions. As they entered the temple, they would have seen sayings inscribed on the columns, including "Know thyself" and "Nothing in excess," which survived as commonly used maxims to this day. Inside the temple, the seeker was led to the sibyl

---

* *Pytho* comes from the Greek, meaning "to rot." It is likely that this is a reference to the smell that emanated from the volcanic fissure, as well as the smell believed to emanate from the underworld.

† The later Delphi, after the ecstatic practises at Lykoria had ceased.

in the adyton. It was dimly lit by oil lamps, illuminating the seeress who
sat on a stool above the volcanic vent in the rocks. Plutarch attributed
the power of prophecy to the volcanic fumes, which emerged from the
fissures. According to one story, the decision for the temple to be built
there was because a farmer found that one of his goats had succumbed
to the fumes. This was considered an auspicious sign by the priesthood,
who decided to build the antechamber used for the oracle over the chasm
where the fumes had emerged. When in 1927 French geologists found
no sign of any fumes of chasm, the story was dismissed as purely myth.
But after a four-year study at the end of the 1990s, a geological survey
published in *Geology* magazine discovered that there were, in fact, two
faults, which intersected each other.[4] These released hallucinogenic gases,
to quote Professor Diane Harris-Cline of George Washington University:
"Ethylene inhalation is a serious contender for explaining the trance and
behaviour of the Pythia."*

Until recently ethylene was used in operating theatres as a general
anaesthetic. In the confined space of the oracle, it would undoubtedly
have resulted in the seeress entering a deeper euphoric trance state
than when she prophesied in the cavern at Lykorei. This would have
also prevented any of the earlier, more active ecstatic rites, as she now
became more dependent on the priesthood. Next to the seeress stood a
three-legged brazier on which bay leaves were burnt, which had a similar euphoric effect. Speaking from experience, this would have made a
pleasant crackling sound, as the leaves were placed on the brazier by
the priests of Apollo, standing on either side of the seeress, ready to
translate her sometimes cryptic answers. The whole oracular chamber
was full of symbolism: the three legs of the brazier could be seen to
represent the sacred three—the Fates or Moerae—as well as the three
oracular centers of Delphi, Dodona, and Delos. There is a suggestion
that if one included the rear of the chamber, the legs represented the
four elements and the four directions, as well as being dedicated to
specific goddesses, but there is little to substantiate that.[5] The seeker
would ask their question directly to the seeress or allow the priesthood
of Apollo to ask it for them. In earlier times, when the oracle was still in
the cavern at Lykorei, the situation was very different with the seeress
preempting the questions and approaching the seeker directly during
a rite, which included singing, dancing, and drumming. The rites were

---

* The use of ethylene gas in this way is potentially fatal, and we cannot recommend
the use of this or other hallucinogenic preparations in this way (see Preface).

more conservative, with any replies being directly interpreted by the male priesthood. Direct contact between the seeker and the seeress as she fell into an intoxicated trance state was forbidden; while in the past this would have been a sexually charged moment. It was in this trance state, what the ancient Greeks referred to as *katoché*,* that the spirit of Apollo possessed the sibyl.

Before Apollo, the sibyl would have been in communication with the original Earth Goddess. It would have undoubtedly been a full possession rather than an act of mediumship; the seeress was possessed or "enthused" (where we get our modern word enthusiasm) with the spirit of the Goddess. In the later period, of course, it merely became an act of what we now call "channelling," where the spirit of Apollo entered but did not fully possess the seeress while she was affected by the ethylene fumes. In this state, she would have at best spoken in cryptic riddles, and at worse in an unintelligible babble which was interpreted by the priests of the temple into an elegant form of hexameter verse. Heraclitus describes this process: "The Sibyl, with frenzied mouth uttering things not to be laughed at, unadorned and unperfumed, yet reaches to a thousand years with her voice by aid of the God."[6] Many of these prophesises became famous and demonstrate the way they were constructed into riddles.

In 547 BCE, King Croesus of Lydia was concerned about the growth of the Persian Empire and what would happen if he instigated a war with them. He sent several messengers to the oracles in the known world, with instructions to keep count of the days from the time of their leaving Sardis. On the hundredth day they were to consult the oracles about what Croesus, the son of Alyattes, king of Lydia was doing at that moment. The messengers were then to return to Croesus with the oracles' answers in writing. The only surviving answer comes from Delphi. When the Lydian messenger entered the sibyl's sanctuary, she preempted his question with an answer in hexameter verse:

> "I can count the sands, and I can measure the ocean; I have ears for the silent, and know what the dumb mean e[i]ther; Lo! On my sense there striketh the smell a shell-covered tortoise, boiling now on a fire, with the flesh of a lamb, in a cauldron. Brass is the vessel below, and brass the cover above it."[7]

---

* *Katoché* can mean confinement or imprisonment, but in relation to trance as being influenced or possessed by a spirit, daemon, or deity, the word *katochos* was used to define the entity involved.

When the messengers returned, only the Oracle at Delphi was correct. On the day they left, Croesus had indeed taken a lamb and a tortoise and cooked them together in a brass-lidded cooking pot, believing that none of them would know what he had done. He was overjoyed with the oracle at Delphi's answer, believing that only she could tell him the answer he sought. Croeus asked the oracle if he should cross the River Halys and attack the Persian king, Cyrus. The reply was that if he did "a great empire will fall." Croesus was promptly defeated in battle; he had failed to ask which empire would lose, and wrongly assumed that it would be the Persians.

In the last one hundred years before the first millennium, the Oracle at Delphi began to decline in importance. During this time it was plundered at least twice, but the oracle continued to be of importance well into the new millennium with many Roman emperors consulting the oracle. In the early second century, the Emperor Hadrian reconstructed some of the site, but its heyday was over. The last advice given by the oracle was in the fourth century, when Emperor Julian the Apostate, in an attempt to revive ancient Greek culture, consulted the oracle. The sibyl responded with a less than promising message: "Tell to the King that the carven hall is fallen in decay; Apollo has no chapel left, no prophesying bay, no talking spring. The stream is dry had so much to say."[8]

The 'stream,' the volcanic fissure which had fuelled the sibyls' trances, had been closing up due to the lack of seismic activity, and the hallucinogenic gases were becoming less and less present over time. The coming of Christianity meant the final end for the sanctuary in 394 CE, when the Emperor Theodosios banned the cult of Apollo and its practises, including the oracle, but the influence of ecstatic trance-prophecy was not to disappear completely. The tradition was to continue amongst the Corinthians who embraced "the Greek ecstatic model."[9]

The Power of the Sibyls: The Sibylline Books, Christianity, and the Modern World

In the summer of 2006, we visited the Vatican and its museum. Our main reason for the visit was to see one of the best collections of God and Goddess statues in Europe. During the tour we saw the collections of art by both Raphael and Michelangelo. It was in these collections that something we couldn't ignore struck us: why were the walls around the Sistine Chapel covered in pictures of the sibyls? Several of them held up the beautiful ceiling, including the Delphic, Cumaean, and Libyan (see Photograph 2), but many of them could also be found in the Library of Pope Julius II.

Why did a place of Christianity, which rejected the idea of the Goddess, end up with so many images of her priestesses? This attitude within the walls of the bastion of Christian thinking can be accredited to a collection of books dating back five centuries before Christ. These were *The Sibyl line Books,* oracular transcripts which played an important part in the history of Rome. The books were acquired by the last king of Rome, Tarquinius Superbus, who ruled between 535 and 510 BCE. Originally, nine books were offered to him by the Cumaean sibyl, but when he refused to purchase them at the price she requested, she started burning them until he relented. Only three were saved, but he still purchased them at the original price offered for all nine. As the belief in their accuracy and their political importance grew, they were entrusted into the care of many custodians. Initially, they were two patricians, but by 367 BCE, their number had risen to ten, and eventually to fifteen custodians. The books had interesting effects on Roman culture, particularly regarding religious worship. They were to introduce Greek concepts of the gods and goddesses to already-existing Etruscan-influenced deities of Rome, particularly Cybele. This affected Christianity, as well as the foundations of the Vatican.

Beneath the Vatican lie the remains of a temple, a place of worship for the same Goddess Cybele connected to the Delphic oracle and *The Sibylline Books.* The Vatican is actually named after the presence of this Goddess and her oracular aspect; St. Peter even adopted

Photograph 2: Michaelangelo's Libyan Sibyl from the Sistine Chapel, the Vatican, Rome
(Courtesy Wikipedia Commons, under public domain)

Cybele's keys as his symbol. *Vatic* actually means "oracle" or "sibyl," while its suffix *-anus* means "mount." In modern English translation, it literally means *the seat of the oracle* or *sibyl*. Clearly, the sibyls played such a strong part in the cultural psyche, they were hard to ignore. Even Christianity found itself having to recognise their importance if they were to gain acceptance as the new religion. This was not a difficult task, since in Virgil's *Fourth Eclogue*, the Cumaean sibyl foretold the coming of a Saviour, and the Tiburtine sibyl predicted the coming of Constantine, the first Christian Emperor of Rome: "Then will arise a king of the Greeks whose name is Constans. He will be king of the Romans and the Greeks. He will be tall of stature, of handsome appearance with shining face, and well put together in all parts of his body."

This legacy always played on the minds of those within the walls of the Vatican; every day bishops and cardinals come face to face with history of the sibyls. It is not surprising that the papacy gets jumpy every time children report manifestations of a prophecy-giving Madonna. They did so at Fatima, Portugal in 1917, and at Medjugorje, Bosnia in 1981.* What concerned the Vatican the most were the prophecies or three secrets of Fatima. The third secret was not released to the public until the year 2000 because they were afraid of its implications. Regardless of the Catholic Church's condemnation of prophetic practise, they still heed the passages from I Corinthians 12:28, Psalm 105:15, and Matthew 5:17, which although subordinating prophecy below that of the apostles, encourages the continued respect of prophets and prophecy within Christianity. We believe this happened because the church built its powerbase upon the prophecies of the sibyls. This allowed their legacy to survive in modern Western culture, in literature and art.

The late nineteenth and early twentieth century saw a new renaissance of interest in the sibyls and their prophecies in art and literature. Artists such as John William Waterhouse (*Consulting the Oracle,* 1882) and John Collier (*Priestess of Delphi*, 1891, the cover art of this book) followed in the footsteps of Michelangelo and brought their artistic interpretations of the sibyl to the general public. The name Sybil was adopted as a forename, and the new mystics of the period, such as William Butler Yeats, studied the classics to understand the nature of pagan prophecy and found themselves coming face to face with the oracle herself. Robert Graves gave the sibyl and *The Sibylline Books* the final say in his work *I,*

---

* In 2014, the church completed its investigation of events in Medjugorje, but has not issued a ruling.

Claudius, and was later to write about her more formally in his seminal work *The White Goddess*. This interest in the mystical nature of the sibyl was to influence occult practise, and was eventually to influence the practises of both the Golden Dawn and Aleister Crowley's Ordo Templi Orientis, as well as the image of the female medium in Spiritualism.

NOTES

1 Joseph Fontenrose, *The Delphic Oracle: Its Responses and Operations* (University of California Press, 1978), 3–4.
2 E. M. W. Tillyard, "A Cybele Altar in London," *Journal of Roman Studies* (1917).
3 R. E. Witt, chap. XI in *Isis in the Graeco-Roman World*, 142.
4 *Geology*, August 2001.
5 Carla Osbourne, "A Short Detour to Delphi and the Sibyls," chapter 6 in *The Amazon Nation* (2000).
6 Heraclitus, frag. 12.
7 Herodotus, chaps. 43–47 in *Histories Book I*.
8 Philostorgius, *Church History 7.1c = The Passion of Artemius (425–423 AD)*. The last prophecy given to Julian the Apostate.
9 David E. Aune, chap. 1 in *Prophecy in Early Christianity in the Ancient Mediterrean World*, 17.

Chapter 2

Mediumship, Spiritualism, and the Magical Revival

T he connections between the modern revival of magic, Witchcraft, and the Spiritualist (or more correctly, Spiritist) movements may not at first be obvious. The link between the three movements can be seen in one of the strangest events in English legal history—the Helen Duncan case—which was not only a turning point for Spiritualism in the United Kingdom but also a catalyst for the rebirth of Witchcraft. After following the spiritual path for a while, one realizes that such connections are not by chance; they are part of a bigger web of events, dictated by the divine in all its forms. For Gavin, this is of particular significance because of the events that took place in his hometown of Portsmouth, Hampshire, England, centering on a Spiritualist medium called Helen Duncan. She had already fallen foul of the law on at least one occasion, when she was accused in 1933 of being a fraud by one of her hosts. Although she lost the case and had to pay a £10 fine, it was not because of fraudulent activity, but because Spiritualism was still a crime under the 1824 Vagrancy Act. On this occasion, as well as other occasions previously, she proved to be a gifted medium. Some even say that, following the verdict, the judge and some of the jury members became her regular customers. This case highlighted the problems Spiritualists faced under the existing laws in the United Kingdom. It was in Portsmouth in 1941 that Helen Duncan was to fall foul of the law again, only this time for being such a good medium.

Portsmouth is a naval town. It is a city steeped in naval history, and as such it isn't surprising that Spiritualism was, and still is, very prominent. During the Second World War, just about every family had connections with the sea and, of course, many had lost loved ones to it.

20

This made it a prime location for a medium like Helen Duncan to ply her trade. It was during one of her séances that she materialized the spirit of a sailor from HMS Barham, who was able to provide the date when the ship sank, names of those lost, and exactly how many. An off duty naval officer present at the séance was not surprisingly curious about Duncan's claims, and on returning to duty inquired about its loss. He was informed that this was not the case, but later discovered that this had been a ruse to cover up the use of intelligence gained from the breaking of the highly secret German Enigma Code. Helen Duncan was already under investigation by Naval Intelligence, following her prediction of the sinking of HMS Hood at a séance in Scotland,* in front of the head of Military Intelligence in 1941. From recently released documents, there is little doubt that British Intelligence considered her a serious thorn in their side, particularly with regards to this latest breach of security. At one point, she was even accused of being a German spy; it was even suggested that she had been in radio in contact with German submarines off the coast of Portsmouth. Of course, nothing could be proven. Her abilities were eventually taken so seriously by British Intelligence that a spy was assigned to her, a Lieutenant Worth of the Royal Navy, whose job was to monitor her activities and report back on her séances. Most of what he reported back were normal messages for the bereaved, which made her of little interest to his superiors. This is something that would change in the near future.

It was the plans for D-Day, the allied invasion of Europe set for June 1944, which sealed Helen Duncan's fate. She was arrested by Naval Intelligence, who had serious fears that she would breach the security of their invasion plans. With the help of Lieutenant Worth, she was arrested on January 19, 1944 during one of her séances in Portsmouth. Initially, she was charged under the Vagrancy Act for fraudulently contacting the dead, then the charge was changed to a breach of the 1735 Witchcraft Act. The authorities did not dispute her abilities as a medium, but accused her of sorcery. The trial was moved from to London, with the intention of preventing sympathetic witnesses from attending. The purpose of the arrest and the trial was to deter others who may have felt inclined to channel classified information detrimental to the war effort. The trial quickly became a media circus; Helen Duncan even volunteered to manifest her spirit guide in the courtroom to prove her authenticity, but to

---

* HMS Hood was considered to be the most powerful Battleship afloat. Its sinking in 1941 by the German Battleship Bismark was considered to be a major loss to the Royal Navy and had a major effect on wartime morale.

no avail. Even then Prime Minister Winston Churchill was aware of the
case and felt it was a waste of the court's time and money. It lasted one
week, with Helen Duncan being found guilty by the jury after only thirty
minutes, and being sent to prison for eight months.

After the Second World War, the Spiritualist movement in the United
Kingdom started a campaign to get her name cleared and repeal the
outdated laws that were used to convict her. They were successful—both
the Vagrancy Act and the Witchcraft Act were replaced by the Fraudulent
Mediums Act in 1951. This obviously gave peace of mind to the genuine mediums who were practising, but it also opened the way for many
modern Witches to become more public, resulting in the growth of the
neo-Pagan movement as we know it today.

The Origins of Modern Mediumship and the Spiritualist Movement

The resurgence of interest in communication with spirits can be traced
back to the 1700s with the writings of Emanuel Swedenborg (1688–1772)
and Franz Mesmer (1734–1815). While many are familiar with Mesmer
and his contribution to what was later to become known as hypnotism,
only a few have heard of Swedenborg. Prior to his work, most Christians
accepted the church's concept of one heaven and one hell. It was Swedenborg who suggested that the reality was more complex. He felt that
there were multiple levels of realities, with spirits acting as intermediaries
on behalf of God to communicate directly with men. He was careful to
point out that this communication must always be initiated by the spirit,
and not the other way around. Mesmer's contribution to the subject is in
the field of mesmerism, a word we still use today as mesmerised to mean
entranced. While Swedenborg suggested that there was a cosmology that
allowed spirit contact, it was Mesmer who believed that it was possible to
communicate with spirits and supernatural beings. He demonstrated this
on several occasions, but his flair for showmanship meant that his work
was not really treated seriously by the professional community. When it
was developed into a therapeutic practise, the word hypnotism was used
so that the techniques would be treated seriously.* Modern clinical hypnosis can trace its origins in Mesmer and his Spiritualist practises.

By the 1840s Mesmer's ideas had spread, including the idea that it was
possible to communicate with the spirit world. In the United States, some

---

* Dr. James Braid developed mesmerism into a therapeutic practice in 1842. It was he
who gave it the name "hypnosis."

practitioners started to combine the ideas of Mesmer and Swedenborg, the most famous being Andrew Jackson Davis. He created the first coherent thesis on the practise of Spiritualism, which he published in 1847 in his book The Principles of Nature, Her Divine Revelations, and a Voice to Mankind. While this book gave birth to modern Spiritualism as we know it today, it was the Fox sisters, Kate and Margaret, who brought Spiritualism to the attention of the world. The Fox sisters claimed that they had made contact with the spirit of a murdered peddler, who made them aware of his presence by making rapping noises, which everyone present could hear.* Due to their friendship with several Quakers, they soon found themselves adopted by the Quaker community. The belief within Quakerism had always been that it was possible to be influenced directly by the Holy Spirit. This sometimes took form of shaking or quaking, and speaking in tongues.[1] Many early Spiritualists came out of this religion for this very reason. By the mid-1800s the Fox sisters were followed by others claiming similar abilities. This growing movement invited more and more scepticism; its popularity had made it vulnerable to unscrupulous elements of society, who saw it as a way of making money and a new form of entertainment. Stage hall acts began to appear, and while some were genuine, others were mere trickery. Even worse, some of the perpetrators set themselves up as mediums, using the opportunity to commit acts of fraud. By the end of the nineteenth century, with claims of fraud rife and several court cases pending in Britain and America, The Society for Psychical Research was founded in London (1882) to investigate claims of psychic ability, thus separating the genuine mediums from the charlatans.

Most séances of this period were a very middle-class affair, consisting of a group of people sitting around a table in a darkened drawing room attempting to communicate with the spirits of deceased relatives. Unfortunately, this attracted just as many thrill-seekers as it did grieving relatives. The medium would sit between them, asking them to touch hands, generally by using their little finger. She would then go into trance, connecting with her spirit guide, who would bring the recently deceased to her. In some cases, table rapping or table lifting would occur, sometimes apports would appear—physical items related to the deceased manifesting physically. This was a favourite tool of the charlatan, who having researched her clients would rig the room with the help of her assistants. In some cases the medium would visibly regurgitate ectoplasm

---

* This took place on March 31, 1848. Spiritualists still regard this date as the founding of their movement.

(see page 124). Witnesses to this would often describe the temperature in the room dropping as the spirit manifested. This gave a further opportunity to the charlatans to dupe the grieving relatives even more. Although certainly many mediums of this period were false, there was a small number of those who were gifted psychics, as is the case today. The one outstanding feature about the mediums then as well as today is that they are not inspired by the need for fame or wealth, but by their desire, in all humility, to serve both the divine and mankind.

Although Spiritualism gained the majority of its converts in the English speaking countries, there was also interest on the European continent. Allan Kardec (1804–1869), a French lecturer and teacher, published the first books to systemise mediumship in a coherent way. It became the guide books for future mediums, particularly in Latin-American countries where it became the basis for Espiritismo (Spiritism). The influence of Western-style Spiritualism and Kardec's work spread to Brazil and the Caribbean, particularly Puerto Rico and Cuba, where although it retained its Anglo-American heritage, it took on a particularly Latin feel. Unlike the Western séance, Espiritistas (Espirito practitioners) gather in a small family group called a misa. While it is monotheistic, as in Western Spiritualism, it has absorbed many of the practises of Santeria and Vodoun, including the creation of amulets dedicated to saints. One modern development is Santerismo, where the tradition becomes combined more fully with Cuban Santeria. The major difference is that the orishas possess the medium, allowing her to directly communicate with the spirits. Similar to Santeria, the area is cleansed before the ceremony, then a prayer is said to Ellegua to open and protect "the gateway" before the orishas are invoked using traditional chants. In many ways it follows the traditional pattern of Santeria, but invocations are replaced with prayers. The removal of evil spirits may also be a part of the proceedings—a *sahumerio*, or exorcism. Holy water is used to wash the possessed person, while herbs, garlic, and incense are burned to drive out the unclean spirit.

Up until the late 1800s Spiritualism remained unorganized, even though there were periodicals such as The Banner of Light (Boston, USA) and The Spiritualist (London, England). The formation of The Spiritualist Nation Union in England heralded the creation of the first societies that studied psychic phenomena as a science—parapsychology—as well as the first ghost-hunting groups. Regardless of increased communication among Spiritualists, they continued to hold a mixture of views regarding religious theology and how to use the techniques that could be found in the newly published books on mediumship.

During this time, one particular technique appeared which was to gain notoriety: the Ouija Board™.* This was originally intended to be a serious tool, but ended up being marketed by several board game companies. It consisted of a board with "Yes," "No" (where the terms oui and ja derive, being the French and German words, respectively), and "Maybe" written on the board along with the alphabet. A planchette, a small heart-shaped board supported on castors was held over the board, with the idea that the spirits would move its pointer over the appropriate letter, thus spelling out a phrase. As it could only be used by two people at a time, a homemade version of the process developed and gained popularity in the late 1960s. This could easily be made by placing individual letters printed or written on paper in a circle on the surface of a polished table. Several people would sit around the table with the index finger of their left hand placed on the glass. The glass would then move, under agency of the spirit communicating with the group, over each letter to spell out a message. Unfortunately, both techniques gained a bad reputation because they tended to be used frivolously. This resulted in numerous horror films being produced around the idea that one's life could be wrecked or that they could be possessed by a demon if they used one of these "talking boards." This was a shame, as both techniques have serious applications if one knows how to use them correctly.

By the 1920s it was apparent that more formal training and vetting were needed within the Spiritualist movement. The result was the formation of several Spiritualist churches, which were all associated with The Spiritualist National Union (http://www.snu.org.uk). They all instituted systems of training based on the Declaration of Principles, which dates back to 1899. It has gone through several amendments over the years, developing it into The Nine Guiding Principles, found in modern Spiritualism today:[2]

---

* American businessman Elijah Bond first marketed the talking board as a parlour game in 1890, with William Fuld taking over its production in 1901 and naming it the Ouija Board™. In 1966 Parker Brothers took over production; Hasbro (1991) currently holds the copyright and markets the game.

1. We believe in Infinite Intelligence.
2. We believe that the phenomena of Nature, both physical and spiritual, are the expression of Infinite Intelligence.
3. We affirm that a correct understanding of such expression and living in accordance therewith constitute true religion.
4. We affirm that the existence and personal identity of the individual continue after the change called death.
5. We affirm that communication with the so-called dead is a fact, scientifically proven by the phenomena of Spiritualism.
6. We believe that the highest morality is contained in the Golden Rule: "Do unto others as you would have them do unto you."
7. We affirm the moral responsibility of the individual, and that we make our own happiness or unhappiness as we obey or disobey Nature's physical and spiritual laws.
8. We affirm that the doorway to reformation is never closed against any soul here or hereafter.
9. We affirm that the precept of Prophecy and Healing are divine attributes proven through Mediumship.[3]

What is obvious to any modern Pagan or Witch is that the principles of Spiritualism are not in conflict in any way with neo-Pagan philosophy. The phrase "phenomena of Nature, both physical and spiritual, are the expression of Infinite Intelligence" is certainly in keeping with neo-Pagan nature-based theology, as well as being the same principle upon which the Universalist Unitarian Church bases its practises. It is, therefore, not unusual to see Hindu, Buddhist, or even Egyptian statues on the altars of modern Spiritualist churches. The principles are well worth studying by anyone who is practising trance-prophecy, as they are clearly relevant to neo-Pagan practise as much as they are to Spiritualism.

What is a Medium?

A *medium* is someone who interacts with spirits through a psychic ability (e.g., clairaudience, clairvoyance, or *automatic writing*—the unconscious ability to write while guided by a spirit). The major difference between a medium and someone who has other psychic skills is that a medium interacts directly with the spirit world, as opposed to a psychic who just uses their own gifts. For example, while a medium and a clairvoyant may appear to have the same psychic faculty, the medium is seeing what is given to them by the spirit world, while the clairvoyant is seeing directly. Being a medium requires some psychic ability, a necessity to communicate with the spirit world. But not all psychics are mediums; they may not automatically have the ability to interact with spirits. It is also important to point out that a medium is not necessarily the same as someone who "channels." *Channeling* is a New Age term related to the ability to relay information from an alleged spirit source, such as an angel or a mythological figure such as Merlin. Spiritualist mediums are quick to point out that they do not 'channel,' but rather act as a medium, a vessel for the spirit world (normally the spirit of a deceased person). By definition this implies that they are filled with the spirit that is communicating through them, an act of positive possession. In this respect, there is little difference between the modern medium and the oracular sibyl.

Within Spiritualism, mediums are classified into different categories depending on the way they manifest spirit communication. Below we touch on a few:[4]

***Auditive* or *Hearing Medium*:** As the name suggests, this medium hears the spirit through their psychic ability of *clairaudience*. The medium either hears a clear voice, as if someone was talking to them physically, or experiences *pneumatophony*—an interior voice speaking directly to their mind. The spirit will either speak directly to the medium, or may relay a conversation from the past that is relevant to the seeker. The medium acts as a relay, which allows him or her to edit detail or more disturbing aspects of the message.

***Talking Medium*:** It is important to point out that a talking medium is not the same as the auditive medium, who is relaying the message they are given by a spirit. The *talking medium* has no conscious control of their ability to speak, but the spirit controls their ability directly. The medium will not actually hear what the spirit is saying until it comes out of their own lips. It is also common for some of the mediums to have no recollection of what has been said (see page 120 for a personal experience of this phenomena). The medium's voice may also change to resemble that of the spirits, who may also say things that are contrary to the personality of the medium or their personal views. (The American poet-psychic Jane Roberts was a Talking Medium.) We have personally witnessed talking mediums on several occasions during trance-prophecy where a deity in possession of a seer has contradicted comments made by her prior to her entering trance.

Seeing Medium: A *seeing medium* is a clairvoyant. They will see the spirit in the physical form it took when it was alive (for a deity this could be its mythological form, contemporary, or other forms. See page 154), or they may see images that the spirit wishes them to see (e.g., incidents in the past, the future, or abstract images, such as a relevant object). Some seeing mediums may only see one particular spirit, normally their guide, while others may see more than one. Some who have this ability only manifest it while in trance state or while they are sleeping, although it may surface while the medium is fully conscious during times of stress, or an emergency when a spirit is desperately trying to warn them of danger.

Somnambulic Medium: Quite simply, a *somnambulic medium* is a sha-man—someone who enters into deep trance and travels to meet a spirit, rather than the spirit coming to them. By definition, this means that they must leave their consciousness behind while they enter into trance. This form of medium brings the information they have gathered back with them when they return to the physical world.

Writing Medium: Often referred to as a *psychographic medium,* this medium has the gift of *automatic writing*—when a spirit controls the me-dium's hand and communicates by written word. There are two distinct forms. The first is *intuitive*, where the spirit works through the medium's mind. The medium has no conscious control of what is written; they are simply relaying a message, which flows out as they write. The second form is *mechanical*—the spirit works directly through the medium's hand, seemingly bypassing the mind. The medium is unaware of what the mes-sage is until it is written. This may even be involuntary, with the medium finding it hard to stop the process.

Modern Spiritualism: The *Platform* and *Sitting Medium*
When most people think of a medium today, they usually think of a *platform medium*. Most people have seen one, not through the hallowed doors of the Spiritualist Church, but on television. These mediums carry on the long tradition of showmanship that has existed in mediumship since the stage hall acts of the Victorian days. Unfortunately, the char-latans are also still present; if these showmen aren't performing on the stage, then they are appearing in haunted castles on ghost-hunting shows,

attempting to communicate with the tormented spirits that haunt the dank walls, normally accompanied by their female "scream queen." Although they have popularized mediumship, they have also resurrected its own "ghosts of Christmases past" in the form of scandals. In recent years, at least two major TV mediums have been discredited, one in the United Kingdom and one in the United States. They were not necessarily charlatans; it was simply as most psychics know: some days you just can't turn the gift on. If asked to perform on one of those off days in front of the camera, there is always the temptation to cheat by cold reading* or making sure that the personal researcher has done the background check on the audience. Knowledge of this temptation is one of the reasons why the most gifted and ethical platform mediums rarely appear on TV or in the stage hall. Their purpose has never been to entertain, but to give comfort to those who lost loved ones.

Platform mediumship is a performance, in the same way that the practises of Delphi were also full of drama and ritual. Table séances, although still practised, have now given way to the medium standing on a stage or platform within a hall or Spiritualist church. Most of the training now centers on this practise, as well as that of a *sitting medium.*

Gavin remembers his mother regularly visiting a sitting medium when he was in his teens. Her name was Mrs. Claire. She would take one client at a time and sit with them. It was a private affair with no one else present. Sometimes she would ask for her client to give her an object that would allow her to connect with them. Sometimes she would hold her own connector (a scarf). Both techniques are, of course, acts of *psychometry*—the ability to read an object psychically. Her guide would then pass messages through her to the client. She would be in a light trance state during this process, but would never actually be possessed by her guide or any other entity. Gavin remembers how accurate she was, particularly regarding what she said about him. She rarely talked about the dead; this is one of the misapprehensions regarding modern mediumship. Today people are just as likely to go to a medium for spiritual guidance, as they are to talk to loved ones who have passed over. In that respect, modern mediumship has returned to its ancient roots similar to the traditional forms of prophecy found in the classical world. This is true for both sitting and platform mediums, but it must also be remembered that contact

---

* Cold reading is the ability to convince someone that you know actually more than you do by careful use of language. The cold reader examines the sittee's age, dress, and language to discern information about them.

with the dead occurred in ancient times as well. While the original reason
for consorting with the dead in modern mediumship was to console the
grieving, this was not the case in ancient times, when it was clearly about
prophecy and spiritual guidance. Since its inception, modern mediumship
has slowly returned to its ancient practise.

Most mediums in the twenty-first century, both sitting and platform,
go through a process of training. The Spiritualist National Union (SNU)
not only runs and regulates tuition programs through their associated
Spiritualist churches or temples, but also produces a course on DVD for
aspiring mediums. These are long courses, many being to diploma standard, designed both for those who wish to be mediums and those who
want to move on and teach mediumship. Similar organizations to the
UK-based SNU can also be found in the United States, and have done
much to move Spiritualism away from the negative image that it had in
the early twentieth century.

Spiritualist influences in Modern Magic and Witchcraft

The magical revival of the nineteenth century ran parallel to the growth
of the Spiritualist movement. It is interesting to note that one of the
major figures of the Golden Dawn, W. B. Yeats, was actively involved in
Spiritualism. His notebooks of automatic writing can still be viewed in
the National Library of Ireland, alongside his ritual tools. He clearly saw
no separation between his ritual magic and mediumistic practises, writing
several pieces on the subject, including an essay on Swedenborg, where
he refers to Allan Kardec and the Chaldean Oracle.[5] He was certainly not
alone: Dion Fortune, who was an occultist and a medium, published a
book on the subject, *Spiritualism in the light of Occult Science,* as well as
several articles.[6] It would be easy to suggest that modern occultism absorbed the idea of mediumship from the Spiritualist movement, as there
was certainly some crossover between individuals in the two movements.
But more likely, they developed independently from each other, although
influenced by the same sources. Both movements were familiar with the
ancient oracles, but the magical revival also drew on two notable occultists of the medieval period: Dr. John Dee, the well-known astrologer and
court magician of Queen Elizabeth I, and his medium, Edward Kelly.
They claimed that the majority of Kelly's communication was with angels, which is how Kelly channelled *Enochia: The Language of the Angels.*
This, they claimed, was the first language spoken by Adam. Most cere-
nial magicians are aware of their contribution because of the continued
use of the Enochian language in ceremonial magic today.

Dee and Kelly suffered accusations of *necromancy*, or conjuration of the spirits of the dead—mediumship by any other name. Most of their messages seemed to come from higher spirit forms, as it did in the ancient oracles and in modern trance-prophecy techniques. This concept of the magician and the medium working together influenced the future generation of occultists into the twentieth century, such as the ritual magician Aleister Crowley.

Crowley was particularly influenced by the work of Dee and Kelly. He built on their work with the *Enochian Calls* and *Enochian Keys,* but was also inspired by Kelly's ability to channel information from higher spirit forms. Although fictional, Dennis Wheatley's book *They Used Dark Forces* is clearly based on Wheatley's contact with Crowley. It contains elements of truth, and examines the relationship between the magician and his medium. The medium helped support the work of the magician: communicating with spirit forms to see if his magical work was effective on the higher levels, the astral planes. Gavin witnessed a similar use of a medium in the first group he joined in 1985. The group used a traditional Spiritualist-church-trained medium who, although a Christian mystic, had no problems working with both ritual magicians and Pagans in the "Great Work,"* as it was called. It is worth examining Crowley more fully because of the way he used his mediums or "Scarlet Women," and the way their use later influenced Wicca.

The term Scarlet Woman originates from the book of John the Divine more commonly known as the book of Revelation: "The woman was clothed in purple and scarlet, and adorned with gold and jewels and pearls, holding in her hand a golden cup full of abominations and the impurities of her fornication; and on her forehead was written a name, a mystery: 'Babylon the great, mother of whores and of earth's abominations'" (Rev. 17:4–5).

In Thelemic practise, "the Mother of Abominations" is the main goddess figure used. The first mention of her by Crowley can be found in his famous work The Book of the Law (1904). For Crowley, she represented the natural feminine libido, which was so repressed within Victorian and Edwardian society. It is interesting to note that sexuality was often associated with mediumship, although in a negative way. Accusations by critics that female mediums were often involved in "lewd sexu-

---

* Aleister Crowley used this term for the heralding of the New Aeon, the Age of Horus. Most work in this group consisted of pushing the human consciousness into this new age.

al behaviour" was commonplace, and echoed the same accusation made by the priesthood of Apollo against the original pythoness. Crowley was not exploiting these accusations; the female psychic ability and sexuality are linked in the patriarchal psyche, with the fear that such women can hold power over men. Mediums were "liberated women" by nature, many being involved in women's suffrage. One leader of the women's rights movement, Annie Besant, was linked to Spiritualism as well as the Co-Masonic Fellowship of Crotona, which is linked with the origins of Wicca. Crowley associated this image of sexualized femininity with the concept of the Great Mother Goddess, which he and many modern Pagans recognise as the "Whore of Babylon" referred to in the Bible. He is, of course, talking about the Great Mother Goddess cult that developed in the millennia before Christ. This Goddess derives from a fusion of several goddesses often associated with sexuality, including Ishtar, Isis, Diana, et al.[7] More importantly, it absorbed their prophetic natures. Evidence of this can still be seen today in the Sistine Chapel in the Vatican in Rome, where Michaelangelo's paintings of the scarlet-clad sibyls still symbolically hold up the famous painting of God and Adam on the ceiling (see chapter 1). Crowley was well read and would have been aware of these connections. "This is Babalon, the true mistress of

Photograph 3: Leila Waddel was Aleister Crowley's most and influential Scarlet Woman and probably one of the first priestesses in modern times to reenact Drawing Down the Moon.

(Photo of Leila Waddel performing during the Rites of Eleusis in 1910)

The Beast; of Her, all his mistresses on lower planes are but avatars" (Crowley, *The Equinox IV*).

Crowley believed that his Scarlet Women were the embodiment of this Great Goddess, as well as her "avatars" manifesting throughout ritual. During the honeymoon with his first wife and Scarlet Woman, Rose Edith Kelly, she directed him while she was in a trance to go to the Cairo Museum. It was here he found a wooden funerary stele, The Stele of Revealing, which was dedicated to the god Horus. The catalogue number of the piece was 666, "the number of the Beast," which he associated with himself ever since his dysfunctional childhood. Later, Rose put him in touch with his guide, "Aiwass," whom he mentions extensively in Liber Legis. He refers to Aiwass as "the minister of Hoor-paar-kraat," which translates as "the minister for Horus the Child." In other words, his Higher Self or Holy Guardian Angel (see page 125).

Several Scarlet Women followed Rose Edith, including Roddie Minor and Mary d'Este Sturges (Soror Virakam). Although there is no proof that Crowley's Scarlet Women were formerly trained in Spiritualism, there is little doubt that both the women and Crowley himself were influenced by the Spiritualist movement. On several occasions, Crowley and his Scarlet Women visited mediums to assist their magical work. Several of these women were quite well known, including Everard Fielding, who was a leading figure in The Society for Psychical Research. Crowley also consulted two famous Italian mediums while in Italy: Eusapia Palladino in Naples, and Caracini in Rome. Apparently, he was not impressed with either one of them. Leila Waddell was the most important of his Scarlet Women (see Photograph 3). She was probably the first priestess in modern times to be involved in the ritual of Drawing Down the Moon. Crowley used her mediumship skills to bring through the Moon Goddess on numerous occasions using ritual drama and ceremony. The Goddess' messages came through Leila while she played her violin. Sometimes this would happen very publically as an act of performance art. One critic from The Sketch newspaper called it a "really beautiful ceremony." Encouraged by such reviews, Crowley rented the Caxton Hall in London for what he called The Rites of Eleusis. The climax of this ritual was invocations to Pan, Horus, and the Moon Goddess. It might seem odd today that Crowley should do such magically intense ritual in public, but this was a period when such acts of mediumship were carried out publically.

Crowley's writings, which came out of this work, of course, were to later influence Wicca. Gerald Gardner, the "father of modern Witchcraft," incorporated much of Crowley's work, including elements of his Gnostic Mass[8] into the Leviter Veslis: The Lifting of the Veil. This was later to become the ritual of Drawing Down the Moon. Crowley's use of mediums, his Scarlet Women, was to bleed over into Wiccan practise through Gardner's use of his rituals. The major difference was that the seer as high priestess was not acting to support the magician, but quite the opposite: the magician, the high priest, was now supporting the seer (see chapter 6).

These connections between Spiritualism, ceremonial magic, and Wicca are rarely recognised in the histories of Wicca or the neo-Pagan movements. But as renowned Wiccan historian Phillip Heselton points out, they do exist:*

> Gerald (Gardner) was certainly interested in spiritualism, as we can tell from his experiences in Borneo and his investigations on his visit to England in 1927. It could be (and, indeed, I think it actually likely) that he got in touch with certain spiritualist groups in the Christchurch/Bournemouth area when he settled there in 1938. . . . In this context, it is interesting that Doreen (Valiente) certainly attended spiritualist meetings in Bournemouth in the 1944 to 1956 period! It is tempting to speculate that she may have met Gerald at some spiritualist meeting there in 1944, before Gerald returned to London, but I doubt it or she would have recognized him when she met him at Dafo's house in 1952![9]

It is very clear that there were links between Gerald Gardner and Doreen Valiente (often referred to as the "mother of modern Witchcraft") with the Spiritualist movement. We also know that his first initiate, Barbara Vickers (who preceeded Doreen Valiente by several years), was a practising medium in a Spiritualist group in Knightsbridge (see Photograph 4). There is a good chance that Gardner's other priestesses were also aware of the techniques employed in mediumship and, like Vickers and Valiente, applied them to the practise of Drawing Down the Moon. In the modern period, there are some more tangible links. Author Ray Buckland, who is considered to be the father of Wicca in the United States, also first explored Spiritualism before embracing Witchcraft. In the 1990s

---

* Philip Heselton is considered the foremost expert on the life of Gerald Gardner and early Wiccan history. He is the author of several books on Gardnerian history, including *Wiccan Roots: Gerald Gardner and the Modern Witchcraft Revival* (2000), *Gerald Gardner and the Witchcraft Revival* (2001), and recently, *Witchfather: A Life of Gerald Gardner*, volumes 1 and 2.

he went back to the Spiritualist movement and, alongside his books on Wicca, for which he is most well known, published several books on the subject of Spiritualism, ghosts, and spirits. These books include *Buckland's Book of Spirit Communications*, *The Spirit Book*, *Mediumship and Spirit Communication*; *Ouija – "Yes! Yes!"*; *Dragons, Shamans and Spiritualists*; and *Weiser's Field Guide to Ghosts*.

Just as links can be found between traditional Gardnerian Wicca and Spiritualism, they can also be found in Alexandrian Wicca, an offshoot of that tradition which appeared in the 1960s. Its founder, Alex Sanders, was originally trained in the Spiritualist Church as a healer and medium. This is confirmed by his ex-wife, Maxine, in her autobiography, Firechild:

> "He did however work enthusiastically in his spare time as a materialisation medium in Spiritualist churches under the name Paul Dallas. He was a natural medium and worked regularly with his spirit guide 'Red Feather'. Together their healing successes came to attention of a famous medium of the time called Edwards."[10]

Photograph 4: Barbara Vickers, Gerald Gardner's first initiate
and a practising medium
(Photo courtesy Miranda Vickers and Phillip Heselton)

Some of the training Alex Sanders received from the Spiritualist Church was included in his early training seminars with his Wiccan students (see page 116), much of the language clearly originating from the Spiritualism of the 1950s. While he did not teach mediumship in his own coven, he taught some of its philosophy and continued to practise as a medium until his death in 1988.

Today we see Spiritualism and the neo-Pagan/magical revival as being two separate entities, but clearly in the past this was not the case. Over the years the crossover between the two movements became undeniable. There is a continual connection between the two groups, from the early days of the Spiritualist movement to the early twentieth century, with such well-known names as W. B. Yeats. All the well-known names of the early magical revival have had links with mediumship and Spiritualism, as shown in this chapter, although by the 1970s, the connections between the two seemed to wane. This was originally a magical revival, which then became neo-Pagan, while most Spiritualist organizations still leaned toward Christian thinking. By the 1990s this was to change: a growing interest in ancient forms of mediumship gained prominence, culminating in return back to the oracular practises of our ancestors.

NOTES

1 Michael Bjerknes Aune and Valerie M. DeMarinis, eds., *Religious and Social Ritual: Interdisciplinary Explorations* (Albany: State University of New York Press, 1996); Martha Ellen Stortz, chap. 4 in *Ritual Power, Ritual Authority*, 105.

2 Todd Jay Leonard, chap. 3 in *Talking to the Other Side: A History of Modern Spiritualism and Mediumship* (Lincoln, Nebraska: iUniverse Books, 2005), 86.

3 National Spiritualist Association of Churches, USA, "Declaration of Principles," https://www.nsac.org/principles.php (accessed May 25, 2015).

4 Allan Kardec, adapted from chaps. 14–15 of *The Book on Mediums* (first published in 1874; current publication by Cosimo Inc., 2007).

5 W. B. Yeats, *Swedenborg, Mediums and the Desolate Places*, 14 October 1914, http://www.sacred-texts.com/neu/celt/vbwi/vbwi21.htm.

6 This book with the articles was compiled and published jointly with Gareth Knight as *Spiritualism and Occultism* (republished by Thoth Press, 1999).

7 Jean Markale, "Our Lady in All Things," part 2 in *The Great Goddess: Reverence of the Divine Feminine from the Paleolithic to the Present* (Rochester, Vermont: Inner Traditions International, 1997), 185–187.

8 *The Equinox* ("*Blue Equinox*"), vol.3, no.1:21; *Liber XV* [The Gnostic Mass].

9 Philip Heselton, e-mail to authors, August 22, 2013.

10 Sanders, chap. 9, page 101. Harry Edwards was a famous Spiritualist healer of the 1950s. He is still revered for his accomplishments.

Chapter 3

Modern Trance Traditions: Shamanic Witchcraft, Seidr, and Vodoun Trance States

Within the Western magical community today, there are several neo-Pagan traditions using trance techniques. Wicca practises Drawing Down the Moon, while Asatru and the Northern tradition (the reconstructed customs of the Norse, Anglo-Saxon, and Germanic peoples) practice *seidr*. There is also a fusion of modern shamanic practise and Witchcraft, which has been developing since the 1980s, often referred to as *Shamanic Witchcraft*. Although not strictly Western tradition, the only surviving unbroken tradition of trance belongs to the African Diaspora religions: Vodoun and Santeria, which have roots going back to the Ifa religion of Northwest Africa. Within these traditions there is an idea of being "ridden" by the *loa*—being possessed by the ancestral deity-spirits.

We also divide trance into two categories: *oracular trance*, where the object is to connect with spirits for the purpose of prophecy; and *ecstatic trance*, where the ritual is more open and allows for multiple trancees and the participants all having personal experience with the invoked spirits, rather than there being a defined seer.

Shamanic and Ecstatic Witchcraft

What we wish to cover here is specifically the development of ecstatic trance in Witchcraft. In Gardnerian Wicca, its use was limited to raising energy—the cone of power—by dancing and chanting of "The Witches' Rune" in a ritualistic fashion. Unlike Vodoun, the use of these techniques rarely went beyond twenty minutes in duration, and was unlikely to induce any form of trance. Some of this is because Gardnerian Wicca embraces ritual magic rather than ecstatic methods. There were those in Witchcraft, spurred on by their experiences with dance and chanting, who started to experiment with trance techniques in the late sixties, which can be attributed to the interest in psychedelics at this time. A good example of this can be seen in one of the first films on modern Witchcraft, *Legend of the Witches* (1970).* In the film, strobe lighting is used to induce trance in an initiation ritual. Many of the younger generation coming into Witchcraft from the '60s hippy movement had already experimented both with psychedelic and Eastern transcendent mind-altering methods, which were the fashion of this time period. Although some of this was undoubtedly frowned upon by the older generation of Wiccans, their disapproval did not affect the new generation or stop them from incorporating some of what they had learned into ritual. The significant changes in modern Witchcraft, though, did not began until over a decade later with a generation that began to challenge the ceremonial nature of Wicca.

In the United States, the development of shamanic and ecstatic Witchcraft began to develop in the late 1970s. It is difficult to separate the two terms, as they are deeply entwined with each other; shamanism being an ecstatic tradition by definition. The major difference between Shamanic Witchcraft and shamanic practise is that Shamanic Witchcraft is a group activity, rather than a solitary practise, although there are some who would undoubtedly argue this point. Shamanic and ecstatic Witchcraft were without a doubt influenced by the interaction with Native American culture, particularly as Americans sought to find their magical connection to the land on which they lived. The drum began to be a common sight in ritual during this time, and it is to this day.

Starhawk was one of the first individuals to write about using ecstatic methods in her book The Spiral Dance (1979). She originated out of Victor and Cora Anderson's Feri (Faery) Tradition. She suggested that ritual should be freer flowing, with the use of drums, dancing, and chanting being an integral part, rather than the more rigid form of ritual found in orthodox Wicca. These techniques became a major part of the Reclaiming Tradition. The Spiral Dance had a major impact on the way people practised ritual and influenced others, such as Sabrina Fox in the US, and Shan Morgain (previously Jayran) in the UK.

---

* *Legend of the Witches* (1970) was written and directed by Malcolm Leigh. It features Maxine and Alex Sanders' coven.

By the mid-1980s the increasing influence of Michael Harner's core shamanism made the use of drumming and dancing almost compulsory in open ritual, and began to be adopted into mainstream Wicca. The term Shamanic Craft first appeared in the 1980s in the United Kingdom, being first used by Shan Morgain in London. As far as we know, this was the first time someone has specifically labelled any form of emerging tradition within modern Witchcraft, which employed shamanic or ecstatic methods as part of its ritual practise, in this way. Even today, people who employ such techniques rarely label themselves. Shan was a major figure in the revival ecstatic techniques in Witchcraft, and was a well-known figure within the British neo-Pagan scene. In 1988 she set up The House of the Goddess in London, one of the first active organizations in the UK that employed trance techniques.

Taking the High Seat: Seidr and Spaework

The origin of modern seidr practise is in the historical reconstruction of past Northern European shamanic traditions. It is important to point out that the term *seidr* (or, in Anglo-Saxon, *seith*) refers not just to trance but also to Northern European witchcraft, as well as sex magic, both being considered in the later patriarchal culture as being a form of negative magic (for more on this see page 241). For this reason, modern practitioners distinguish between seidr as a whole and the trance-prophecy aspect, which they refer to as *spaework*, or *oracular seidh*, which survived as the only accepted aspect of the seidr tradition well into the eleventh century.

The practitioners of spaework do not claim an unbroken lineage, nor complete accuracy in their historical representation. What is important to them is the result of the practises, the connection with guiding spirits. The biggest exponent of this method of practise is Diana L. Paxson; her importance in the revival of trance-prophecy cannot be underestimated. She has an MA in literature, specializing in the Middle and Dark Ages. Before beginning to write nonfiction, she was known for her novels, her first being *Brisingamen* (1983), which delved into the mysteries of the Norse myths. This novel was the beginning of her serious exploration of Norse mythology. During a shamanistic workshop led by Michael Harner, Diana had a spiritual experience, an encounter with the Norse God Odin, which led her to start studying runes and seidr as magical practise. In addition to Asatru, she studied other magical traditions including Wicca, ceremonial magic, and Umbanda, which have all contributed to her knowledge of trance techniques. In 1988 she set up the group Hrafnar, in Berkley, California, with the intention of recreating ancient practises of Norse and Germanic peoples. Seidr was an important, if not the core ritual element of this group. It was from this work in Hrafnar that she developed a Core Oracular Method. More recently, in addition to giving lectures and workshops at private and open events, she has written two books on the subject of seidr and trance: *Trance-Portation: Learning to Navigate the Inner World* (2008) and *The Way of the Oracle* (2011) both published by Samuel Weiser. *The Way of the Oracle* includes history and the full text of Diana's spae ritual. She is currently working on a book on possessory trance.

Modern spaework is as much a historical reconstruction as it is a mediumistic practise. Generally, participants will be dressed in traditional costume, and the ritual will be organised around traditional guidelines drawn from historical material, such as the Poetic Edda and the Saga of Erik the Red. A special elevated chair is also used. Paxson considers this an important part of the ritual, helping to put the practitioners into the correct mood:

When participants wear authentic clothing, they can make that psychological transition, just as a shaman wearing a cap or cape with skins or pictures of her power animal and other symbols helps her to function. A great deal of this could be classed as theater, but any analysis of the shamanic literature will make the dramatic element in most traditional practices quite clear.[1]

Photograph 5: Diana Paxson in traditional Norse dress at Thingvellir, Iceland, 2002
(Photo courtesy Diana L. Paxson)

All of this comes together to create a powerful and atmospheric ceremony.

Like Drawing Down the Moon, it is helpful in modern seidr practise to define sacred space for consecration and protection. In modern Norse practise, one way to do this is by calling of the dwarves who uphold the four corners of Midgard (our world): Nordri (north), Sudri (south), Oestri (east), and Vestri (west). The World Tree, Yggdrasil, is the sacred center. The purpose here is to also spiritually orient the practitioners, particularly the seers who are using the traditional cosmology of Norse practise. A circle is not cast, although the area may be cleansed with incense or water "from the Well of Wyrd," which is also used to purify the seers.

The invocation of the gods is an important aspect of spaework, particularly those who will be called during trance. The invocation of both Freya-Vanadis (see page 283) and Odin is essential, as both are patron deities of this practise. Other spirits, including those of the ancestors, may also be called. The use of music, chanting, singing, or drumming is at the heart of the trance technique employed, raising energy to be used by the seer to get answers. Much of the music used comes from traditional Scandinavian folk tunes, such as the music for the "Summoning Song" (based on "Heimo and the Water Spirit"). The song itself has a hypnotic quality, and at some points it is quite discordant:

> Make plain the path to where we are
> A horn calls clear from o'er the mountain
> The gods do gladden from afar
> And mist rises on the meadow . . .
>
> The hounds and eight-legged horse we hear
> A horn calls clear from o'er the mountain
> The heart beats quick as Yggr draws near
> And mist rises on the meadow . . .

Drumming is also an important part of the spaework technique devised by Paxson, which clearly derives from Harner's core shamanism (although the reference to Odin "drumming with the voelvas" in *Lokasenna* may indicate the Norse used it as well). The general format for her style of seidr ritual is as follows:

- Purification with the use of herbs or incense. Quarter Guardians and spirits may be called to center and balance the group. Warders watch over participants.

- Invocation of the gods and goddesses, particularly those associated with seidr/seith, plus ancestors and allies.
- The guide begins induction of the seer and participants by narrating a pathworking based on Norse cosmology. She may also use the drum, starting with a slow beat and building.
- The pathworking leads the group to an appropriate place in the otherworld, such as the Well of Urdh or Hel. At this point, the seer is "sung through the gate" and into a deeper stage of trance, while everyone else waits outside. The guide now acts as an intermediary for the seer. Participants are encouraged to ask questions, which may involve contacting ancestors or gods, as well as getting simple answers.
- When all the questions have been asked, the guide talks the seer back through the gate and narrates a pathworking to bring everyone back to ordinary consciousness.
- All the powers who were invoked are thanked, and the warders make sure that everyone is grounded.

Being "Ridden": Vodoun and Santeria

In recent years, there has been a growing interest in African Diaspora practises among neo-Pagans of both African and Hispanic origin. We first came across this in the United States in the 1990s, and discovered that it was becoming increasingly common to find lectures, workshops, and rituals on the subject being conducted at neo-Pagan events. Clearly, an overlap between neo-Paganism and these religions was occurring, but why? We asked one practitioner this question, and his answer was not what we expected. He said it was due to the import of *djembés*, the West African drum, customarily used in traditional ritual. These drums had become very popular at Pagan events in the 1990s. He stated that in his tradition, it was believed that djembés contained a spirit, an *obé*, and the use of the drum invoked the spirit. While we agree with this viewpoint, we also believe that these traditions offer immediate experience with spiritual entities, something which had been lacking in the neo-Pagan movement up until recently. It also offered a tradition that is not "in the head"; where experiencing is more important than the collection of knowledge, which was the basis of Western occult thinking. At first, this crossover did concern us, as most occultists with any experience know there are no quick fixes, particularly in adopting a culture one may not understand. We were concerned that there would be problems in this crossover, but

as time goes on, we have become less concerned. This is mainly due to
our contact with neo-Pagans of Afro-Caribbean background, such Ivo
Dominguez and Lilith Dorsey, who have seamlessly taken their cultural
backgrounds and combined them with the ethos of modern Paganism.
Since this time, interest in Vodoun and Santeria has spread to the United
Kingdom and Europe.

Vodoun, Santeria and their many derivates originate from the Caribbean, particularly the islands of Haiti, the Dominican Republic, Cuba,
and Puerto Rico. Other forms can also be found on the West Coast of
South America, particularly Brazil (Umbanda and Candomble). When
slaves were brought from the west coast of Africa to the Americas during
the sixteenth and seventeenth centuries, they brought with them their
own spiritual and magical practises. These practises continue today with
several names. The pure form, still practised in West Africa is known as
Ifa, but in the Caribbean and in the American state of Louisiana, it has
developed into two distinctly separate forms. When slaves were brought
to the colonies, they were converted to Christianity and, like early Christian Europeans, refused to give up their pagan practises very easily. They
hid their magical beliefs and practises behind the culture that enslaved
them. In French colonies, such as Haiti and New Orleans, this was less of
a problem, as the French had a much more laissez faire attitude towards
religion; in these areas it developed into what we call Vodoun. In the
Spanish colonies, Christianity was less forgiving. It became necessary for
the slaves to hide their deities behind saints, just as the early pagans did
in Europe. This practise is commonly known as Santeria, literal translation being "the way of the saints."

Within a Vodoun ritual or Santeria bembé, it is common for a participant to be possessed by a spirit, either a loa or orisha, respectively
(see Photograph 6). In Vodou, the participant is often referred to as a
"horse," as they are "ridden" by the spirit. On the surface this seems
to be reflected in the Wiccan Drawing Down the Moon, in which the
high priestess allows a deity to speak through her. There are, however,
some major differences. The first is that in Vodoun or Santeria, the
orishas or loa are not regarded as gods or goddesses like they are in
the Western and Northern magical traditions. This can become confusing to Western practitioners, and it is best to consider them to be like
ancestral spirits. In some traditions, such as Cuban, they are considered
to be "families" (multiaspected), hence one may get several forms, or
"avatars," of the same deity. For example, Osun, a water divinity, who

governs love, beauty, and marriage can also manifest as Oshun Ibu Ikole I ("the Vulture"), Oshun Ibu Yumu ("the Elder"), Oshun Ololodi ("the Diviner"), etc. The second and most important thing is that a bembé is considered to be an ecstatic ritual more in keeping with the Dionysian practises of ancient Greece (see chapter 14), rather than being an oracular trance ritual, such as Drawing Down the Moon and seidr. Drumming, dancing, and the use of alcohol (traditionally rum) are all part of the ritual, as well as the use of cigar smoke as a purifying sacrament. There is a definite structure and ritual frame, while there is still room for spontaneity, which allows any invoked spirits to steer the ritual. Raymond Buckland once told us about his experiences on Haiti, where he attended a bembé.

The ritual Buckland described to us is important, as it shows both similarities and differences between Western trance traditions and those of a long-surviving contemporary tradition. Buckland was in Haiti exploring the spirituality of the Vodoun tradition, particularly in relation to Spiritualism and mediumship. He was invited to a ritual to explore the processes involved. He watched the whole process from beginning

Photo by Doron

Photograph 6: Vodoun ceremony, Jacmel, Haiti. Trance-possession, or being 'ridden,' is an essential aspect of Vodoun ritual.

(Photo by Doron, under license: https://en.wikipedia.org/wiki/GNU_Free_Documentation_License)

to end: from the invocation of the spirits and the use of vévés (traditional symbols representing the spirits or loas), through the traditional
sacrifice of livestock and, of course, the possession of individuals during
trance and drumming. It is the latter description which is of most interest: during the dancing and drumming in a packed and crowded ritual
space, a particular participant caught Buckland's eye. He was, to quote
Buckland, "a very large gentleman" who was clearly native to the island.
Buckland remembers that he was a truckdriver or of a similar occupation.
As the man was dancing to the drums, his whole demeanour changed.
From a stomping dance, he suddenly changed to more smooth and gentle
movements. Buckland noticed the change immediately, as did two priestesses—two mambos—who were sitting in the corner, dressed in their
traditional white dresses and headscarves. After some whispering, they
stood up and approached the truckdriver. As Buckland remembers, he
was oblivious to their presence and clearly in trance. They escorted him
out of the ritual space and into a side room. About ten minutes later, the
two mambos returned with the truckdriver. He was still in trance, but had
been dressed in a red dress, high heels, and a wig. They had recognised
immediately that he was being ridden by an aspect of Erzulie, a female
(or more correctly a family of female) loa. For the rest of the evening, he
continued to dance possessed by the spirit, flirting with all the men, who
did not consider this to be unusual at all. He did this into the early hours
of the morning, when she finally left him. According to Buckland, when
Erzulie left, he was somewhat surprised to find what he was dressed in,
much to the amusement of all present!

Buckland's story shows several interesting similarities to Western ritual trance practise. The first is that there are individuals acting as guides
in the trance experience at the ritual, even though this is not apparent at
first. These individuals are the mambos and houngans who are conducting the ceremony. The major difference is that they put more trust in the
invoked spirits to maintain the safety of the Vodouisant, or participant,
than we do in Western magical practise. Some of this is probably due to
the level of commitment a Vodoun or Santeria priestess or priest make to
their deity, compared with the level we take it to in neo-Paganism. Very
few Wiccan high priestesses would be willing to shave off all their hair,
as is the practise for dedicants of Erzulie. The second difference, outlined
by Buckland's story, is regarding gender. Within neo-Paganism there are
defined gender roles, such as in Drawing Down the Moon; a woman is
always possessed by a goddess, and a man by a god. This is not the case
in older traditions, such as Vodoun, or even traditional spaework.

The reasons a ritual may be performed are numerous, but in all instances the loa are invoked. The reasons for invoking the loa include healing, protection from 'black' magic or protection in general, bringing good luck, giving thanks, marking a particularly special date (e.g., an anniversary), satisfying the demands of the loa (as an initiate), and for the purpose of initiation. The spirits are invoked for just about any reason; not just to assist in magical or spiritual undertakings but also those in mundane life. No separation is made between the two in these traditions. Most rituals are communal events, with the exception of initiation, where the event is purely attended by the priesthood of the tradition.

Over the years, we have attended several Vodoun or Santeria rituals. There are differences between the two main religions, as there are in the different localized forms. We have outlined the most general forms, such as found in Haitian and Louisiana Vodoun. Please bear in mind that this is generalised, for the reasons we give above:

- **Preparation:** This is very important in Vodoun ceremony. In Haiti, this may take several days. It consists of erecting altars with statues, icons, and ritual items, as well as bowls of offerings.
- **Drumming with djembés:** This starts almost immediately and continues throughout the ceremony. It may pause at times for invocations of the loa.
- **Invocation of the loa:** This starts with the drawing of vévés on the ground. The most common items used to draw are corn and wheat flour. Offerings and sacrifices to the appropriate spirit are made on the vévé, as is the appropriate invocation. It always begins with Legba (Vodoun loa) or Ellegua (orisha), who is the "opener of the gates."
- **Continuation of drumming, and commencement of dancing over the vévés:** Meanwhile, the Vodouisant may be ridden by the loa. This may go on for several hours.

The experience of being possessed in Vodoun or Santeria may vary depending on the individual, but in all cases there are no halfways. These are trance-possession traditions, and although an individual mambo or houngan may have mediumship abilities, these are not part of the traditional ritual where only full possession takes place. Anyone entering a ritual becomes a participant, a Vodouisant, and agrees to be ridden by a loa or orisha if it so chooses. They do not have to be a trained priest or priestess for this to take place. There is no such thing as an onlooker in ritual rituals; everyone is involved in the process, and it is not unusual for first-timers at such rituals to be ridden, to become the horse for a spirit. Such an event, if one is unprepared, can be quite traumatic. Gypsy, who is experienced as a high priestess and sibyl in Drawing Down the Moon and Hellenic (Sibylline) trance methods, describes such an occurrence when she inadvertently was ridden at a ritual in New Orleans:

> This deity (Erzulie) I fought more than anything, not really knowing anything about Voodoo and quite confused at what was hitting me or shall I say, literally slamming into the back of my head and my back, then into the front of me and I hit the dirt flopping like a fish out of water, I really didn't expect it at all. The visions I saw I can't interpret either, I spoke fluent Creole and I don't speak Creole. That was interpreted just yesterday and it was when she didn't see her offerings or an altar to her, she said in Creole, "My anger will come down on you" maybe just as a saying? I am learning she has many aspects, I think after the very loving aspect came in, that one went out and her aspect of Dantor possibly showed up?[2]

In Gypsy's case, her negative experience occurred simply because she wasn't expecting it and wasn't prepared for it. She was used to the controlled (Apollonian) nature of trance in Western neo-Paganism. In Vodoun and Santeria, being ridden by a loa is considered to be an honour, and they certainly don't expect to be fought against, as Gypsy did against Erzulie (it is important to point out that she later ritually apologized). It is clear that this possession was much stronger than the ones she experienced in Drawing Down the Moon or in the method she used when acting as a sibyl. This is probably due to Vodoun and Santeria being ecstatic (Dionysian) rather than an oracular trance traditions (see chapter 14), which combines multiple trance methods, including dancing, singing, and drumming.

One other noticeable aspect of possession in Vodoun and Santeria is the demeanour of those possessed. While multiple techniques can be found in seidr, in both Drawing Down the Moon and seidr, the possessed tend to generally remain static during the ritual. This is not the case in being ridden, where the possessed individual may continue to dance and move around the ritual space. In some instances, the loa may sit down and take a particular pose, or insist on a particular item of clothing or ritual tool. A good example of this is Legba, who when possessing an individual, will consistently insist on sitting on a chair with one leg crossed over the other. He will often rock the chair, and insist on having a cigar. A similar parallel exists in modern seidr, where Odin insists on having a hat, and Freya insists on taking the nearest priestess' amber necklace to put around her own neck.

Michael Harner's Core Shamanism

Although not strictly a trance-prophecy tradition, core shamanism is important to mention because of its impact on those interested in trance work in the neo-Pagan community, both in the United States and Europe. We are aware of several neo-Pagan trance traditions that have their roots in core shamanism-trained practitioners, or those inspired by Michael Harner's work. For this reason, its importance cannot be ignored if one is to look at the modern history of trance in neo-Paganism. Unlike trance-prophecy and ecstatic ritual, core shamanism tends to take a purely therapeutic approach, revolving around a shaman-/client-healing relationship. Although the training may take place in groups, it is centered on the shaman, eventually acting in a solitary fashion in this role.

Michael Harner gained his PhD in anthropology in 1963, and went on to found the Center for Shamanic Studies in 1979. It was later established as the Foundation for Shamanic Studies; a nonprofit charitable and educational organization. He is considered by many to be the foremost expert on the practise of contemporary shamanism, publishing his first book on the subject Hallucinogens and Shamanism (Oxford University Press) in 1973. In 1980, he published *The Way of the Shaman: A Guide to Power and Healing* (New York: Harper & Row Publishers), the book he ultimately became most known for. It was one of the first books to give people a flavour of practical trance techniques, being based on his shamanic experiences with Jivaro and Conibo tribes of the Amazon.

Harner suggests that there was a core to all shamanic work regardless of culture, which has been lost in Western religious practise. This is important to remember when practising his techniques, since it is a synthesis of many cultures, rather than being based on only one. Although it is a broad overview, it has encouraged many neo-Pagans to study and adapt Harner's core shamanism techniques, in particular his use of drumming, rattling, journeying, and power animal retrieval, in a European magical context (although many are uncomfortable with the appropriation of techniques from cultures outside of their own).

By the mid-1980s, Harner's work had encouraged and inspired many to look at the lost trance traditions of Europe. Quite a few people became disenchanted with the existing traditions they came from, such as Wicca or ritual magic, feeling that they lacked the connection to Spirit and trance work, something many were beginning to yearn for.* In the United States, the previously mentioned Diana Paxson used core shamanism as a basis for her study of seidr, while in the United Kingdom, individuals such as the late Richard Westwood and Alawn Tickhill were reviving Native British and Anglo-Saxon shamanic practises.† Moonshine Publications published several booklets that encouraged practical exploration of Native British shamanism. These included *Riding the Horse*, *Weaving the Web*, and *Banging the Drum*, written by the previously mentioned Richard Westwood. To quote him from chapter 1 in *Weaving the Web*:

> We follow the shamanic path in Britain, and draw on that to energise and inform our lives . . . and look for inspiration from traditions which are native to Albion (Britain). This has come about for two reasons; one being that we don't have direct access to existing shamanic traditions such as the Native American, and the other which stems from that, is that we have an awareness of our own native traditions as being "right" for our land as they sprang from this land of Albion.[3]

Alongside *The Way of the Shaman* by Harner, *The Way of Wyrd* by Brian Bates encouraged many to look at Anglo-Saxon shamanism or seith as a valid magical path. Although an academic like Harner, who clearly inspired him, Bates took a very different approach. He decided to turn the knowledge he had gained from his study of several historical Anglo-Saxon manuscripts of the sixth century into a novel.‡ The result was a book that in many respects is similar to the writings by Carlos Castaneda about the shaman/sorcerer Don Juan, although it is based purely on academic research rather than personal experience, as Castaneda claims for his works.§

---

* Gavin was part of this movement, and joined Pagan Link as a contact in 1989.

† Richard and his wife, Kate, ran an occult bookshop in Selly Oak, Birmingham, UK, called Prince Elric's in the 1980s. He established the Pagan Link network.

‡ Brian Bates bases much of his research on *The Lacnunga Manuscript* (Harley 585), an Anglo-Saxon manuscript of herbs and their associated charms and magical practises.

§ Carlos Castaneda's first book on his training as a shaman/sorcerer under Don Juan Matus were first published in 1968, and was followed by several others. They became incredibly popular throughout the seventies, even though many claimed they were purely fictional. Many point to his fusing of several aspects of different Native American traditions as proof.

NOTES

1   Diana L. Paxson, "The Return of the Volva: Recovering the Practice of Seidh," *Mountain Thunder* magazine (1993).

2   Gypsy and Monte Plaisance, personal mail to the authors, 2002.

3   From chapter 1 in *Weaving the Web: An Introduction to Native British Tradition* (Birmingham, England: Moonshine Publications, 1987), 4.

Chapter 4

Dancing With the Divine: Personal Experiences of Trance-Prophecy

This chapter will give the reader an idea of the varied experiences that one may face when embarking on a journey into trance, prophecy, and deity possession work. Personal experience will always be different from what you read in a book, which is why sharing these experience is essential in understanding trance and what to expect during it. For this reason, we tried to include accounts of trance from individuals of diverse backgrounds. Some are from traditional Wiccan backgrounds, such as Alexandrian or Gardnerian, while others come from Norse seith/seidr, Vodoun, Santeria, eclectic Pagan trance-prophecy, and even Christianity. Some have trained with us over the years, learning the techniques we teach in this book, while others are traditionally trained or have developed their own techniques. Regardless of their credentials or training, what is important are the similarities in the experiences they describe.

Gede Parma—a Hereditary Seer

Gede Parma (Fio Santika Akheron) is a Witch, singer with spirits, mystic, priest, and award-winning author. He is an active initiate of the Wild-Wood Tradition, as well as the Anderean Craft, and a Reclaiming Witch and teacher. Gede is a hereditary healer and seer with Balinese, Gaelic, and English ancestry. He is a proactive and dynamic teacher and an enthusiastic writer, and travels internationally to serve and listen with magical communities. Currently, he calls Ubud, Bali, home and has returned to the island of his birth. A devoted priest of Persephone, Hekate, Hermes, Aphrodite, Dionysos, and the four Witches' gods of his traditions, his spiritual path is highly syncretic and ecstatic and fuses spirit-led gnosis as well as inherited and older lore and customs.

I was born a vessel of the spirits by virtue of my father's line. At a very early age, my younger sister would become possessed by the spirit of my late grandmother, who was a renowned medium and a powerful healer. In Bali, spirit possession is a 'side effect' of any ceremony that may involve trance elements. Due to the culturally contextual cosmology, individuals who are entrenched within Balinese ritual and magic are highly susceptible and open to the wandering beings of the island's diverse cornucopia of spirits.

I began to experience trance possession at the age of fifteen. It started while I was alone and usually in the middle of ritual. My mind and heart would begin to throb, as my body rocked back and forth, and my eyes would flutter rapidly. I would slip in and out of consciousness as spirit-forces and beings sat within me and granted visions or spoke charges. It was a strange and delicate time. I trusted these forces because of the Great Powers and my ancestors who watched over me. I was being prepared, lubricated by the spirits. My life changed dramatically and powerfully because of these interactions. I teach what I have learnt from my practise of possessory rites only after I have passed my basic teachings to my students, and anchored them in their own sovereignty of self, self-possession, and integrity. We are coconspirators with the spirits—as Witches and sorcerers—and they respect us more when they can tell we are in our power, consciously participating and negotiating our boundaries.

During this preparatory period, I was also psychokinetic and received visitations from serpentine-angelic beings that had no precedent in my personal spiritual and magical explorations. I was not raised in any Abrahamic tradition, nor did I feel the least bit inclined to study the heavily Hebraic angel lore. As I now say, however, "the angels chose to work with me, not me with them." And I have discovered the hidden angelic lore in the traditional streams of Old Craft.

When I was sixteen and seventeen, I experienced trance possessions that culminated in foreign languages spouting from my tongue, my hands plunged into fire for lengths of time, and I experienced total physical displacement. While I recall some of the events, the details are always vague and most of my memory is supplemented by witnesses. I felt overwhelmed, challenged, frightened, yet oddly familiar with these consciousness-altering experiences.

The WildWood Tradition, of which I am an initiate and helped to mid-wife, is decidedly supported and informed by trance experiences ranging from the visionary and oracular to the possessory. Our Sacred Four, the divinities we hold especially hallowed in our lore and cosmology, would (and still do) possess individuals and convey techniques, lore, stories, and wisdom. Drawing Down the gods is a consciously cultivated and seriously appraised skill within our tradition, though it is by no means the only re-lationship we have with our gods, and we are very aware of the spiritual codependency that can develop between any vessel and deity.

Ultimately, what must come first is the divinity of self. It is through ecstasy that we find that self is embodied All-Self. To know the boundar-ies and edges of self is to respect our individuality held within and deriv-ing from the matrix of All-Self. Any vessel who hopes to partner with a deity or other spirit in possessory work must know this; both parties must treat the experience as a holy communion—the temple of flesh meeting with the mantle of spirit. The truth, of course, is that the flesh is the im-mediate and direct expression of the spirit, and that the spirit is the con-sciousness of flesh. To become 'possessed' by any spirit-force or being is a delicate dance of surrender rather than submission, of Perfect Love and Perfect Trust, which holds and facilitates a union and dance between the consciousness of the vessel and the consciousness of the deity.

In the WildWood Tradition, we work with a method that was passed to us directly from our Crescent-Crowned Goddess, one of our Sacred Four. She referred to it as the "3 x 3 method," and we have codified the technique into nine steps. The vessel would have most likely entered into an intense rapport with the deity for a solid period—praying, meditat-ing, sharing dialogue, and making devotions. The vessel would have also been previously trained in the arts of Drawing Down during their aspi-rant training. The twenty-four-hour period before the possession is spent fasting and drinking water (some will measure their own capabilities and judge for themselves exactly what to fast from or what to eat and focus on the mythos of the deity and incorporating it). The vessel is then attended to by "tenders" who will aid in the trance induction (usually through the 3 x 3 method) and stand by the vessel's side as they move, speak, and act for deity in the ritual.

The 3 x 3 method is expertly crafted to allow for a guided and grad-ual refinement and deepening of the consciousness of the individual into a space of deep trust, love, and surrender. For those of us who are natural vessels, this kind of preparation is not always necessary, though it is preferable to deepen and guide the experience. Personally, I will simply eat lightly, pray to the deity beforehand and affirm the allyship/partnership, and then breathe into my center, embrace my soul-shape as a vessel, and call out to the deity/spirit. For me, the transition in consciousness is quite physically demonstrable, as I will start to uncontrollably shake, writhe, or even slump. This passes and my consciousness recedes and I float in a comfortable, dark space until the deity leaves. At times the deity/spirit will leave suddenly and my body will collapse; at other times the transition is gradual. Generally speaking, I retain little to no memory of the proceedings; however, there are times I can recall events and information if witnesses remind me.

Other techniques I teach and practice allow for memory recall and are less intense. In Reclaiming Tradition (popularized through Starhawk's and others' writings) we call this "aspecting," in common with other revivalist Craft traditions. Aspecting is not full possession but is a skill to master in that it requires anchoring, negotiating with spirit-beings, knowing one's current and deep edges, and running and holding life force. It takes a little more focus on the part of the aspector or vessel, in my experiences, than just stepping aside and letting the spirit take you, which is valid as well, of course. I also teach something called double-headed trance possession and facilitate rituals known as the Three-Circle Possessory Rite, which Hecate gave to my southeast Queensland community. These are powerful rites that I describe in my essay in the 2014 Llewellyn Witches' Companion.

As a vessel that manifests divinity, it is part of my magical vocation to offer my services in ritual, privately or publicly, when called for. I have been working consciously with possession for nearly a decade, and while there is skill to it, it is also simply another mode of my being. I work in partnership with the gods; we respect one another.

Diane Champigny—Mantle of Stars:
Drawing Down the Moon

Diane Champigny is a third-degree high priestess of the Alexandrian tradition of Witchcraft. She runs an Alexandrian training coven in New England. She is also an accomplished trance medium, occult bibliophile, and contributing author to Priestesses, Pythonesses, Sibyls; From a Drop of Water; Hekate: Her Sacred Fires; *and* Vs.: Duality and Conflict in Magick, Mythology and Paganism, *published by Avalonia Books, Glastonbury.*

My background and training is that of an Alexandrian priestess. I was originally trained in an Alexandrian-based coven with ceremonial overtones due to our heralding from a magical order in Boston, Massachusetts. I have since retrained in an Alexandrian coven in the United Kingdom. In both instances, Drawing Down the Moon is central to the practice.

Drawing Down the Moon is a form of deity assumption in which the priest invokes the power of the Goddess into the body of the priestess [*see* chapter 12]. How this ultimately manifests varies from priestess to priestess and from occasion to occasion. At its core, Drawing Down the Moon is a specific occult method that depends heavily on the rapport of the participants, especially that of the priest and priestess, who bring through the godlike dynamics of a deep polar relationship, mediating to all men and women via the group soul/collective.

What happens prior to the rite is of utmost importance. I try to eat as little as possible beforehand and remain in a state of repose/meditation for much of the day. The process starts before we enter the temple, as stage by stage I attempt to prepare myself as a channel or vessel of our Divine Mother in order to identify with the cosmic archetype. The trance state deepens via the familiar atmosphere: chanting, incense smoke, flickering candle flame, and the company of well-travelled companions.

What I am attempting to do is gradually have my personality temporarily step aside to allow the divine to enter—to surrender my individual consciousness from the outset. Women are naturally suited to this service. Humility is essential for those following the path of the mysteries. It is a matter of backing into the god-form. The priest's words and ritual gestures all add to this process, forming a current of force in circuit. I initially make energetic contact with the priest before I move inward, envisioning myself as a hollow reed or straw. Aleister Crowley describes this feeling quite aptly in his *Book of Lies*: "The seed thereof is that which

I have borne within me from eternity, and it is lost within the body of our Lady of the Stars. I am not I; I am but an hollow tube to bring down the fire from heaven."

Her energy moves first through the top of my head or crown, radiating downward toward my throat, heart, solar plexus, legs, and feet. Feelings of detachment from the body, increase in physical height, and a shift in consciousness of more celestial proportions manifests. The state that I slip into is not unlike the cosmic stellar void that I was able to enter into easily as a child. The Source of All. The Temple of Nuit: "I am the blue-lidded daughter of Sunset; I am the naked brilliance of the voluptuous night-sky" (Crowley, *Liber AL vel Legis*, 64).

I oftentimes do not remember many details after coming back to my normal state of consciousness. Fragments of the rite sometimes do stay with me, but most times my fellow companions are the ones to describe the changes in my face, ethnicity, and age. Over the years it has been noted that I seem to channel a very Grecian presence. Recently, I was told that my entire face disappeared, which I've also experienced many times in a ritual context due to energy passage and shifts.

I tend to use The Charge as a jumping-off point only, with my goal being to have the divine speak through me. She can give advice, omens, portents, or warnings. In my experience, and that of my companions, it is wise to heed these precious and fleeting messages.

For me, it's a method of surrender and of mutual trust and understanding. Entering the process with great humility and trust are essential to a successful Drawing Down. It is the ultimate surrender of your being to the divine. The blessings of such a brush with Her are truly invaluable and not something to be taken lightly. It is a matter of suspending disbelief and literally stepping aside or dropping your personality of this incarnation (or incarnations). Through years of this type of ritual possession or contact, the method deepens to the point where between trained and well-worn initiates, the mere touch of the priest's hand upon the priestess will incite the process to begin. To a certain extent, we can bring the process into our everyday lives, making each interaction we have on the mundane plane throughout the course of our day a spiritual experience. I consider it to be a walking, living, breathing meditation or mediation.

One calls the forces positive and negative, and realizes them in good and bad, emission and reception, life and death, idea and action, man and woman (positive and negative magnetic poles) in the material plane and, conversely, the woman (active pole) and man (negative pole) in the mental plane. As Dion Fortune mentions in *The Demon Lover*: ". . . a pouring forth of power (from the male) that quickened the life within her, causing it to flow forth in response to him." Her later novels, *The Sea Priestess* and *Moon Magic*, illustrate this cosmic law and its effects very clearly.

The male and female aspects of the Supernal Triad, Chokma and Binah of the Tree of Life, illustrate the technique quite well. They represent the opposing principles of the universe, which I bear in mind upon entering the Work. Once the Goddess has flowed through you, there is a veil that has been crossed that can never be completely closed. My worldview has become broader, and there is a certain part of me that stays in that "other" hidden world of the astral light. It can sometimes be a lonely existence, as not many people in everyday life have the same knowledge or experience. It is both a sacrifice and a service I am honored to have made my life's vocation.

Courtney Weber—Intimacy with the Gods: Trance-Prophecy

Courtney Weber is a priestess, writer, tarot advisor, and activist from Portland, Oregon. She received ordination as a priestess of Pan from Rev. Cyn DeFay of the Cluan-Feart Mystery School in 2005, and third-degree initiation from Janet Farrar and Gavin Bone in 2009. She is the high priestess of Novices of the Old Ways, a progressive Witchcraft community based in New York City. She is the producer and designer of Tarot of the Boroughs, a contemporary, urban tarot deck set in New York City. Her articles on Witchcraft and tarot have been published by Llewellyn, US Games, and Circle Times.

Our coven has had deeply profound experiences with trance-prophecy. We have had gods and goddesses prophesy the birth of twins, warn about ecological disasters in places near and far, deliver messages from the dead, bless, and heal. I have seen staunch skeptics walk away believers. I personally have received the same message numerous times from the same deity, coming through different people in different trance-prophecy (TP) rituals. I am a believer. I have seen the power of this work.

The transformation is visually remarkable and energetically palpable. Faces, whether behind the veil or not, tend to change. Individuals' bodies can also appear to expand or shrink, depending on the shape of the deity. Traces of the person's personality remains, but like an essential oil scented by a carrier, the personality of the deity may be "scented" by the personality of the seer, but the true nature of the deity shines through.

Hekate, for example, routinely plays with words and becomes giddy over offerings. Two Samhains in a row, we brought Hekate through two seers. Neither of these seers had met before or seen the other bring through the Goddess. The second seer was new to our circle on the night she took the chair and had not heard our tales of the prior year. Both times, Hekate giggled over play on words, and both times she became ecstatic over certain offerings, bouncing up and down in the chair at receiving chocolate and smearing elderflowers over her lap. Both women were vegetarians, but both times the women enthusiastically ate greasy chicken while bringing through Hekate.

When selecting our seers, we most often draw names randomly, which we believe allows the God or Goddess to decide who will bring them through. Quite often, the person most reluctant to take the chair is the one chosen, and, most often, those most reluctant are the ones with the most powerful experiences. This is not a practice in which ego proves an asset. Humility, groundedness, and easy ability to let go of personal masks allow the process to happen best. Attention seekers usually have weak experiences that lack the kinetic quality of the authentic experience. I do recommend people use the veil. The person's eyes and face can become glassy or stone-like, which can be eerie and uncomfortable to view. The veil also helps the seer better lose their normal consciousness to allow that of the being to take over.

The sights of the bridge and the gates are subjective to the person in the chair; however, the reactions post-TP are quite similar. Most people come out slightly disoriented as though they have just awoken from a deep sleep. Many are emotional. I've likened it to the emotions one has when they dream of someone who has passed away. The embrace of the person in the dream state is very powerful and very emotional when the dream is over.

As I'm writing this, I realize I'm spending a lot of time comparing it to a dream state, but it's far more tangible. You can feel another consciousness settle into you. You begin to share memories and associate colors with objects in an unusual way. You can see the pasts and glimpses of the future of those who come to speak to you. Words come out of you that make no sense to your waking consciousness but make perfect sense to the person hearing them. Even though your eyes are closed, it is as though you can 'see into' those who are around you, to their ailments, their suffering, their gifts, their blessings. Some of the images are very strange.

The first time I took the chair, it felt like I was suddenly sharing my blue jeans with another person. My body felt tight. Sensory-wise, it was as though I was sleeping and people were still talking to me. I could hear what was said, but the words came through a filter and seemed more like pictures. I remember seeing a great deal of the color red and hearing a single voice in the back of my head telling me what to say, but it was hard to move my mouth. I didn't have full control of it. The main characteristic I've experienced is that once the being is settled in, I've been aware that something is going on and have even wondered a few times, "Is this really happening or am I just playing along?" But it's not until the being leaves, when you feel the energy get pulled out of you and you're suddenly back in your normal state that you realize something happened. It's like being in a realistic dream and wondering why things are just "slightly off," only then to be awakened and realize you really were somewhere else.

One of my favorite stories is when Brid came through; I walked around the circle "on chicken legs." I remember having difficulty walking, as though my body was suddenly too heavy to carry. Some of the things were relayed to me, later. In one of the stories, Brid thanked a woman present "for the lavender." The woman was shocked because privately, she had been offering lavender to Brid on her home altar. This wasn't something I knew. I didn't even know the woman. All I could see was red, even behind a white veil, so I did not even know what she looked like. At the end of the circle, I struggled to release Brid, and it wasn't until Gavin tapped me on the forehead that I finally did. I could not catch my breath, even though I had no problems breathing until the being was released. It was as though I could not connect with my lungs. I've been in the chair numerous times, but that was the most powerful. I've often wondered if it was because that particular ritual happened on the first day of my menstrual cycle. Afterward, I was very emotional and cried for at least an hour. It solidified my relationship with the Goddess and with being her priestess. I felt as though I knew her better than ever and firmly had her guidance on my journey.

Leading and doing trance-prophecy has brought me to a level of intimacy with the divine that was never possible before. It takes the divine out of the ethereal and makes it accessible through sight, sound, scent, and touch. As I said before, I am a believer. I have seen the power in this work. I can attest to its abilities to empower a ritual, empower Spirit, and empower the Craft.

Gayleen Jacobs: From Christian to Pagan: The Toronto Blessing

Gayleen's experience has been included to show that trance and connecting with divinity goes beyond any one religion or tradition. In her case, she was unable to find what she needed in the way of training in trance from the church and instead turned to Witchcraft. She is now a second-degree high priestess, having trained with us for over six years, where she trained in trance-prophecy more formally. She was already making connections with other deities before leaving the Christian church, so it was a natural step for her to move toward neo-Pagan trance tradition.

I was a Christian charismatic Catholic missionary, with my husband and our seven children, for a total of sixteen years. I served in the Philippines for most of that time, and worked in Germany and Ireland. I spent nearly two years in training in Hawaii (yes, a brilliant place to train)! We moved to Ireland and worked there for eight years, where we trained other people. It was there that we encountered the "Toronto Blessing" [see Glossary]. It has other names, including Father's Blessing, the Anointing, the Awakening, the River and the Fire (Wikipedia).

I first heard about it from a charismatic Church of Ireland, where the Holy Spirit seemed to be pouring out this blessing on them. I went to a meeting with my husband and saw people responding to this anointing of the Spirit.

Steve and I were training people for missions, to be able to tell other people about Jesus, so we asked the priest there if he had someone to come and teach us about it. The man who spoke to us (about forty people) told us how to ask properly for the Holy Spirit and to not be afraid of our physical responses, but to go with them.

So he started with a prayer with great expectation of God's willingness to share his goodness with us, then the worship group, who had been told some of the better songs to play, started in. We started with fast, joyous songs, working to slow, deep, worship songs, with most of us having hands in the air, or down on our knees deeply lost in who God is. At the same time, the speaker came around and started to lay hands on us. The next thing I knew I was laughing hysterically, and so were many others. I felt a pull in the middle of my stomach causing me to bend over. These two symptoms happened every time I prayed this way. It did not hurt; in fact it almost felt good. Then many of us started to get visions that were spoken, and to prophesy. Sometimes it was for an individual in the group, sometimes for the whole group, and many times just to edify the group as a whole.

I walked away from this first meeting a changed person. I have in the past regularly received visions or prophecies, but have felt very much alone because very few of my fellow Christians also received them. This time was different, as everyone felt it, had visions, and prophesied.

As a group we met regularly to pray for about two months, at which point the community split into two. People started thinking that maybe it was really the devil and not the Holy Spirit. We had times where people would hoot like owls, neigh like horses, bark like dogs, howl like wolves, and even hiss like snakes. We were suddenly banned from praying in the community building.

So I invited those who were still interested in being immersed in his incredible baptism of the Spirit to come to my house. We ended up with about eight people who were still interested. With a tight-knit family of eight, and three of them being good worship leaders, it took off like a wildfire.

One of the symptoms of this wildfire was the inability to sleep. I would shiver or shake constantly. I lost about thirty pounds, as I felt no hunger. The visions would hit me without warning; I could be on a bus, in a store, at a mass, and so forth. We were praying nearly every day, and we couldn't figure out how to turn the visions off. One time I was on a bus and all of a sudden I started laughing hysterically and literally rolled out of the bus. Talk about feeling a bit stupid! I have to say, though, I was so happy for the way that God (Jesus) was pouring out his love on me. I didn't mind; I felt the Holy Spirit had taken control of my life! I was privileged.

Our little group met for about eight months, although I experienced this outpouring for about a year. I had some personal journeys that I was taken through during that time. I will share a few of these. I usually had them after the worship time, but it got to a point where I could praise God by myself and be taken away. It was like the little steps had been learned, and I practiced daily to enter into this world that the Holy Spirit had prepared for me. Many of the other people experienced the same thing and were walking upon their own path, of course, as long as it was Christian.

Over the course of the year, I always came to a river that wound around, the scene would change, and the importance of the day I was there would also change. There was always a veil that was pulled back, silk, lace, but always white. After the veil was pulled back, I always felt help given me intellectually, emotionally, or physically, or even ways in which I could help others. I even felt, in some small way, that I was helping the Trinity in their great work.

The first time I was allowed through the veil, I met Jesus.* It was a glorious, joyous, and full of light time, in which I had sex with him. My life was mixed with fire and water, in a way that is incomprehensible and difficult to describe. It has marked me. I am not ashamed of this mark, one called to serve the god(s)!

Another time he took me to a mountain top, I saw the beauty of creation and all that was in it. The two of us danced together in joy, and the air was intoxicating. He took me back a few days later, and a city had been built. Factories had black smoke rising, and paved streets went out to all parts of the world. I sat on the mountain and cried. I felt like we were losing everything. He told me that this was my responsibility. I remember being depressed for days.

Another time I was floating in my little canoe, I looked up, and saw an old ornate church on a hill. I also saw a 'Jesus' that looked like the ones in the pictures, not like the one who had befriended me. This other Jesus came down, took me out of my canoe by force, dragged me half way up the hill, and raped me. At this point, the real Jesus came and cleaned my wounds, washed me, gave me fresh clothes, all the while weeping about the harm that was done to me. (I believe this is the organized church, different from those who know Jesus as the Healer.)

The last journey I will share is the last vision I had. I had many others, but I don't share much on these.

First, as always, I went through a silken veil, found myself in my canoe, but instead of being in my river, I was in a very dark, black, and turbulent bay. It was like I had found the ocean, but on a moonless night, with dark, dark clouds. The water was swirling, with huge white caps. The wind was blowing and bitterly cold. The water was splashing into my little boat, which had other people in it. I remember hanging onto the side of the canoe so I wouldn't fall out or be washed overboard. Suddenly we were hit with a large wave and the whole canoe capsized. Everyone fell out, and I didn't see them or the boat again. I thought I was going to drown. It was so real. Then Jesus appeared to me and took my hands

---

* Gayleen described this to image of Jesus on several occasions. She described him as young and Asiatic Indian in appearance. He did not fit the traditional Caucasian image. She later associated this Asiatic image with the Vedic god Shiva.

and pulled me to a circular, white sand beach that was about nine feet around. In the middle was an obelisk with writing on it that I did not understand. There were jewels at the top, but I could not see color or shape. It stood about fifteen feet. It was still dark and slightly stuffy, but I felt safe. Jesus put my arms around the obelisk and said to me, "This is your God now. Follow me." After laying there for a while, I slowly drifted back to where I was.

I have never stopped having visions or hearing things for others who ask or need to know. I had the side effect of sleepless nights until I learned how to ground. Long after I left Christianity, I still have a love for my Jesus. I do have "other" gods now who also speak to me. I still have problems dealing with the high I get from doing actual trance work. It really does give me joy to see others touched by something bigger (although not necessary more powerful) and know that they are loved. I also get a sense of destiny when I hear or get something that brings change into my or someone else's life, even if it is bitter medicine.

I personally believe the "blessing" that came to the Christian churches was good and brought change. It is now rejected by most at this time.

Lilith Dorsey: Possession and the Experience of Being "Ridden" in Vodoun

Lilith Dorsey, MA, hails from many different magical traditions, including Afro-Caribbean, Celtic, and Native American spirituality. Her traditional education focused on plant science, anthropology, cinema, and fine arts at the University of Rhode Island, New York University, and the University of London. Her magical training includes initiations in Santeria, Vodoun, and New Orleans Voodoo. Dorsey has been doing successful magic since 1990 for patrons of her business, Branwen's Pantry. She is editor of Oshun-African Magickal Quarterly, *and author of* Voodoo and Afro-Caribbean Paganism. *Most recently, she has been performing with the legendary jazz musician Dr. John, choreographing and dancing in his Night Tripper Voodoo show.*

Trance, possession—the words connote images of darkness, demons, and a dissolution of control, but in fact the exact opposite is what is really happening when an individual becomes possessed. Possession is a state of in-between, of liminality, the borderline or veil, if it were, that separates the worlds.

Many years ago, as both a scholar and a seeker of spiritual knowledge, I began to study traditional African religions. My anthropology professor had mentioned to our class that there was no such thing as modern American divination practices, a statement that struck me as false and one I wished to disprove. I had already made an undergraduate student documentary about tarot cards and Wiccan divination systems as practiced in late 1980s New York City, and was aware of many friends and fellow Pagans who used divination practices as part of their daily spirituality. Eventually my personal and academic investigation led me to the psychically charged city of New Orleans. The crescent city, where up is down, down is up, and the surreal becomes real. New Orleans is the place where the great Voodoo queen Marie Laveau was the first American to hold open pagan ceremonies and charge money for psychic divination. Many of Laveau's early ceremonies took place in Congo Square, an area where nineteenth-century slaves and free people would come to eat, celebrate, worship, drum, and dance in their traditional ancestral ways. In modern times, located across the street from Congo Square, is the Voodoo Spiritual Temple and Cultural Center. As a member of the Voodoo Spiritual Temple, I had my first encounters with possession. I saw people speaking in tongues, dancing with fire, and drumming the path to the divine.

When the gods descend, all that they do is writ large. The extraordinary becomes commonplace, this is foremost how they distinguish their majesty. In my work with the gods and goddesses of Voodoo, I have personally seen individuals under the influence of trance lift four times their body weight and roll through flames unscathed. One of the first times I experienced the phenomenon, I dropped to the ground, curled into a ball, and rolled at top speed to one side of the field, where I began to speak in languages I had no knowledge of. All of this occurred while another member of the temple mimicked my actions in real time and rolled to the opposite side of the field. Needless to say, possession is an interesting and confusing endeavor. In Haitian Vodou and New Orleans Voodoo, both religions that I have initiations in, possession is brought about with specific ritual combinations of aromatic herbs and oils, sacred waters, magickal baths, artfully drawn *vévé* symbols, complex rhythms and chants, happy accidents and intelligent designs. Every detail is controlled to produce the desired result. A possession experience is thought to give special blessings to both the participant and the observer. It is a way for an individual to access the divine. There have been numerous times when I have undergone a possession experience in order to help heal someone attending a ritual observance with their trauma, be it physical, emotional, personal, or professional.

Many people ask me about what the possession experience is like. Numerous people have even asked me if it was just like Linda Blair in *The Exorcist*. Again, for the record, no—it is not like that. In fact, there are many different stages or levels of possession. Afro-Brazilian practitioners of Candomble have listed them, ranging from mild nausea, all the way to body and language changes. For me, the experience is most often a combination or progression through several of these stages, and it is dictated by many factors: the god, goddess, ancestor, or entity involved; my own personal intent in the situation; the participants involved in the ritual; the other possessions that occur at the time; and what I like to call the "Q factor." The Q factor is how I refer to the unknown, which is always a force at work in the overall creation of any ritual experience. It is a process of discovery.

For example, one ritual I took part in took place on a sunny afternoon in a building with latticework walls. As we began to lay out the cornmeal vévé patterns on the ground, the shadows formed another image, that of a boat with a thatched sail, very similar to the vévé for the Haitian deity Agwe, so we added the cornmeal to the shadowy image and went on to include Agwe in the ceremonies that day. From adept to novice, no one is ever sure what they are going to encounter. One possession experience I had involved a family of Voodoo Loa, or deities, known as the insect Gede. The ritual was designed so that several people would simultaneously become possessed by insects. What ensued was a craving for sugar and a connection to the hive mind. I have met several of my fellow bugs over the years, and an odd kinship is still felt.

Possession in many ways is both a supreme expression of personal identity and a complete loss of self. In the Afro-Caribbean religion of Vodou, many believe that the first Loa, or divinity, to possess a person is the one that is their ruling spirit, above all others, guiding their destiny. Simultaneously, the possessed person is also called a "horse" and is "ridden" to whatever destination the universe chooses. The best advice is to keep an open mind and know that both the rider and horse have special blessings to give and receive.

Chapter 5

The Philosophy and Purpose of Trance-Prophecy: Prediction or Divine Direction?

T
he question posed in this chapter's title is the most important question to be answered in this book. Without a purpose, modern trance-prophecy techniques are just an act of amusement, a trivial sideshow in the history of neo-Paganism. It is far from that, and has, in fact, as we have previously shown, been a core practise of Paganism, ancient and modern.

The ultimate answer is that trance-prophecy is part of a bigger process, our cultural and spiritual evolution. The scientific rationalists would say that trance-prophecy has had its day, which ended with the death of the last of the classical sibyls or the last vala in the tenth century. Such irrationalism has now been replaced by science and a logical process. Regardless, scientists are still fascinated by the paranormal, particularly psychic ability. This is probably because scientists are still trying to come to terms with whether the universe is run by determinacy or random occurrence. During the writing of this book, a paper by respected academic and parapsychologist Daryl Bem of Cornel University appeared in *The Journal of Personality and Social Psychology*. He claims to have proven the existence of psychic ability.[1] As much as his critics have scrutinised and attempted to trash his evidence, they have found no fault with any of his findings. Of particular interest is how Bern finishes the article; he quotes from Lewis Carroll's *Alice through the Looking Glass*:

> Near the end of her encounter with the White Queen, Alice protests that "one can't believe impossible things," a sentiment with which the 34% of academic psychologists who consider psi to be impossible would surely agree. The White Queen famously

retorted, "I daresay you haven't had much practice. When I was
your age, I always did it for half-an-hour a day. Why, sometimes
I've believed as many as six impossible things before breakfast."

Clearly, even in this age of reason, some scientists still feel the need
to question the possibility of psychic ability. Why then do so many quite
rational people still go to those who can purportedly talk to the spirits
and guide them? Why is it, in an age where we view the universe as a
mechanism, where everything can be explained rationally, that we still
need those who can look one step further: the Spiritualist mediums, the
New Age channellers, or the new wave of neo-Pagan seers and oracles?
We can certainly see that there is still a need, even though we may not
be able to give an answer that fully satisfies the scientific rationalists, who
will undoubtedly critique Bern's findings. It is undeniable from the viewpoint of sociology when this need in our culture manifests.

It is apparent when you read the classical accounts of the oracles
and sibyls that they were at the height of their importance during times
of social stress. When the whole of the ancient world looked as though
it was going to burst into the flames of war, when people struggled to
survive famine and pestilence, and when natural disaster threatened to
destroy the tenuous fabric of ancient society, the oracle, the sibyl, and the
seer were there with messages of hope for the future. The most notable
of these, as every school child knows, is the story of Joseph, found in
Genesis 41:37–47. Joseph's dreams predicted seven years of fruitful har-
vests followed by seven years of famine; it mobilised the whole Egyptian
culture to prepare for the worst. Such messages did not just give people
a reason to look forward to the future, but collectively caused the social
structure to survive. Rather than resorting to "every man for himself,"
ancient cultures saw a reason to work together. It is clear that the sibyl
was as much a part of the prophecy as was the recipient—the two could
not be separated. Such self-fulfilling answers create their own questions,
one being whether they are prophecy or divine direction.

The question we are now faced with is: what is the oracles' or seers'
true purpose? Are they here to prophesise, or are they here to allow us to
receive direction from the Ultimate Divine, manifesting through the gods
and goddesses? Or is it both? This naturally leads us to also ask: why are
we seeing a resurgence of interest in trance-prophecy now? Clearly, the
world is going through some changes.

Spiral Time Theory: What Can and Can't Be Prophesied

Before we look at what possible purpose the seer or prophet may have, we first need to look at what can and cannot be prophesied. We would like to mention that like much of the more arcane material in this book, the following information is theoretical. Regardless of that, it gives an explanation from an occult viewpoint on why it is only possible for a seer to see certain events at certain times. It is first important to explain how the following theory came about. This is significant because we are not the only ones who have come to similar conclusions regarding the spiral in both the occult, New Age, and scientific communities. The spiral appears continually in nature, as the golden section, and in art as far back as the building of the Neolithic burial tombs of Europe. It has always held a fascination for occultists and scientists. Our modern scientific understanding of the spiral nature of DNA only came about because of a dream James Watson had of two spiralling staircases, linking both the previously mentioned snake as a symbol (as the caduceus) and the spiral.

We were in Palermo, Sicily in September of 2011, visiting a particularly special place where several fig trees grew together in a most fascinating and marvellous way. After a long walk, we turned a corner into the Piazza Marina where the trees grow. At this moment, Janet took on a vague expression, walking right out into the traffic. Luckily she was caught in time before she was hit by the cars. When we sat down with our Italian hosts, Janet recounted what had happened. As she turned the corner all the traffic disappeared, as well as all the people. The buildings appeared younger, without the weathering of time; there were no railings around the buildings as there are today, and the road was cobbled rather than tarmacked. During the discussion of what and why Janet had seen these images, Gavin started to scribble an image of a spiral on a napkin. Gavin had the epiphany that time was a spiral, which explained why only certain things at certain times could be seen during any form of prophecy or divination. In the past Gavin had toyed with the notion that time consisted of three spirals: past, present, and future, but now this new vision had filled in the gaps of his understanding making his theory more complete. In this reality, there was only one spiral.

Consider that time is a tightly coiled spring, with the seer sitting on one of the coils looking along the spring. She sits in the moment, the present, but she sits facing the future, which is ahead of her, with things yet to be experienced buried in the Akashic (see page 124), in the deepest recesses of the collective unconscious. Coiling behind her are those things that have gone before, and are already in conscious experience. From where she is sitting, she cannot see along the length of the whole spring, but only a linear vision of the tops of the coils as they move from left to right ahead of her. If she turns around from where she is sitting and looks into the past at those things that are history, she still cannot see everything from where she is sitting; she cannot see all of the coils as they bend around the spring. In fact, at best, she can only see possibly a third of everything that has gone before. All historians know that what is recorded is never complete, with secrets lost to time. But as time goes on we learn more about our past. As she turns around and looks into the future, she can see nothing, unless she has made herself receptive to the Akashic memory. Of course, this can happen naturally within prophetic dreams or psychic flashes, or by entering trance using the techniques described in this book. Depending on her vision, and the levels of her psychic ability, the seeress may see some distance along the top of the coils. She may do this by herself or with the help of a *guiding spirit* (a spirit guide or a deity). The guiding spirit would, allegorically speaking, sit above her crown chakra, allowing her to see more, but she will still only see the coils that are visible in a straight line ahead of her. She will only be able to prophesize about certain things in the future at certain times. She may have to move slightly further ahead into the future, travel along a coil slightly more, to see more clearly what is happening. As she travels in time along the spring, the coil beneath her will be turning and moving into the past, while she moves along the same coil into the future. The coil she is sitting upon is a spring, and, as such, those hidden things will now be in linear vision.

But does this make future time set? Is everything predestined? We discuss this in our next section about *wyrd*, but according to quantum physics it isn't, as there are multiple realities according to theory now accepted by many physicists as the many worlds interpretation.* These multiple realities also relate to this concept of spiral time as we describe it here. Many people have dreams about what could have been. What if they made a different decision in their lives? What if they married a different person? What if . . .? These are more than our unconscious minds dwelling on the past and reconciling choices. They are, in fact, visions of

---

* Hugh Everett III first proposed the "relative state formulation" in 1957. Originally, physicists scorned it until Bryce Seligman deWitt popularized it and renamed it in his book *The Many Worlds Interpretation of Quantum Mechanics* (Princeton Univ. Press, 1973).

other realities. At least, theoretically they could be. According to current quantum theory, every time we make a choice, several other different quantum realities come into being.

For example, in one reality John F. Kennedy was not shot, resulting in a complete change in world and personal history. Once this new reality occurs, it takes on a different quantum reality, a different frequency occurs. Of course, this means we exist in a specific frequency which is the same as the past, but changing as we make decisions in our present. This means that a seer sees into the future those frequencies that are strongest, those frequencies closest to those at her present time. This forces us to revise our view of how the spring is coiled.

Rather than it being one spring coiled tightly all the way along, it is, in fact, an infinite number of springs all coiled together. As decisions are made, the spring with the same frequency is the one the seer is most likely to see, but the coils of the spring are no longer tightly packed together. Between those coils exist coils of other realities, other possibilities which never came into being in this reality. Once a decision is made, the repercussions exist in the same quantum reality as the seer, and she will only be able to see these. But as other possible choices come into view, she will be able to see them, as they open to her or the questioner. There is one other interesting aspect to the coiled spring analogy of spiral time. Sometimes a coil can "slip." This means a coil from the past may accidentally slip along the length of the coil and may, in fact, become closer to the present. This may be temporary or permanent, and may be detectable to a sensitive or psychic. Janet was not the only one to have that experience at Piazza Marina in Palermo. Another accomplished Witch and writer had the same experience, which leaves the question as to why this happens at certain places. It could be that the energy of the place causes this to occur. In the case of Piazza Marina, it could be that the fig trees, which are seen as *axis mundi* (see page 105) in Mediterranean culture, acted as a magnet, psychically causing the coil from the past to be drawn to it. This does explain some reported 'ghost' sightings where people seem to slip into the past particularly at emotionally, psychically, or spiritually charged places.

The spiral time theory makes sense from an occult viewpoint, as it obeys *the law of reflection, the law of microcosm and macrocosm* ("As above, so below"). The spiral appears in DNA, as previously mentioned, but also in ancient cosmology as the spiral path, which intersects the realms and worlds of the unconscious mind and the astral realms (see chapter 7). This theory, whether you regard it as literally true, is irrelevant. The important thing is that it gives a model that is helpful for anyone working in trance-prophecy. It also explains one reason why a seer, a Tarot or rune reader, or any other diviner cannot see everything. Another reason is found in ancient concepts related to how we perceive fate.

Trance-Prophecy, Fate, and Chaos Theory

The most important concept in understanding the purpose of trance-prophecy is the concept of fate and its complex relationship with time. Many see the idea of fate as if everything in our lives is fixed from the moment we are born to the moment we die. From a spiritual viewpoint this is clearly untrue, for if it were true, there would be no point of getting out of bed in the morning. Everything would be fixed; it really wouldn't matter what you did, as everything would happen, as it should. This would also mean that there would be no free will in our lives as everything would be predetermined. Of course, what we are really talking about here is the nature of time. Many scientists in the field of quantum physics are debating whether time travel is possible and, if it is, whether we could change the past by travelling back to it. One argument is that yes, we can, but the big problem is that it results in a paradox: the individual travelling back would not be able to return back to the time they originated from. For example, if you went back to assassinate Adolph Hitler and succeeded, then historically you would have had no reason to go back in time in the first place!

The second argument is that although you can travel back in time, you cannot change it, because of this paradox. If you were to travel back in time to assassinate Adolph Hitler, it wouldn't matter what you did, as something would stop you from succeeding. The moment you go back into that period of time, you are a part of its enfolding events. Your failed attempt would be a historical event, which you may not have necessarily been aware of in your own time. Of course, this last thought really upsets the scientists, as it means there is no free will and the old concept of fate is correct! The third and most interesting concept, divergent dimensions in time, has recently become a favourite of science-fiction writers, something we briefly discuss in spiral time theory.

Quantum physicists believe that the universe consists of layer upon infinite layer of other universes identical to our own, except that in each one a minor change occurred that affected the whole universe. These divergent universes come into existence every time a decision or action is made. For example, say in Texas, in 1963, a mother brought her son a bottle of Coke. The boy drops the Coke, resulting in it smashing on the road. Later that day, John F. Kennedy, then president of the United States, starts his motorcade through the streets. Unfortunately, his car drives over the glass, resulting in a puncture, thus delaying the motorcade. Because of this incident, a policeman who is bored waiting for the President's procession strolls over to the other side of the road and sees a gun barrel protruding from a window. The would-be assassin is caught. The assassination is thwarted, and Kennedy remains in power. He institutes a nuclear disarmament policy with the Soviet Union, which now has more resources for its people. In the early 1970s, it starts the process of democratization in the USSR. The political situation in the world has changed, and all because a mother buys her son a bottle of Coke. Of course, this is an example that could be true in another divergent universe, which shows how one small detail changes the universe forever. This obeys the occult law of unity or connection,* which echoes modern chaos theory. There is a nursery rhyme, sung by children for centuries in Europe that echoes the point:

> For want of a nail, the shoe was lost.
> For want of a shoe the horse was lost.
> For want of a rider the battle was lost.
> For want of a battle the kingdom was lost,
> And all for the want of a horseshoe nail.

By now you are probably thinking: "This is all very interesting, but what does it have to do with trance-prophecy?" There are very important ways. The first one has to do with the nature of our own lives. We are all journeying in time, altering the world and the direction it is going in every day, within the confines of both the physical and magical laws. This means that we are altering the future of our lives and creating new possibilities for our future. As the smallest action, therefore, changes the universe, it means that fate is not fixed. This leaves us with a dichotomy, because if this is true, then why is it possible for the future to be predicted using systems of divination? The ancestors of the modern German, English and Scandinavian peoples knew why, and they gave this concept of changeable fate a name: *wyrd.*

---

* The occult of law of unity or connection states that everything in the universe is connected. All past, present, and future events are linked. This law, in fact, parallels modern chaos theory and the butterfly effect, which can be seen as this law in its most subtle form.

Wyrd, Reincarnation, and Fate

The word *wyrd* is Anglo-Saxon in origin; it is the origin of our modern word "weird." Although wyrd is Germanic in origin, derivations of this word can be found all over Northern Europe. The concept it represents would be familiar to almost every practitioner of magic around the world. It is similar to the idea of fate, but the major difference is that it allows change and the ability to grow from lifetime to lifetime. The normal concept of fate is that everything is fixed. In wyrd it is not; only pivotal moments are immutable. Referred to as *orlog* ("immutable fate"), they are often a result of actions in this or a past life. When doing magic, it is, therefore, important to understand the concepts behind wyrd if we are to practice magic ethically.

The idea of "the web" is synonymous with wyrd; threads like a great web interconnect all life (the Web of Wyrd). The web as a concept related to fate is found in Greece, in the myth of Ariadne, all the way to the ancient peoples of the Americas, where Grandmother Spider was said to be responsible for weaving the fates of men. In Norse/Anglo-Saxon mythology, this web is weaved by the Wyrd Sisters or the Norns. Interestingly, they are often portrayed as three witches (e.g., in Shakespeare's *Macbeth*). Clearly, it was believed that witches and magic users in general had the ability to shape the web.

As a symbol, the web is a perfect way of illustrating how wyrd works. The web shows that important aspects of our lives are connected, being the nodes where the threads of the web cross and join. Our journey in life always starts from the point in the center and works its way out. As we progress, we make choices as to which way to go—straight ahead, to the right, or to the left—but we always cross the circular threads, the *weft*, as we progress. These mark the parts of our lives we cannot change. They are the previously mentioned orlog—karmically predestined events, dictated by the actions of others or our own actions in past lives. For example, how many times have you noticed that you have met someone of importance in your life and later discovered that if you had not met them at that time, you would have met them in another way? Ever thought this was *weird* (wyrd)? You were destined to meet that person, possibly because of karma related to a past life. Very few people will take the direct route out of that web, straight ahead—the thread that you were first on when you were born. Throughout our lives, we zigzag our way out from the center of the web, meeting people and being involved in events that were predestined. Of course, not all the events in our lives are predestined; we do have free will. There are events that happen because of our choices rather than any form of orlog or immutable fate being involved. This means we do retain control of some of our own fate (wyrd), but it also means that our actions in this life may also create our own cross threads in future lives, things we cannot change in our next life. When we do finally reach the outside of the web, it is, of course, our own death, and we subsequently reincarnate. Any future life will have these previously mentioned cross threads. To use the Vedic term, they are karmic and we cannot pass over them until we have dealt with the previous issue from the previous life.

It is important to point out that these threads are not a measurement of time, but rather a measurement of our own development and growth in this life. Unfortunately, this means we can sometimes get stuck in a cycle if we do not learn a lesson in this life; this is called *the law of cyclical return** (see Illustration 1, The Web of Wyrd) and will carry it over into our next incarnation as the new threads of our next web.

If we have learnt the life lesson that the circular thread (the weft) of the web represents, an event that was karmically predestined, then we will move forward to the next event or the edge of the web. But, if we haven't learnt the lesson, we will move sideways along the circular threads of the web until we have learnt that lesson. Our lives will be stuck in a holding pattern until we learn what we need to know. Unfortunately, as all events are connected, if we do not learn the lesson but actively ignore it, we may find ourselves backtracking and going round and round on the web, and being given the same lesson to learn until we have learnt it, before going forward again. We will find ourselves in a *negative karmic cycle*—a karmically damaged stream of time. If we do not learn the particular lesson, we will die still stuck in that cycle not reaching the edge of the web, and the lesson will continue in our next life. The purpose of trance-prophecy on a personal level must be to help someone learn that lesson and move forward. Therefore, trance-prophecy cannot just be about giving an answer; it must also be about giving a direction to the querent. This was well known in ancient times, where it was believed that oracles were used as voice instruments for the gods, who used seers to make their followers aware of their wishes. This is best shown in the paradox of the Greek myths related to self-fulfilling prophecies.

---

* The law of cyclical return dictates that if you are unable to overcome a karmic obstacle, or unable to learn from the mistakes in your life, you will continue to face that obstacle until you overcome it.

Paradox: Self-Fulfilling and Directional Prophecy

A self-fulfilling prophecy is one that directs an individual in such a way that they fulfil the prophecy; if they had ignored the prediction, the events would not take place. For example, at a trance-prophecy ritual an individual is told that they will "win the lottery." The next day he or she rushes out and buys a lottery ticket, and lo and behold wins the lottery! Such prophecies are not so much a prophecy but the individual being directed by deity, spirit, or fate to fulfil their destiny. Of course, if the individual did not believe that the prediction would come true and refused to act on it, it wouldn't have! It is, therefore, incredibly important to be positive about predictions that one wishes to come to pass; this is particularly important if they appear to be negative.

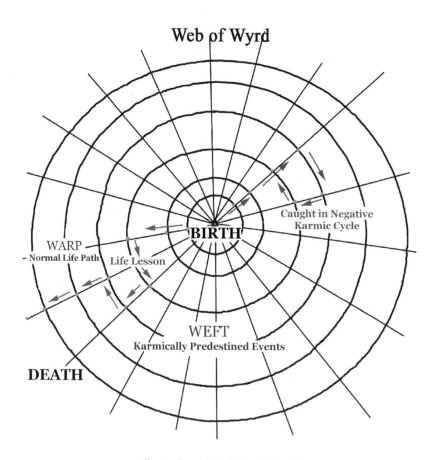

Illustration 1: The Web of Wyrd

The idea of self-fulfilling prophecy, dichotomies, and the paradoxes they create are not new. One of the most well-known Greek myths is about the dangers of believing a negative self-fulfilling prophecy, and acting in a negative way to prevent it from coming true. The myth is more commonly known for its use in psychology as a warning about the taboo love of a son for his mother. This is, of course, the myth of Oedipus, which we have summarized as follows:

Oedipus's parents, King Laius and Queen Jocasta, abandon their newly born son because of a prediction by the Oracle of Delphi that he will kill his father and marry his mother. A shepherd is ordered to take him out and kill him, but unable to do so, he is given to a shepherd from Corinth and ends up being adopted by the King and Queen of Corinth. They bring him up as their own son, unaware of his true origins. On reaching adulthood, Oedipus visits the Oracle himself and is told he is destined to kill his father whom he believes is the King of Corinth. He leaves Corinth in a chariot in order to avoid this fate, and during his journey gets into an argument with another charioteer, who will not give him the right of way at a crossroads. A fight ensues in which hot-headed Oedipus kills the other man, who (unknown to him) is, in fact, his biological father, King Laius.

Upon reaching Thebes, he is confronted at the city's gate by a sphinx, which terrorizes the city by asking a riddle of all travellers who attempt to pass through the gate and killing them when they cannot answer it. Oedipus is able to beat her in this contest of wit and will, and the outraged Sphinx leaps to her death hurling herself against the rocks below the gates. Oedipus is proclaimed the city's saviour and proclaimed king by the queen's brother, Creon, who is its regent. Oedipus marries Laius' widow, his own mother, and has four children with her.

After a plague suddenly descends upon the city, Oedipus is informed by Creon that the Oracle has instructed them to find and punish the murderer of King Laius, as only this will end the plague. Oedipus sets out to solve the murder, first summoning the blind prophet Tiresias who at first refuses to speak, but then tells him that it is he, Oedipus, who is responsible and that he will be condemned for it. Oedipus refuses to believe him and mocks him for his answer. Jocasta, his queen and true mother, encourages him to ignore such prophecies, and she tells Oedipus about the prophecy about her own son and how it never came true. She, explains that a prophet once told her that Laius, her husband, would die at the hands of their son, but her baby son died abandoned, and Laius himself was killed by a band of robbers at a crossroads. Oedipus becomes distressed by Jocasta's remarks, because just before he came to Thebes he killed a man who resembled Laius at a crossroads. He remembers that as young man, he had been told that he was destined to kill his father. Oedipus is now determined to learn the truth.

He learns from a messenger that his adopted father, the King of Corinth, had died of old age. Jocasta tells him that this is proof of the inaccuracy of the prediction, but Oedipus is still concerned. Overhearing the conversation, the messenger informs them that they should not worry, as the King and Queen of Corinth were, in fact, his adopted parents, and that he was a foundling brought to them by a shepherd. Jocasta begs him to stop, but Oedipus is determined to find out the truth, confident that he will find out that he is of low birth. The shepherd refuses to speak until being threatened with death, and he finally tells Oedipus of his true origins as the son of King Laius and Queen Jocasta of Thebes. Queen Jocasta, in her grief, kills herself and Oedipus, tortured and in frenzy blinds himself so he cannot look upon the misery he has caused. He begs Creon, now King, to kill him, but Oedipus is condemned by the Oracle to walk alone as a blind beggar until his death.

Regardless of all his precautions, Oedipus was unable to stop the prophecy from coming true. He had inadvertently, in an attempt to escape his fate, actually created it and discovered that he had indeed killed his father and married his mother.

This myth can be interpreted in many different ways:

- It can be seen as a warning of the futility of trying to change or avert one's fate;
- that this was a test by the gods who used prophets to manipulate the fates of Oedipus and that of the other characters for their own sublime purposes;
- that negative deeds carried out because a prophecy predicts a negative outcome, result in that negative outcome. Such a negative approach will, in fact, cause a self-fulfilling prophecy; it will cause the events to happen. Sometimes it is better to ignore such prophecies; and
- that trying to lead one's life by continually heeding prophecies is unhealthy and unproductive. It is ultimately one's own decisions that direct one's life, not those of the gods.

We disregard the first analysis for the following reason: what is the point of warning you about something if you cannot change it? This is illogical from the viewpoint of fate. It seems more logical that the gods manipulated Oedipus, his mother, and his father. But why would they do such a thing unless it was a form of punishment? This leads us to ask another question: why and what had they done to upset the gods so much? We should remember that the story of Oedipus is a morality tale that probably has no historical reality to it. We do believe that the gods will always use prophecy to bring about a positive outcome. It is the last two points that are the real lessons of the Oedipus myth and self-fulfilling prophecy: that negative reaction to a prophecy causes a negative outcome, and that by abdicating responsibility for your life to prophecies and oracles, you will suffer the same fate as Oedipus. It is also important to remember that negative prophecies do, of course, serve a purpose.

Negative prophesies are warnings, sometimes to prepare you for what is about to happen or allow you to change the outcome. The clue as to which it is will depend on the way the prophecy is worded. Again, there is no point in being given a prophecy that you cannot change or prepare for. Prophecies about the self are, therefore, always mutable; change in some form is always possible. For example, a warning of a car accident will give you the opportunity to change the outcome by being more careful while driving or avoiding a route you take daily. Janet once gave a Tarot reading warning that an electrical fire might start in the office where the person being read for worked. The next day, the person checked all the electrical sockets at work and discovered one by the electric kettle sparking and smoking. Of course, the paradox here is that by being positive there is a chance that you may never know if the prophecy was correct. Would that socket have caused a fire, or would it have just blown a fuse?

Self-fulfilling prophecies are rarely negative, regardless of what Hollywood movies suggest! Unless, of course, a negative attitude is taken (e.g., "It's fate; I can't do anything about it!"). Some predictions are warnings to emotionally prepare you for the worse; for example, the death of a relative by natural causes, which is unavoidable. Again, such prophecies will not be about the self, but someone you know or who you are close to. Whether the negative prophecy is a warning or preparing you for an event is not as important as keeping a positive attitude and taking positive action, just as you would if given a positive prediction. Sometimes, like in the myth of Oedipus, deities will use the ritual to "direct by prophecy." In other words, they may use prophecy to "tweak the web of wyrd," to influence the natural course and flow of fate. But unlike in the myth of Oedipus, it will always be for a positive outcome.

So What is the Ultimate Purpose of the Seer and Trance-Prophecy?

So far we have discussed what the seer is capable of and why. While we had suggested that originally their role developed to predict the cycle of tectonic changes, it took another function over time. One decade into the new millennium we face the onset of a possible new dark age: an ongoing cultural conflict between east and west; a never-ending recession; changes in social values, which are causing social upheaval; and the potential spread of new plagues caused by international travel. Just as in the fifth, sixth, and seventh centuries, we now face new challenges. During those times, the seers and oracles of the classical world appeared. They served a particular purpose: to give divine guidance during the times of distress the humanity was facing. In the times of strife and change, we can see the same thing happening today: a new cycle of resurgent interest in trance-prophecy manifests. People are again looking toward the words of the divine to guide them. It is the role of the seer to give those words of warning and consolation as they are needed, but also to perform a more important function that is to be part of the Great Work of the new millennium. For centuries we have been without our ability to be fully guided by the divine. We say fully because at different times individuals have been influenced: Copernicus, Galileo, and Steven Hawkins, to name a few. One of the best examples of this is the Indian mathematician Srinivasa Ramanujan.* A devout Hindu of the Brahmin caste, his groundbreaking theorems have continued to influence modern mathematics, and he credits the visions given to him to the goddess Namagiri (an aspect of Lakshmi). He is one of the few figures, including such spiritual leaders as Gandhi, who realised what was taking place. Now this ability to consciously communicate has returned in trance-prophecy, its purpose to affect the evolution of ourselves and our world, to heal us in the true meaning of the word, to bring us to wholeness. Change one person's direction in their life for the best, and you change the world—an act of universal healing. This is not separate from the evolution of man but part of it. These words come from the forces of evolution, personified as divinity. To be a seer is, therefore, not a path of ego, but a path of service to mankind, divinity, and evolution.

NOTE

1 Published in *The Journal of Personality and Social Psychology*, vol. 100 (March 2011), 407–425.

---

* Srinivasa Ramanujan sent his theorems to eminent Cambridge University mathematician G. H. Hardy in 1912–1913. Hardy considered him to be a natural genius and in the league of such contemporary mathematicians as Euler and Gauss.

Part II

The Four Keys to Trance-Prophecy: The Methodology of Oracular Work

Chapter 6

The Seer and the Psychopomp: Roles and Training in Trance-Prophecy

With the exception of sitting mediums, there are two active roles in almost all modern traditions that use trance-prophecy. This is most evident in Wicca, with the roles of the high priestess and high priest in the ritual of Drawing Down the Moon. In spaework (seidr), there is always an accompanying priestess or priest responsible for the conducting the ritual, and in Vodoun there are always priestesses and priests (mambo or houngan, respectively) who perform similar roles in conducting the rites and ensuring that the 'ridden' Vodouisants (Vodoun practitioners) are treated appropriately. The same can be found in other traditions around the world, even in ecstatic rituals, such as Harasiddhi in Nepal (see chapter 14), where multiple individuals go into trance. Even in some Spiritualist churches, these two roles can be found: there are those who act as mediums, and those who act in support, particularly in platform mediumship, where the medium performs on stage supported by an assistant who forwards questions to him/her.

Both men and women can be found practising trance-prophecy (see Photograph 7). For this reason we have opted for the term seer as a gender neutral term, while referring to them in the feminine, as "she." The reason for this is the majority of practitioners tend to be women. After all, it has always been a feminine, lunar practise, although this is not necessarily true of ecstatic ritual. We have treated the role of ritual psychopomp as being masculine; this is purely because of history rather than any gender bias. At the Temple of Apollo in Delphi and similar oracles in Greece, the priesthood took on the role of the ritual psychopomp, which was certainly regarded as a purely masculine role. Within Wicca, Drawing Down the Moon followed suit and maintained this idea, particularly as it was believed that the high priest manifested the Horned God, who within Wiccan mythology acts in this role. Certainly in other ancient traditions this division of roles by gender may not necessarily been the case. In traditional Thracian and Etruscan Drawing Down the Moon, women may have assumed the role of the psychopomp, and this could have been the case with the sibyls of the later Greek and Roman period. Within contemporary trance traditions, the issue of gender is unimportant, particularly in Vodoun where a female loa may possess a male Vodouisant. It is, therefore, important not to get caught up in dogma and gender stereotypes when dealing with trance and possession work. For example, a priestess of Hekate may be more suitable to act as a psychopomp than a priest when attempting to bring this goddess through.

Within contemporary trance traditions, when it comes to the deity communicating or possessing, the gender or sexual orientation of the seer is really unimportant, particularly in Vodoun, where a female loa may possess a male heterosexual Vodouisant or a male loa may possess a female. We have also found this be true in all trance-prophecy and possession work. The idea that a goddess can come through a man or a god through a woman is not new, although the perception of it is often clouded by a cultural bias or outright prejudice. In the past it might have been assumed that any man who was capable of psychic ability or prophecy or even being possessed by a goddess was homosexual. As Sybil Leek writes in *The Complete Art of Witchcraft* (1971):

> My researches took me way back into antiquity and resulted in the curious and interesting conclusion that there is a connection between the Uranian, or homosexual, temperaments and religion— especially the gift of prophecy and divination. . . . These youths became the high priests or medicine men of the tribes, with no depreciation of respect for them as individuals. This fact has been lightly glossed over by historians and theologians, and few people have commented on the link between the functions of homosexuality and psychic powers. What we do not want to see we can easily become blind to. . . .

Even up until the 1980s, men who exhibited feminine traits were often considered to have "homosexual temperaments," even though their actual sexual orientation was heterosexual. The ability for a man or woman to be able to balance their own anima/animus is essential when it comes to trance-prophecy. In a man, this may result in traits seen as being "Uranian," such as increased emotional sensitivity, which in a patriarchal culture was considered to be effeminate. It is fair to say that homosexuals were more likely to be drawn toward the prophetic traditions before our present culture of sexual acceptance because they had already embraced their animas and had nothing to lose by showing the repressed aspects of their character. Some of the best priests we have trained have been homosexual for this reason. Of course, our new culture of sexual acceptance has allowed more heterosexual men to exhibit these "feminine" traits, which would previously have resulted in them being labelled gay. The reality is that labels related to gender or sexuality such as heterosexual, homosexual, or lesbian are irrelevant to a possessing deity, as they are purely cultural labels and have little to do with whether a person is spiritually suitable to be a vessel for their essence. Any blocks a man may have to allowing a goddess to come through them, or a woman, a god, are purely spiritual or psychological caused by the social norms and values of the culture in which they have been brought up. Although there is still resistance to the idea that a man or woman can bring through a deity of the opposite sex, it is seen more often and slowly becoming more accepted. We have seen men bring through goddesses and women, gods, which has taught us that trance-prophecy is no place for dogma relating to gender or sexual orientation.

The Seer

The sibyl, the pythoness, the vala, the high priestess, the medium, the channeller—these are all cultural terms to define a role carried out by a particular person who is capable of bringing messages across from the divine, manifest as a spirit, a god or goddess, or even in the form of abstract images. They are literally the see–er. This is why it is important to ignore the terms and look at the role itself and its immediate purpose.

The primary purpose of the seer must be one of healing. This must seem an odd statement at first, but any positive form of divination (the term being used in the true sense of the word) must be about healing an individual mentally or spiritually in some form. Of course, there are also those who are capable of physical healing, like the healing mediums found in Spiritualism. This act of healing is most evident when a medium channels the spirit of a dead relative allowing closure for members of his/her family. This is of particular importance during times of war, when a loved one may be lost on the war front and never seen again. This explains why there was a substantial growth of interest in Spiritualism during and after the American Civil War, the First World War, and the Second World War. Although some neo-Pagan seers may take on this role of dealing with the spirits of the dead, most will deal specifically with prophecy and spiritual guidance. These too can be seen as acts of healing if you take the holistic view that any act that brings an individual into harmony with nature and the divine is an act of healing. The seer, the spirits, and the divinities that talk through her seek to do so, not just for the benefit of the individual, but also for the world in general. This is because the holistic principle and wyrd dictates that if you heal one person, you affect not only the immediate world of the individual but also the greater world beyond, like the ripples caused by a stone dropping into a pond. Therefore any seer, if she is to be capable of doing this, must be in harmony herself, with nature, and the divine. What makes someone a seer therefore becomes a major question for anyone who wishes to pursue the path of the oracle.

For a seer to perform her role of causing positive change in the world around her, she must have several attributes, the first of these being knowledge of the self. This was a well-known fact in ancient times, particularly to the ancient Greeks. Above the temple at Delphi, three statements were carved into the stone: "Know thyself," "Nothing in excess," and "Make a pledge and mischief is nigh." These three statements are, in fact, far older than the temple, and according to Plato originated from one of the seven sages of Greece.* Knowing thyself is of extreme importance if someone is going to train and take on the role of a seer. To have no self-knowledge of "what makes you tick" is inviting disaster. A seer could easily succumb to delusions of grandeur; to their ego, as they connect with the divine on a regular basis. In her book Wicca: The Old Religion in the New Age, Vivianne Crowley, a well-respected Wiccan high priestess, quotes the psychologist Jung on the dangers of connection with the divine if you are not internally balanced: "To quote Jung, coming into contact with the divine part of ourselves creates feelings 'even of omnipotence'. With the confines of the circle, as we speak as the Goddess or God, this is what is meant to happen. The danger of such mystical experiences is, as Jung points out, that an archetype can take over the ego" (152).

---

* Socrates mentions the Seven Sages in Plato's *Protagoras*. They are Thales, Pittacus, Bias, Solon, Cleobulus, Myson, and Chilon.

Photo by Gavin Bone

Photograph 7: Priest possessed by Dionysus during a neo-Pagan blessing of the vines, Tuscany, Italy, July 2010.

Although she talks in psychological terms (e.g., archetypes), the same can be applied if you believe that the deities and spirits invoked are real personalities. Vivianne Crowley, in fact, agrees with Jung when he said that there are "beneficial" effects to such a union if the individual is in balance. Wiccan training has always emphasised the need to achieve psychological self-awareness by the "balancing of the four elements," or in the case of training regime in our own temple, working with and balancing the chakras (see chapter 8). The first part of any training for the would-be seer must be to develop an understanding of self. This means coming to terms with who she is and dealing with her own personal 'demons.' If she doesn't, these demons will start to manifest during trance in negative ways such as manifestations of 'evil spirits,' frightening visions, etc. This is well known to anyone with experience in dealing with individuals who have used hallucinogenic drugs. A "bad trip" is often caused by unresolved problems, which have been repressed in the individual's shadow. During the 'trip,' these emerge out of the individual's subconscious mind and are often of a religious or occult nature—for example, images of demons, the devil, etc. A seer must therefore have the ability to be positively critical of herself in a constructive way. This can be a fine 'tight rope'; the seer needs to balance the ability to self-criticise against the belief in her own abilities. At some point every seer will ask herself: "Was that the Goddess I brought through or an aspect of my own personality, my ego?" As she develops her own psychic abilities, such questions are a healthy sign.

While some seers are born with natural psychic abilities, others will find the need to develop them. Those who are naturally visually imaginative, artists in particular, make excellent seers. These skills can also be developed using creative visualization techniques, such as pathworkings, a form of guided meditation. In the trance method we have developed, the Underworld Descent Technique (see chapter 11), these techniques are essential. Of course, the reality of life is that some individuals will simply not have the abilities to be a seer. In our experience with running workshops on this subject, however, those drawn to trance-prophecy tend to have inherent abilities even if they don't realize it.

Medical and Psychiatric Conditions That Affect Trance

The issue of mental health comes up regularly regarding the suitability of individuals to become seers, particularly if they suffer from some form of mental illness such as bipolar disorder or epilepsy. This is a complicated issue to say the least, both from a historical and practical viewpoint. Historically, it is well known that some mental conditions have often been attributed with having the ability to allow people to see between the worlds. Mircea Eliade remarks on this in his important academic work on ecstatic states Shamanism: Archaic Techniques of Ecstasy: "The only difference between a shaman and an epileptic is that the latter cannot deliberately enter into trance . . . Among the Subanun of Mindanao the perfect magician is usually neurasthenic or at least eccentric. The same thing is found elsewhere: in the Andaman Islands epileptics are considered to be great magicians . . ."[1]

While Gavin worked as a registered nurse, he dealt with epileptics on a regular basis. It was well known that they often see an aura around things before going into a grand mal fit; this in itself is a change in consciousness. On recovering and regaining consciousness, they always found themselves in a euphoric, ecstatic state. Gavin remembers one young man who fitted for over twenty-four hours and then slept for two days afterwards. When he awoke, he was unable to stop laughing at everyone and everything for at least another twenty-four hours. Gavin came across many epileptics who often described having visions, which were often predictive. Some patients also talked about meeting relatives who had passed over years before. While we have never dealt with epileptics in a trance-prophecy setting, we can see potential dangers in teaching them trance techniques, as it is possible that they may encourage a potentially dangerous grand mal fit. There is a more dangerous form of this condition, which has been mistaken for demonic possession in the past:

frontal lobe epilepsy which causes nightmare-like waking dreams.

What is clear, anthropologically speaking, is that the ability for some individuals with mental conditions to see "beyond the veil" is well accepted. In fact, in some cultures these individuals are considered to be natural shamans or seers, but it is important to point out that this is certainly not true of all cultures where ecstatic states are practised. The Jivaro shamans of South America are expected to be "reserved and taciturn in temperament."[2] Apart from his experiences with epilepsy in general medicine, Gavin also witnessed the psychic nature of mental illness during a psychiatric placement. Some of his patients were clearly psychic, being able to predict when visitors or incidents were going to occur unexpectedly. Certainly there were those with psychosis, who had auditory hallucinations emanating from their own subconscious minds, but there were also those hearing voices who were certainly not psychotic. As part of Gavin's training, he was taught that the diagnosis of mental illness is not an exact science, and that what makes somebody "mentally fit" in society is not a medical judgement but a social one when it comes to organic disorders.* This left Gavin wondering what the mechanisms were from a psychic and spiritual viewpoint. His conclusion is that these individuals have what is often referred to as "a blown crown chakra." Simply put, the spiritual chakra that connects us to the astral level is unable to close; a symptom of this form of mental illness but not the cause. It isn't that they aren't hearing voices, but individuals with these conditions are unable to control consciously, unconsciously, or astrally the process of closing this chakra center. The natural filters that allow them to operate in the everyday world become inoperable; they simply aren't able to block out any interference from the other levels of reality.

Speaking from personal experience, one of our most competent and gifted seers is bipolar. Her competence is due to the fact that her condition was stabilized, since it is an organic disorder. She has never suffered any ill effects from doing trance work. In fact, she claims it helped stabilize and control her condition. Of course, this may not be true for everyone, and certainly individuals with extreme forms of this condition and others, such as schizophrenia, would not be suitable to undergo training as a seer. It would undoubtedly cause them more harm than good, as they faced the problem of having to differentiate between

---

* Modern psychiatry classifies mental illness into two categories: organic, which means that there is a physiological cause (e.g., chemical imbalance), and inorganic, which means that the cause is purely psychological.

genuine experience and delusion. It is vitally important to point out that trance-prophecy will not cause these conditions, but it can exacerbate them if the potential seer has not already dealt with the instability. This is best summed up again by Mircea Eliade: "The medicine man, or the shaman is not a sick man (or woman); above all he is a sick man that is cured, who has succeeded in curing himself. Often when the shaman's or medicine man's vocation is revealed through illness or epileptoid attack, the initiation of the candidate is equivalent of a cure."[3]

While practising trance-prophecy may not cause mental illness, it is essential for the purpose of maintaining the ability to function in the everyday, mundane world that one understands how to close the crown chakra, and open the root chakra. This is essential for any seer. This is an important part of training in the Spiritualist church who use the "Trap Door" method to open and close the crown (see page 189). Although it may not cause mental illness, there are several potential side effects if trance is carried out on a regular basis. The first of these is that the seer opening up psychically causes any psychic ability to become enhanced and awakens any dormant ones. While this sounds desirable by anyone who has spent years trying to become psychic, the reality is very different. Being woken up at 3 a.m. by the spirit of Granny who wants to have a quick chat about your nephew can get quite tiresome after a while, and it doesn't make for a good work experience the next day! Even with the best training, such experiences are inevitable, so anyone going on the path of the seer needs to be aware of the downsides: not just being more open psychically but also being more susceptible to hypnotic suggestion.

Long- and Short-Term Side Effects of Trance States

Ask anyone who has been hypnotized on several occasions—after the first time it just becomes easier to "go under." This phenomena is well known by therapeutic hypnotists. As hypnosis and the trance techniques mentioned in this book work in basically the same way and are, in fact, the same thing, anyone who is involved in trance-prophecy regularly will find themselves able to slip into trance more easily. The downside is that they may trance out at an inopportune moment and find that they are more susceptible to subliminal suggestion, particularly when carrying out everyday chores that are repetitive. In the most extreme cases, even driving can be a problem, as a driver regularly experiences the strobing effects of trees and lampposts by the side of the road. They, therefore, have to be continually aware of their mental state. This is why being balanced as an individual is so essential and must be part of any training. It can affect the seer not only mentally and emotionally but also physically and socially.

One side effect that is of more concern is trance addiction. Alcohol and drugs are often initially partaken to escape the stress or reality of everyday life. A person susceptible to addiction may soon find that they become more and more dependent on them psychologically, and eventually this dependence becomes physical. The same is true of trance if used too often, although the addiction is more mental-emotional than physical. A person at risk from trance addiction may find it hard to cope with the everyday world and will slowly put themselves into trance more and more to escape from the issues surrounding them, making him or her more and more addicted to the experience. We have only come across one case of this personally, as it is very rare, but we have come across it in discussion with other trance teachers. Someone we knew who was practising shamanism went from trancing once a week to almost daily in order to escape an unhappy relationship and home life. Eventually the person was unable to distinguish between what was a genuine spiritual message and what was coming from her own subconscious mind. Ultimately, she began to exhibit paranoia and sociopathic behaviour, which started to affect others as she struggled with her own inner conflicts. This situation highlights the dangers of doing trance work when you have not trained or balanced yourself mentally and emotionally. If you do not work on this, you exacerbate your own issues. You also need to make sure there are substantial gaps between trance sessions regardless of your level of competency. Of course, this is a rare and extreme case, most side effects of trance are minor and transient.

The minor side effects of trance work normally occur during or immediately after trance. Everyone who does trance-prophecy may experience at least some of these at some time, particularly in the early days of training when one is still learning to shut down the appropriate chakras and ground. These effects include

- dizziness and light-headedness;
- shaking and trembling. In some cases, this can appear almost like a mild fit; and
- feelings of disassociation. A feeling that you aren't quite back in the mundane world.

All of the above effects can be resolved by grounding. Other effects can also occur and may require other forms of intervention. These include

- cravings, particularly sugar and water, during the dancing and drumming in an ecstatic ritual (see chapter 14). Having warm beverages and a blanket ready is always useful;
- a drop in body temperature. This is common after any form of possession where the deity/spirit leaves suddenly, taking some of the participant's energy from their etheric body;
- euphoria, laughing, or crying. A person in trance may commonly enter into an ecstatic state after coming out of trance; and
- collapse and temporary unconsciousness. This is common during ecstatic ritual after entering a trance state. The individual should be placed in the recovery position* and attended to until they revive. They should then be given water and encouraged to ground.

Most of these side effects will not affect the seer in the long term. Most are temporary and controllable with common sense, for example water and sweet foods should be readily available during prolonged ecstatic rituals to deal with dehydration and hypoglycaemia. Some effects, though, may follow the seer throughout her or his life: shaking and trembling is a common and well-known side effect in trance traditions. Rather than being seen as a problem, it is actually seen as indication of the presence of spirits wishing to communicate. In most cases, these symptoms are merely cathartic release—a healthy release of repressed stress and emotional issues built up within seer in everyday life. These are stored in the solar plexus, causing what is normally known as a "chakra blockage." In rare cases where people have deep-seated issues they have not dealt with, the result will be release of this energy post trance or at a slower pace. This can result in digestive problems, and in more extreme cases symptoms resembling Irritable Bowel Syndrome (vomiting, diarrhoea, etc.). We have witnessed this on several occasions with seers capable of deep trance, who have not dealt with their deeper issues before trance. It is, therefore, important for any seer and trance guide to be aware of any issues that they are going through before trance, and if necessary deal with them beforehand.

If you have been put off by our warnings regarding the side effects and are having second thoughts about exploring the path of trance-

---

* A standard first-aid technique. The unconscious individual is placed on their left side, their right knee being bent and brought up to their chest. Their right arm is brought forward, pushing left shoulder back to the left side of their face, which is flat on the floor. This technique keeps the individual's airway open if they vomit.

prophecy, we would say, "Good!" This is a vocational path and may not be for everyone. It is a path that takes over your life; it effects your family and social life and how you view the world. It is not for everyone. If you decide this is the path for you, that it is your vocation, then you should listen to some of the advice that was given to Gavin at the Spiritualist temple he use to attend: "Open the bottle slowly." Like all good things, this discipline takes time. And it is a discipline; it takes patience, dedication, self-awareness, humility and training. It is not a path that can be taken up and dropped at a whim. There is a tendency in recent years by some to think that you can pay your money and take a course or buy a book and you will instantly be a master at your chosen occult skill. This idea comes from a fast-food generation, who think everything should be instant. To quote A. J. Drew from one of his books: "Would you like some fries with your McWicca?" Of course, this is not just true for Wicca, but any occult path, and most particularly trance-prophecy, where time and experience is as essential as knowledge of the subject. Training is, therefore, an essential part of any seer's life, as it not only gives knowledge but also builds essential experience.

Training and the Four Keys to Trance-Prophecy

It was because of the positive and negative experiences we have had with trance that we developed our own system of training in trance-prophecy, which we call the Four Keys. These are not based purely on academic knowledge but also on our practical experiences in this area since 1993. Undoubtedly, others created similar systems, and have undeniably come to the same conclusions we did regarding what is required in safe trance-prophecy work. They may use different names, but basically the conclusions and, therefore, methodology will be the same—"a rose by any other name," as the saying goes. Some of our techniques originate from a fusion of practises from contemporary traditions, as well as the modern Spiritualist Church, Norse seidr, and Vodoun/Santeria.

Our method of teaching the Four Keys can be found in the following chapters and comprises

1. The First Key (chapter 7): Understanding Spiritual Cosmology and Psychology. An understanding of the mythological universe both microcosmically and macrocosmically. This allows the development of creative visualization techniques to induce trance, and how they relate to personal psychology.

2. The Second Key (chapter 8): Understanding Spiritual and Magical Energy. How these relate to trance, particularly in the way the aura and the chakras act in relation to mediumship and possession work.

3. The Third Key (chapter 9). Understanding Trance. How trance works from a psychological and physiological perspective, and what techniques can be used and combined safely.

4. The Fourth Key (chapter 10): Understanding Divinity and Spirits. What the spirits and the gods and goddesses are. How they can be understood, connected, and communicated with.

We do need to point out that the training given in this book is not enough to make one a seer. It must be preceded by some basic occult training, as well as training in Shadow work, as it is often referred to. This is where the individual comes to terms with their own inner workings, their ego, Shadow, and id, and becomes aware of their own inner nature. This enables them to put these into balance, which prevents any of the more negative side effects we have previously mentioned in this chapter. In Wicca this is often referred to as second-degree training, but such training also takes place in Michael Harner's core shamanism. Although this is best learned in a training group, it can be undertook by oneself, but it is a much more difficult path.

Tools and Dress of the Seer
Specific dress for a seer depends very much on their own connections with divinity, as well as their cultural leanings. This is very simple if you are following one of the Mediterranean paths: Greek, Roman, and even later Egyptian, where the sibyls and oracles of the ancient world classically wore red robes. Images of the sibyls of old are found everywhere, as they were a particularly popular subjects of Victorian artists, such as John Collier. Such works of art give an indication of the style of dress, although it must be remembered that they are often Victorian interpretations. It is relatively easy to make a toga from a single piece of red cotton material, and if long enough will naturally provide the traditional veil. This dress is always a good start for beginners, whatever their personal cultural path. As time and connection with specific deities progresses, dress can change appropriate to the culture. For example, the traditional Norse dress of a white robe covered by a blue tabard, if one is connecting with Freya, Odin, or any of the Northern deities.

If the seer is bringing through a specific deity in possession work, it might be appropriate to dress as that deity. In some cases, those who made this connection and work with a specific deity on a long-term basis may wish to ask the deity what dress is appropriate. This may sound simple enough but can result in some embarrassing situations. In 2009 we attended an event in Belgium called Pagan Gathering Europe. We conducted a trance-prophecy ritual with several seers who had over some years been learning our techniques (see Photograph 9). Several weeks beforehand, we asked our students to connect with their specific deities to see if they wished to come through at this event. They were also asked what dress would be appropriate for the seers to wear. One of the seer-esses found herself in an embarrassing situation having to negotiate with her deity, Aphrodite, who wished her to go naked in front of two hundred people! It took some negotiation until finally Aphrodite agreed that it would be acceptable for her to wear a very revealing cerise-coloured open-cut dress! Be aware: the gods may not always want to wear the classical styles, and they do have an eye for fashion!

There are no specific tools required for a seer, with the exception of such traditions as the Wiccan Drawing Down the Moon, where the high priestess often carries the crook and scourge. Like dress, tools will depend on cultural leanings and the deity you are bringing through, particularly in trance-possession. A good example of this is Odin who will always insist on wearing a wide-brimmed hat. It is therefore important to be aware of the specific needs of the divinity you are bringing through.

The Ritual Psychopomp: The Role of the Trance Guide
There is plenty of evidence for the role of the ritual psychopomp and of the priesthood of Apollo within classical accounts of the Oracle at Delphi (see chapter 1), although there is no specific name given, just "priest." We decided to define it by giving the two possible descriptive terms in the title of this chapter. We used the term *ritual* in front of the term *psychopomp* to differentiate it from the term used for gods or goddesses such as Anubis, Hekate, etc., who guide the souls of the dead into the underworld. The use of the term ritual implies a presence in this world rather than any other, as well as suggesting that the user is a priest or priestess. Our reasons for the use of the term *trance guide* is more obvious: it implies someone who guides the seer while they are in trance. The term you wish to use is really up to you ("a rose by any other name . . ."); as what is really important is the role itself, and the knowledge and skills required to do it.

What is clear is that the minimum number of individuals involved in the trance-prophecy process is two—the seer and the trance guide.

Without the trance guide, the process becomes simply one of psychic pathworking; if the seer works alone without the support of a trance guide, there is the possibility she will become more absorbed in her trance experience than the needs of those who have come to ask questions. There would also be problems with order, as people try to bombard the seer with questions all at once without the intervention of a third party. In such a situation, the seer would also have problems maintaining a trance state and would be distracted by the resultant disorder. This could easily result in her coming out of trance too early and too fast, particularly if possessed by a deity, so the use of a trance guide also becomes an issue of safety. This two-person process is evident in ritual magic, where the magician acts as the trance guide to his medium, as well as in the relationship between the high priestess and her priest in Drawing Down the Moon.

In Wicca, the process repeats the same roles found in ritual magic, although there are some differences in emphasis. When the high priest performs the rite of Drawing Down the Moon (see chapter 12) on the high priestess, he acts in the role of a trance guide. The major difference with ritual magic is that he is openly recognised in ritual by the high priestess as the trance guide when she invokes the following onto him, using the Invoking Pentagram of Earth:

> Of the Mother darksome and divine
> Mine the scourge, and mine the kiss;
> The five-point start of love and bliss—
> Here I charge you, in this sign.[4]

She, as high priestess, "charges" him to undertake this role as the embodiment of the Horned God, as psychopomp, just prior to her ritual possession by the Goddess. This role is enforced later again in the ritual, when a fuller invocation of the Horned God takes place: "Great God Cernunnos, return to earth again! . . ." It must be remembered that the Horned God Cernunnos is the Lord of Death and Initiation. Like the Norse god Odin and the Greek Hermes (with whom he is sometimes equated), the Horned God performs the same roles as they do, but within the context of Wiccan theology. Clearly this ritual indicates that the high priest is expected to perform this role ritually during the process of Drawing Down the Moon. It is very likely that this role within Wicca did not originate in any particular ancient source, but from the ritual practises of magical orders such as the Golden Dawn and Crowley's Ordo Temple Orientis. In both orders, mediums were used to chart the progress of any ritual on "the other levels" and then to relay information back to the magician. This role can be seen quite clearly in the relationship between Crowley and his "Scarlet Women." As previously mentioned (on page 31), Crowley borrowed the term Scarlet Woman, or Whore of Babylon, from the Bible, specifically the book of St. John the Divine, more commonly known as the book of Revelation. There is little doubt among scholars that whore does, in fact, refer to the sibyls and oracles of ancient times, who traditionally wore red. The major difference between ritual magic and Wicca is the emphasis of the roles. In the magic of Crowley and his predecessors, the seer served as medium to the magician, similar to the earlier relationship of sibyls with the patriarchal priesthoods of classical times, which undoubtedly Crowley based his practise on. In Wicca, the role of the priest as trance guide is reversed: his primary role is to serve the high priestess as she manifests the Goddess, rather than her assisting him magically.

As we have mentioned in chapter 1, the rites at Delphi were originally very Dionysian and orgiastic in nature, but in the eight century, when they became more organised, the rules of practise around them became more restrictive due to the nature of the patriarchal Apollonian priesthood. This priesthood, unfortunately, took on the role of interpreting the prophecies for political and financial ends, so regarding its ethics, it is not necessarily a good role model for anyone taking on the role of a ritual psychopomp. It is likely that prior to Apollonian takeover, the other seers at the oracle took this role in turns, as the ritual practises were more ecstatic.

The role of the trance guide can be defined in five points, although these roles may differ according to tradition and culture:

- To protect the well-being of the seer: This is done by questioning any entities present and protecting her/him from lower spirit forms or suffering from energy drain.
- To guide the seer into the underworld: Knowing how to use the correct trance technique and their effects to ensure that he/she enters the appropriate realm(s).
- To maintain order in the ritual space: Conducting rituals and proper etiquette related to any incumbent deity, including the correct way to approach the seer by those wishing to ask questions.
- To relay and translate answers: Where necessary, acting as a mediator between the seer and the querent. Interpreting answers, which may not necessarily be comprehensible to the querent (see page 183).

- To train seers: The minimum number needed for the trance-prophecy process is two, so the role of training the seer must naturally fall upon the trance guide.

There is also a particular level of knowledge and accumulated skills required to act in the role of trance guide:

- Comprehensive knowledge of the Four Keys: Magical Energy, Cosmology, Trance Techniques, and the Nature of Spirits and Deities.
- Empathic abilities: The ability to sense the progress and well-being of the seer while he or she journeys into the underworld.
- Ritual abilities: Knowledge of how to conduct ceremony and ritual practise, and how to maintain order.
- The ability to translate and interpret abstract, dream-like symbolism: particularly important if doing pure trance-prophecy where there is no interaction with deities or spirits (see page 181). This is so the trance guide can translate symbolism coming from the Akashic/collective unconscious. An understanding of Jung's theories on symbolism is useful, as is studying dream symbolism.

Tools and Dress of the Ritual Psychopomp

There is little information on what magical tools or items the classical trance guides used. The most likely item is, of course, a staff or stang—a traditional symbol of wisdom and priestly authority. The staff is traditionally carried by several gods and mythological figures who have associations with this role, such as Odin, with his spear *gunginir*; and Hermes/Mercury, with the caduceus. Unlike the previously mentioned deities, the god of ecstatic trance, Dionysus, carried the *thyrsus*, a wand tipped with a pine cone. Like the staff, it was also tool of the element of air and a symbol of the axis mundi. Because of these associations, it is obvious that the staff is the appropriate magical tool for the role of trance guide, as he works in the realm of the mind by inducing trance in the seer and conducts her in the process of exploring the cosmology of the spiritual realms. Another reason is that traditionally weapons were banned from oracular sanctuaries, so the staff would have been used to sanctify the sacred space. In Wiccan parlance, it is used similarly to cast a circle and control any spirits that may have manifested. As these spirits would have been of a divine nature, a sword or dagger (athame) would have been inappropriate, since higher spirits forms, like gods and goddesses, are never commanded by the use of a sword or ritual knife, but politely and respectfully asked by the use of a staff or wand.

The stang differs slightly from the staff in that it is bifurcated. The main difference in use was that it was traditionally placed in the center of circle in Witchcraft to represent the Horned God who, as we mentioned earlier, is a psychopomp. By placing it in the center, it also becomes the axis mundi, the "center of the world," for any group working in circle. For this reason, the stang or staff is particularly useful as a tool for grounding and centering the seer when she comes out of the trance. This is done by getting her to place both hands on the top of the staff/stang, while the guide holds it. The guide can then encourage the seer to visualize the staff/stang as the axis mundi and imagine herself standing in the middle world (see page 106) while visualizing any access of energy grounding downwards. This action will ground the energy downward through the chakras. Decoration of the staff will depend on the cultural practises of the trance guide using it. For example, in seidr it may be decorated with runes. Regardless of tradition, it should certainly have symbols of protection inscribed on it, as well as the names of the specific divinities the seer or trance guide works with.

Like the staff or wand, how a trance guide dresses depends on the cultural inclination of the practitioner, and the nature of the ritual. For any form of ceremonial trance-prophecy ritual, a white robe is always a good investment, as it is the most commonly used dress found in classical times, in African diasporic religion, and modern Wicca. White is a colour of purity, so you can never go wrong using it. As time goes on, a guide may find themselves with a collection of robes for specific invocations of divinity.

The Roles of Seer and Trance Guide in Ecstatic Ritual and Sex Magic.

While the two roles we have described seem more relevant to traditional ceremonial magic, Wicca and seith/seidr, they are just as relevant to ecstatic ritual (see chapter 14), as found in the traditional rites of Dionysus and contemporary religions such as Hinduism and Vodoun. If you examine these religions, you will find those roles are there but are often assumed by more than two individuals in the ceremonies. Within Vodoun there may be multiple individuals performing the trance guide role in ritual, ready to work with anyone who is "ridden" by a loa. These are the trained priestesses and priests who are often found at the edge of any ritual. Which mambo or houngan (priestess or priest) works the 'horse'—

the individual who is being possessed—will depend on which loa is in possession, as there are priesthoods for each. Of course, Vodoun is an unusual situation since there is no pre-chosen seer within the ritual; all participants or Vodouisants have the potential to be ridden. The priests must wait to see which loa decides to possess whom during the intense ritual and drumming. Rather than being purely oracular traditions, African diasporic traditions put a strong emphasis on the ecstatic connection with the spirits, the loa; any prophecy that takes place, therefore, tends to be secondary to this goal. Regardless of the differences with Western and Northern oracular tradition, the basic role of the trance guide remains the same in any form of ecstatic ritual. In trance techniques related to sex magic, a major shift in emphasis occurs. In case of such practise, both individuals take on both roles for each other—the couple are both seer and trance guide at the same time (see page 243). Any individuals involved in this practise must have a more advanced understanding of trance-prophecy that can only come from several years of experience.

NOTES

1 Eliade, *Shamanism: Archaic Techniques of Ecstasy*, 26.
3 Eliade, in chap. 1 of *Shamanism and Psychopathology*, 27.
4 Janet and Stewart Farrar, part 1, chap. 1 in *A Witches' Bible: The Complete Witches' Handbook* (Phoenix Publishing), 41. It first appeared in the Gardnerian Book of Shadows in 1957.

Chapter 7

The First Key: Understanding Spiritual Cosmology and Psychology

When it comes to magical and spiritual practise, spiritual cosmology and psychology cannot be separated. Our inner world is reflected in how we view and shape the outer world around us. In occult terms, this is the theory of microcosm and macrocosm, summed up in the old occult law of reflection: As above, so below; or, in the case of trance-prophecy: As within so, so without. This can often be seen in the folk and fairy tales of old, such as "Sleeping Beauty," a tale that is as much about our internal psychology and need to balance our masculine and feminine aspects—our anima or animus (as the psychologist Jung called them—as it is a story of love and chivalry. Such tales are strongly rooted in our psyches. This is why we have been using storytelling to teach cosmology for several years now, although to a lesser extent, we decided to do the same here. Please bear in mind that like all stories, there is a level of artistic license needed to convey the intended message, which is not necessarily historically accurate.

Once upon a time, ancient humans commenced their journey toward full sentience. At this stage, humans were little more than apes. The first realisation they had was that if one turned in a 360-degree circle, one was at the center of the world, and the world was round—the horizon is curved. As the individual looped around the world, wherever he or she went, they were still at the center of his world, and the world was still round. From his viewpoint, everything in the world literally revolved around him or her, just as a child sees the world. Early humans also noticed that there were four directions: ahead of one, behind, to the left, and to the right. They divided the world into daytime and nighttime. Ancient humans feared the night.

During daylight hours, ancient humans looked into the sky and saw the friendly ball of yellow—the sun. It was warm, benevolent, and its light allowed them to see what they were doing so they could survive in an otherwise hostile world. They could see their enemies—the wolf, the bear, the lion—before they saw the humans, and evade them. They could also see to gather food. The sun was a powerful friend, and quickly humans began to believe that it was somehow looking over them, protecting them. Perhaps it was like them; perhaps it was caring for them. So every morning when the sun rose, they would raise their hands and thank it. And every evening they would have to say farewell to it, which made them unhappy. Ancient humans feared the night.

The night was a dangerous time. Humans couldn't see their enemies: the wolf, the bear, and the lion. Their enemies could hunt the tribe members; they could kill them. Therefore at night, humans hid, listening in fear to the strange sounds of the night, as the wolf, the bear, and the lion prowled looking for food. They noticed that attacks from evil spirits that caused illness and disease were at their strongest at night.* As the predators prowled, humans wondered where their friend the sun had gone. They wondered whether it would return the next morning and became scared when, as the year progressed, it seemed to take longer and longer for their friend to return. They decided that when the sun returned they would hunt and find where it hid, so they could ask it to return during the hours of darkness. Ancient humans feared the night.

Of course, every so often, the night became a safer place. The great white orb, the moon, would rise and light the trees with silver light and cast long shadows. During this time, man could see the wolf, the bear, and the lion hunting, and he became the hunter himself. He learned to hide in the shadows as he hunted the deer and the hog. The moon was like the sun, only gentler and more fickle. She did not appear as much as the sun, but when she did she offered protection in the darkness of the night. Like the sun, she descended and hid. Clearly they were partners—lovers—who could only be united at certain times when they ceased to chase each other across the sky. Ancient humans feared the night.

They realised that the sun and the moon lived in worlds different to theirs, two different realms. The sun lived in a world above theirs, a world of order, but where did it descend to at night? Humans set upon a quest to find where the sun and the moon were hiding. Clearly, they

---

* This is an experience that many who work in the medical and nursing professions can attest to. Illness normally reaches its peak during the hours of sleep.

were hiding under something—in the underworld (under the world). Every evening they watched the sun descend; it went underground. They searched everywhere. Was it hiding in the river? No, because surely the water would quench its flames. Was it hiding under the tree roots? Possibly, but if it was, how could they reach it? Was it . . . was it . . . in the cave! But ancient humans hesitated in descending into it, as even during the hours of light, the cave held dangers. It was dark and foreboding. It was home to the creatures of the night—the wolf, the bear, and the lion—which slept there during the daylight hours. Even though they knew that down in the long, descending tunnel, the sun rested at night, they were unwilling to venture in as they knew this was where death dwelt in the form of predators and disease. It was for this reason ancient humans feared the dark of the night and the cave.

Now, humankind realised there were three worlds: one above them where the sun dwelt during the day—the upperworld (one he lived and survived in)—the middle world; and one where the moon slept during the day and the sun slept by night—the lower world or underworld. But soon, they were no longer alone. Humans had always lived in family groups, in tribes that were becoming more important. In family groups, there were more hands to search for food, more eyes to look for enemies in the night. Now the individual was no longer the center of the world. He or she was part of a family, a clan, a tribe; and with this awareness came the realisation that they were others. There had to be an agreement on what was at the center of their world. Was it to be a particularly large tree? That would be ideal; they could send messages up the tree to their friend the sun. Or was it to be a large gathering of rocks? They reached the sky as well. It was irrelevant what they decided. What was important was that it marked the center of their world; it marked their cooperation as a family. It would be a meeting place to discuss matters of importance: where the best deer roamed, where the best berries and nuts could be found, how they would deal with those who broke the laws and taboos of the tribe—those who they saw embracing the values of the night rather than those of the day. Now ancient humans didn't fear the night so much.

With this need for cooperation came problems for humankind. They couldn't do just whatever they wanted anymore. One could in the past when there was just oneself and the sun, but now one had to behave, to cooperate. He couldn't just take food from someone else in the tribe, nor could he just take a woman when he wanted. If he tried to, he would be hurt by an angry fist or worse, be outcast from the tribe and have to face the world and the night alone. His chances of being eaten by a wolf, a bear, or a lion would be great. So he learned to control himself, to push his desires down, to push them deep within himself, in the same way that the sun descended every evening into that cave. Ancient humankind was losing their fear of the night. Perhaps it was time to explore that cave, but before doing this, they had to have an ally, something that could drive the night and their fears away. To do that they would have to learn how to relate to the world around them, the four directions, and elements.

When the sun set, the family was most anxious. This was a time of change for ancient humans, when they would have to prepare to face the dark, to face the night and all their fears. This was the direction from which those fears emerged. It was the direction of spirits but also the direction of emotion. The westerly winds brought the rain, whose drops reminded them of their own tears of happiness and sadness. When they turned to the north (in the Northern Hemisphere), they knew this was when the dark was at its height and from where the cold winds blew. When he looked to the north in daylight hours, he saw the mountains and the rocks—the bones of Mother Earth herself. The north and the earth represented that which they could see in daylight hours (the material world around them), but at night it represented the height of their fears: the return to the earth, death itself. But as they turned once more, they faced the east. For ancient humans, this was the time of the release of their fear of the night; it was the time of beginnings; it was the morning. They would feel the wind blowing in their faces, which like thoughts they could neither see nor touch. With these thoughts came plans—plans on how to find the sun and how to conquer the night, to conquer his fears. When humans faced the sun at its height, at midday, they would be facing the south (in the Northern Hemisphere). Here they felt the heat of the sun, and wished to harness that power, that fire. When the grasslands caught fire, they edged toward the burning brush and, overcoming their fear, they grasped a burning stick from the edges. They were as Prometheus who had taken fire from heaven. Having succeeded in this trial, they were now ready to face their other fears.

Humans entered the cave with a new gift—fire—a gift given to them from the sun. They now had the will to overcome their fears. They pensively entered the cave. There was nothing there. They went deeper into the darkness. No sign of any wolf or sleeping bear or lion, no sign of the evil spirits of illness, which plagued members of the tribe. But even if there had been, they had their friend fire. Together they could drive anything out. Ancient humans were proud! They had overcome fear. They had entered the darkness. To mark their success, they filled their mouths with red ochre dust from the floor of the cave, put their hands on the wall of the cave, and blew the mix of dust and saliva around their hands. A perfect imprint of their hands was now on the cave wall. It would last thousands of years—a testament to their courage. Perhaps the story of this heroic adventure would be told around campfires—their journey into the underworld—and be recorded in the future mythologies of their people, gaining a new meaning. Very soon they realised that this is a place where the spirits of illness and animals dwell and where they could communicate with them. So they devised elaborate hunting rituals to tell the spirits that they wanted to catch the deer or the hog.

The tribe was growing. The food from hunting deer and hogs was not enough. The gathering of berries and nuts was not enough. Cooperation meant they had learnt much; they had exchanged information with each other at the gathering place, at the center of their world. Now they tried new things. They planted their own crops, grew their own food. Hunting was productive but couldn't sustain them through the winter, so they caught young hogs and tamed them. They turned from hunting and gathering to agriculture. Their priorities and views of the world were changing. They were developing common beliefs, agreed ways of behaving, and now the center of their world was decorated with the symbols of their collective beliefs and culture. They carved symbols of the animals which they hunted onto the trees. The Sun was seen as the lord of order; it commanded the hours of daylight and all things that were positive, including the need to control those desires that had to be pushed down; it established law. Darkness was the opposite; it was the time of desires unleashed, a time to hide from those desires, a time to sleep, except when the Moon was full. The Moon guided humans in the darkness, and it came to represent hidden things within them, as well as allowing them access to the hidden realms below, the underworld and Realm of the Ancestors.

Ancient humans now grasped that the world outside and the world within were separate. The wind and one's thoughts were not the same thing, neither was fire one's will, nor water one's emotion, nor was one's body actually the conscious self; it was just a shell. It made no sense that when one died, one ended up in the place of their fears, in the underworld. Perhaps they went somewhere else? Perhaps they had to journey through the underworld to reach the realm where the spirits of his ancestors gathered—a Realm of the Ancestors. Likewise, he wondered again about the gods. Was the Sun really God; was the Moon really Goddess? Were the Moon and the Sun just a manifestation of those great spirits from somewhere else? Humans came to believe that the gods had their own dwellings, which manifest on the edge of the middle, physical realm, a place that humans shaped in their dreams. Perhaps they descended from the Realm of the Divine through the realm of dreams, the Astral Realm, to manifest on the mountaintops to the north.

During this journey, ancient humans made a leap in understanding between the magical realm around them and their own inner natures. They had gone from one realm—a Middle Realm, with themselves at the center—to three realms (still found in shamanic practise) including one where the spirits dwelt below; a lower or underworld where their fears manifested; and a world above, a place of hopes and aspirations driven by ego. They then began to explore their own inner natures through the four elements of earth, air, fire, and water and their connection to the four directions; their emotions; physicality; mind; and will. Now the tribe was centered within these seven worlds; they were ready to descend to face their fears. Having descended into the underworld, their consciousness also expanded, allowing them to realise the existence of two other realms—the Realm of the Ancestors and the Realm of the Divine—totalling nine realms, which they saw around them. They now shaped the outer world in the image of their inner world, which we can still see today in the way that we build tall central structures, the axis mundi, at the center of our cities, such as cathedrals, monuments, and commercial buildings, and align them with the four directions.

As you can see from our story, it is impossible to separate how we view the world, our cosmology, from our own internal psychology. Our world and our need to survive in it has shaped us externally and internally, macrocosmically and microcosmically. The stories we created in ancient times to explain our world, our mythologies, were also explanations about our own inner selves. We discussed this overall view of spiritual and magical cosmology in our previous work, *The Inner Mysteries* (chapter 7). We do not wish to reiterate much of what we have written there, just the major points that are important for anyone involved in trance-prophecy. It does, of course, center on the lower rather than higher realms: the underworld and the Realm of the Ancestors.

The Realms of Trance-Prophecy

Regardless of which path you follow—be it Greek, Egyptian, Norse, or Celtic—the traditional mythological realms of these cultures can be applied to the cosmology we describe below. Trance work focuses on the axis mundi of this cosmology—the five realms surrounding the trunk of the tree. The four elemental realms are less important in the process, except during training when preparing somebody for trance by balancing the elements within them.

The Middle Realm, the World of Experience (the Celtic/Druidic Abred, the Norse Midgardhr): This is the central realm on the axis of the tree, and corresponds with the *id*, the element of our psyche that strives for the most basic needs: food, shelter, procreation, etc. The id forces us into the world and causes us to experience it. The id is satiated or repressed by the effects of the other five realms that intersect it, such as the Realm of Water, which makes us feel emotion. This intersection of realms is symbolized by the crossroads, a traditional meeting place of witches and sacred to the goddess Hecate, where she was traditionally invoked by Drawing Down the Moon. In any trance journey, this is your starting point.

The Astral Realm (the Celtic/Druidic Gwynfyd, the Norse Ljossalheim): This is above the central Realm of Experience. In Freudian and Jungian terms, it is the abode of the ego, and thus anything we perceive here is clothed by our ego. Unfortunately, this makes our understanding of this realm subjective, so in order to fully realize the experiences here, it is necessary to descend into the underworld, Jung's Shadow Realm, as well as pass through the elemental realms. The Astral Realm is where one finds the World Tree, with which to travel between the worlds. The Astral Realm intersects the world above it, the Realm of the Divine, where many of the entities and symbols found on the astral plane originate. When initially going into trance, you must first ascend to this realm by entering into an *alpha* then *theta* state (see page 136). From here you can "descend the tree" into the underworld.

The Underworld (Norse Niflehiemr/Svartalheimr): This corresponds with Jung's *personal unconscious*, where the Shadow dwells. It is here that the ego sends the impulses it wants to repress. Deep within this realm are all the fears and negative aspects of the self rejected by the personality. Not surprisingly, many of the images are frightening, but to understand what you see here, you must face yourself. The anima and animus, our repressed contrasexual selves, exist here in an area the neo-Jungians call the *Bright Shadow*, which is often symbolised as a pleasant, peaceful area hidden among the dark images of the Shadow (for more on this see page 252). In Michael Harner's core shamanism, this is considered separate from the underworld and is referred to as the lower world. The moon is an important symbol in trance because it acts in this world of repressed emotion and desire as a guide and protector, guiding the individual safely through the underworld.

The Realm of the Divine, the Abode of the Gods (Celtic/Druidic Ceugant, Norse Asaheimr): This is what Jungian psychologists refer to as the *Superconscious*, or what occultists refer to as the Higher Astral. It is found above the Astral Realm, and is the Realm of the Divine, the unknowable force that is the intelligence of the Universe itself. To understand it, think of heaven and God as, in fact, the same thing. Cabalists call this *An Soph Aur*, the unknowable. It has no form as such until it descends into the realms below where it takes on the forms that human consciousness has assigned to it. For example, in passing through the Astral Realm, it becomes what we know as a god or a goddess. It cannot manifest without this mediation first taking place; hence, deities have associations with the elements, the underworld, etc. It is an unattainable realm, which means we cannot enter it in our normal state of consciousness, although a gifted traveller or psychic may catch a glimpse of this realm. During trance, an invoked deity may descend from this realm, passing through the Astral Realm on its way to meet the invoker, the seer.

The Realm of the Ancestors (Celtic/Druidic Annwn, Norse Helheimr): This is the collective unconscious, where the many images of what Jung calls the *numinous archetypes* are stored. It is positioned below the underworld. This is the true Realm of the Dead and the ancestors, and in many myths can only be accessed by dying, by crossing the river of death itself. A good example is the Greek myth of crossing the river Styx. The Realm of the Dead/Ancestors has been portrayed in many ways, as Helheim to the Norse and Annwn to the Druids. The Greeks saw it as Tartarus, the abode below Hades. It is important to recognise the culturally different ways to view it, as it is easy to confuse this realm with the underworld. Like the Realm of the Divine, it cannot be accessed directly from the Realm of Experience. Its passage through the other realms shapes the images originating from it, just as it happens with the Realm of the Divine. It is possible to stand at its gates and see some of the images within it, but it can be dangerous to attempt to enter. In the flood of imagery that would overcome your senses, you would literally risk losing your mind. In all cultures, this is a realm of danger, death, and horrific images.

The Biggest Obstacles:
Overcoming the Ego and Persona

When we analyse the techniques used to create trance and ecstatic techniques, they all have something in common. They all attempt to sublimate the ego of the individual to allow trance to take place. In trance-prophecy traditions, this sublimation is paramount. If this isn't the case, as we witnessed on several occasions, what comes through is not the divine but the individual's ego, sometimes appearing to manifest as a spirit or god form. At best, it can be no more than fantasy, with the individual's ego playing out its own needs, but at worst, it can take the form of a Shadow entity (see page 166) if the individual is disturbed, which will disrupt any serious trance working. This is why any practitioner of trance-prophecy must be willing to examine their own nature and deal with their own repressed issues. This is not always an easy thing to do, but it is one of the foremost aspects of trance-prophecy training. It is summed up by that statement found in the pronaos (forecourt) of the Temple of Apollo at Delphi: Know thyself.*

In nearly all magical traditions, as well as trance-prophecy, there is a negating of what we perceive as the self, which is at the core of techniques for creating enlightenment and connection with the Divine Spirit. A good example of this is found in Buddhism, with chanting of the mantras; in shamanism, it can be seen not only with chanting but also drumming or rattling, dancing, and the use of hallucinogens and masks. In Western occult practise, other techniques have been used: in The Sacred Magic of Abramelin the Mage (edited by MacGregor Mathers), the use of sleep- and food-deprivation techniques are encouraged to connect with one's Holy Guardian Angel—one's Higher Self—while also facing one's own demons; a technique really no different to the path of the shaman into the underworld.

In early Gardnerian Wicca, the scourge or whip, and *ligature* (binding with ropes) were used at initiations to create a euphoric state by encouraging the production of endorphins and, therefore, hopefully putting the initiate into a communion with divinity. In recent years,

---

* Recorded by Pausanias, a Greek travelogue writer of the second century.

New Age techniques have appeared, which include *circular breathing*, or *rebirthing* as it is sometimes called, based on Vedic pranic breathing. Circular breathing increases carbon dioxide in the blood while decreasing oxygen. In this respect, it is no different to the Native American *inipi* or sweat lodge, which does the same thing using steam. A guided visualized journey, a pathworking, can also be undertaken. This process is used in seith or seidr, along with singing. All these techniques are listed below:

- ritual invocation
- visualization/pathworking
- intoxicants/hallucinogenics
- food/sleep deprivation
- hypnotic induction
- drumming and rattling
- sex (tantric techniques)
- masking
- chanting and singing
- dancing
- ligature and scourging
- breathing patterns

All these techniques are discussed in more depth in chapter 9.

Understanding the Psychology of Trance

Jung believed that human personality consisted of two components, the ego and the id. These terms are Latin and mean, respectively, "I" and "it." In everyday life, we normally refer to ourselves in the context of the semiconscious ego; hence, we refer to ourselves as "I."

If we become controlled by our instinctual impulses—for example hunger, thirst, or sexual and aggressive instincts—we fall under the control of our id. When this happens, we may very likely refer to these forces as "it." In a normally adjusted individual, the function of the ego is to serve and, to a certain degree, control the instinctual id. Thus we are prevented from taking off all our clothes in a public place in hot weather by our ego, fearing ridicule. This is a good example of the ego defense mechanisms that develop in an adult, but in a child the ego has not yet developed, so a child may very likely do such things without fear. When the ego finds itself trying to cope with the demands of the id, which is only interested in satisfying itself, the ego's copes by using several strategies. It may repress the unwanted impulses, thoughts, and ideas into the unconscious—the Shadow Realm.

We develop personas, our personalities, at the outer edge of our functioning egos. These are masks, a compromise between what our egos aspire to be and the limitations and social functions imposed upon them. If there is no compromise between the ego's aspirations and the social limitations, then the persona becomes a rigid stereotyped mask. In a balanced state, it is supple and pliable, being able to adjust to life's everyday situations.

The Shadow is the antithesis of the persona. Just as the persona lies in front of the ego, the Shadow hides behind it in the deep unconscious mind. It is the part of the ego that has been rejected, its unacceptable face. This concept has appeared in mythology and literature for centuries; in modern writing the concept is typified by the characters of Dr. Jekyll and Mr. Hyde. Because of the ego's rejection, the Shadow is often found portrayed as evil in nature, as can be seen from the examples given previously. This is an oversimplification, because unfortunately when the ego sublimates some of its aspects, it may sometimes "throw the baby out with the bath water," so to speak—it develops what neo-Jungians call the Bright Shadow. It is within the Bright Shadow that the *anima/animus complex* is found—our constrasexual selves. In a man it is the buried feminine, and in a woman the buried masculine.

It is significant to understand why it is important to sublimate the ego. The ego in the adult does not like to give up control and will fill the individual with doubt regarding their ability to trance or connect with spirit. We have found statements such as "I don't think I'm capable of doing this" coming from some of the most gifted trancers we have come across before they have actually tranced. The main reason this occurs is because a journey into trance inevitably leads to a journey into Shadow, which the ego firmly rejects. The ego has spent most of its adult life suppressing its Shadow and trying to protect the individual from the repressed demands of the id that it has stored there. It has developed several strategies and tricks over the years to prevent the persona and the Shadow meeting, one of these being the aforementioned self-doubt, the other being creating a distraction.

Anyone who has meditated is familiar with the ego's attempts to retain control. It may cause several different types of distraction to maintain its control. These include physical distractions, such as the sudden occurrence of itches (particularly in the legs) and psychological distractions, such as the nagging voice that asks just at the moment a deep meditation is reached: "Are we there yet?," causing a lapsing back into the fully conscious mind. Likewise, the ego can also be distracted to cause trance to occur, which many techniques used to create trance and ecstatic techniques do. Dancing, for example, which focuses the ego on the physical activity, or chanting, which focuses the ego on the verbal activity, are some examples. Sometimes the technique may use the body's own biochemistry to circumvent the ego. For example, scourging or ligature, thus releasing endorphins, a natural analgesic and sedative that are actually stronger than most opiates. Artificial chemicals are also used, such as hallucinogens, which will have a similar effect. They all do the same thing: allow the individual to enter the unconscious world of the mind and allow access to other states of being.

Mythical Cosmology and the Mind

When you apply an understanding of spiritual cosmology to trance, something else becomes very clear: those who formulated such cosmologies have a practical understanding of the mind, even though rudimentary when it came to trance. Anyone entering a deep trance state enters their own underworld, the unconscious Shadow within his or her own mind. Of course, in lighter trance states, such as traditional Wiccan Drawing Down the Moon, the individual only enters the boundary between the conscious and unconscious mind, and never fully enters the Realm of the Shadow. Wiccan priestesses often describe the feeling of this as "withdrawing into the back of their own heads" as the invoked goddess enters, but they do not get the same level of underworld visions as other traditions. This is why in deep trance techniques, such as in shamanic culture, it is important to have a guide (e.g., a power animal) when exploring such realms: not only to guide but also to protect, as the ego is no longer in a position to do this. As a result, the person trancing may see quite disturbing imagery, much of it coming from their own repressed natures. We have one account of such an event from a trance priestess we have known for some time. She is used to entering trance states for prophecy using Western techniques, but was not prepared for what happened when she attended a Vodoun ceremony. She, much to her surprise, was ridden by one of the loa:

> We attended a Voodoo ritual . . . During the ritual, I was very
> coherent and everything was fine . . . (during it) I became "pos-
> sessed." I was in a white dress with a great pedicure and manicure,
> and I do NOT normally lose control and go down to the dirt. And
> I did, and I was dancing and doing other odd things. We are Greek
> Hellenic; I do invocations of the Greek female deities, and those are
> not as harsh as this was. This actually scared me, along with the
> vision quest I seemed to be on during the possession.

There are several reasons why this experience was more intense for
her. The first and most obvious is that Vodoun practitioners are much
more experienced at putting individuals into trance than most Western
magical practitioners. Most of us are trying to relearn these skills, which
were lost after the coming of Christianity to Europe. The other is that
like most shamanic cultures—and much of Vodoun is an evolved form of
shamanism—a combination of techniques are combined to create a deep
trance state, with drumming, dancing, and chanting being the most common. The priestess, although she was used to trance, and as such already
susceptible to the impact of these techniques, was thrown quite literally
into her own Shadow, and taken on a journey into the underworld when
the loa possessed her. It is for this reason that trance techniques should
not be undertaken lightly. Regular induction into trance states over time
results in personality changes, as the person comes to term with what is
referred to as "the mysteries" in modern occult practise.

The underworld, borders on the collective unconscious, what was
known in different cultures as the Realm of the Dead or of the ancestors.
In trance, a psychological bridge can occur between the underworld and
the Realm of the Ancestors. Rivers traditionally mark the boundaries between realms in many mythical cosmologies. It is across this boundary,
from the Realm of the Ancestors, that the deity-spirit, be it a goddess,
orisha, or loa, comes. Sometimes the boundary may take another symbolic form. It European mythology, they cross what are often referred to
as "the gates of death." Like the symbolism of the river and the bridge,
it is useful in facilitating trance-prophecy and trance training techniques
(see the Underworld Descent Technique, page 172).

The Personal Evolving Cosmology

Most people at some point have a dream that they are in a house that
seems familiar. In most cases it is a recurring dream. This is personal cosmology. We create our own cosmologies around us, both internally and

externally, microcosmically and macrocosmically. The house represents the individual's mind, as well as different levels of reality: the basement the underworld (Jungian Shadow), the lower floor with the kitchen the Middle Realm (id), and the attic the Astral Realm (ego). Symbolically, the use of this is well known to any fan of the horror film genre; the axe murderer is always hiding in the basement, and the beneficent spirit of granny is always hiding among her old clutter in the attic.

It has been our experience that when you begin to study cosmology, be it the Norse Nine worlds or the concentric circles of the Druidic cosmology, as much as you try to stick to them, when you start to work on the other levels, personal symbology starts to intrude. You have to remember that these ancient cosmologies were based on the world of yesteryear; they are no longer necessarily relevant to our modern experience. While they can be initially used to map the other realms used in trance, the seer's experience will begin to morph into the world she experiences every day. A good example comes from Gavin's experience with one of his own students. Initially she studied the Norse cosmology of Yggdrasil. While this worked for pathworkings, what she experienced when she tranced and dreamt was very different. She worked in the theatre in the physical world, so this was reflected in her personal symbology. When she dreamt or tranced, she went to the theatre: the stage was the Middle Realm, the flies (above the stage) were the Astral Realm, but most interestingly was what was beneath the stage. When she explored beneath the stage, she found at the back a door and a spiral staircase going down into the basement. She followed it down where it led to the props room. There amongst the props was a seamstress at work, sewing the costumes. The symbolism was not lost on her, as it cannot really be lost on anyone who understands cosmology. This was her personal underworld, her Shadow that influenced her waking life and the "costumes" she wore.

If you will excuse the pun, we used this example to dramatically show how personal symbology can affect you when you practise trance. Many new practitioners, while in trance, expect to see the mythical and historical cosmology they have been studying, and often become confused when it doesn't materialize. Our personal symbols are drawn from our personal experiences, our memories, so it is not unusual to find that places from our past and places we visit regularly become the stage for these realms if they are strongly associated psychologically. Rather than fighting against this by trying to imprint a mythological cosmology, it is more practical and effective to work with it during any imaginative induction into trance. One of our students regularly visits an ancient site related to a specific goddess, unaware of this process at work. She had several problems connecting with Deity during trance, until we realized that she was, in fact, describing the tomb and the hill that it was on. Once we realized this, and went with the flow of the symbology of the trance states, she was immediately able to make the link with the divinity concerned. This is why an understanding of cosmology (and symbology) is so important in trance-prophecy work.

Chapter 8

The Second Key: Understanding Spiritual Energy

E
verything is energy—this book you are reading, the ink on its
pages, even the thoughts that are going through your mind while
you read these words. It is the basis of modern physics, of quantum theory.[1] Some have described quantum mechanics as being the new
philosophy where religion and science meet. There is good reason for
this, as most of the theories of modern science are not new. They can be
found in the old magical philosophies of the world. A good example of
this is the structure of an atom compared with that of our solar system.
Both are reflections of each other due to the effect of energy, in the case
of atomic structure electrochemical bonds, and in the case of planetary
bodies, the effect of gravity. Most occultists would say that this is the old
occult law of reflection at work; microcosm and macrocosm. Such an
understanding of the similarities between science and traditional magic
resulted in the creations of a new form of magical tradition in the 1980s:
Chaos Magic. This in turn, encouraged more traditional magical practitioners to reexamine their relationship with modern scientific theory
from the viewpoint of hermetics, including the magical use of energy by
creative visualization. It became common place in the 1980s and 1990s to
find occultists quoting quantum theory (often badly) to prove the existence of magical energy. These crossovers between modern science and
magic are just as relevant to trance work. An understanding of our own
energy fields, our auras, and our chakras is essential if we are going to
understand how we trance and the nature of the spiritual world that we
wish to communicate with.

The idea that a form of natural energy is connected to trance is also not new. In the late 1700s, a student at the University of Vienna, Franz Mesmer (whom we previously mentioned in chapter 2), put forward this idea in his published thesis Dissertatio physico-medica de planetarum influxu (*The Physical and Medical Effects of the Planets*).[2] The main thrust of his work is that just as lunar gravity affect the seas, so the gravity of the other planets affect the human body. His thesis was heavily influenced by the work of Issac Newton, particularly his theory of gravity, which he initially referred to as "animal gravity." He later came to believe that this was a magnetic rather than gravitational effect, so he changed the term to the more familiar "animal magnetism." His theories were particularly influenced by his witnessing of exorcism and *stroking*—the use of hands passed over the body without touching the skin to draw out negative influences. Many strokers believed that magnetism worked, as they saw similarities between their method and the way metal bars could be magnetised by stroking them with a magnet—they believed similar forces were at work. In one exorcism ceremony, Mesmer watched a priest tell people that if they remained unaffected, their disorders were physical; but if they went into trance, they were diabolically possessed and suitable for exorcism.

Mesmer's ideas influenced the new generation of occultists who emerged in the 1800s, particularly those in the Spiritualist and Theosophy movements. Mesmer's terms, *magnetic* and *electrical*, were to be used extensively as a way of describing the energy field or aura around and individual's body. Within the Spiritualist movement, these terms continued to be linked with trance in the form of mediumship. They were later linked to the emerging neo-Pagan movement of the 1950s, as many of those coming into Witchcraft had backgrounds in the previously mentioned movements. This crossover in ideas can be seen in the teachings of Alex Sanders, in regular talks to his coven in the 1970s about the *electrical and magnetical fluids*, as part of their training:

> There are two main kinds of fluid originating in the four elements of earth, air, fire and water. These are known to occultists as the electric and magnetic fluids. The electric fluid comes from the fire principle; the magnetic one from the water principle; the air principle is the mediating element between the two; and the earth element is bipolar, hence it contains both the fluids—it is electromagnetical, electrical in the center, and on the periphery, magnetical. According to all natural laws, these two fluids are working in

all of the spheres, in the Mental as well as in the Astral Sphere, and in the material world too. These fluids are the cause of everything being as it is.[3]

Of course, the four platonic elements of Earth, Air, Fire, and Water that Sanders mentions are just metaphors for the states of matter that we are taught in science at school. Earth is solid, air is gaseous, water is liquid, and fire is plasma; energy manifests in the material level. Within Wicca we were trained to master these elements psychologically, magically, and spiritually. This mastery is even more important for someone who is to enter into trance states; because these elemental analogies also apply to the levels of consciousness, we must become aware of if we are to travel between them. Our ancient forebears were well aware of this, and evidence can be found in the writings of Lucius Apulieus, who wrote the classic description of Isian Initiation mysteries *The Golden Ass* in the second century: "I made my way to the verge of death, I trod the threshold of Proserpine (Persephone), I travelled through all the elements and made my return."

Modern Pagan thought tends to revolve around the idea of four elements and Spirit. This derives from the ancient Greek perception of the elements, particularly those of Plato, but compared with other cultures, it is quite simplistic. Other cultures developed different perceptions of the elements far from what is the norm in modern Pagan practise. For example, the Chinese have five elements: Fire (huǒ), Earth (tǔ), Metal (jīn), Water (shuǐ), and Wood (mù). In ceremonial magic teaching, there is the doctrine that the elements exist within each other; for example, Earth in Water, Fire, and Air, as well as its pure form. This gives us, including Spirit, twenty-five possible subdivisions of elements. Some would say that this is overly complicated, and we would agree. The existing elemental systems are humankind's own perceptions of the universe on a philosophical or magical level. This is one of the reasons that we have moved toward the use of the Vedic chakra system for magical and, more specifically, trance work in the last few years.

Our conclusion that understanding this energy is vitally important tool came about from our experiences and conversations with numerous participants of Drawing Down the Moon and seidr rites during the 1990s. Many of them described particular occurrences, which could only be explained by applying the principles of energy we outline in this chapter. Generally these occurrences can be described as following:

- An individual observing a trance-prophecy, seidr, or Drawing Down the Moon rite would see a "shadow" they perceive as deity prior to it entering the priestess or seer.
- The priestess or seer would describe the feeling of a presence behind her, often but not always behind her left shoulder.
- When an individual was possessed by a deity, those present would see a change in the face of the priestess or seer. This was often described as being like a transparent mask, which changes the shape and appearance of some of the facial features.

One priestess we talked to described two of these occurring as she watched her own high priestess being drawn down upon:

> I was watching my HPS (high priestess) having the Moon drawn down on her by our HP (high priest). We had seen it done several times on her, but on this occasion something had changed. There was more intensity to the ritual for some reason. The first thing I noticed was my HPS's aura highly noticeable in the candlelight. It hugged her body around her head and shoulders like a grey mist. I then noticed a shadowy figure behind her. As the invocation by the HP continued with the invoking triangle, I noticed that the shadowy figure had disappeared but her aura had seemed to grow larger. At first I thought it was an illusion until I looked at her face; it had changed. She had a beautiful glow around her, her cheekbones seemed to have become higher on her face and she appeared to have a more classical shape to her face. I will never forget it; it was one of the most beautiful things I have ever seen.

What is initially being seen behind the priestess is the aura of the divinity. It is attempting to access the priestess's crown chakra and align its own chakras with its own mental-emotional body (we discuss the idea of deities having their own energy systems in chapter 10). When this happens, the mental-emotional body of the deity enters through the priestess's crown chakra. For this to happen, the crown chakra must be open on both the spiritual and mental-emotional level of her aura. This allows the deity to overlay its mental-emotional body over that of the priestess's. This causes the aforementioned effects, particularly the changes in the priestess's face. Many priestesses describe the same experience, as one priestess who wrote to us describes:

Illustration 2: Deity Aligning with Chakra System

"It normally occurs about a few seconds into the invocation. I start to feel a presence behind me. Slowly as the invocation continues, I can feel the presence begin to merge with me. I feel a slight pressure at the top of my head, and I begin to feel as though my consciousness is being pushed into the back of my head. It is like looking at the world through a pane glass window; I am here but am not here. My mouth seems to go into automatic, words come out but I don't seem to know where they come from. Normally at this point I begin to lose any memory of what has happened. I just retain fragments."

What is being described here is the alignment of the deity's chakras with that of the priestess (see Illustration 2). In this case it is a full alignment, the root center is open, and the crown is open, as are the brow and throat centers. Full possession can only take place if all these are open. Different combinations of these alignments can result in different effects:

- crown, root, brow, and throat: Simultaneously opened on the spiritual level of the aura: possession of the mind occurs. This happens in Vodoun and Santeria and is often referred to as being "ridden."

- crown, root, and brow: Simultaneously opened on the spiritual level: the seer sees the deity in her mind's eye—her "third eye." She can communicate with a divinity if one is present, or can see psychic messages emerging as images from the Astral Plane/collective unconscious (pure trance-prophecy). She is able to relay messages from the deity, or the meaning of these images, to a questioner if present. The relaying of messages from a deity is the easiest form to manifest.

- crown, root, and throat: Simultaneously opened on the spiritual level: this is actually described in the above account where the priestess suddenly starts talking and not knowing where the words come from. It is what is commonly referred to as *glossolalia*, or "speaking in tongues." In most cases, it is intelligible, but sometimes the priestess or seer has been known to speak in a language they are unfamiliar with.

There is also another final stage, which we have only just begun to understand in recent years. It came about from Janet being possessed by a divinity and walking around the circle. This can only occur if the deity takes full control of the seer's body, which is certainly rare. Our conclusion is that for this to happen, the deity must align all its chakra centers with that of the seer. Not only would crown, root, throat, and brow have to be open and aligned with those of the deity, but so would the remaining chakras: heart, solar plexus, and sacrum.

Of course, we are here talking about connection with Deity and possession taking place. In some traditional forms of trance prophecy, such as seidr, this does not always occur, with the seer only seeing images which have to be translated. In this case, only the third eye is open; the brow chakra is open on the level of the spiritual body.

In ecstatic ritual (see chapter 14), energy becomes important because so much is released during the rite as an effect of dancing and drumming. The ritual area fills with etheric energy generated by the auras of the participants. It is palpable to anyone who is there or who enters the ritual at a later time. This assists the participants entering into an ecstatic state of consciousness, allowing them to fully trance to the point of becoming possessed by the divinities they have worked with. This is what occurs during a Vodoun ritual when the loa possess *Vodouisants*, or individual participants. Historically, it also occurred in the original pre-Apollonian rites of Delphi. Like trance-prophecy, understanding the energies involved in such ecstatic rituals allows possession to happen safely, as well as allowing correct grounding at the end of any such rites.

Let us now look at what is happening from the viewpoint of the chakra system. We use the Eastern chakra system, as it has several advantages over the other systems, including Cabala, when it comes to understanding energy and trance. The first advantage is that it is a tried and tested system. Secondly, it is a wholly pagan system, and thirdly and most importantly, it works. It explains many occurrences that individuals describe during trance and magical states of being, as we have previously mentioned.

We have covered the basics of chakras and the aura in our previous work, *The Inner Mysteries*, so it is not necessary to go into detail regarding their roles in the body and aura. But to reiterate, there are seven major chakras starting at the feet and working to the top of the head:

- root chakra (the feet or the perineum): the element of Earth. Colour: red.
- sacral chakra (the sacrum/pelvic girdle): the element of Water. Colour: orange. Relates to emotion, fertility.
- solar plexus chakra (the abdomen): the element of Fire. Colour: yellow.

- heart chakra (center of chest): the element of Air. Colours: green/turquoise.
- throat chakra (throat): Ether. Colour: Blue.
- brow chakra (forehead): the Mind. Colours: Purple/Indigo/Mauve.
- crown chakra (top of the head): Spirit or Akasha. Colours: bright white/silver/gold or multicoloured.

The last three chakras—the throat, the brow, and the crown—are often referred to by New Agers as the higher chakras. It is these three chakras that are responsible for the creation of the three levels of the aura in Western tradition: Ether: etheric body, the Mind: mental and emotional body, and the crown: the spiritual or astral body. Each chakra, therefore, has three different associations related to these and, of course, a fourth, the physical body, which is generated by the four lower chakras. While all of the chakras are important in the process, it is the following four centers: the root, throat, brow, and the crown that are of specific importance in mediumship and trance-prophecy. For any technique to work, it is necessary for these four centers to be fully open. Study of all the chakras and the practise of opening and closing them regularly is essential in the preparation to practise trance-prophecy. It is essential for any practitioner to be able to balance their own chakra centers.

The chakras are, in fact, vortices of energy in the body: energy coming in from the back and out from the front forming a reverse funnel as it is spun out into the body. This is best described using the bath tub analogy, which we created ourselves to explain what the chakras are in energetic reality rather than symbolically as they are often described. One of the best ways of doing this is the visualization we give below. This is best done in a semi-meditative state, with eyes closed in a relaxing atmosphere.

1. First visualize a bathtub, and then visualize it in the shape of a person. Imagine there are not one but seven plugholes and place them appropriately in the positions of the seven centers.
2. Secondly, fill the bath with water. Imagine the water spiralling down the plugholes in a clockwise fashion as it normally does (if you are in the Northern Hemisphere). Now visualize that this flow alternates with each chakra: root center turns anticlockwise; the sacral turns clockwise; and so on up the body.

3. Thirdly, now imagine this process in reverse, as if watching a film backwards, with the water spiralling out of the plugholes into the bath. Now take away the bath, but keep the water there so that you have a figure of a person made of water.

4. Finally, imagine the water coming up, out of each plughole in the appropriate colour of the chakra. We often suggest visualizing drops of ink being dropped into the middle of each center. Now imagine the water flowing from the front of each center, being pulled into the other centers from the back and being pushed out the front.

What you are now visualizing is the flow of energy around the aura, as it comes out of each center resulting in a cascading flow of colour around the body. By visualising the chakras in this fashion, it is possible to understand the way energy flows up and down the body, which is particularly important in trance possession work, as we explain later, and how the aura is generated. It is also more obvious what happens if the energy flows faster through one center than another; it begins to pull in more colours and converts them to its own.

The Root Center (Muladhara): Earth

This is the seat of the mystical kundalini, which in Hindu religion is traditionally believed to be a goddess.* There are differing views about its actual position. If the body is in the *lotus position*, it is certainly at the base of the spine (the fourth sacral bone). There is also the view that the normal position of this center is at the base of the feet. This makes sense to us, as it is the center, which links us with the earth. It is normally seen as a rosy red colour when at rest, and fiery orange-red when active. It is divided into four segments or petals, representing the four elements in the material world. As the center is principally related to the Element of Earth, it is responsible for the disposal of unwanted, impure energies, which pollute the three bodies of the aura and the other centers. It is therefore of vital importance in the act of grounding. Within the physical body, it governs the spinal column and the urinary system, including the kidneys. This chakra is also associated with physical sensations like pain and pleasure. In trance work it is essential to have it open for grounding, to allow any passage of energy from above to earth, and thus create a spiritual current.

* Originally, the chakra system was associated with the Goddess Kundalini, according to Anodea Judith in *Wheels of Life*. "She becomes the coiled serpent, Kundalini-Shakti, wrapped three and one-half times around the *Shiva lingam* in the Muladhara. . . . Her name comes from the word *kundala*, which means 'coiled'" (pp. 36, 416–417).

The Throat (Vishuddhi) Center: Ether

This is the first of the upper or higher centers, and is positioned at the throat. It relates to the concept of Ether: the old-style Spiritualists (see chapter 2) often referred to Ether as ectoplasm, and it was commonly manifested during séances by trained mediums, particularly when they were vocally possessed by a discarnate spirit. This center is responsible for generating and connecting us with our etheric body. It is positioned over the larynx and has obvious associations with communication and speech, the power of the word, listening to others, and taking responsibility for what we say. Physically, it is related to the respiratory system, the upper alimentary canal, and the vocal apparatus. The throat center also affects metabolism due to its relationship with the thyroid and parathyroid glands. All traditions agree on its blue colour, and it is divided into sixteen petals. During trance work this is the center that governs communication with the spiritual world on the *akashic,* or spiritual, level of the aura.

The Brow (Ajna) Center: Mind

This is the mystical "third eye," and is positioned on the brow. It rules the mind, and is responsible for generating the mental body. It is well known as the center that controls clairvoyance and psychic experience. For this reason, it is referred to by some as "the doorway to eternity." Within the physical body, it affects the lower brain, ears, eyes, and nervous system. It is positioned perfectly over the pituitary and hypothalamus glands, which control the whole endocrine system. Again, there is no dispute among traditions about this center's colour, which is violet or indigo, although there is some disagreement regarding the number of petals. There are two differences in thought. According to the Rev. C. W. Leadbeater, there are ninety-six petals,[4] but according to most Hindu and Buddhist traditional writings, there are only two. From the perspective of the seeker of the mysteries, this chakra has two petals, for the brow chakra governs the psychological processes. The idea of two lobes, therefore, gives us polarity: positive/negative, right brain/left brain, yin/yang, and, of course, Jung's concepts of anima/animus and ego/Shadow. An understanding of this polarity and the ability to internally polarize is essential in ecstatic states such as trance-prophecy, as it allows the individual to open this center on the akashic or spiritual level of the aura (the opening of the third eye). Being able to open this center on this level rather than the mental level allows genuine visualization of any spirit or deity, or messages that are coming from the astral planes. If they are not successful in opening on this level, all they will see will be filtered images generated by their own ego.

The Crown (Sahasrara) Center: Spirit

This is the final center, known as the crown because of its position at the top of the head. It is the ultimate link with the person's astral body, and is where the soul enters. It is therefore governed by Spirit. It is the abode of what is often referred to as the Higher Self, or Holy Guardian Angel. This is the Astral Guardian, which monitors and protects us when we venture into the spiritual realms. As such, it is essential for anyone doing trance-prophecy to have contacted and worked with their Astral Guardian if they are to have any success in contacting a deity-spirit. Its colour varies, depending on the individual's spiritual development. It is generally visualized as white, which is made up of all the colours of the spectrum. In a spiritually developed person it becomes quite large, and when fully open, it covers their whole head, producing the classic halo effect. This effect is also produced by its staggering 972 petals. In oriental pictures and statues, this chakra is often shown quite prominently, as it is in early Christian iconography. This is considered to be the highest chakra, since it connects the individual to divinity, which is Kether (the crown) in Cabalistic terms, or God and Goddess in general Pagan terminology. In the physical body it controls the nervous system and the higher functions of the brain.

There are three levels to the aura, and each energy center or chakra also exists on each of the auric levels. They are the same chakras but at different frequencies; hence, there are seven associations related to them in the etheric body, seven in the mental/emotional, and seven in the spiritual. This is important to understand if you are working in trance-possession states. In order for a deity to enter into a seer, the crown center must be open. Not just on the spiritual level of the aura, but also on the mental/emotional level. The aura bodies have the following associations and functions.

The Etheric Body

This is often seen as a grey misty area closest to the body, and is generally referred to as the etheric body. It normally extends about one to three inches over its surface. The term ether refers to a state between energy and matter. Gifted psychics often describe the etheric body as being composed of energy lines forming a sparkling translucent web along which sparks of bluish-white light move, which gives a pulsating effect.

It is generated by the first four chakra centers, which are associated with the elements of Earth, Air, Fire, and Water. This is important to realize when doing any magical work, as we explain later. The action of these four centers in conjunction with the fifth, the etheric chakra, results in the formation of this part of the aura. The etheric body vibrates at the same frequency as Spirit, and acts as a vehicle for it. It therefore helps to shape and anchor the physical body, which is why it hugs the surface of the body so closely. For this reason it is sometimes referred to as the etheric double. Its main purpose is to feed the body with life force or *prana*.

The Mental/Emotional Body

The second part is the mental/emotional body, which is generated by the sixth chakra. It is made up of even finer energy than the etheric body, and unlike that body, it is normally ovoid in shape. How far it projects depends on the immediate mental and emotional state of the individual. The aura of an extroverted person can project out as far as several feet, but that of an introvert may remain always close to the body, almost withdrawing into the etheric body. A trained psychic sees this part of the aura as made up of a variety of colours. Like the size of the aura, they indicate the mental, emotional, and occasionally the physical state of its owner. During possession states, it is overlaid by the mental/emotional body of the deity, which enters through the crown center in the mental/emotional body of the seer.

The Spiritual Body

The last body, and the least easy to see even for a sensitive, is the spiritual body. This connects with the last of the chakras, the crown. In a spiritually developed person, it can extend from the body for some distance. This part of the aura exists on the Astral Plane and is the individual's connection with the world of spirit. The individual's consciousness moves in this body, combined with the mental/emotional body, during astral travel in the higher planes. But during out-of-body experiences on the physical material plane, it is only the mental/emotional body of the aura that detaches from the physical body. This happens involuntarily, sometimes during sleep, giving what is often referred to as lucid dreaming or rapid eye movement (REM) sleep by scientists (for more on this see page 136). This is important to understand, as it is a state the seer may enter into during trance.

In traditional Wiccan Drawing Down the Moon (see chapter 12), the technique for opening the body's energy centers was the Fivefold Kiss, which has its origins in the Middle Pillar Ritual of Cabalistic ritual magic. The main problem with this was that it only opened five of the seven centers, mimicking the Middle Pillar of the Tree of Life. There was actually no problem with this happening, as it is only necessary for the four centers we mentioned previously to be open to allow this to happen, but it gave an incomplete picture of the energy centers of the body, particularly when training in trance work.

For all intents and purposes, we are a tube of energy due to the effect of the energy flow up the body via the chakras: one flow of energy going up from the root to the crown, and another vice versa, going from the crown to the root: from earth to Spirit and from Spirit to earth. For this to happen, both the root and the crown chakras have to be fully open, particularly if any other form of energy, such as that of a deity-spirit, is to enter. It is not essential for the other chakras to be fully open, but as we mention further on, it will be necessary for either the throat or the brow to be open for trance-prophecy, or both for full deity possession. Quite simply, you cannot put a quart in a pint pot; it is necessary for energy to be grounded. The energy comes in from the crown chakra; hence, the importance of having the root chakra open. This is the feeling of "withdrawing" into the back of the mind that a seer feels when being positively possessed by a divinity.

When trance possession takes place, be it Drawing Down the Moon, being ridden by the loa, during spiritual mediumship, or even being taken in ecstatic dance by one's power animal, the same mechanisms are at work related to the body's energy system. In all cases, the spirit or deity enters through the crown chakra, which is why it is essential for it to be open, as we have previously mentioned. The deity-spirit then attempts to align its chakras (see Illustration 2) and spiritual and mental/emotional bodies with that of its host. This can result in several effects:

1. The person in trance may meet the deity-spirit in a trance state in another level of reality, such as the Astral Plane, the underworld, etc. who then relays important messages to them. The trancer may either sense the deity being present and hear them, or see them with their mind's eye. Whether one or the other takes place depends on which lobe is dominant in the brow chakra. This is a prophetic act of clairaudience or clairvoyance respectively, and occurs because only the crown and the brow chakras of the host and deity-spirit are aligned, but there is no alignment of the auras.

2. The deity-spirit speaks through the host, often feeling them, but retains his or her control and memory of the entire event, although
he or she does not have voluntary control of speech. Sometimes this
can be what is called in Christian terminology speaking in tongues;
a garbled language, which appears to mean nothing (until the host
translates it afterwards), or sometimes a very definite message may be
given to those present. This occurs because only the crown and the
throat chakras are aligned.

3. The deity-spirit totally overwhelms the host, sublimating the personality completely (causing it to withdraw into the unconscious), and
possesses the body. The deity-spirit may prophesize, dance, or lead
the ritual; whichever is in its nature. They become 'enthused' by the
spirit as an act of "inspirational possession."[5] The host loses complete
control and memory of the events that transpire. This occurs when all
the higher chakras are aligned; the throat, the brow, and the crown,
along with the root center being open. This allows the aura of the
deity-spirit to also align itself completely with the seer/host.

For any of these processes to take place, the host must have had some
form of spiritual training, particularly in internal elemental balancing
and polarity, to be able to fully open the throat, the brow, and the crown
chakras. Training in dealing with one's own *Shadow*—one's own personal
repressed issues—becomes essential, as does understanding of what is
often referred to as the "mysteries" in occult speech.

Opening and Closing the Chakras

Being able to open and close the chakras is absolutely essential in any
form of trance work, which is why it is necessary that both techniques are
mastered. We would recommend using the following opening and closing
exercise on a daily basis until you are adept at the processes involved.
It takes about twenty to thirty minutes. We would recommend having
somebody present who is sensitive and able to see the chakras the first
few times you do it. For example, if you are taking on the role of the seer,
you may want your trance-guide to do this. He or she can confirm when
the centers are open. With practice it takes less and less time to open your
centers, and you will eventually find that you can discard this exercise
completely and open them by willpower alone.

Opening the Chakras

1. The first stage is to find somewhere quiet and comfortable to sit. The
best position to sit in is the well-known lotus position, used in Eastern

yoga, because it has the effect of bringing the *muladhara*, or root center, into line with the other chakras. If you are not supple enough to use this position, sitting cross-legged or kneeling will have the same effect. The important thing is to stay comfortable for a reasonable period of time.

2. The next stage is to breathe regularly. There are various breathing patterns used, but we have found that breathing out for seven seconds, holding for two seconds, breathing in for seven seconds, and finally again holding for two seconds, is the most effective. It is important to breathe from the base of the lungs, by expanding the stomach first and then the ribs. It will take a while to get used to this, so give yourself time to master it. Now visualize that you are breathing in light. Initially this should be white light, before going on to the next stage.

3. Energizing the chakras, one by one, is the third stage. Continue the breathing pattern that you began with, which by now should be natural and rhythmic. Visualize the root center at the base of the spine as a red, glowing, spinning ball. As you breathe in, visualize the colour of your breath as the same; in this case red. After several minutes, this should have the effect of making the chakra expand while spinning faster and brighter.

4. Finally, imagine the energy from the center you have just energized moving up to the next chakra (in this case the sacral center), but change the colour of the light you are breathing to that of the new chakra (in this case, yellow). Again, it should take several minutes to energize the chakra, which should behave in the same way as the first center. You then simply repeat the process until you reach and energize the third eye or brow center. Then visualize all the colours from each of the energized chakras moving swiftly up to the crown center at the top of the head. Allow the energy to leave the top of the head like a fountain and bathe your aura.

Closing the Chakras and Grounding

It is important to ensure that your chakras are closed after you have finished any form of trance work or mediumship. This is commonly called *grounding*. Leaving them fully open can result in a loss of vitality, higher risk of disease, and mental stress. Most people who are not grounded describe a feeling of disconnection with the world, a feeling of light-headedness. The easiest way to close the chakras down is to eat. This is the purpose of Cakes and Ale ceremony found at the end of most neo-Pagan rituals, as the ingestion of food closes the solar plexus chakra, while replenishing any energy loss. One other method commonly used is to place the palms of the hands flat on the ground to remove any excess energy left in the system, and visualizing the energy going into the ground (*earthing the power*). This is commonly used while visualizing the root center.

If you are new to trance work, we would recommend the following technique. Visualize the energy draining back down from one chakra to another. Once you have drained the energy from each chakra to the one below it, visualize a shutter closing it from vision. Repeat this center by center. When you reach the root center, remember that it is the only one you leave open all the time, because it acts as the body's grounding point and helps to prevent mental and psychic overload. It is important to pay particular attention to closing the crown, brow, and throat chakras—the upper chakras. This is because these are the ones that are predominantly used in trance-prophecy and trance-possession work. Making sure the crown is fully closed is the most important thing to do.

Because each chakra center opens up on different levels of the aura, it is important after any form of trance work where there has been spiritual communication to make sure the "gates" (crown chakra on the level of the spiritual aura) are closed. This is done by using the following exercise, while closing the crown chakra. It is a variation on a technique commonly taught in Spiritualism:

- Spend about a minute or more visualizing that your mind is a white room.
- Now look at the ceiling. In the ceiling, there will be a set of trap doors ("the gates") opening into the "loft" (the Astral Plane).
- Now visualize that you are pulling the trap doors shut. Once they are shut, bar them.
- If you find that you have problems closing the doors, call your spirit guide or the deity you have connected with to help you close the doors.

These gates are, in fact, synonymous with the gates taught in the Underworld Decent Technique, described in chapter 11.

Deities Related to the Chakras

There is another factor that needs to be taken into account, particularly in trance-possession. It could be that specific deities are attracted to the energy emanating from particular chakras, especially if a specific chakra is more developed in the individual who is calling or acting as host for the deity-spirit. Certainly in the Vedic system of correspondences related to chakras, specific deities relate to particular centers, with the exception of the crown center:*

- root (Earth): Brahma
- sacral (Water): Vishnu
- solar plexus (Fire): Rudra
- heart (Air): Isha
- throat (Ether): Sada-shiva
- brow/third eye (Mind): Shiva

All deities, regardless of cultural origins share the same archetypal energies. For example, Freya, Aphrodite, Venus and, of course, the Hindu Shakti, are all deities of love and sex, and as such all relate to the sacral chakra and would be attracted to anyone who has a well-developed sacral chakra or is well in balance with the element of Water. Taking this into account, it is therefore more likely that a deity-spirit will come through if ALL the chakras are opened. It is for this reason we introduced the idea of the Sevenfold Kiss, which is chakra- rather than Cabalistic sephira-related. We assumed that we were the first to develop this technique, but during the research for this book, we came across references to the Seven Points of Brotherhood, used by the O.T.O. This is hardly surprising, as Crowley used chakras as an important part of his practise.

The Sevenfold Kiss

The Sevenfold Kiss revolves around the use of a pranic breath technique to charge another individual's chakras. We developed it specifically for use in trance-prophecy. The pranic breath used is paced by breathing in to the beat of seven, holding for two, breathing out for the beat of seven, and then holding for two. During this breath, blue etheric energy should be visualised emanating from the throat chakra and up into the mouth as the giver of the kiss breathes in and out. When kissing each chakra point, they are in fact breathing and visualizing this energy entering their partner's chakras, thus charging them. Like the traditional Fivefold Kiss,

---

* Valerie Walker, a Faery (Feri) initiate and elder of Compost Coven (in San Francisco), independently created a similar system she calls the "Ladder of Hestia," using Western deities. For more info, visit her website at http://www.wiggage.com/witch/feriladder. html .

it can be done as a ritual with the priest starting by kneeling at the feet
of the seer and working up the body.

Priest kisses feet (root chakra):

"Blessed be thy feet, which connect you with
earth from which we come."

Priest kisses above pubic bone (sacral chakra):

"Blessed be that from which flow the waters
of pleasure and birth."

Priest kisses abdomen (solar plexus chakra):

"Blessed be that which brings forth the fire
and energy to sustain life."

Priest kisses center of chest (heart chakra):

"Blessed be that which brings love on the air
to all that seek it."

Priest kisses lips and side of neck (throat chakra):

"Blessed be thy lips, which breathe in the
ether of life."

Priest kisses between eyes (brow chakra):

"Blessed be thy eyes, which see the truth in
the many realms."

Priest kisses top of head (crown chakra):

"Blessed be thy spirit, from which all light
shines as the doorway to the divine ones."

We'd like to point out straight away that this is a much more powerful
act than the Fivefold Kiss; it suffuses the chakras immediately with etheric energy, opening them rapidly. The receiver of the kiss may initially
feel lightheaded and off balance as the chakras open, but they will then
rapidly feel the chakras go into natural balance again.

NOTES

1 The term *quantum* or *quanta* derives from Max Planck (1858–1947). He and Werner Heisenberg (1901–1976) are accepted by most scientists as the fathers of quantum theory.

2 This was published in 1776 as part of Mesmer's doctorate work at the University of Vienna.

3 Stewart Farrar, "Wicca Transcriptions," personal training notes, 1970.

4 Rev. C. W. Leadbeater, *The Chakras: A Monograph*. His rationalization for this number of petals relates to energy rather than symbolism.

5 Mark Bancroft coined the term "Inspirational possession" in his thesis paper, "The History and Psychology of Spirit Possession and Exorcism," published as a book by EnSpire Press (no longer available).

Chapter 9

The Third Key: Understanding Trance and Its Techniques

Many of the techniques we mention in this chapter are not necessarily ones we would use ourselves or even condone. If people do decide to use the techniques mentioned here, they do so only *after* serious thought about the consequences, taking adequate preparations and precautions. Even if these techniques are not used, it is important for anyone who is going to study trance to understand them, including their history, how they work, and why they are used. This knowledge will give a better understanding of other trance techniques available to them.

If you are going to practise trance techniques, it is, of course, important to look at what trance actually is. In simple terms, it is a change in consciousness, where the individual's conscious self, their persona, is sublimated for a period of time, allowing direct access to the subconscious or unconscious mind. Most people will think of hypnosis and induced trance, which we talk about specifically in this chapter, but we also enter natural trance states, frequently. We take these states for granted not realising they are, in fact, trance states, and use other terms for them such as "daydreaming," "turning off," or "chilling out." What they all have in common is a relaxed state where we lose consciousness of time, and particularly our perception of it. We enter into an alpha brainwave state or deeper (see below). This can happen when we are watching TV, listening to music, or relaxing in the bath. While most people have heard of *circadian rhythms*, our daily body clock, we also have another cycle, the *ultradian rhythms*, which are less well known.

While circadian rhythms go through a twenty-four-hour cycle, which includes our sleep and waking phases, ultradian rhythms are shorter, going through one-and-a-half to two-hour phases, with rest phases of approximately fifteen minutes. It is during these rest periods that you may naturally trance, entering into an alpha or possibly deeper, into a theta state, with the assistance of specific techniques (see below). During this time, to use a term from hypnosis, you are naturally suggestive and able to absorb information and ideas directly into the subconscious mind. This is because your persona, your consciousness, sidesteps—you literally lose yourself. This is experienced in the examples we have previously given, but also in such activities as prolonged dancing to rhythmic beats (see below), where the individual enters into one of these phases, and it is then prolonged by the rhythmic beat of the music and dance, making them enter into the deeper theta state.

Being aware of your personal cycles is obviously useful to know if you wish to enter into trance. You can choose a particular time to enter into trance when you know you are about to enter into one of the ultradian rest phases, assisting the trance techniques we mention later in this chapter. Most of these techniques we mention here induce the rest phase and prolong it by affecting brainwave activity, which is important to understand. Because the rest phase normally lasts only twenty minutes, this can be taken into account when inducing that state for trance-prophecy or ecstatic ritual. The period a seer can be kept in trance should therefore be no longer than twenty minutes unless other techniques are used towards the end of the session to maintain the trance state. In ecstatic ritual, such as the Vodoun ceremony, techniques such as dancing, drumming, chanting, etc., should be maintained throughout the whole ritual to keep the individual practitioner in that state of consciousness. In Vodoun ceremonies, this can go on as long as six hours or more, although we recommend that any prolonged trance method should not go on any longer than two hours, keeping in tune with the active phase of ultradian rhythm and, therefore, allowing the practitioner to go back into tune with their own cycle.

Brainwave Activity related to changes in Consciousness and Trance

Brainwave activity is measured with the use of electroencephalogram. It measures the brain's electrical activity cycles. This activity is measured in hertz (Hz), which is a cycle per second. It is known that there are four main states of brain activity, which are directly related to the state of consciousness of the individual: beta, alpha, theta, and delta. Generally, the lower the brainwave frequency, the more the individual turns his or her awareness to the inner world, the subjective experience, and is able to access other realties including the spiritual realms. The deeper the individual goes into these realms, the lower the brainwave activity will become, and the more profound the experience will be.

Beta (14–40 Hz)	This is the full consciousness, as we know it in everyday life. We are fully awake, and as such it is generally associated with the left, logical hemisphere of the brain. Your attention is focused outward, on the world around you. The border between beta and alpha states is the doorway to your subconscious mind.
Alpha (8–13 Hz)	This is a relaxed state; for example, when we are daydreaming or contemplating artistic ideas, which bubble up from our right brain. It is the first stage needed to achieve any form of trance or creative visualization, as it is in this state that you turn inwards. The border between alpha and theta states is the doorway that allows you to access your psychic abilities through your unconscious mind.
Theta (4–7 Hz)	This is deep relaxation and is generally associated with the deeper areas of the subconscious mind. The right brain function tends to take over completely. We enter this state when we first fall asleep.
Delta (0.5–3.5 Hz)	During sleep and deep trance states we enter two stages of brain activity. In delta the brain cycles regularly into rapid eye movement (REM) followed by nonrapid eye movement (NREM) sleep at roughly twenty minute intervals. While REM is well known as the dream state, NREM is much deeper and dreamless. It is in NREM that the individual may access the Superconsious.

Trance Techniques

Ritual and Ceremony

Religious rites have always been an important aspect of trance, regardless of whether they take place as part of ancient tribal shamanism, or the practises of modern Spiritualist mediums. Repetitive ritual is particularly important for trance, as it causes the individual trancing to enter into a pre-trance state of expectation. From setting up a temple space, the donning of special dress (like a ritual robe), to the creation of "sacred space" and invocation of the spirits or gods, all are important in creating the right state of mind for trance.

Special Dress

Most modern Pagans and Witches are used to seeing ritual robes being worn for any ceremonies. These are generally a medieval style, but other traditions of trance wear other types of clothing. In shamanic practises, a special cloak or jacket may be worn. These are often made of skin, and may be adorned with totems or power items representing the spirits the shaman works with. In Asatru, it is very common for practitioners of seith to wear a dress, which is historically accurate for the period of ritual they enact. Using a special dress works very closely with wearing the masks (see below) in helping to change the perception of self and sublimate the ego/persona complex. For those who are experienced with trance, they act as a trigger, the donning of special clothing having a Pavlovian effect.* Such an effect is important to remember regarding all aspects of trance.

Creation of Sacred Space and Psychic Protection

In trance, sacred space is created for three reasons:

1. as a protective barrier to prevent interference (i.e., from unwelcome lower spirits),
2. to maintain the energy within the ritual space, and
3. to consecrate the space, which literally moves the space being used to a different level of consciousness.

Most who have worked in magic circles have experienced altered perceptions of time, with participants often describing that time feels as though it is running faster or slower in ritual. This often goes along with

---

* Ivan Pavlov (1849–1936) was the first to research *conditioned reflex*—the unconscious reaction to an action caused by prolonged ritualistic behaviour.

the comment that the act of correctly casting the circle changes the "feeling" of the ritual space. This is a result of it shifting to a different level. Sacred space is created in nearly all magical trance traditions, although we may not notice that this act is taking place. For example, in Spiritualism a circle is formed by the joining of hands, fingertip to fingertip, around the table.

One other form of protection commonly used is the contacting of a guardian spirit—a spirit guide, power animal, or familial spirit. Traditionally, this is one of the first actions any would-be shaman or spiritual medium takes. Contacting a patron god or goddess early on in trance-prophecy training is, of course, performing the same action.

Ritual invocation of the Spirits or Gods
Ritual invocation is essential if spirits or deities are to be communicated with in trance, as it not only calls the spirit forms to enter the sacred space, but also opens up the mind of the seer to be receptive to their attendance. This can be clearly seen in the traditional Wiccan Drawing Down the Moon, where they are verbally invoked, but also in Vodoun practise, where it is the nonverbal with the use of *vévés* (symbols of the loas), which are formed on the ground or floor of the temple. An important part of this process in more traditional trance work is the making of offerings to the spirit form, whether it be an animal sacrifice (as in Vodoun) or the offering of wine and herbs into a bowl (Romano-Greek). What is important is that the correct offerings are made for that spirit or deity.

Visualization/Pathworking
Meditation and its deeper counterpart, pathworking, has been the mainstay of occult practise since the nineteenth century and, of course, before that in Eastern culture. It is from these cultures that it probably originated before being introduced into Western occultism. There are different forms of these practises, each taking the individual deeper down into their unconscious. The use of visualization techniques uniquely developed in European-based culture. While Eastern techniques are based on clearing the mind and focusing on a single thought or object, a mantra such as Om/Aum, or the image, say, of a rose, visualization uses a *pathwork*—a continual dialogue or story rather than a static image. There are several advantages to using such techniques, the first is that it is easier to focus on the pathway and therefore less easy to become distracted. It can also be used to take the participant to "places," allowing him or her to explore

their own aspect of their psyche, and going deeper into other spiritual dimensions. When combined with an understanding of psychology and mythic cosmology, pathworking becomes particularly potent (see chapter 7). At its deepest level, it is, of course, akin to self-hypnosis. The Underworld Decent Technique (covered more fully in chapter 11) is one such method.

Entheogens: Intoxicants and Hallucinogens

The use of ingested substances to cause change in magical consciousness goes back to the very dawn of time. The term *entheogen* (see Glossary) is used to define their use in this way. Recorded history is full of accounts of their use in almost every culture, from the ancient Persians' and Greeks' use of *Soma Elixir*, to the modern-day use of peyote by the Native American Church. There is little doubt that almost all ancient cultures had some form of cult-related use of a hallucinogen or psychoactive substance. Psychoactive substances such as lysergic acid diethylamide (LSD) and mescaline (an alkaloid derived from certain fungi and cacti) directly affect the brain's chemistry, specifically the enzymes of the neuroreceptors. It is this which causes the hallucinations; it causes these receptors to fire off randomly. The biggest problem with their use is that their effect is difficult to control in any ritual way. It is also difficult for any user to differentiate between a genuine vision caused by the psychedelic opening of the psyche on other levels of reality, and what comes from the individual's own unconscious mind. Although frequently used in traditional shamanic practises, **we do not recommend their use in any form of ritual trance-prophecy**, as the effects are often uncontrollable. In the long term, apart from the psychological and physical damage they can cause (see Introduction), they can also effect the energetic body of the individual, causing damage to both the individual's aura and chakras.

Aside from the use of hallucinogens, alcohol, tobacco, and mildly psychoactive herbs have also been traditionally used. Wine, mead, and beer were once believed to be a gift from the gods in ancient times, and their intoxicating effect was once believed to help connect with the divine force. Alcohol was particularly important in the cult of Dionysus, the god of wine and wild nature, and was used extensively in his rites. These rites were eventually to degrade into the orgiastic rituals of the Roman Bacchanalia, but its sacred use was absorbed into the Christian Church with the taking of wine at Mass. Its use in modern Pagan ritual as a sacrament can be found in Wicca with the consecration of wine, as well as in Asatru with the passing of mead. In trance, it can be used in moderation to make

the participants more susceptible to entering a trance state, but it should
not be used in excess.

Food and Sleep Deprivation

Alongside the use of hallucinogens, both of these techniques are some
of the most hazardous if used to induce trance. **We do not recommend
the use of either.** We have seen dire consequences resulting from their
misuse, including the onset of physical and psychiatric conditions, as well
as psychic dangers. While basic twelve-hour fasting is quite safe, doing it
any longer results in particular physiological changes to the body, including changes in the body's chemistry. These changes include ketoacidosis,
the breaking down of muscle tissue resulting in a chemical (ketones) entering the bloodstream, which upsets the blood's pH balance. Extreme
fasting can also cause hypoglycaemia, or low blood sugar, which effects
the brain's ability to function. Both of these can result in psychological
changes, which can be used to induce trance.

Sleep Deprivation, particularly when the individual has missed sleep
for over twenty-four hours, can result in a euphoric state caused by a rise
in serotonin and dopamine levels in the brain.* Sleep deprivation was,
in fact, a common technique used in psychiatric hospitals to lift clinical
depression for this very reason. It can also result in visual and auditory
hallucinations; from a psychic viewpoint, these hallucinations occur as
the crown chakra opens up. Unless trained, the individual will not only
find it difficult to control these hallucinations, but also find it difficult to
distinguish between what is psychically real and what is fantasy.

Hypnotic Induction and Invocation

The term *hypnosis* derives from the Greek god of sleep, Hypnos. English
surgeon James Braid used this term to differentiate it from *mesmerism*.
Although the techniques of trance inductions used were basically the
same, Braid believed the cause was a form of physical "nervous sleep" as
opposed to Mesmer's theory of *animal magnetism*. Braid suggested that
hypnosis was "a condition resulting from the mind being possessed by
dominant ideas,"[1] that it was caused by suggestion. This remains the main
theory of hypnosis even today.

Ritual invocation can be seen as a form of hypnotic induction, as can
any form of repetitive ritual that causes a change in consciousness. James
Braid believed that focused attention was essential for creating hypnotic

---

* Serotonin and dopamine are both *monoamine neurotransmitters*, chemicals released
by nerve cells to send signals to other cells, particularly in the brain.

states, which he also stated were none other than "a state of extreme focus." Invocation of a deity into a person by repetitive ritual (e.g., the Wiccan Drawing Down the Moon) clearly does the same things and is no different to hypnotic induction if performed by a skilled ritualist. It relies on the individual's willingness and desire to enter into that state and the belief of the possibility of it happening. Quite simply put, you can't hypnotise someone against their will, so likewise you cannot put someone into trance by invocation without their willingness to sublimate their will to the person putting them into that changed state of consciousness. The more someone is put into trance through hypnotic induction or invocation, the easier it gets each time.

Hypnotic Induction is, of course, a two-person technique, requiring someone to induce the trance in the participant. That person has to have studied the various techniques, including the use of voice technique developed both by Braid and Milton Erickson. While Braid used a direct authoritative approach that relied on commands, Erickson and proponents of Ericksonian hypnosis use an indirect technique that encourages cooperation with the unconscious mind to put the participant into trance. Although this may appear to be at odds with the ritual approach to trance, such techniques can also be used, as can the Ericksonian use of the *Confusion Technique*. To use this technique in ritual, such as Drawing Down the Moon, the priestess continually repeats a specific piece of prose or ritual poetry, while the priest invokes, resulting in the confusion and mental overload in the priestess, which will cause her to slip into trance.

Drumming

Drumming is one of the commonest forms of trance induction and the most popular form in the neo-Pagan movement (see Photograph 8). It was one of the first musical instruments used by man (e.g., the beating of a hollow tree trunk with a log) to create a repetitive beat for dance and, of course, trance. Later on, the drum was developed into two specifically noticeable forms.

1. The first is the barrel-type drum: a wooden log carved to make a deep body, with a skin strung or nailed over the open end. The West African *djembé* (pronounced jem-bay) and many Native American drums are of this form.
2. The second is the ring-type drum—shaped wooden strips creating a wooden ring, with a skin that is strung or nailed over it. The Irish/Celtic *bodhran* (pronounced *bow-ran*), and the drums used by the Tuareg and other North African tribes are of this type.

Photo by Gavin Bone

Photograph 8: Neo-Pagan Blessing of the Vines, Tuscany, Italy, July 2010.
Drumming is found in almost every world culture,
being the commonest form of trance induction.

In many magical traditions, be they European, African, or American, the drum is believed to possess a spirit. Gavin once asked a practitioner of Santeria why West African magical traditions were becoming so fashionable among Western neo-Pagans. He was told that it was not that people were following fashion, but that they were being subjected to "the spirit of the drums" due to the number of cheap djembés that were being imported, and it was these drum spirits that were causing people to look to practises such as Vodoun and Santeria. Djembés are, of course, an important part of West African diaspora practise where they are used to induce trance states.

In shamanic practise, it is said that the roundness of the drum represents the world that we live in, that the sound the drum makes is the beat of the universal heart, that the drum is the shaman's "horse" he or she uses to travel the worlds on. The magical drum is traditionally decorated with symbols representing the shaman's guides, guardians, and the worlds in which he travels. It may also be hung with feathers, sacred stones, etc. Drums induce trance in people by changing the brainwave frequency and, therefore, activity of the brain. A beat of 220 to 240 beats is normally needed to achieve this, and it is no coincidence that this 4.5 beats per second corresponds to the trance-like state of theta (4–7 Hz or cycles per second. A drum being used for trance will generally be "warmed up" first with a gentle steady beat, and as time progresses, it will be increased to a desired speed and then maintained. Once the individual enters trance, the beat may be slowed down.

Rattling/White Noise

During the Second World War, radio technology was in its infancy. To ensure that radio equipment being carried by the radioman in each squad of soldiers was working correctly, a continual noise, a hiss, was fed into his ears during the whole time he was using the equipment, which could sometimes be as much as eight hours. It was quickly noticed that these men seemed dazed during the whole time they were using the equipment and for some time after. In fact, it resulted in many of them being killed due to poor reaction times in battle. The men were being subjected to white noise, which is known to cause changes in consciousness by putting individuals into a theta state. Of course, the knowledge that white noise does this has been known for a long time. The African, Eurasian, and Native American shamans have been using rattles for centuries. The use of the rattle has always been associated with water. There are two main reasons for this: first is that water has always been an important means of travel physically, resulting in the idea that you can also travel by water spiritually. And secondly, the idea to use a rattle probably came from the experience of trancing near waterfalls or rivers, both of which cause white noise. It is therefore not surprising that two of the most traditional ways of making a rattle were using a turtle shell or a gourd, which can normally be found floating down a river; both having water associations.

Depending on the type of rattle, it is used slowly by rattling it back and forth (or up and down) to create the right frequency of sound and induce a theta state in the user. This sound can only really be created by experience, so it is difficult to describe the process here, considering the different types of rattles and the different types of noises they make. The correct use of rattles can only be achieved by trial and error by the person wishing to trance, but what we can say is that the sound should be very similar to that of a television after the program channel shuts down. A rattle is one of the simplest trance tools to make. Even an empty can filled with dried peas will suffice. Needless to say, most rattles in general use are decorated appropriately for their purpose, with invocations and symbols representing the spirits and gods their owner works with. Of course, other methods can be used to create white noise apart from the rattle, including the taping of white noise or music, which has the right frequency of sound in its beat.

Sexual Activity/Tantric Techniques
The belief that a spirit or god/goddess could possess you during sexual activity can be traced back thousands of years, not just within Vedic culture, but throughout the world. This could be what the writers of the Greek myths are pointing at when they talk about the gods, particularly Zeus descending from Olympus to make love to a mortal woman.

In tantra/Shaktiism, it is believed that you are possessed during the act of union through the specific rites that they teach. This belief has filtered into Wiccan practise, specifically the Great Rite, where it is believed that it is not the high priestess and priest coming together in spiritual union, but the Moon Goddess and Horned God manifesting through them. The origins of this in Wicca can probably be traced through Gerald Gardner's clear interest in tantra and sexual magical practices, which originated from his time on Ceylon (modern-day Sri Lanka) where he was a regular visitor to many of the temples. We have two pieces from that time that belonged to him; cast iron statues of tantric design.

The sexual magic side of tantra or Shaktiism works almost completely by the use of tantric yoga positions, pranic-breathing technique and, of course, chakra energy work. If done properly, most Wiccan priestesses and priests are already doing this work in its most rudimentary form when they consecrate wine (or water) with the athame. The next natural stage to this ritual is the previously mentioned Great Rite. Sexual union releases endorphins as well as several other hormones, which can place the individual into a theta trance state, making them open to deity possession.

Masks
Going back to the first hunter-gatherers in human history, masks have been used in magical practise. In the cave of Les Trois Frères in France, a cave painting over fifteen thousand years old shows a shaman wearing the mask of a stag, probably used for invoking the Stag spirit prior to hunting. Masks have always been an important method in magical practise of sublimating the personality and ego of the wearer; so much so that they are closely linked to both the histories of magical trance and the theatre through the Greek Dionysian mystery play. In trance-prophecy,

veils were often used to cover the face of the seer, which has the same affect. The sublimation of the personality by covering the face can have a strong psychological effect on the wearer; even the shyest of person may suddenly "get into the role" of the mask and become more boisterous and outgoing. In some cultures it is actually believed that the mask contains a spirit in its own right, and literally possesses the individual when they don the mask.

The use of masks today can still be seen in Native American and African tribal practises, as well as in Japanese Kabuki, a form of Shinto Mystery Play. In modern culture they have become, not surprisingly, closely associated with Halloween, the remnants of the old pagan festival of Samhain. Their use is unknowingly a revival of old pagan rites, where spirits manifested through the wearer of the mask at that time of year.

It is impossible to cover the process of choosing and making a mask in one whole chapter let alone a paragraph, so for this reason we do suggest further reading on the subject and heartily recommend the book *Sacred Mask Sacred Dance* by Evan John Jones and Chas Clifton (see Bibliography), particularly chapters 7 and 8. This book is also invaluable when it comes to the use of masks in the previously coverer subject of dance. We can give some limited advice here though. A mask should be chosen to specifically represent the spirit you work with, be it a deity, spirit guide, power animal etc. Make the mask yourself is possible as part of a sacred act. By doing so you imbue the mask with not only part of yourself but also part of that spirit. Masks are easy to make. Most costume and novelty shops stock white plain plastic masks, which are effective just as they are, or can be painted and decorated with feathers, fur, horns, jewellery, etc. It is important that they are comfortable for the wearer.

The process of masking can be an important part of the ritual leading to trance. Masks also have a strong effect on those witnessing a trance-prophecy ritual, as they lose conscious perception of who is behind the mask. Makeup can perform the same role, and was often used in ancient ritual for the same reasons. Even when veiled, the sibyls of Rome would wear elaborate makeup, whitening their faces and highlighting their eyes.

Chanting and Singing

Chanting and singing is another well-known method of inducing a change in our mental state. This is the secret of the ancient Masons who knew how to construct temples, and later churches and cathedrals, in a way which would affect the frequency of sound to create a feeling of holiness within the building, particularly when singing takes place. This can still be felt today when entering an old church or cathedral compared with a newer one where this knowledge has been lost.

It is well known by psychologists that different frequencies of sound can affect our minds, just as the previously mentioned drumming and white noise do. It must be remembered that sound is energy, so not surprisingly, there is a correlation between the body's energy system, the chakras and the aura, and different frequencies of sound. Traditionally, chakras have different mantras associated with them. In Eastern mysticism, different mantras are believed to have different effects on us. The most commonly known mantra is "Om" (related to the brow center) associated with the mind and connection to Spirit, but there is also "Lam" (root center), "Vam" (sacral center), "Ram" (solar plexus), "Yam" (heart), and "Ham" (throat). All tend to work on the etheric level of the aura and, as such, affect the body's energy levels and ability to manifest energy.

Neo-Pagans use a variety of chants and songs, which work at different frequencies of this energy. Most are more orientated toward the wording rather than the frequencies they induce, so a certain amount of experimenting is needed to see whether they will assist in trance. Rhythm and repetition is always essential to induce a trance state, at which point a chant or a song work the same way as an Eastern mantra. In our experience, they correspond with the frequencies used in traditional chakra work.

Dancing

Like singing and chanting, dancing is a common core human experience when it comes to religion. There is not one culture in the world where dancing in some form does not exist. In many cultures, the cosmos was believed to have been created by a sacred dance, as in the dance of Shiva Nataraja in Hindu mythology. Dancing is believed to mimic this act of creation and, therefore, empowers the dancer with the divine:

> In this way the body is the whole range of its experience, is the instrument for the transcendent power; and this power is encountered in the dance directly, instantly and without intermediaries. The body is experienced as having a spiritual inner dimension as channel for the descent of power.[2]

In most modern Witchcraft covens, very little dancing is taught; most modern Wiccan practitioners only being familiar with the famous spiral dance. It was certainly not intended to create trance states, as it relies on a specific method used for raising external magical energy, rather than rhythmic moves designed to cause trance induction. This is not to say that Witchcraft groups do not use dance techniques for trance. A good example is the Reclaiming Tradition, where free flow dance is encouraged for the purposes of invocation, which can result in trance, but it is not their primary intention. In most cases, the modern Witch's or Pagan's first encounter with trance-dancing is when experiencing drumming at an open Pagan festival or during a Vodoun ritual.

Dancing works to create trance in several ways. The first is to amplify already existing techniques such as drumming. The movement of the body with the rhythmic and hypnotic drum beats causes the individual to slip deeper from an alpha into a theta state, as the mind focuses on dancing as well as the beat. In this respect, it works the same way as the previously mentioned Ericksonian Confusion Technique: as the conscious mind tries to focus on both the dancing and the drum beat, the unconscious mind takes over. Dancing as a trance technique is by definition Dionysian (see page 219) and ecstatic, although it may contain ritualistic aspects. It is not a technique that could easily be incorporated into any heavily ritualised practise, since it relies on the individual being able to flow freely with both the music and the dance. It is, therefore, one of the primary techniques used in ecstatic ritual (see chapter 14).

One of the first Pagan writers to talk about trance dancing in ritual was Ed Fitch in his magazine *The Crystal Well*, first published in 1965. A whole section was later dedicated to *Magical Dance* in a compilation of the magazine in 1984. Fitch mentions the use of dance to call the elements, raise energy, for sexual magic and for "attaining altered states of consciousness and an ecstatic trance-like state,"[3] but the most comprehensive source for understanding ecstatic dance we have come across is from the late author and shaman Gabrielle Roth. She created the "5Rhythms" system of trance-dance. It consists of five movements: flowing, staccato, chaos, lyrical, and stillness used in a sequence known as a "wave" (for energy waves in ecstatic ritual, see page 229). This normally lasts an hour, although they may last longer if being used to explore emotions and induce visions.

Ligature and Scourging
Both of these techniques have origins going back certainly as far as classical times. Images of a young woman being initiated into the cult of Dionysus can be found at the Villa of the Mysteries at Pompeii. They continued to be used by Christianity in the medieval period and are, in fact,

still used by some Christian sects today. Both have gone out of fashion as techniques within the neo-Pagan community. In many cases, their use is now merely symbolic, although some Gardnerian covens do use them in the correct fashion to create changes of consciousness. Within the neo-Pagan community, their use has become too associated with the bondage, domination, sadism, and masochism (BDSM) scene and are considered to be too sexual and risqué among those who wish wider acceptance among the ecumenical religious communities.

Ligature, more commonly called bondage, uses cords or rope to restrict blood flow. This induces a light trance state by increasing levels of carbon dioxide in the blood and decreasing levels of oxygen and affecting the blood chemistry (see Breathing Techniques below). In this respect, it works no differently than many breathing techniques, although it tends to be more intense psychologically; the individual has to willingly give up their will (and the drives of the ego) to the person tying them. It is still used today in Japan as Japanese rope bondage. It is still considered to be an art form and is used within more traditional geisha houses.

Various Christian orders (including Opus Dei) still practice scourging, the use of a whip or cat-o'-nine-tails, as an act of penitence. Of course, as a magical technique, its use can easily be traced back to ancient Greece, and was a known rite in Rome carried out by devotees of Cybele. It is not heavy whipping, but a light repetitive technique used on certain areas of the body, such as the lower outer buttocks. This releases endorphins, the body's own natural narcotic. The use of endorphin-inducing techniques is also common among contemporary Hindu practitioners (see page 222). The repetitive strokes of the whip also result in a hypnotic effect and a change in consciousness. In the BDSM scene, this state is often referred to as "subspace," but it is the same light theta trance state that most shamans and seers enter into at the beginning of their trance journeys.

Care should be taken with both techniques, as both are capable of causing harm if not used safely. In ligature, ropes should not be so tight as to cause areas of the body to go white due to restriction of blood flow. As a rule, it should be possible to get three fingers underneath any rope knot. In scourging, the whipping of certain areas of the body are taboo, such as the kidney area, etc. It should be remembered that both are learned art forms and there is plenty of literature available on the Internet regarding their use if you search the pages of any serious BDSM website.

In recent years there has been a crossover between the S/M and neo-Pagan scenes, as members of the BDSM community find themselves having trance and spiritual experiences due to the use of these techniques. It resulted in a comeback of these techniques in the more adventurous areas of the neo-Pagan community. It has caused some controversy, but the BDSM community has far more experience in the use of these techniques.

Breathing Techniques
Breath control is important in trance, as it can directly affect our physical and mental state by altering our body chemistry. Of course, this is well known in Eastern traditions such as yoga, where it is linked with the concept of *prana*, or life force. Breath is believed to be able to alter our life force. In trance, deep relaxed breathing allows us to enter initially into an alpha state, where we feel relaxed and calm. Sustained breathing in this way will help us become even more relaxed, so that we go into a theta state, a state of trance. Breathing alone can put someone in trance, particularly using a circular, or holotropic, breath pattern. This is commonly used in a popular practise called rebirthing, where the individual is encouraged to overbreathe, by inhaling and exhaling deeply without interval for a sustained period of time, while visualizing their breathing pattern as a circle.

All breathing techniques affect both oxygen (O) and carbon dioxide (CO_2) levels in the bloodstream. When it comes to trance, it is the carbon dioxide metabolism that is more important to understand, as it is not just a waste gas but also affects the pH, the acid/alkaline balance, in the body. We give off more CO_2 in our breath, not just as a waste product but also to maintain the balance in our cells. If it is too acidic, then CO_2 is released and we breathe deeper and faster. If too much O2 is in our system, then we breathe shallower and less. Therefore, by affecting our breathing pattern consciously, we can, in fact, reduce or increase the levels of these gases in our system. With the exception of such techniques as holotropic breath work, they will have no adverse effect on the pH metabolism in our bodies. Deeper and shallower breaths result in more relaxed states because less O2 gets into our system, allowing our brainwave patterns to change appropriately as we enter into other states of consciousness. All breathing patterns work in this way.

One of the commonest and most effective breath patterns we have used over the years is the 8-4-8-4 breath. In this pattern, you breathe in for a count of eight, hold for four, breathe out for a count of eight, and hold for four again. This, and any other breathing pattern for that matter, while initially being the focus of the participant's attention, should eventually become second nature. It should flow naturally, allowing the participant to focus on the meditation or other trance techniques they are engaging in (for information on more complex breathing patterns, see chapter 15).

Aspecting, Embodiment, Channelling, and Possession

It is important to discuss these three terms in relation to trance-prophecy. Although all three derive and are more often associated with the New Age movement, they are also often used by neo-Pagans.

Aspecting and Embodiment: These are, in fact, both the same thing. In aspecting/embodiment, the individual takes on or aspects or embodies an archetype rather than actually being in contact with or possessed by a spirit or deity. The participant may enter into a light trance state, an alpha state, but rarely do they enter into full trance. This is because the process is not about the sublimation of the ego or personality, as it is in both traditional and contemporary Pagan traditions; in fact, we know of one teacher of this technique who very clearly states that the participant must not "let go." We believe that some of this comes out of the New Age community's fear of possession; a fear, no doubt, left over from and bringing in a Judeo-Christian culture, where the concept of demon possession exists in religion and in the popular media. It can, therefore, not really be seen as a form of trance-prophecy, as no contact is made with any form of exterior entity; it has more in common with method acting than actual seership.* Regardless, it has its uses in neo-Pagan ritual, particularly when working such archetypes as the Triple Goddess.

Channelling: This term is also often used by the New Age movement, and is really a replacement for the older term mediumship, which in some circles was considered to be an outdated term. There is often confusion about the actual meaning of the term *channelling*. As yet, *The Merriam-Webster Dictionary* doesn't have a definition of the term from the occult viewpoint, although there is a general meaning given: "to serve as

---

* Lee Strasberg developed "The Method," as it was called, with The Group Theatre in New York from the 1930s to '50s based on Constantin Stanislavski's system.

a channeller or intermediary." The ancient Greeks, and the early Greek Christians, referred to this as *enthousiazein*, or *enythsiasmos enthusiasmos*. In fact, our word *enthusiasm* comes from this ancient Greek word, which literally means "to be enthused by (to be full of) spirit." This term was used to generally mean that the individual was influenced, but not the necessarily possessed, by a divinity or spirit.* Likewise, the term *channelling* has come to mean anything from purely relaying a message to intermediate possession. Its use is quite recent, only becoming popular from the 1980s onward. Judy Zebra (J. Z.) Knight used the term to describe her encounter with a spirit called "Ramtha" in 1977. Her subsequent TV appearances and books popularized the use of the term in the New Age movement.† The term is often applied in retrospect to Jane Roberts and her body of work, as it was with the rerelease of her book *Seth Speaks*, which was first published in 1972.‡ Since then it has continued to be used by channellers claiming to bring through everyone from the spirits of the dead, Arthurian figures such as Merlin, and even aliens. It is not surprisingly an unpopular term among serious mediums and trance-prophecy practitioners.

Possession: This is, in fact, a much easier term to define, but unfortunately stereotyped due to misinformation. The idea that a spirit can actually take control of our bodies and our minds has been around for a long time. The ancient Greeks used the term *katoché* to define a full and controlling possession by a divinity.[4] This was always done with express permission of the individual, and always had a positive effect on their well-being. The term 'possession' in its modern context is, therefore, a very misleading one, as there is, in fact, no ownership of the host's body,

---

* David E. Aune, *Prophecy in Early Christianity and the Ancient Mediterranean World*, page 33. Aune suggests the term *enthusiasmos* had more in common with inspiration (*in-spirato*) rather than possession: "This kind of direct divine inspiration is thought to be normally clearly expressed in the terms *entheos* and *enythsiasmos*."

† Knight appeared on such shows as Larry King Live and The Merv Griffin Show, and influenced such high-profile figures in the show business world as Shirley MacLaine.

‡ Beginning in December 1963, Roberts communicated messages from an "energy personality essence," or entity, called "Seth." Roberts and her husband, Robert F. Butts, went on to publish more than twenty-two books of Seth's wisdom, known collectively as the "Seth material," before Roberts died in 1984, and many more Seth/Jane books were published posthumously. The term "channelling" is not used in the original editions, but has often been attributed to them in retrospect. Jane called herself simply a "medium."

which remains their spiritual property. The spirit is only temporarily in control, and except in extraordinary circumstances, possession only occurs with the express permission of the host. It is important to point out that the level of possession may also differ from individual to individual in any form of oracular or ecstatic spiritual work. Dependent, of course, on the level of their training and experience, it is quite common for aspects of a seer's personality to sometimes filter through into that of the deity if the seer's ego/persona is not fully repressed or if proper chakra alignments do not take place. Unfortunately, in modern culture, it is now generally accepted that there are two types of possession: positive or *inspirational possession*,[5] where the individual has an experience that benefits them spiritually and emotionally, and negative or *malevolent possession*, which, of course, does not benefit the host. Due to the influence of various horror movies such as *The Exorcist*, most people immediately assume that possession is negative. The reality is, of course, very different. Throughout history, people have been temporarily possessed by divine spirits who have not only entered their physical bodies but also have inspired them to commit great deeds.

We feel it is important to point out that there are different levels of possessive trance.

In pre-Christian times, possession was not immediately assumed to be negative. This change occurred much later, not just because of a change in Judeo-Christian values, but primarily due to the strengthening of the individual psyche. Individuality became more important in modern culture, and the idea of personally giving up control either to a spirit or even another person such as a hypnotist was considered frightening and even repugnant—a classic ego reaction. It is, therefore, not surprising that in modern times traditions such as Vodoun, which espouse trance-possession, developed a negative reputation. The fact is malevolent possession is rare, and when it does occur it is generally associated with mental illness. It does not occur in trance-prophecy traditions because the environment is almost always controlled in a ritual fashion to prevent this from happening. **For this reason, nothing in this book nor the techniques we teach will induce a negative, malevolent possession. If a possession does occur because of what is being taught in this book, it will inevitably be of the positive, inspirational form.**

NOTES

1 James Braid, *The Discovery of Hypnosis: The Complete Writings of James Braid,* page 31, and *James Braid: His Work and Writings* by Dr. John Milne Bramwell (1896).

2 Maria Gabrielle-Wosien, Sacred Dance: Encounter with the Gods.

3 Ed Fitch, *Magical Rites from the Crystal Well* (Llewellyn Publications, 1984), 84–92.

4 David E. Aune, *Prophecy in Early Christianity and the Ancient Mediterranean World,* page 33. Aune defines full possession as *ek tou theo katachos.*

5 Mark Bancroft, MA, *The History and Psychology of Spirit Possession and Exorcism,* http://www.markbancroft.com/info/spirit-possession.

Chapter 10

The Fourth Key: Understanding Divinity and Spirits

Over the past two decades of practising trance-prophecy and giving public workshops, we noticed that spirits and deities seem to manifest in several specific forms to individuals. Most of these forms are related to the manifestation of a particular spirit or deity during trance, although they also seem to apply to physical manifestation, as well as the lower spirit forms such as the sídhe, as well as the lower elemental fairies. These forms seem to manifest for specific reasons, according to the psychic abilities of those perceiving the divinity, and the environment in which it appears.

Energetic Form: This is the purest form, the "soul" of the divinity, manifesting as light and energy. As such, it manifests directly from Superconsciousness, or in Cabalistic terms they are a glimpse of Kether as it manifests in Chokmah and Binah. A good example of the physical manifestations are the sightings in Ireland of the Madonna at wells and shrines, as a figure made of bright white light with only her face visible. The Madonna is a divinity, with origins in Isis as much as in the Christian concept of Mary. In trance, the energetic form may initially appear as a speck of light that slowly takes on the form of the Akashic or mythological archetype. This is the least easy form to communicate with, unless the individual is a highly gifted psychic, as it will try to communicate on the spiritual level via the aura of the seer, rather than their mental-emotional body.

Akashic/Mythological Form: These are the cultural memories of the divinity, which have been recorded for eternity in the Akashic Records, where the deity's personality dwells in the Collective Unconscious. It is important to point out that this is not a historical perception of the divinity; hence, a deity may appear to someone in a guise that the person does not expect. A good example of this is Hekate, who most expect to appear as an old hag, but for many, much to their surprise, she appears as a much younger woman. Just as people wear different clothes for their different roles in life, so too may the goddesses and gods. For example, in her mythological form, Freya may appear as Vanadis, a love goddess and a warrior (a later form); the goddess of seith and trance; or even as the older Vanir goddess, Gullveig, the old hag of chaos and wisdom. This is the form anyone doing any form of trance-prophecy should aim to work with, as it is able to communicate directly with the seer.

The Subjective Forms: These require interaction with the individual or the environment they are in. Unlike the previous forms, the deity has no control over how it manifests in the subjective forms. These are generally the commonest and easiest forms to see.

1. **Intellectual (Expectative):** This form is dictated by the expectations, experience, and knowledge of the perceiver; the individual acts as a filter. The goddess or god will, therefore, take the form the seer has read or heard about. The problem here is that the deity may filter through the individual's ego, particularly if they have not gone into deep trance, which sublimates the ego.

2. **Contemporary (Modern cultural):** The deity will access the cultural memory of the individual; in fact, the perceiver may not even be aware that they are seeing a deity. It must be remembered that the gods were always originally perceived in this way. The classical dress of Aphrodite is completely contemporary for the period in which she was originally worshipped. A goddess or god may, therefore, appear in modern dress, which is role-appropriate. For example, Aphrodite may update her wardrobe to appear in high heels and slinky black dress, while Mercury may appear as a telephone repairman or even a computer geek! Janet once saw in a dream "the restaurant at the end of the universe" where all the different Pagan deities were in modern dress, while Gavin had some friends who saw Odin manifest in a long leather trench coat and hat. He had inadvertently invoked him while preparing his rune staff. His friends were totally unaware of the identity of the spirit until Gavin informed them.

3. **Animistic:** The deity will manifest according to the interaction of the individual and the environment she or he is in. Of course, some deities are only able to manifest this way, such as *genius loci* and cannot manifest in the previously mentioned two forms. Animistic forms may appear in their animal as well as human forms; for example, Bast as a cat, Freya as a hawk, etc. Historically, the idea that deities can manifest as animals is well known; Zeus appearing as a swan, and the Morrigan as a raven. Shamanic power and totem animals can, of course, be seen historically as the first stages of this process of the divine manifesting through and as animals.

The Order of Spirit Forms

It is important for anyone who is dealing with spirits to understand the natural order of spirit forms that exist. Natural order is the correct term rather than hierarchy. All naturally occurring spirit forms exist for a good reason, and this applies just as well to created thought-forms. There is very little sensible information written about this subject, only material from medieval grimoires with their hierarchies of archangels, angels, and demons; all inspired by a Judeo-Christian theology based on fear of the unknown and redacted at different times by individuals to suit their particular worldviews.*

In any ecstatic state or, for that matter, any form of spiritual work, you may find yourself meeting any of these entities, so it is important to know how they will react to you. All you have to remember about spirit forms is that they follow the most important occult principle: As above, so below; and, likewise: As below, so above.

1. **Ground-Feeding Entities:** In nature, bacteria slowly breaks down vegetation to create rich, fertile soil, which feeds the new growth of trees. In fact, they are the same bacteria that you are likely to find in your compost heap at the bottom of your garden. In their own domain, they go safely about doing their job. Nobody would call them 'evil'; they perform an important function. But stick your hand in the compost heap and you risk infection. Ground-feeding spirits are no different. Their job is in the 'forest' of emotions, and their role is to break down negative emotions, such as fear, hate, etc. that appear

---

* Pope Gregory the Great (540–604 CE) wrote that heaven and hell are structured into the current form that we know today, with specific choirs of angels (cherubim) and demonic legions, still referred to ceremonial high magick.

on the lower astral realms. These are recycled and used to build that realm. In Cabala they are called *qliphotic* and are found in every sphere on the reverse of the Tree of Life—the Qlipoth.* Often referred to as "shells," they are attracted to the negative emotions, and while they are in the qliphotic compost heap, this is fine, but if these emotions become the basis of any magical practise, these "ground feeders" will be attracted. There are two specific forms:

a. **Intelligent:** These will set about manipulating and generating the negative emotions that they need to feed upon, thereby showing a level of intelligence. This way they can guarantee getting a really good feed (see talking boards, page 268). It is possible to interact and communicate with them, although this communication is really a reflection of the individual's own Shadow.

b. **Non-Intelligent:** These are often referred as auric leeches or limpets. This is the lowest form of ground feeder, showing no level of intelligence and being only interested in feeding directly from an individual's aura. They are specifically attracted to 'dirty auras,' where fear or emotions are ingrained due to one or several negative incidents. They are easily removed, by the individual dealing with these emotions, or by energy healing and spiritual cleansing.

2. **Lower Elementals:** In Shamanism they say "rocks breathe." In the world of spirit, this is true—they do! But, they breathe so slowly we do not notice them. The spirit of a rock is a spirit of earth, a lower elemental form, sometimes appearing in mythology and folklore as a "troll." Likewise, trees, flowers, rivers, lakes, and even mountains have spirits, referred to as *genus loci* (Latin for "spirit of the place"). It is also important to point out that in animism, the basic belief structure of shamanism, that inanimate objects are also possessed of spirit. This means that spirits can also develop in manmade structures, such as houses, from the interaction of the occupant with the spirit of the house; hence, the concept of brownies in Western Europe and, in Lithuania and Latvia, the *žaltys*—a small snake spirit that lives in the home. In Celtic lands they were the sídhe, the fairy folk; in ancient Greece, the dryads and nymphs; in Scandinavia and England, the elves and dwarves; and in India, the devas, a term now found commonly in the New Age movement. They are all the same

---

* In Judaic mythology this literally means "husk" or shell. These are the lower, impure, demonic, or negative forces that are referred to in Cabala.

thing, whichever culture they hail from. The only difference is that
different cultures perceive them differently and clothe them according to their mythology and folklore. Like their manifestations in the
physical world, they are amoral—they have no human concept of
good and evil or right or wrong as such. They care only about their
own existence and survival; if it is in their interest to work with you,
they will; otherwise, they will ignore you. But if you threaten them,
then expect them to defend themselves just like any wild animal in
the natural would.

3. **Animal Entities:** Regardless of Judeo-Christian propaganda, animals do have a soul and a spirit. When you see your pet, you see
   only a fraction of their intelligence, as the rest is on another level.
   This, of course, is not news to most cat owners, so it is hardly surprising that they became the witches' favourite familiar. This understanding is what made the witch choose such animals as familiars in
   the first place, as cats are aware of things psychically that humans
   are not and are willing to work with them in a symbiotic partnership. Animals also have a closer connection to their own group soul,
   or collective consciousness, than do humans. It is this which the
   shaman calls upon when he summons his power animal: he does
   not call "his" wolf, but calls Wolf; he calls upon the collective soul
   of all of them. You could even go as far as to say that this is 'the
   Wolf God,' which would explain such deities as Bastet, the Egyptian
   goddess of cats. This is the highest form of the animal entities, and
   links shamanic practise with the practise of witches traditionally
   keeping familiars.

4. **Higher Elemental/Lower Deity Form:** In Wicca and neo-Paganism,
   magical working groups and individuals invoke the higher elemental
   forms of the spirits all the time, as the Lords of the Watchtowers, the
   Guardians of the Four Directions, etc. These higher elemental entities are a development from the lower elementals, which we mentioned earlier. The purpose of invoking the higher forms is to control
   these lower forms in magical work. They also appear in occult work
   in other forms. For example, they appear as the *psychopompous*, the
   spiritual guide to the mysteries, and as Gate Guardians, entities that
   guard access to spiritual realms. Over time, they can develop into
   god forms, in the same way as it can happen with genus loci. In
   traditional folklore, higher elementals were often referred to as the

kings or queens of the fairy or elven folk—the "Lords and Ladies" as they are sometimes known, best typified by William Shakespeare's portrayal of them in *A Midsummer Night's Dream*. As a place becomes magically charged due to worship or recognition of the spirit that is present there, it becomes a higher form of the genus loci. This can very quickly develop into a fully fledged deity form, a good example being the Irish river goddess Boann, who became one of the Tuatha De Danann of Gaelic legend. Both the Romans and Greeks referred to these as *daemons*, but they are not to be confused with Judeo-Christian concept of demons.

5. **Discarnate Entities (Voluntary and Involuntary):** When most people talk about these, they mean human spirits who are between worlds; they are neither in the land of the living, nor have they "passed down the tunnel to the other side." They, therefore, can be categorized into two sorts:

    a. **Voluntary:** they may have decided to act as a spirit guide, as they have reached a higher level of spiritual development, in which case they are able to travel freely between worlds. There are also some that may have decided to stay behind out of emotional attachment, such as love or even guilt.

    b. **Involuntary:** these are trapped and unaware of their predicament; for example, due to sudden death in car accident or similar.

While it is obvious that voluntary discarnate entities that act as spirit guides are not really a problem, those that stay out of emotional attachments such as guilt and those that are involuntary are obviously of most concern, as these entities may end up attaching themselves to the living and feeding off of their energy (see page 263). They are not evil, just lost souls desperate for attention. These are, of course, the classic "ghosts" who cause the room to go cold, a symptom of this feeding. Involuntary entities may, in fact, cause disruption and exhibit poltergeist-type behaviour because of their frustration at a lack of communication. The ethical responsibility of anyone contacting such entities is clear: to assist them on their way down "the tunnel" to "the other side" (see page 258).

6. **Thought-Forms:** These are created spirit forms from human interaction with spiritual and elemental forces. There is always a physical object, individual or place that tends to be their focus. There are two forms:

a. **Intentional:** These are the basis of many forms of magical practise, where an entity is created within a magical circle to do the
magician's bidding (i.e., a magical *fetch*). In modern magical practise, they are created by the fusion of the four elements (Earth, Air,
Fire and Water), and Ether (life force). It is then given a purpose,
a "programme." This was one of the favourite magical methods of
Alex Sanders, who had several brightly coloured cards of abstract
design, each related to a thought entity he had created. Janet has
used a similar method by producing a painting of the actual entity
she or her coven created.*

b. **Unintentional:** Many ghost sightings are, in fact, unintention-
ally created thought-forms. The best way of describing this is the
"haunted house" phenomenon. A group of children decide that an
old house is haunted. Their psychic energy feeds into this belief,
resulting in psychic activity around what was once nothing more
than a derelict building. When a medium comes to investigate,
she picks up on the entity and is able to communicate with it. The
myths and psychic energy directed at the property actually creates
a 'ghost.' T. C. Lethbridge describes this phenomenon in his book
Ghosts,[†] and how it seems related to damp atmospheres. The story
of Philip is well known in paranormal circles.[‡] In 1972, members
of the Toronto Society for Psychical Research created a 'spirit'
purely by discussing his fictitious history over a year. At the end
of this period, several séances were conducted. Several different
mediums, unaware that he was a created thought-form, found they
were able to contact him. This form of created spirit can explain

---

* For an example of one of Janet's spirit paintings, see *A Witches' Bible/The Witches' Way*.

† Born 1901, died 1971. An accomplished English author on occult subjects, he wrote several books on ghosts, witchcraft, dowsing, psychic phenomena, and archaeology. He was known for his unconventional approach to academia, often challenging many conventional theories of his day.

‡ Philip was a totally created entity, fictionalized as a seventeenth century cavalier who had a torrid love affair with a gypsy called "Margo," who was denounced as a witch by Philip's wife. Margo was burnt at the stake and Philip, tormented by his lost love and his guilt, took to wandering the battlements of his home (in Diddington Manor, Warwickshire, England) and finally committed suicide by plummeting to his death. It took a year for Philip to actually contact anyone. He became a celebrity on Canadian and American TV, as the group regularly demonstrated their séances. No doubt this fed the Philip thought-form even more!

imaginary friends, as well as poltergeist activity around troubled adolescents.

7   **The Gods (Primal, Ancestral, and *Genius Loci*):** In British Traditional Wicca (BTW), there is an idea of duotheism, of God and Goddess, rather than of polytheism, or the idea of many gods. (We discuss this in more detail in our previous work *The Inner Mysteries,* as well as how deities are created, particularly ancestral.) What is important to understand is that it is not possible to contact either "The God" or "The Goddess" as entities if they are only perceived as concepts, as duotheism is really no more than an extension of monotheistic thought. Contactable deities must have faces (we explain why below). It is important to realise that the deities of Paganism are real personalities and are spirit forms in their own right. Each form generally fits into at least two of the categories below:

a.   **Primal:** These are deity forms that represent natural forces, both macrocosmic and microcosmic, such as the sea, the wind, or even natural human drives or aspects, such as sexuality and creativity.

b.   **Ancestral:** These are the deities to which you are genetically linked, as well as the deities of craftsmen and craftswomen—deities who manifest human skills. The goddesses of Witchcraft fit into this category, such as Aradia, as do the gods and goddesses of smithcraft, such as Bríd. Most of the gods and goddesses of trance and prophecy fit into this category.

c.   **Genius Loci:** We have mentioned these previously and how they develop from higher elemental forms into lower deity forms due to worship and incorporation into culture by man.

8.   **The Ultimate Divine:** This is "God," but even this word has been corrupted by monotheistic religions to mean male, as well as being anthropomorphised. In Cabalistic terms, this is *Ain Sof*, the Unknowable. In all the mainstream monotheistic religions, it was the intention that "It" should remain as such, but this does not take into account human nature, which needs to put a face on the divine to make it more reachable to human experience. The main problem is that when this happens, it creates another god form; it pulls the energy from the Ultimate to create this new face, but this 'god' is not the Ultimate itself; hence, the use of prophets, messiahs, and saints as intermediaries in monotheistic religions. In pre-monotheistic religions, of course, this

process was known, and no attempt was made to worship the Ultimate, as it was considered to be omnipresent, manifesting in its highest accessible form as the gods and goddesses of the ancient world.
It is not possible to understand God, and this is often pointed out in
all of the holy books of Abrahamic religions; hence, originally it was
taboo to create images of God, which is still true in modern Islam
and Judaism. To use an analogy that we commonly use, we are ants
trying to understand a computer. It is beyond our level of intelligence
or experience. To an ant, therefore, a computer must be seen as some
form of strange tree or rock structure. The same is true of ourselves
if we try to understand the Ultimate Divine; it is beyond human collective experience or our ability to articulate what it is we are seeing.

Angels and Demons

It is impossible to discuss spirit forms without discussing angels and demons. How they are viewed by most people in modern culture is very
different from the way our pagan ancestors would have viewed them. A
great deal of misunderstanding has occurred mainly because of semantics
and mistranslation. A great deal of semantics and mistranslation regarding the meaning of the words *angel* and *demon* have occurred over several hundred years, resulting in a misunderstanding in our present culture
of what they actually are. For this reason, before discussing angels and
demons and the pitfalls of seriously working with them, it is important to
understand the origins of the two words. It is important to point out that
what we write in this section is not about the minor dalliances people
have had with angels in recent years (for example, *Angel Cards* and the
like), but the deeper work related to Western magick.

The word angel derives from the Greek *angelos*, and is believed to
be the translation of the Hebrew word *mal'akh*,* which literally means
a "messenger," be it human or supernatural from God, although the
Greeks tend to use the word specifically for the latter, as a supernatural
messenger and servant of the divine. In Gnostic belief, angels, being of
higher essence, were not supposed to touch the corrupt earth; hence,
they were never shown in paintings as touching the ground. In the case
of the *theophanic* angels, they were believed to be an aspect of God. The
concept of angels as supernatural guides or guardians didn't appear until
much later in Western thought, being derived from the positive aspects

---

* *Mal'akh* derives originally from the Tanakh, the Hebraic Biblican (The Torah, Ne-
vi'im, and Ketuvim). A similar term can also be found in the Qur'an.

of the Greek *daemon*, who may come to the aid of an individual, acting as a guide or guardian on their behalf. It is this division between one being higher essence (the angelos) and one being earthbound (the daemon) that was later to perpetuate the idea that the daemon was by nature evil.

Before and up to the time of Homer, the word daemon was originally applied to spirits of nature that interacted with mankind in a helpful and generous way. Often these were *genius loci*, or "spirits of a place." It was believed that they were the spirits of fallen heroes or rulers who remained to aid mankind, hence the term could be applied to both elemental spirit forms and discarnate entities. This makes them little different to the genius loci and ancestral deities that we find all across the world. Shrines erected to them were venerated, and in return it was believed that these spirits would become "good beings who dispense riches."[1] They were regarded as being *agathodaimon*, or "noble spirits," and they were originally seen as being little different than what we call guardian angels. The Greeks used a different word to define an evil spirit or lesser god—a *keres*, such as those released by Pandora when she opened her box—but the word daemon was also used to describe a *kakódaimon* or "malevolent or evil spirit." They could fit into several categories depending on their nature and interaction with humanity, ranging from the qliphotic, intelligent, ground-feeding entity, through to both lower and higher elemental spirit forms.

The use of the word daemon in a negative sense does not appear until later among the Greeks and Romans. Plutarch later wrote that they were "malevolent and morose, who rejoice in unlucky days, religious festivals involving violence against the self." This switch occurs as religion in the West begins to polarize towards a monotheistic and dualistic belief system rejecting the balance found in the old Dionysian religion. A result, no doubt, of the influence of new ideas coming from the Middle East. Deities and spirits related to the earth in any form were seen as base by their very natures, corrupt and, therefore, evil; hence, the meaning of the word daemon was corrupted into the concept of demon.

Our current concepts relating to angels and demons derive from the incorporation of the Egyptian and Assyro-Babylonian gods into the theologies of Judaism, Islam, and Christianity, which in turn were influenced by the dualistic tradition of Zoroastrianism. A good example is the traditional form of the winged angel that we are all familiar with. Clearly this image has strong links with Egyptian goddesses such as Isis and Nephthys, both found in winged form. The Ark of the Covenant was described as having two such figures on its lid, often referred to as cherubim by Christian and Judaic scholars, but it is clear from the imagery they are of the aforementioned origin. The Judeo-Christian concept of the demon literally originated from the demonization of the old gods of the Middle East. A good example is Baal, Lord of the Animals, who became Beelzebub, simply because his main temple was in a desert region known for its fly population.* An even better example is Ashtarte, whose demotion from a goddess of open sexuality and love to the demon Ashtaroth demonstrates the suppression of female sexuality in Judaism and Christianity to the point where it became a sin. A goddess of that sin was clearly a demonic influence, particularly one who had encouraged open sexual practise; the temples of Ashtarte were known for their prostitutes. The symbolism of that demon, its serpent nature reminiscent of the serpent from the Garden of Eden, and its smell of rotting fish, were all ways of symbolizing and condemning feminine sexuality. The final change was to change the demon's sex to male, as sex was considered to be a purely male concern.

The example of Ashtaroth is important esoterically as well as psychologically. It clearly shows the polarisation of angels and demons into Jung's concepts of ego and Shadow respectively. The suppression of female sexuality into the cultural shadow of the Judaic peoples resulted in the creation of the demonic Ashtaroth. Demons do, of course, have their polar opposite—angels. The polar opposite of Astaroth became the virtuous goddess and Queen of Heaven, Ashera. She represented the female cultural ego of Judaism and what every good Hebraic woman should aspire to be. She was later to evolve into one of the most popular religious figures in modern Christianity—the angelic, virtuous and desexualized Virgin Mary—while her demonic opposite was to fall by the wayside:

> "The emergence, development and evolution of both angel and demon in history holds up a mirror to the collective psyche or soul of the time. It reveals how we have polarized the cosmos into black and white, good and evil, and now long for anything other than that polarity, ironically through the angel without the demon."[2]

Much can be learned from the mythology relating to angelic entities, particularly the stories related to fallen angels. The best but not the

---

* Remains of the Temple of Baal can be found in Ugarit, Syria. Baal was worshipped by the Canaanites enemies of the Israelites, and reference to him can be found in the Bible.

only example is Lucifer. Here is a demonstration of what happens when ego gets carried away and challenges "the throne." Lucifer, the "light bringer," the most radiant and beautiful of the angels, is a clear example of the dangers of inflated ego that allows the darker and more dangerous aspects of the Shadow to manifest—the bigger the ego, the bigger the Shadow! As we have seen in recent history, evil men do not clothe themselves in ugliness or openly pursue evil for its own sake. They are led by uncontrolled egos, which tell them to act by brandishing the "sword of righteousness." If at the time you were able to ask such maligned historical figures as Adolf Hitler or Saddam Hussein if they were guilty of doing evil, they would probably have rebuked you by telling you that they were acting out of the highest and purest of motivations. In the 1930s Hitler clothed himself in propaganda pictures with the shiniest armour of the Teutonic knights, giving the impression of a code of chivalry and behaviour, which his own order of knights, the SS, alluded to while committing the most evil acts. They were the modern "Lucifers" who unwittingly fell under control of their own darkest fears. Their egos, so concerned with themselves, allowed the floodgates of the darkest areas of the Shadow to open, clothing the basest of instincts in light.

Herein lies the problem when working with angels and demons. Pagan gods are by their nature balanced entities. All the pagan myths of the gods show that they have their failings. They are complete entities in their own right, just like people. This encourages individuals to understand their own Shadows, egos, and personas. Angels and demons, however, are split, polarized, dualistic forces. To work with one, you must work with the other to balance them, but the two are never able to integrate with each other; it is an eternal battle of dualism, which is found in the theology of the monotheistic religions rather than the nature-based traditions.

We have been discussing angels and demons in the context of the Abrahamic traditions. This does not include the concept of the Holy Guardian Angel—an aspect of the higher self that merges with the divine—or the concept of demons or angels as they are viewed outside of Judeo-Christianity. There is no quandary for the practitioner of trance when it comes to these entities manifesting during shamanic journeying or trance-prophecy work. These words mean something very different in other cultures, such as Buddhism or Siberian Shamanism, where they are viewed in a more balanced way. The only way their existence can be reconciled in trance-prophecy work is if they are viewed in this way, rather than the Judeo-Christian, which we recommend against. In these cases they represent the buried id within the Shadow, the deepest dark-est impulses, best depicted in our culture in Robert Louis Stevenson's fictional character of Dr. Jekyll, who becomes possessed by his own inner demons or Shadow as Mr. Hyde.

Shadow Entities
We have included Shadow entities because they have the potential to manifest during trance-prophecy in individuals who have repressed any form of abuse or trauma. Some would argue that these are separate enti-ties that attach to the individual, going as far to say that they are "de-mons," while others would suggest (including ourselves) that they are akin to the previously mentioned unintentional thought-forms. Unlike those, they specifically manifest on the mental or emotional level during trance or magical work. They develop or attach (depending on your viewpoint) during a period of stress, abuse, or trauma. The ego will repress this into the individual's Shadow to allow the person to function in the everyday world. If someone doing training as a seer does not deal with their deep-rooted issues, the repression will start to manifest with a personality of its own. The entity, through the individual's ego, will try to repress the aforementioned trauma and will often masquerade as another spirit or deity form. It is important to point out that this is not an expression of schizophrenia or multiple personality disorder, but an expression of the individual's Shadow, which is quite different.

Ghosts—Categories of Hauntings

It might seem odd that we have included this section in a book ostensibly on the subject of trance and Witchcraft, but in the modern period there has always been strong connections between the Witch and the "ghost hunter." In fact, one of the most widely known authorities on dowsing, ghosts, and hauntings, the previously mentioned T. C. Lethbridge, was also a founder of the Witchcraft Research Association. Lethbridge's theo-ries relating to hauntings remain the foundation for parapsychology even today, as famous occult investigator and writer Colin Wilson states:

> "No one who is interested in the paranormal can afford to ig-nore Tom Lethbridge . . . Today many of his admirers believe that he is the single most important name in the history of psychical research. His ideas on dowsing, life after death, ghosts, poltergeists,

magic, second-sight, precognition, the nature of time, cover a wider field than those of any other psychical researcher."[3]

As Witches can testify, sooner or later they find themselves being asked to help deal with a discarnate entity or similar spirit activity. We have been approached on several occasions both by concerned home owners as well as parapsychology groups to intervene on their behalf with earthbound spirits, and found ourselves dealing with poltergeist activity or a discarnate individual who, for some reason, was not able to pass over to the other side. Understanding the nature of hauntings is, therefore, essential if engaging in such efforts. The need to understand such phenomena becomes apparent when you do this kind of work. While some ghost sightings and hauntings are related to discarnate spirit activity, some are most definitely not. For example, poltergeists may be due to psychic activity from an individual or from a ley line. It is, therefore, important that you are able to differentiate between the different forms.

Poltergeist: This German word means "noisy spirit." A house or building becomes subject to noises: bangs, raps, and tapping, as well as telekinetic activity—objects moving of their own accord, such as tables, chairs, and ornaments. There have even been reports of people being physically harmed; for example, thrown out of bed or scratched. It is generally accepted among parapsychologists that there are three reasons for such phenomena:

1. Human: An individual in the house may be releasing large amounts of psychic energy due to the stresses they are going through. The most common person is an adolescent going through puberty, but it can also be caused by a person who is psychiatrically ill.

2. Leyline: A house may be built on a bad location, such as on a negative *leyline* (also known as a "black stream"),* which can cause such activity in a house even when it is not occupied. In such a case, it is necessary to call a dowser who will repolarize the line by redirecting it around the cause of the negativity, by using copper nails.

3. Frustrated spirit: A discarnate entity that is seeking attention. Such spirits are almost always unhappy with their lot, being stuck between

---

* The theory is, that black streams are created when a building, road, or similar structure is built on an existing ley line. This results in the ley line repolarising from positive to negative.

worlds by having missed the chance to pass over to the other side. It is very likely that they are unaware that they are dead, and are frustrated at being unable to communicate with the living. In such cases, it is necessary to communicate with them and assist them to pass over.

Both human and leyline forms of poltergeist activity can result in the secondary creation of an unintentional thought-form (see page 263).

Recordings: Many of the most commonly seen ghosts are, in fact, recordings. This does explain the strange incongruity of sightings of such historical figures as Ann Boleyn (the beheaded wife of King Henry the VIII), who appears to haunt several places at once. Such recordings take place because of the social and cultural trauma that is associated with the incident, which has resulted in the death of one or several individuals, which subsequently produces a recording of the incident in the ether of the place and replays under certain circumstances. Lethbridge suggested that damp atmospheres were more susceptible to such recordings. For this reason, ghosts of individuals who are not killed may sometimes be seen; they may even still be alive at the time! The most famous ghost sighting of this form was seen in Northamptonshire, England at the sight of the Battle of Naseby (14 June 1645); one of the bloodiest battles of the English Civil War. For several years after the battle, local people reported seeing a ghostly reenactment of the battle, complete with cavalry, canon, and most disconcertingly for them, people they knew to be still alive, such as Prince Rupert. Similar occurrences were reported at other Civil War battle sights, including Edgehill and Marston Moor. King Charles II took the reports so seriously, he conducted an investigation into them. It is important to point out that the English Civil War was one of the most turbulent periods in British history, where families were torn apart and brother fought against brother across England. It is this social trauma that resulted in these sightings.

Crisis Apparitions: This happens when someone at the moment of their death decides to inform their loved ones of their demise. Such apparitions are very common during times of war. In fact, almost all recorded cases occurred during wartime. They tend to take the same form: a loved one appears suddenly to one or many members of their family as if they have returned home from the battle. They may even enter into a conversation with them saying how much they love them; in some cases, they even say good-bye. They always end the same way, with the ghost disappearing the moment eyes are taken off of them. One of the most well-recorded accounts of this happening was in Ireland, at Glaslough Castle, County Monaghan. In 1914, Norman Leslie was killed in action in Flanders. His ghost appeared at the castle. He was seen to walk through the grounds and talk to estate workers before appearing before Marjorie Leslie, his mother.

Succubus and Incubus: This form of haunting was more commonly recorded during the Middle Ages. People believed that the succubus was a demon, which took female form. It then sexually raped the individual at night while he slept. The demon would then take on a male form—or incubus—and rape a female victim. In both cases the victim would claim that they were paralysed and felt the weight of the demon on their chest. Of course, such stories were more common among the sexually repressed members of society at the time, such as Christian monks, priests, and nuns. It was also a good way of explaining why women under celibate holy orders suddenly became pregnant! A celibate priest would clearly not do such a thing, so it was most probably a "demon" taking the form of a priest, who perpetuated the crime. There is now a physical explanation for some of the genuine cases: that of sleep paralysis (muscle atonia), where the individual becomes physically aware of their environment while sleeping, but is unable to move.

NOTES

1   Hesiod, *Works and Days*. Written in 700 BCE, it is a didactic poem consisting of over eight hundred lines.
2   Sarah Bartlett, chap. 1 in *A Brief History of Angels and Demons* (London: UK: Constable and Robinson, 2011).
3   Colin Wilson, *The Unexplained File: Cult and Occult*, Peter Brookesmith, ed. (London, UK: Orbis Publishing, 1985).

Chapter 11

The Underworld Descent Technique: Creating an Oracular Ritual

W e started developing this spiral descent pathworking technique some years ago when we recognised the need for a safe, systematic way of teaching Drawing Down the Moon (see chapter 12) to be used in a coven or a group setting, suitable for practitioners of varying experience levels. We discovered very quickly that this technique can be used for personal connection with deity and underworld guides. From this stage, it developed quite organically into a method of talking with the gods and goddesses. It quickly became apparent that if it was placed at the core of any oracular ritual, and combined with other trance induction methods, such as chanting, drumming, and ritual invocation (see chapter 9), it would become a trance-prophecy ritual in its own right.

Pathworking techniques and rituals that involve descent into the underworld are not new. In 1985, R. J. Stewart published a book titled *The Underworld Initiation*, which used a similar descent pattern, although based on Celtic fairy faith symbolism.[1] Of course, the Second Degree Initiation ritual in Gardnerian/Alexandrian-based Wicca uses "The Descent of the Goddess" into the underworld as its main theme. We drew our inspiration from such contemporary work and from several other traditions, the most noticeable being Norse/Anglo-Saxon spaework.* We also drew from the teachings of Spiritualism and shamanism, particularly when it comes to approaching the gates of death. One of the most interesting things we discovered after we developed the technique was that

---

* This includes the early work of Diana Paxson on seidr and spaework (see page 40).

there was a parallel in hypnosis called "the Spiral Staircase Induction."* Perhaps those who developed this technique actually drew from past occult practise without realizing it. As we have shown, the origins of hypnosis are in the occult world of trance mediumship.

In 2004 we started to incorporate this technique into our public Inner Mysteries Intensive workshops in Europe, Australia, New Zealand, and the United States. We did not expect to have such staggeringly successful results from its use. Initially, we would take three people from the audience: one with no experience, one with limited experience, and one with much experience with Drawing Down the Moon. With few exceptions, nearly always all three volunteers experienced meeting a divinity or a guide, and in quite a few instances this developed into an act of mediumship or *inspirational possession* by the divinity. This naturally led to the demonstration, turning into a full-on trance-prophecy ritual. The technique is simple: by following a left-handed spiraling path downward, it should be possible to sublimate the ego/persona complex. This path uses the Wiccan cosmology, which we covered in our previous work, *The Inner Mysteries*,† but has origins in several cultures. In Norse myth, the god Hermod (who is believed by some to have derived from the earlier Hermes) rides into Helheim to arbitrate with the goddess Hel for the release of Baldr.[2] But more relevant is the Greek myth related to the descent of Persephone into the underworld. In the classic Greek myth *The Odyssey*, a direct link between descent into the underworld and prophecy can be found: "And come to the house of Hades and dread Persephoneia to seek sooth saying of the spirit of Theban Teiresias.‡ To him even in death Persephoneia has granted reason that . . ." (Homer, *The Odyssey*, Book 10, card 473).

Similar parallels can be found in other ancient cultures, and in some cases they relate to real physical places in the ancient world. At Baia, just west of the Bay of Naples, Italy, postulants and seekers would actually descend into the underworld via an underground maze-like complex at the Oracle of the Dead (see page 260). In Ireland, Owenynagat (the "Cave of the Cat"), in County Roscommon, relies on a left-hand descent into the cave, where in myth the dark mother goddess Morrigan ascends into this

---

* The power of this technique is evident by its appearance in other systems, including *David St. Clair's Instant ESP*.

† Originally published as *Progressive Witchcraft* (New Page Books, 2004).

‡ Teiresias was the prophet of Thebes who Athena blinded when he saw her bathing. In compensation she gave him the gift of prophecy.

world. She is a deity often associated with prophecy,* as were her priest-esses, the *ban-tuatha* ("battle sorceress") and *ban-saitha* (often translated as "witch" or "fairy-woman").[3]

The technique we developed follows a traditional path downward into the underworld, the realm of Jung's Shadow, and then finally onto the "bridge" between this world and the world of death and the ancestors: Jung's *collective unconscious* (see Illustration 3). In the example we have given below, we used the imagery of a pathway down a hill into the underworld, with the participant being guided by the moon, which represents the positive aspect of the individual's *Shadow*. In the terminology of Jungian psychology, it represents the *Bright Shadow*. In contrast,

---

* The Morrigan makes several prophecies in Irish myth, the most important is after the defeat of the Fomorians following the Battle of Moytura.

Illustration 3: The Path to the Bridge and Gates

the sun is used in the return journey as it represents the return of the sublimated ego-persona complex. When it comes to the journey, there is no reason other symbolism could not be used. For example, a descent down a tree trunk or through the roots of a tree, and eventually exiting into the underworld or down a spiral staircase, in a castle where a door opens up to a drawbridge with a gate on the other side. Regardless, the symbol is taking the seer to the same place—the underworld. It is here that it is possible to meet divinity, in the act of communing with it and, if the individual is adept enough, becoming its spokesperson or oracle. Ultimately, the traveler in this realm becomes a vehicle, or as they say in Vodoun, a 'horse' for the divinity: the deity's spirit temporarily possessing the physical body of the seer. Alternatively, it can be used for pure trance-prophecy, in which case the seer, rather than being possessed or relaying messages from a deity, can look beyond the gates for symbols to answer questions.

We recommend the use of this technique in a group setting if it is to be used for training in Drawing Down the Moon or for trance-prophecy. Certainly, when it is used for the first time, there should be at least one person acting as the ritual *psychopomp*, or trance guide. It is not unsafe for someone to use it by themselves as a personal pathworking. The effect will be the same, but there will be no reason for the deity to come into the person if there is no one to talk to. Of course, it is a very useful technique for personally connecting and finding one's individual deity. With practise and experience, the rite can also be used to invoke a specific deity.

Regardless of how it is used, there are several rules to follow for the reasons of safety. The first is casting a circle for protection, for without it, the individual using the technique may suffer from interference on a psychic level in the form of a lower spirit, which will be able to access the process. It is the same thing that happens if a Ouija Board™ is used without a circle, and most people are familiar with those stories. It is not essential to call the elemental quarter Guardians, although it does add to a more secure atmosphere, particularly if one is used to calling them in ritual. The second consideration is comfort: if the Underworld Descent Technique is being used purely as a personal working—for example, connecting with deity—the participant can be lying down. But if it is being used for trance-prophecy or full possession, sitting in a chair is preferable, as it eases communication between the seer and the questioner. Initially, we recommend for this work to be done indoors, purely for reasons of comfort. Once the seer or seers are more experienced, there is absolutely no reason why it cannot be an outdoor event.

Preparation

If this technique is being used as part of an oracular ritual, the audience can be standing or sitting. Sitting is preferable if there are going to be several seers taking turns in the chair, in which case the seating arrangement should be in a horseshoe pattern around the chair. It should be positioned in the center of the room, draped with a piece of velvet or a decorated bedspread (there are some very nice ones with batique knotwork) to give it the appearance of a throne. An altar may also be set up, particularly if there is a plan to invoke a specific deity into the seer (see Photograph 9). The altar should be decorated appropriately for the divinity who is to be invoked, and should be approximately six feet behind the chair. Some deities like specific objects on the altar, which they may wish to use once invoked. For example, Odin likes to wear a brimmed hat and Dionysus

Photo by Gavin Bone

Photograph 9: Three seers—priestesses of Freya, the Morrigan, and Aphrodite— prepared for trance-prophecy ritual before their appropriate altars. Pagan Gathering Europe (PaGE) 2008.

will want a goblet of wine and his *thyrsus*.* Some research may be necessary to find out what each deity requires.

There should be low lighting (candlelight), incense, and appropriate music, preferably related to the deity. If a decision was made to have chanting or singing, the participatory audience should be made aware of it before the ritual, with song sheets handed out to them. The seer should be sitting in the chair before the audience is permitted to enter the room. She should be robed in an appropriate way if a specific deity is being invoked: red robe for Hekate, green robe for Brid, etc. If no specific deity is planned to be invoked, we would recommend a white robe for the seer. She should also be veiled (for the reasons given on page 145). The role of the trance guide in the ritual is to work with the seer. He is her invoker and grounder, as well as her priest (see chapter 6). His role is also to be the master of ceremonies for the rite; he cues when people are to chant or sing, when drummers are to drum, and when people may ask questions of the seer or deity who is manifesting through her. He also assists the seer in journeying to the gates of death by reciting the Underworld Descent Technique to her as a pathworking,† as well as respecting the wishes of any divinity when and if it manifests. Most importantly, he is responsible for the safety of the seer; he ensures that not too many questions are asked of her, and will ask the deity politely to separate from her if the process becomes too tiring for her. He will also interpret what she sees visually while she is in trance, and direct her when necessary to ask the right questions of the entities she meets that come through the gates from the Realm of the Ancestors.

Circle Casting

Once all the preparations have been made, the audience can be permitted into the space and the circle can be cast. As we mentioned previously, the circle should be cast for protection to prevent psychic interference, but there is also another reason. The casting of the circle, particularly if the visualization of energy is used, connects the individuals present—a temporary *gestalt*.[4] This also has the effect of connecting those present with the seer, which results in a greater probability of a stronger deity manifesting, as more energy is available for this process to occur. This tech-

---

* The thyrsus is a phallic wand made of large fennel and tipped with a pinecone. It was also covered in ivy vine leaves.

† Of course, with an experienced seer this becomes unnecessary; his role is just to ensure she arrives at the gates.

nique is very simple and consists of everyone present holding hands, just as it is done during a séance, and visualizing blue energy circling around the room, from person to person clockwise: from the throat chakra down the left arm, while receiving energy from the person on the right. Everyone visualizes their crown chakra and root chakra opening. At the same time, a sphere is visualized, forming around the ritual space. The circle can be cast in a traditional Pagan way simultaneously, with the elemental quarter Guardians being invoked if desired.

The Underworld Descent Technique

If being used in a trance-prophecy ritual, it is essential that the chakra centers of the seer are first opened to permit the deity to manifest in the body. There are two approaches to this: either the seer can open her own centers, or the trance guide can open them using the Sevenfold Kiss, which uses pranic breath in a ritualistic fashion. It is particularly important that the crown, brow, throat, and root centers are open fully for the reasons given in chapter 8. Once the chakras are open, the trance guide kneels in front of the seer, holding her hands so he can "feel" her downward descent. At this point he may signal to the audience for chanting, singing, or drumming to begin. He then begins to journey the seer downwards using a soft voice:

I want you now to listen to my voice—nothing else but my voice.

You are standing in darkness. There is nothing, nothing but my voice.

Any sounds that you hear I want you to list in your mind. Do not attempt to block them out; just accept that they are there and are of no consequence.

As you stand in the darkness, you slowly become aware of standing on a path, a path of pebbles.

You can feel the pebbles beneath your feet. You can feel them grinding against one another, beneath your heel and beneath your toes.

As you look up, you can now see tiny pinpricks of light emerging out of the darkness—stars—and you begin to see recognizable constellations form in the sky.

Your eyes slowly adjust to the darkness: slowly ahead of you, you can see the gray outline of a path winding ahead, going downward and to the left.

The path descends downward: downward into the darkness, downward curving to the left. You decide to follow the path: downward into the darkness, downward to the left.

Now as you look up, you can see a sliver of silver ahead of you, a new moon beckoning you to follow the path.

Can you see the moon? (Seer replies.)

The moon is here to guide you and protect you on your journey; it is the light in the darkness, your guardian and your guide.

You now put one foot forward and can feel the pebbles beneath your feet, as you follow the path; always downward, always to the left.

As you descend—always downward, always to the left—you can feel the coldness of the air around, which you breathe into your lungs, but you continue your journey; always downward, always to the left.

As you look up, you can see the stars and the moon, now waxing and growing, which beckons you down the path.

You descend downward, always downward, always to the left, into the dark, feeling the cold air around you, always downward and always to the left.

The moon is always ahead of you, always guiding you. It is now almost a quarter full, as you descend always downward, always to the left.

Slowly you become aware that the cold you feel is from a gray mist forming around you, but you continue on: always downwards, always to the left.

Can you feel the mist? (Seer replies.)

The moon, now half full, is guiding you along the path, as you descend, always downward, always to the left.

As you descend, you become aware that as you are walking into this gray mist, the sky is now glowing with a strange light, and the path is levelling and straightening.

Above the mist you can still see the moon, which is now almost three quarters full, as you continue to follow the path into the gray mist.

You continually follow the path, never deviating from its course: you continue onward into the cold gray mist, and your eyes adjust to the twilight world you have entered.

Now the moon is full. You can hear strange sounds and see strange images in the mist that surrounds you, but you know you are safe as long as you follow the moon, which continues to guide you along the path.

As you follow the path into the cold gray mist, slowly you can make out a sound: the sound of trickling far off in the distance, the sound of water.

You follow the path toward this sound, as you walk through the realm of mists. You can make out a line in the distance. It is the bank of a river, the river where this sound emerges.

Can you see the river? (Seer replies.)

The moon leads you along the path to the river; as you follow it through this mist, the sound of the river grows louder, from a trickle to a roar as you slowly approach it through the rolling mists that surround you.

As you approach the river on your path, you can make out an object crossing the river: a bridge.

Can you see the bridge? (Seer replies.)

I want you to follow the path to the edge of the river; follow the path to the bridge until you stand at its end.

Are you there, at the edge of the bridge? (Seer replies.)

What is the bridge made of? (Seer replies.)

I want you to look across the bridge and look for the gates. Can you see the gates? (Seer replies.)

I want you now to cross the bridge and wait at the gates.

Are you at the gates? (Seer replies.)

What are the gates made of? (Seer replies.)

In a moment I will ask you to push open one of the gates, but you are not to pass through to the other side. Do you understand? (Seer replies.)

What do you see? (Seer replies.)

At this point, the trance guide will need to interpret seer's experience. For this reason he should be constantly asking the seer about her experiences and what she sees.

The Condition of the Bridge and the Gates:
Translating Symbolism

It is important to understand that all that the seer sees is symbolism. This is particularly vital when the seer first approaches the bridge. The bridge is, of course, a symbolic analogy for the connection between this world and the world of spirits—the Realm of the Ancestors. The condition of the bridge can tell the seer and the trance guide how strong the seer's connection is with this world. If the bridge is in bad condition, if it is impassable, it clearly indicates that the would-be seer requires more training in personally balancing the elements within as part of their own personal growth. They are simply not ready to "pass beyond" at this stage. If the bridge is old but strong, it can indicate that they have already been doing this work without realizing it, or that they have a natural gift. This can also be indicative, particularly if the bridge is strongly built (metal), that they have a past-life tradition of being a seer. Similar rules apply to the *gates.*

The gates are, of course, the final barrier to the other realm. They are directly related to a medium's ability to open their crown chakra on the level of the Spiritual Body. Therefore, when the gates are opened, so is the spiritual level of the chakra in the aura. If it is not possible to open the gates, or they are difficult to open, it means that the individual needs to do more chakra work, specifically opening their crown chakra. If the seer can see through the gates to the other side (e.g., if they are metal railings), it means that the seer is a natural psychic and they often get messages through on a regular basis, whether they realize this. On one occasion during a trance-prophecy workshop, we came across a set of gates metaphorically "blown off" their hinges! At first it may appear as if the individual had "blown" their crown chakra in some way, damaged it due to forcing the gates open too early. Actually, this was not the case; the individual was, in fact, a natural medium and had been denying their ability, keeping their crown chakra closed—to all intents and purposes, "locking their gates." In the end, the pressure from the other side to communicate with her left the gates hanging in the wind by their hinges! Of course, this left her with the problem of constant communication. We instructed her, with the help of the deity she worked with, to rebuild the gates by visualizing their reconstruction. After this, she was able to communicate with deity in a more controlled way.

Experiencing Deities and Guides

Sometimes the seer will see nothing but darkness, a void when the gates are first opened. In such instances the trance guide will encourage her to look into the darkness for a spot of light and encourage her to draw it to her. In many cases, we have experienced this spot of light turning into a guide, guardian, or a deity (see Energetic Form, page 154). Sometimes the seer will see a realm through the gates, green fields of flowers, buildings, etc. On many occasions, we have had seers met by a guide, guardian, or deity at the gate almost immediately or even on the pathway down. On very rare occasions, the seer was instantly possessed by deity if he or she is a priest or priestess of that god or goddess. We have even had deceased loved ones meet the seer in quite emotional circumstances. There are no hard-and-fast rules as to what will happen; it will depend entirely on the adeptness of the seer. It is important to point out that in some traditional forms of trance-prophecy, deities may only be invoked to bring images to the seer, and the seer may not see or communicate with them. Instead, she may see abstract dream-like images that need to be translated by the trance guide or relayed directly to the questioner.

Sometimes if a guide appears but not a deity, the guide can be asked with due reverence to fetch a specific deity. If there is neither a guide nor a deity present, the seer can invoke a deity by calling their name three times (out loud or in their mind) into the realm beyond the gates. We have found both of these approaches to be effective. If a deity does not appear, all is not lost, as the seer can still read from what she sees beyond the gates in the way of symbolism when individuals ask her questions. If a deity does manifest, the first thing she should ask the deity is its name and why it has come. They will never lie, although they may sometimes not wish to answer. If the seer is experienced enough and comfortable with the idea, the deity can be asked if it wishes to come into the seer's body. The seer should visualize the deity coming in from behind and embracing her. As the deity does this, it will be aligning its chakras with those of the seer's. Again, the feeling the seer encounters is subjective, but is often described as a feeling of warmth as their auras merge and the seer feels her consciousness withdrawing. Some have described this feeling as though they are slowly slipping into a warm bath with the water slowly covering their heads, while descending into a trance state.

Even when a deity is successfully invoked, it may not necessarily be willing to enter the body of the seer. If it refuses, it may be that it is uncomfortable with the audience or the ritual setting, or that it does not feel compatible with the seer. For example, the seer may not yet be experienced enough to deal with possession by that deity. Generally, the deity will tell the seer why. We have heard the words "You still have a lot to learn!" given to seers on several occasions when this happens. Deities are always willing to give good advice on such matters, particularly if it is a specific god or goddess of trance. Whatever happens, the trance guide and audience should welcome the deity in an appropriate fashion. Sometimes an offering may be made to the deity or just a "hail and welcome." The deity can then be asked if it wishes to address the audience.

Questioning the Seer and the Deity

The next stage, regardless of whether the deity is present in the seer or if the seer is mediating, is to ask the deity if it is willing to answer individual questions. Obviously, if the deity is present in the body of the seer, this is the role of the trance guide. If the seer is just mediating, then the seer must ask the deity. If the deity says no, then the seer or the trance guide must ask why. It could be that the deity is just there to give a message to the seer or one specific person in the audience, but there could be a number of different reasons. Regardless of the reason, the deity's wishes must be respected, and it should be thanked before it leaves. The seer and the trance guide do have the option of asking the deity to find another god or goddess, either by name or not, who would be willing to answer questions. There will be an inevitable pause in proceedings while this deity searches the realms for another deity, and for the new deity to manifest.

Once any deity is ready to speak, the trance guide should ask if there are any priestesses or priests of the divinity present and allow them to approach the seer to commune with their god or goddess. Although this is not essential to do, we do feel it is a matter of correct etiquette when dealing with deities to allow those dedicated to them to approach first. We do recommend that they do not touch the seer while possessed by a deity. We have witnessed situations in the past where a deity has actually transferred from a seer into their priest or priestess through touch. Although quite dramatic, it can also disrupt any oracular ritual. It is better if priest or priestess touches the seer only at the deity's request.

Once the priests and priestesses have approached their deities, the trance guide should ask the members of the audience for their questions. He can then relay the questions to the seer/deity. Sometimes the answers can be quite personal, so it is important that the priest brings the seeker to the seer/deity for their answer. It is also not unusual for a deity to call the person forward. It is important, as we previously mentioned, that the inquirer does not touch the seer unless beckoned to do so. Sometimes the answers will be very clearly understandable and quite blunt, other times very cryptic. For example, the deity may say: "You are walking along a wall of great height; if you are not careful, you may fall onto either side, but at the end of the wall is the treasure you seek." Such answers are usually only meaningful to the person asking the question. Generally, such questions can fall into the following categories:

- Normal Speech: The deity will come through and reply in normal speech to any questions asked.
- Cryptic/Symbolic: All replies to questions will be in symbolic language or analogies, as mentioned above. It may have a double meaning or its meaning will become apparent only after the fact.
- Archetypal: The reply will be in keeping with the nature of the deity. For example, the Morrigan may say, "Stand up and fight" in reply to a question.
- Rhythmic: The deity replies in rhyme or quatrains.

It also becomes noticeable to anyone who does oracular possession work that the deities may sometimes take on specific poses while possessing a seer. We have seen Lakshmi possess a seer and spend the whole session balanced on her hip to avoid touching the ground due to the fact that she is a transcendent goddess (traditionally she is pictured sitting on a lotus). We have also witnessed the Norse god of fertility, Frey, sit in the same pose (stroking his beard) as found on traditional amulets, which date back to the Dark Ages. Obviously, Odin asks to wear his previously mentioned hat and commonly puts both hands on the arm rests of the chair and leans well forward when speaking. Such poses are well known in Vodoun and Santeria, the most obvious example being the way Papa Legba sits in a chair with one leg crossed over the other while leaning back. Hatha-Yoga uses a system of poses called *asanas*, which are used to honour and invoke the gods. The trance guide must also be prepared should the deity, while possessing the body of the seer, decide to walk around the room and pick people out to talk to. It is also not unheard of for them to do spontaneous healings or rituals.

At all times the trance guide should be aware of the well-being of the seer, particularly if there is a full possession. He needs to watch for any signs of distress or tiredness. For the first few times, we recommend the seer/deity answer no more than three questions. More experienced seers will be able to answer questions for longer periods without getting tired, but if the trance guide is concerned, he can ask the deity to leave, saying that he is concerned about the well-being of the seer. Very rarely do they say no, although it is not uncommon for them to want to complete what it is that they were doing or saying. The deity should be encouraged to leave the seer the way it came in—by pulling back and out of the seer as gently as possible. The trance guide should then confirm with the seer that the deity has left. Once this is confirmed, the seer should take the opportunity to allow the deity to speak to them one last time. The trance guide should then thank the god or goddess and bid them hail and farewell or similar, with the rest of the audience.

Pure Trance-Prophecy

In this technique, a deity is not called to possess or answer questions; it was a common practise of the later oracles of Delphi under the influence of the Apollonian priesthood and is a common practise in modern spaework. It is based purely on the psychic skill of the seer and relies much on her skills at opening her third eye (the brow chakra on the akashic level of the aura) rather than her fully opening her crown. For this reason, it is much more difficult than working with deity, which is why we have put more emphasis on deity connection. On reaching the gates, the seer informs the trance guide with a predetermined signal (e.g., lifting her hand). The guide then asks the audience if there are any questions. He relays the question to the seer, and the answer back to the audience member. This is done so as not to distract the seer, which may bring her out of trance. The seer focuses solely on the images she may see when she receives the question. Often a seer may describe quite lucid imagery as though she is watching the answer on a television screen, or she may see images that are more dream-like and abstract. These later images may not mean anything to the seer or the trance guide but often makes sense to the questioner.

The Return Journey

Once the deity has returned to the Realm of the Ancestors, the trance guide should ask the seer to visualize the gates closing. Once this is done, he can commence the journey with her back to this world:

Bid farewell and thank the deity and any other spirits you have been communing with. Now close the gates; visualize them closing firmly.

Are they closed? (Seer answers and confirms.)

Turn and start your journey back across the bridge, back across the bridge into the Realm of Mists.

As you look up, you can see the first light of the dawn on the horizon. Can you see this light? (Seer answers.)

This light is here to guide you back to the world of the living. Just follow the path to the light, to the rising sun.

Follow the path that led you here, guided by the light of the rising sun, which is always a head of you. Cross the bridge back into the Realm of Mists, always following the path.

Through the rolling mists follow the path, always onward, always toward the light of the rising sun through the cold mist.

Follow the path as it begins to climb, always upward, always to the right, always through the mist toward the first rays of the rising sun.

As you follow the path—always upwards, always to the right— you become aware that the mist is parting and it has become less cold. You can now see the top of the sun on the horizon as it begins to break through the mist.

Continue to follow the path, always upward: always to the right toward the rising sun.

The air around you becomes warmer, and the light returns to this place as the sun rises more fully on the horizon.

Slowly the path comes to an end in a place of warmth, a place of light. You return back now to the place that you started from, bathed in the light of the fully risen sun.

> Very slowly, return back to us now, opening your eyes and see-
> ing the world around you.

It is important that the seer grounds immediately after this experience.
She should go through the process of closing her chakras and grounding. If she is still having problems grounding due to her crown chakra
being open, the trance guide can also try the Trap Door Technique to
close it (see page 129) The seer is likely to feel light-headed and initially
tired. Both these feelings will quickly pass. It is not unusual for her to feel
full of energy and quite ecstatic. If possessed—although she will initially
remember the whole experience, including the questioning—it is quite
common that within ten minutes these memories will have faded (for the
reasons why.

Going Further: Offerings, Libations, and Healing

So far we have talked about the Underworld Decent Technique being
used for oracular work, for prophecy, and asking questions. But if a full
possession of the seer is possible, then that is far from being the only
purpose open to both the seer and trance guide. As anyone who has
practised modern trance-prophecy can tell you, sometimes the questions
put to a possessing deity can quickly evolve into a petition for their help.
We have seen this so many times: a question going from "How can I
solve this problem?" to "Can you help me with this problem?" or even
the deity itself volunteering help. The latter is rare. In most instances
the deity will tell the querent how to help themselves, rather than intervene, but this can be instigated in a traditional way if proper preparation takes place before any oracular session. The use of offerings and
libations in Paganism is, of course, traditional, and can be found both
in ancient culture and in contemporary tradition. It can be seen prominently in the practises of Santeria and Vodoun, where there are specific
offerings for each loa or orisha. When the same practise is combined in
the technique we describe here, it can become a particularly powerful
ritual experience. The deity will feel obliged to reciprocate if the offering is made correctly. Just as in everyday life, where you do not get
anything for free, the same is true on the spiritual levels: there needs to
be an exchange of energy between those asking for assistance and the
deity or spirit who is being asked to assist.

As previously mentioned, preparation is essential. For a session that
involves libations or healing, the seer must be familiar with the deity and
know that it will come through. He or she should preferably be a priest

or priestess of this deity, or have brought that deity through on several occasions before. The appropriate offerings must also be collected, and must be suitable for that deity. It is well worth looking at how this works in Vodoun and Santeria where there are specific offerings to each loa or orisha. For example, Oya likes to be presented with an eggplant and anything purple. With European deities, things are somewhat easier and less rigid than in the African diaspora traditions. For example, nearly all Norse or Saxon deities are happy to accept mead, but it is always good to be as specific as possible. Sometimes the offering may not be an actual object but an obligation to perform a task—with Bast, a promise to give a donation to a cat sanctuary. Hardly traditional, but very acceptable to the goddess of cats nonetheless. Obviously, some research may be necessary if the correct offering is going to be made to a more obscure god or goddess.

In a session where only one deity is being invoked, the whole ritual should naturally orientate around them. It is pointless doing a Celtic or traditional Wiccan ritual around a Greek deity. All the symbolism in the ritual, such as the circle casting and calling of quarters, must be appropriate for that divinity. Chants and songs related to that deity should also be used wherever possible as a form of invocation. Again, research may be necessary. There will also be some extra items needed in the ritual. Obviously the offerings, possibly changes of magical tools and, if offering fluids, such as wine, mead, beer, then a libation bowl to pour and catch the liquids will be needed. Robes and dress may also need to be amended to fit the ritual, although white robes are always a good fallback and essential for anyone doing trance-prophecy. A seer who is likely to be possessed by Hekate would need to be in a red robe veil, while a priest of Dionysus who is to be possessed would want to wear a leopard-skin print toga. Working with Celtic or Norse deities is even easier, and traditional dress can be researched and used. Obviously, colors are important: Brid has a preference for green, the Morrigan for black, and Freya for white with a blue tabard, as is described in Norse tradition.

NOTES

1   First published in 1985 by The Aquarian Press (Wellingborough, UK) and subsequently by Mercury Press in 1990.

2   Found in The Prose Edda, the *Gylfaginning*, section 49.

3   The word *saitha* or *sithe* can be found in *A Social History of Ancient Ireland*, vol. I, by P. W. Joyce (1903). It is very similar to the Norse word *seidr* and the Anglo-Saxon *seith*. It is possible that it has the same origins etmologically as the Germanic words seidr and seith. If correct, then *ban-saitha or sithe* would literally translate from the ancient Irish as "woman of prophesy." Saint Patrick is said to refer to them as "pythonesses" in the same text, which supports this hypothesis.

4   Psychologist Max Gurtheimer coined the term *gestalt*: "The whole is other than the sum of the parts." The term is used in modern occult practise for the concept of the group mind, which forms on the astral or collective unconscious.

Part III

The Practice of Trance, Prophecy, and Possession in Modern Paganism and Witchcraft

Chapter 12

Wiccan Drawing Down the Moon: Understanding and Enhancing the Experience

R itual that included trance was present in Wicca from its inception, making Witchcraft, or Wicca, unique among neo-Pagan traditions today. Although the Golden Dawn made use of some techniques, including deity assumption, most practise centered around pure mediumship. Certainly, this influenced Wicca in its early days. Although some would still argue whether Wicca is an 'ancient tradition,' nearly all would accept from the amount of evidence available that there is nothing ancient about its most important and central ritual: Drawing Down the Moon. Even though the term can be found in the classical world, it clearly consists of elements of ritual derived from Aleister Crowley, Gerald Gardner, Charles Godfrey Leland, and Doreen Valiente (we cover this in more detail in this chapter). For most Wiccans, the most important aspect of the rite is reading of The Charge. This was originally known as the "Leviter Veslis (Lifting the Veil)" and derives from Gardner. What inspired him to include a rite, which by its very nature incorporates mediumship, is now lost in the mists of time, but it is very likely he was inspired by Crowley and his Scarlet Women.

What may be of interest to many is the fact that use of the term "Drawing Down the Moon" within Wicca is historically incorrect. The ritual used in Wicca to "draw the Goddess" into the high priestess bears little resemblance to the historical method used in the Mediterranean. In their book *Wicca: Magical Beginnings*, Sorita d'Este and David Rankine make the same observation stating that the "use of the term *'drawing down the moon'* had a different meaning in classical times to the Wiccan usage today." They go on to point out: "However there was a practice which involved reflecting the full moon into a bowl or jug of water, and this may well have been what was referred to as a drawing down the moon."[1]

Regardless, we are now stuck with the term Drawing Down the Moon to describe the ritual technique in Wicca. It is not our intention here to try and change this, but we do feel that it is important for people to realise the true origins of the term, as the techniques used for Drawing Down in ancient times are very different to the ritual magic techniques employed in the Gardnerian-based Wicca and Witchcraft of the twentieth and twenty-first centuries. These ancient methods also offer the opportunity to learn and enhance the existing Wiccan technique (for more on this, see chapter 13).

At the time of writing the modern ritual in the early 1950s, Wicca was one of the only traditions in Western magic that had a ritual whereby a deity was invoked into a priestess. It was this that made Wicca unique in neo-Paganism, and it continued to be unique in this respect up until the early 1990s, until the advent of the seith/seidr spearheaded by Diana Paxson. When Wicca first incorporated Drawing Down the Moon into modern Witchcraft, at least a few of Gardner's high priestesses had some experience in modern mediumship techniques from other sources. Many Gardnerian Witches moved freely between their own groups, and those of Spiritualism, Theosophy, and the existing Western tradition magical groups. Although there is no proof that Gardner's priestesses of the time were involved directly in such groups, one of his initiates does stick out as having a background in Spiritualism and mediumship—Barbara Vickers. She was one of his earliest initiates, and no doubt her mediumistic abilities influenced Gardner's development of the Drawing Down process (for more on the influence of Spiritualism and mediumship, see chapter 2).

Drawing Down the Moon as a Ritual

As we mentioned, the ritual of Drawing Down the Moon is the defining rite that separates Wicca from Druidism and ceremonial ritual magic. Unlike the other traditions, Wicca introduced the idea of *deity assumption*, or possession by a god or goddess, into modern Witchcraft. Although there are minor differences between Gardnerian and Alexandrian methods, it has basically remained the same in those traditions, with only minor changes since the early 1960s. It is not our intention to go into too much detail: The "prose Charge" has been published several times, including within the works of Janet and Stewart (Farrar). What we want to do here is examine its magical rationale. Although we do not intend to examine the whole ritual, it is necessary to include some historical material related to the Wiccan ritual, but only in context of trance experience.

The general format for Drawing Down the Moon in the Alexandrian and Gardnerian traditions is now widely published and no longer oath-bound. This has resulted in several derivations of the original ritual. All follow the same basic format. It can be summarized thusly:

- The high priestess stands with her back to the altar in the *Osiris Slain Position*, holding the scourge and flail, as the high priest kneels and gives her the Fivefold Kiss.
- The high priest then invokes the Goddess: "I invoke Thee and call upon Thee, . . . ," etc., using the downward-pointing Triangle of Water, which he draws across her breasts and abdomen. She then opens her arms in the *Osiris Risen Position*.
- The high priest continues the invocation: "Hail Aradia! From the Amalthean Horn, pour forth thy store of love . . . ," etc., with his arms outstretched outward and downward.
- The high priest stands up and takes a pace backward, still facing the high priestess. She then draws the Invoking Pentagram of Earth in front of him and invokes: "Of the Mother darksome and divine . . . ," etc. (We examine the possible reasons for this part of the ritual on page 95.)
- At this point, the Drawing Down is complete. In traditional Gardnerian Craft, the Goddess should now begin speaking through the high priestess. If she fails to do so, then The Charge of the Goddess is recited: "Listen to the words of the Great Mother, . . . ," etc., with a brief invocation interruption by the high priest: "Hear ye the words of the Star Goddess, . . . ," etc., before she continues: "I who am the beauty of the green earth . . . ," etc. This completes The Charge, but not the end of the ritual.
- The high priest then faces the coven with arms raised and recites the *Bagahi Laca Bachahé* chant.
- The high priestess and high priest then face the altar, and the high priest invokes the Horned God: "Great God Cernunnos, return to earth again! . . . ," etc. This ends the rite.

Symbolic Ritual Invocations

Apart from the initial invocation (more on this later), there are two symbolic invocation methods that have been used at different times in British Traditional Wicca (i.e., Gardnerian and Alexandrian) to invoke deity into the high priestess during Drawing Down the Moon: the Lesser Invoking Pentagram of Earth and the Invoking Triangle of Water.

The Invoking Pentagram of Earth is present in all Drawing Down (or Lifting the Veil rituals, as it was originally known) from Gardner's 1949 Book of Shadows (*Ye Bok of Ye Art Magical*) and onward.[2] The rationale behind its use is self-explanatory—the invocation of Spirit to Earth symbolised by the downward stroke from the topmost point (Spirit) to the bottom left as you face it (Earth): "Spirit to Earth." This certainly remained the only symbolic method of invoking the Goddess into the high priestess up until the 1960s when it is changed in favour of the Invoking Triangle of Water.

The Invoking Triangle of Water appears sometime after 1961. In *Lady Sheba's Book of Shadows* (rituals of Gardnerian origin, published 1971), the technique consists of "touching her on the breast and womb with the wand,"* but there is no reference to the anointing of a triangle "with right forefinger on the right breast; left breast and womb; the same three again and finally the right breast," as is used commonly today. It was used and taught in this fashion by Alex Sanders during the time Janet and Stewart Farrar were part of his coven. Its definitive origin is none other than an adaption of the Triangle of Art, the Triangle of Evocation, used in Cabalistic ceremonial magic. This was commonly drawn on the ground outside of the Circle of Art to invoke angels and demons into, but it could also be used to directly invoke such entities into a human host, which clearly has its origins in Traditional Wicca. Of course, it also defines the high priestess as "the Chalice," the vessel into which the Goddess descends. The question really is, who introduced it? Either Lady Sheba's ritual is incomplete, or the invocation used was a direct line from center of chest to womb. If it was the latter, then it is highly likely that Sanders introduced it, as he had done much reading on the subject of high magic technique.

A twist on this is that Janet and Stewart reintroduced the Invoking Pentagram of Earth for invoking deity when they published *Eight Sabbats for Witches* in 1981. In their ritual of Drawing Down the Moon, the

---

* Lady Sheba (Jessie Wicker-Bell) founded the American Celtic Wicca Tradition and the American Order of the Brotherhood of Wicca. She was the first person to make the Book of Shadows publicly available.

priestess performed it with the wand directed at the priest after the Invoking Triangle of Water. Their rationale behind it was to maintain the
balance of polarised energy by invoking the God into the circle through
the priest. They were, in fact, invoking the God as psychopompous into
the priest (discussed in chapter 6).

Regardless of the use of triangle or invoking pentagram, the invoking gesture is accompanied with an invocation, which generally consists
of the following (although there are minor differences in that the high
priestess' name was included in the original [1949] Book of Shadows):

> I invoke and beseech Thee,
> O mighty Mother of all life and fertility.
> By seed and root, by stem and bud,
> by leaf and flower and fruit,
> by Life and Love, do I invoke Thee
> to descend into the body of Thy servant and high priestess, (name).

The Charge

The Charge (see Appendix II) is preceded by the previously mentioned
invocation by the high priest, the invocation to the Great Mother, and the
symbolic ritual invocation techniques (the previously mentioned Fivefold
Kiss and the Invoking Triangle of Water) all preceed the charge. These
were originally intended to be followed by the first part of The Charge,
which the high priestess recited only if the possession by the Goddess was
unsuccessful (we discuss this more fully later on in this chapter). The high
priest would then recite: "Hear ye the words of the Star Goddess, . . . ,"
etc., before she completed the second part of The Charge.

The modern Charge of the Goddess derives from three main sources.
Gerald Gardner drafted the first version of The Charge, known as "Leviter Veslis" (see Appendix I), which translates as "Lift up the Veil," in
his first grimoire, *Ye Bok of Ye Art Magical*. It included material taken
from Charles Godfrey Leland's *Aradia*, as well as material from Aleister
Crowley's work. The Charge first appeared in this form in all the Books
of Shadows predating Doreen Valiente's initiation into the Craft in 1953.
By 1961, Doreen's "verse Charge," as it was known, was now appearing
in all the Books of Shadow given to Gardnerian initiates. The original
"Leviter" clearly included some phrases from Crowley's Gnostic Mass
(first published in 1913), particularly his Ceremony of the Opening of
the Veil.[3] It was her disapproval of the misogynistic aspects of Crowley's

verse that may well have been her initial inspiration behind the creation of the first draft of The Charge. She made a point of excluding Crowley's more sexually graphic phrases from it, such as: "I love you: I yearn for you: pale or purple, veiled or voluptuous." Doreen told Janet and Stewart that her reasoning behind it in a letter during the writing of *Eight Sabbats for Witches* in 1980: "This was not really suitable for the Old Craft of the Wise, however beautiful the words might be or how much one might agree with what they said; so I wrote a version of The Charge in verse, keeping the words from *Aradia*, because these are traditional."[4]

Valiente did not exclude all of Crowley's material though. She kept two important pieces from his work: the phrase: "Nor do I demand (aught in) sacrifice" from his *Book of the Law* and "Keep pure your highest ideal" from his poem "Law of Liberty."[5] She clearly felt that these were in keeping with Wiccan philosophy.

There are also some similarities in the language of Valiente's Charge with the elements of the *Papyri Gracece Magicae* (see Appendix III). One phrase particularly stands out (line 42): "For All Things are from You, and in You do All Things, Eternal One, come to their End," which bears a striking resemblance to: "From me all things proceed, and unto me all things must return" in The Charge. As this phrase doesn't appear in the "Leviter Veslis," we would suggest that it originated from the *Papyri*. Valiente rewrote it, putting it into the first person and then used it to replace the material from Crowley that she had removed.

Gardner's adaption of Crowley's writings followed by Valiente's adaption have resulted in the modern Charge remaining one of the most popular and most beautiful pieces of Craft liturgy used today. It is used in ritual, and Wiccans of the Gardnerian and Alexandrian traditions, as well as others within the neo-Pagan community as a whole, quote it regularly. Its use has now evolved beyond being part of the Drawing Down the Moon ritual; it has been incorporated into other rituals because of its power. For many, it has all the hallmarks of a credo, particularly Doreen's inclusion in the second part: "that if that which thou seekest though findest not within thee, thou will never find it without thee"—an important statement regarding the mysteries.

Trance and the Experience of Drawing Down the Moon

This influence of mediumship training within Gardnerian Wicca, if it did truly exist, died out by the end of the 1960s. As early Drawing Down the Moon depended on it, it never developed into a coherent system of inducing trance within Wicca, relying purely on the mediumship abilities of the high priestess, and the ritual itself. Even Alex Sanders failed to pass on his mediumship training within the Alexandrian tradition. This meant that by the 1970s, Wiccan high priestesses relied purely on their natural psychic abilities, which they brought into ritual. While this worked for some, it didn't work for others, and The Charge of the Goddess became more and more important in the minds of most Wiccans as the high priestess failed to fully enter any form of trance and fell back on the reading of The Charge. We've been lucky enough to talk to many Wiccan elders who all confirmed to us that the use of The Charge was a last resort, used to fill that embarrassing void when on occasion the Goddess didn't grace their coven with her presence. Although its use indicated a failure of the Goddess to come through the high priestess, this was considered to be in no way a reflection on the ability of the high priestess. It was accepted that this was something that sometimes just happened. Unfortunately, the knowledge that The Charge was originally developed to be used for this purpose was lost among many covens; this became compounded with the emergence of new traditions that adopted the Gardnerian style of ritual but lacked any training within it. Where both trance and the real purpose of The Charge was lost, covens started to teach that reciting The Charge was all that was required to successfully bring through the Goddess and no other techniques were required. It was for the above reasons Doreen Valiente once said to us that she was sick of hearing The Charge, as well as the fact that it was often recited in a monotone fashion with little feeling. Regardless, Drawing Down the Moon for many remained a powerful ritual, even when it lacked the trance component. High priestess and author Margot Adler sums it up best:

> I have seen priestesses who simply recited lines and priestesses who went through genuinely transforming experiences. I have seen a young woman, with little education or verbal expertise, come forth with inspired words of poetry during a state of deep trance. I have heard messages of wisdom and intuition from the mouths of those who, in their ordinary lives, often seem superficial and without insight.[6]

Adler's experience was a common one in the 1980s. While some priestesses did genuinely bring through a deity in trance, the majority did nothing but follow the pattern of the ritual laid down in the Book of Shadows, which in the majority of cases resulted in an act of embodiment rather than trance-possession (see page 150). This experience and lack of expectation of what happens was passed on. Increased communication via the World Wide Web from the 1990s on, resulted in priestesses sharing their varied experiences. It created confusion in many as to what was actually supposed to happen during Drawing Down. One of our own students in our Progressive Magic course sums it up best:

> I am not sure what Drawing Down the Moon (Goddess) is really like; I always pictured it would be like a trance state, but I think that maybe on some level that is what happened to me. Partway through the ritual, I was visualizing using a sickle to cut away the negative and draw the positive, but instead of it being on a personal level (which is what had bothered me before . . . making it all about me), somehow I felt myself merging with Demeter, Gaia, the Goddess. And I cut away the negativity of the world and drew the world to myself. And I held it in my arms, and it rested there as a blue ball, and I looked down on it . . . not really able to see "people" but more looking on the energy. And the message was "Love them all as I do." So I held this planet for a while and released it.

The lack of use of any of the techniques, which are common to all genuine trance traditions, resulted in another problem within Wiccan Drawing Down: the lack of sublimation of the ego/persona complex during the ritual. It was more likely to evoke aspects of the priestesses' own unconscious rather than an exterior spiritual force such as a deity, which should occur in a true invocation. During the 1990s, the late Isaac Bonewits, a well-respected writer on the subject of the neo-Pagan movement and an initiated Gardnerian high priest, began to examine the whole issue of whether Drawing Down the Moon was actually successful as a ritual. As he travelled to different covens in the United States, he asked individual members whether they actually believed that their high priestess was successful in truly bringing through the Goddess. He was quite stunned by the results—the majority said "no," and, in fact, believed that their high priestess was just bringing through their own ego. To put Bonewits' experience into context, he visited only a small selection of covens in the United States. While his experience was not unusual, it cannot be applied to the experiences in all covens, as many have instituted their own systems of training for Drawing Down the Moon, which include trance techniques as part of the process.

A major contribution to the lack of trance technique in modern Drawing Down the Moon within Wicca was that many had come to believe

that the ritual in the Book of Shadows was all that was needed to invoke
the Goddess. In fact, many had not only come to believe that The Charge
was the invocation, but also that it had to be read out loud at every Drawing Down of the Moon ritual. Historically this is incorrect; it was never
intended to be used in this way. Wiccan elder and author Ray Buckland,
of the Gardnerian Tradition, who was originally initiated by Monique
Wilson, best sums up its true purpose: "Sometimes, however, although
invoked, the Goddess does not appear and possess the priestess. When
this happens, the priestess will recite what is known as 'The Charge', a
poetic address that was written by Doreen Valiente for Gerald Gardner's
Book of Shadows."[7]

The Charge is, in fact, a way out of embarrassment for the high priestess if the ritual doesn't work. If Drawing Down is successful, The Charge
should not need to be read aloud, as the Goddess would speak directly
through the high priestess in her own words and create her own Charge.
Doreen once admitted to us that its dogmatic and systematic use in this
way at each ritual quite infuriated her, particularly as it was often recited without any feeling. Over the years we have heard the same statement from several first-generation Gardnerian high priestesses and priests.
This was clearly considered normal doctrine regarding Drawing Down the
Moon. It should be noted is that Buckland uses the term "possess." It is
obvious that there were clear expectations of deity possession quite early
on in Wicca's development, but as we have previously mentioned, very few
high priestesses get the full possession experience that can be seen in Vodoun—the experience of being "ridden." The experience of most is probably best summed up by the use of the now common term *aspecting* (see
page 150), where the recipient of the deity-spirit retains some consciousness
and is in control of the proceedings. Although there are high priestesses
within Wicca who do get full possession experiences, these are very few
and far between. When it does occur, it is mainly due to the natural gifts
of the priestess or the fact that they had received training outside of Wicca
in mediumship or similar trance traditions. This has resulted in a wide
range of experiences with a few priestesses getting full possession, while
the majority enter into lighter states—the aspecting just described. In some
extreme cases, Drawing Down the Moon is taught as being nothing more
than a symbolic ritual, with no expectation of any form of embodiment,
aspecting, deity assumption, or psychic manifestation whatsoever.

The varied training and experiences of priestesses is best summed
up in the following quotes. To try to understand what was happening in

the Wiccan community with Drawing Down the Moon, we asked people about their experiences. They can be summed up in three forms. The first is that some continue to be trained in the traditional teachings of Gardner and Valiente regarding the possession aspect of Drawing Down·

> I'm a Gardnerian witch, and I was taught to memorize The Charge as a tool to learn Drawing Down, and as a backup for when the Goddess did not choose to enter the priestess. I'm currently trying to gather more information about trance possession so that I can better understand what I am connecting to and what is happening to my mind and body during Drawing Down.[8]

This is clearly no different from Buckland's statement that The Charge was only to be used if no possession took place, but also it shows that in some traditions and lines of Wicca, there is still no understanding taught of how it works.

The second type of experience is even more interesting as The Charge now seems to have evolved into an invocation in its own right. Undoubtedly, this wasn't its original intention, but some are being taught that this was how it was traditionally used:

> I've seen The Charge used in many ways and all are legitimate as far as I'm concerned. But I was taught, and I taught my priestesses, that The Charge is learnt by heart and known so well that it is used with ritual and invocation by a proper priest to cause the priestess to step aside and allow the Goddess to speak through her. Reciting The Charge becomes a kind of mental trigger. Hence, in practice, the priestess often begins with some of The Charge, but as the Goddess takes over, the words may change; certain aspects may be given more importance, and occasionally the priestess will mediate something completely different. Obviously, this is not always appropriate and depends on the grade of the participants. The important thing to remember is PL&PT [Perfect Love and Perfect Trust]: no HPS should feel inadequate if "only" The Charge ever comes out; not all of us have or are able to develop mediumistic or mediating abilities. I was put under pressure and made to feel a failure when I couldn't do it, which was pointless and unfair. Priests support your priestesses, and vice versa! In my opinion, there is a great deal of substandard teaching and ignorance of proper practice in modern-day covens.[9]

What is clear is that this approach—using The Charge as an invocation—does seem to work for some people, and is quite fairly pointed out. Not everyone will have the ability to trance. In our opinion, this development should be seen as an evolution of the process rather than a degradation of it.

The third quote is really more disturbing as it shows that in some areas of the community, Drawing Down the Moon became nothing more than purely symbolic ritual, with those who have genuine ability to trance facing exclusion:

> I was taught The Charge in my earliest Wiccan training about twenty years ago, and have used it, or variants of it, regularly since then. The group I was with at the time, and from whom I received that training, considered all the invocations (deities and elements) to be "strict invocations" in which the Powers are symbolically invited into the ritual and nothing more. All the Wiccan groups in the area had similar views.
>
> I was also taught that Drawing Down the Moon is symbolic as well, though the groups I worked with used it less often than they did The Charge. From the very first time I spoke The Charge in ritual, I experienced what most people would call possession. I had the same experience with Drawing Down the Moon. I got into arguments with a lot of people who insisted I was "imagining it" or "just getting theatrical," to the point that I eventually left the Wiccan community, and not just that one group, because the attitude here (I'm in the southeastern US) seemed to be that possession, as such, just doesn't happen. Since then I have trained as a shamanic practitioner and have learned much more about possession, or being "ridden," as it is called in many traditions, and experienced it many times under many different circumstances. I have my opinions about why possession and other powerful magical aspects of Paganism in general, and Wicca in specific, tend to be downplayed to such a great extent. I don't know if the same situation holds in Europe, but here I think it has a lot to do with "cleaning up" Wicca so it's more palatable to the general public.[10]

The most fascinating aspect of Laura's statement is that she felt that she had to go outside the Wiccan community to get an understanding of the experience she was having; something we felt we also had to do. We are pleased to say that since the 1980s, Laura's attitudes have changed, but there is still no overall coherent system of training in Drawing Down. Very few priestesses are experiencing full trance-possession, as would have happened in ancient times. This was not the case in the classical Drawing Down the Moon practised in ancient Greece and Italy They undoubtedly combined several techniques: the use of the mirror (hypnotic induction), singing and chanting, dancing, and possibly even the use of hallucinogenic herbs or fungi. It was because of experiences like Laura's and other priestesses that many, like ourselves, started to draw from both ancient and contemporary trance techniques in the 1990s to teach successful Drawing Down the Moon rituals.

The 1980s saw Wicca incorporate practises that were both contemporary, and ancient in origin. This was to herald a new wave of creativity, which gave birth not only to the new traditions that were appearing but also from the older ones. Many, such as Vivianne Crowley and, of course, ourselves, felt that there needed to be deeper training within the modern Witchcraft movement, particularly in areas such as the use of magical energy, application of Jungian psychology, and, of course, Drawing Down the Moon. Although the rituals changed very little in Traditional Wicca, the systems of teaching evolved beyond the purely ritual component. In some cases, integration of new techniques, such as shamanism, were successful, particularly by those who wanted to go beyond the normal rituals of the Book of Shadows and experiment in new methods. In some cases, it even led to new traditions, and eventually the concept of shamanic and ecstatic Witchcraft. Unfortunately, the downside was that the use of psychological principles, particularly Jungian, put forward the idea that divinities were just "archetypes" and nothing more. This was at odds with both ancient and contemporary traditions, which believed that deities were, in fact, spirits not merely a psychological aspect of ourselves. Of course, both points of view are true, but among individuals brought up in a "one truth" culture, it is difficult for many to come to terms with. Psychology has its place in understanding Drawing Down the Moon, but the spiritual aspect must not be forgotten as it has been in some cases.

Using the Underworld Decent Technique as a Form of Training

We discussed this technique fully in chapter 11. Our development of the Underworld Decent Technique was originally created to teach priestesses Drawing Down the Moon, but quickly developed into a stand-alone method of trance-prophecy. This technique can be used for training any priestess in Drawing Down the Moon.

Initially she sits in a chair (as described on page 173) or lies down, and the technique is used to take her to meet the goddess she wishes to work with. It is very likely that this will be a deity with whom she is already familiar; she will already be working with them as a personal deity, or it may even be the coven's patron deity. It is important to remember that Drawing Down was originally a deity-archetype-specific technique. As the name suggests, a lunar goddess was always invoked, such as Diana, Artemis, Selene, or Hekate. Although lunar goddesses are not the only ones who can be invoked in this way, they will, of course, come through stronger than any other archetypal form. If the high priestess is not making contact with the coven's patron deity or a lunar deity, she does have the opportunity, using this technique, to ask whichever deity is present to bring the coven's patron deity to her (never, of course, forgetting to say "please"). This connection with a coven patron or lunar deity can then be used in the Wiccan Drawing Down ritual.

As this technique is just being used for training, she should not allow possession in the early stages, but she will become familiar with the "feeling" of that connection. In a later stage, she can allow possession under controlled conditions. After using this technique for a while, the next time the high priestess enters circle, she can bring that connection with the deity with her. She can have her priest act as the trance guide (see chapter 6) and take her "down" before the ritual in preparation for Drawing Down. She can then ask the deity—the goddess she meets at the gates—to accompany her back along the spiral path in a clockwise fashion. She can then bring the deity into circle, ready to possess her at the appropriate moment, during the traditional rite, and it inevitably will. At a later stage, she can go one step further by visualizing the Descent Technique during Drawing Down. Since it is necessary for the chakras to be open to allow deity possession, it can also be incorporated into the Fivefold Kiss preceding the Drawing Down, either by the high priestess visualizing the chakras opening or replacing the Fivefold Kiss completely with the Sevenfold Kiss (see page 131).

One thing that can happen both in traditional Drawing Down and trance-prophecy is that as time progresses, a process of conditioning takes place. Simply put, the traditional words of the Drawing Down the Moon ritual will psychologically trigger the effects of the Underworld Decent Technique in a Pavlovian way.* The high priestess will find herself stand-

---

* Ivan Pavlov (1849–1936) was a Russian psychologist who studied conditioned behaviour. He is famous for his experiment in conditioning dogs to react to a bell. Repeated ritual can work in the same way.

ing at the bridge and the gates, as described in the technique, in the presence of the deity she has been connecting with. In most cases, this will progress so that eventually she feels the presence of the deity standing behind her. She can then allow the deity to possess her at appropriate moment of the Drawing Down the Moon.

There is no reason other trance methods cannot be incorporated into the Wiccan Drawing Down the Moon ritual. Drumming, chanting, and singing are all appropriate methods of inducing trance (see chapter 9). But whatever is decided to be used, the high priestess must be familiar with the effect the trance method has on her; some techniques work better on some people than others. Chants or songs must also be deity-specific whenever and wherever possible. For example, "The Dark Mother Phantom Queen" chant is appropriate for the invocation of Hekate but not Selene who is a "bright" goddess, and is very likely to bring her through regardless of your intentions. It is worth researching or creating specific chants for specific goddesses.

NOTES

1 Sorita d'Este and David Rankine, chap. 10 in *Wicca: Magical Beginnings*, 129–130.

2 Aidan Kelly, chap. 2 in *The Original Gardnerian Documents for the Book of Shadows, Ye Bok of Ye Art Magical (BAM)*, 1993.

3 *The Equinox*, vol. 3, no.1 ("*Blue Equinox*"), 21; *Liber XV* [The Gnostic Mass].

4 Doreen Valiente, personal correspondence with the authors, 1980.

5 *Equinox*, vol. 3, no.1 ("Blue Equinox"), 7; *Liber DCCCXXXVII* [The Law of Liberty].

6 Margot Adler, chap. 7 in *Drawing Down the Moon: Witches, Druids, Goddess Worshippers and Other Pagans in America Today*, 168–169.

7 Ray Buckland, personal e-mail to Gavin Bone, 2004.

8 Angela Zamora, Gardnerian high priestess, Long Island line.

9 Kate Elizabeth Lander, third-degree Alexandrian high priestess.

10 Laura Perry, Wiccan initiate and author.

Chapter 13

Drawing Down the Moon: Its Origins and Practises

Historical evidence for Drawing Down the Moon as a trance technique is quite sparse. Very few sources actually talk specifically about it being used in this way, which leaves a big question as to whether the concept of it as it is known in the neo-Pagan movement is actually valid. Most references seem to relate it to the idea of the moon being involved in sorcery or, in later more critical sources, the ability to actually physically cause the moon to descend to earth. For the most part, they come from later Greco-Roman writers of the first centuries BCE and CE, causing most researchers to assume the ritual's origins are Greek. If Drawing Down the Moon was a genuine trance tradition involving deity assumption and prophecy, then it is necessary to look at the cultures that such a trance tradition would have emerged from rather than any literary sources. We would like to point out that in the following paragraphs, these connections are theoretical on our part, but it does seem to make sense when you look at the cultural origins of the peoples of Greece.

The most compelling evidence for Drawing Down the Moon as a trance tradition is in the cultures that migrated into ancient Greece before the Trojan wars, which are believed to have taken place between the twelfth and eleventh centuries BCE. We believe the most likely origins for any such trance tradition is in the cultures of Southwest Asia, particularly the Scythian/Thracian culture. The Thracians originally inhabited a large area of central and southeastern Europe around the Black Sea. A large region of their settlement included many of the areas that border on what we now know as Greece, including Macedonia, Scythia, and Dacia. The Thracians were later to settle in eastern and central Greece, known as

Thracia (hence the name Thracians). Historically then, Drawing Down the Moon (although this term might not have been used) did not emerge out of Greek culture, but from a separate Indo-European culture—the Thracians.

Peter Levi, in his book *Atlas of the Greek World*, notes "The strange ornaments, the parallel stripes on the woman's head, represent tattooing. Thracian witches who could enchant the moon out of the sky, and the tattooed faces of Thracian women had been proverbial in Athens in the 5th century."[1] Many of the descriptions suggest a shamanic culture borne out by the fact that similar tattooing can be found in the cultures of Southwest Asia, Siberia, and the area around the Black Sea particularly. The "Ice" or "Ukok Princess," as she is known, is a good example. Discovered in 1993 in a burial *kurgan* (mound) in Pazyryk in southwest Siberia, this mummy found in the permafrost was covered in tattoos of animals similar to the ones that have been described as being on the witches of Thracia. The remains also date back to the same period, the fifth century BCE, and were found in an area with a long and ancient tradition of shamanic trance practise, which can be traced back thousands of years. It is important to point out that it is also likely that, rather than being Thracian, she may have been Samartian. The Scythians, Thracians, and Samartians shared a common language and culture. There is also the possibility that seidr or spaewifery and Drawing Down the Moon have origins in central Asian shamanic practises, as it was from this area that those tribes that were later to became known as Teutonic or Germanic pushed west, and many of the Germanic deities, including Odin (Wodenaz) and Freya have origins with these peoples.

It is very likely then that Drawing Down the Moon, as it later became known, was not just a way of empowering spells, as some later Greek and Roman evidence suggests, but a genuine development of shamanism, whose ancient practises would have inevitably influenced neighbouring cultures. Those cultures include the Greeks, and may have also influenced those of Thessaly and possibly even the early practises that took place in Delphi at the cave of Lykorei. The connection between the Thracian witches and the Goddess Bendis is also of importance. She is often portrayed in writings as a Thracian form of the lunar goddess Artemis, and it is believed by some academics that she was imported into Greece by the Thracians, where she evolved into the Goddess Hekate.[2] This is supported by the fact that in prehistory the cult of Bendis-Hekate and her maenads spread alongside the ecstatic god Dionysus-Sabazios to the

Islands of the Thracian Sea (Thassos, Samathraki, and Imraz).[3] This link between Bendis-Hekate and Dionysus-Sabaziso leaves little doubt about the ecstatic trance nature of her cult.

One of the most compelling pieces of evidence for the idea of ancient Drawing Down the Moon being a trance practise does not come from literature but archaeology. A Greek vase from the second century BCE shows what appears to be an illustration of Drawing Down taking place.

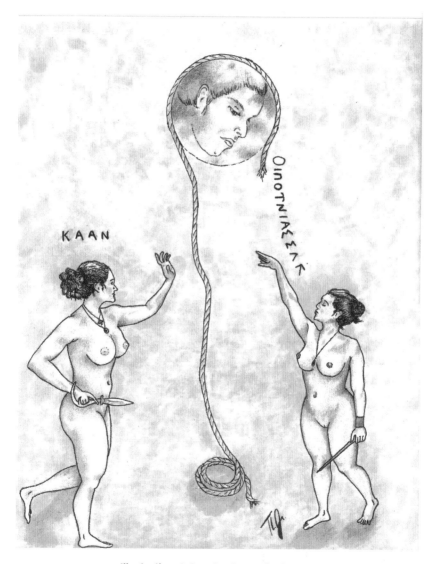

Illustration 4: Drawing Down the Moon

This piece of art is commonly cited as proof that such a practise existed, although this is not conclusive. It shows two priestesses in the act of Drawing Down—one with a wand in her hand on the right, and one with a sword on the left who appears to be saluting a disc with a face—the Moon. What appears to be a rope is draped over it with one end touching the ground. The face on the Moon appears to look at the figure on the right who holds the raised wand. The illustration appears in Margot Adler's book *Drawing Down the Moon: Witches, Druids, Goddess Worshippers and Other Pagans in America Today*.[4] In her article "Greco-Roman Drawing Down the Moon," Myth Woodling suggests the following interpretation of the illustration:

> This depiction has some Greek lettering near both of the figures. As I do not read ancient Greek, I sought the help of someone who could. The word on the left translated as, "beautiful." The words on the right were more difficult to translate. Not all of the handwritten letters were very clear, but apparently translated as, "who [are] of the Moon mistress." Armed with this probable translation, I will speculate about the two figures.
>
> The woman on the left seems to have raised her left palm in salutation to the Moon disk. Did she speak the word, "beautiful," to the Moon disk or to her partner on the right?
>
> The feminine face in the Moon disk gazed directly at the face of the woman on the right. In turn, the woman on the right extended her right hand almost as though trying to touch the Moon disk. Did she speak the words, "who [are] of the Moon mistress"? Or did the spirit of the Moon disk speak through her?
>
> The presence of a rope around the disk is very interesting. It may represent pulling the spirit inhabiting the Moon down out of the sky.
>
> What about the sword and the wand? Both ritual tools were used in magic practiced in the Mediterranean for invoking or evoking spirits, yet neither sword nor wand were being held up.
>
> It is possible this drawing depicts two figures who were performing a rite to draw down the Moon spirit from the sky.
>
> It is also possible that the two women were simply giving adoration to the Moon. Perhaps the Greek inscription referred to the two women. There is no way to be certain.[5]

One of the earliest known references to Drawing Down the Moon dates back to 423 BCE .in a work by Aristophanes. It relates particularly to the witches of Thessaly. He states that "if I could purchase a Thessalian witch, I could make the Moon descend during the night and shut it, like a mirror, into a round box."[6]

One of the most important pieces of evidence that suggests a trance component to Drawing Down comes from a more obscure source of Greco-Egyptian origin, The Fayum Papyri: "If I command the Moon, it will come down; and if I wish to withhold the day, night will linger over my head; and again, if I wish to embark upon the sea, I need no ship, and if I wish to fly through the air, I am free from my own weight."[7]

The first reference by Aristophanes shows no evidence that trance was part of the original Drawing Down the Moon, but was about harnessing its power in spells or potions. The last one though, from The Faylum Papyri does seem to describe an individual in a state of trance. "Night will linger over my head" can be interpreted as a description of being in a trance state, confirmed further by what are descriptions of an out-of-body experience, or astral travel. Aristophanes' description of the use of a mirror in Drawing Down is also of particular interest to anyone doing trance, as it hints at a known method of trance induction still used by modern hypnotists today. Such techniques are important to know if you are going to perform traditional Drawing Down the Moon as a trance-prophecy technique.

As we mentioned at the beginning of this chapter, later sources during the Roman period tend to see Drawing Down the Moon as a delusion at best, and a form of deceit at worst. Horace refers to the Thessalian Witches and Drawing Down in his satirical work *Epodes*,* where a witch called Canidia "spirits away the stars with Thessalian Charms, and steals the Moon from the sky."[8] The same source states that Diana and Proserpina granted these powers to the witches who worshipped them. Of all those who have written about Drawing Down the Moon, Plutarch (46–120 CE) is the most scathing because he is both a follower of Plato's logic and a writer in the later patriarchal period. In both his *Conjugalia Praecepta* and *De Defectu Oraculorum (The Obsolescence of Oracles)*, he makes the following observation: ". . . As the women of Thessaly are said to draw down the Moon. This cunning deceit of theirs, however, gained credence among women when the daughter of Hegetor, Aglaonicê, who

---

* Quintus Horatius Flaccus (8 December 65 BCE–27 November 8 BCE) was a Roman poet famous for his satires.

was skilled in astronomy, always pretended at the time of an eclipse of the Moon that she was bewitching it and bringing it down."[9]

What Plutarch and Horace are commenting on is not the original ancient technique, but the degeneration of the practise in the first century CE within the city states of Rome and Greece. By this time, every soothsayer and fortune teller in Rome, and in some cases even some members of the Roman Senate, were pretending to Draw Down on themselves for either financial or political gain. There is also an obvious misunderstanding by Plutarch, along with others, of what the practise actually entailed, with a literal interpretation being employed—the belief that witches actually thought they could make the physical moon fall from the sky. The true meaning of Drawing Down the Moon, as observed in *The Fayum Papyri*, is ignored, perhaps out of expediency. If the genuine trance tradition that emerged out of Southwest Asia into Greece and finally into the Italian peninsula, survived, it was among the olive groves of the pagans—the people of the countryside whose practises were scorned by the city dwellers. What became known as Drawing Down the Moon would have been practiced secretly, while the evolved practises of the sibyls continued to be accepted within later Greek and Roman culture, as they could be controlled politically by a patriarchal culture (see page 12 on the Apollonian priesthood). This is what some modern Witches claim, including both Wiccan and modern Strega (Italian Witches), suggested in what was one of the most important books in the revival of Witchcraft, Charles Godfrey Leland's *Aradia: The Gospel of the Witches*.

We personally do not believe that Leland's *Aradia* can be taken as a valid source for the ancient practise of Drawing Down the Moon, for several reasons. The primary reason is that its providence is suspect; there is no evidence it is a piece of genuine ancient literature.* Serious questions remain concerning whether it is genuine, and this is still debated among Wiccan historians, including Professor Ronald Hutton and others.† According to Leland, it originated from a woman called

---

* There are two other reasons we cannot cite *Aradia* as evidence of a traditional form of Drawing Down the Moon. The first one is that even if it is genuine, the material in it only goes back as far as the thirteenth and fourteenth centuries and cannot be considered an ancient source for the practise. Secondly, and more importantly, although there is reference to the moon and Diana within the manuscript, there is no reference to the term Drawing Down the Moon within it nor a description of any trance technique.

† Ronald Hutton discusses three theories on the origins of *Aradia* in his book *Triumph of the Moon* (1999), pp. 144–147, including: a) that it is the survival of a goddess cult, b) that it Maddalena concocted it to dupe Leland, and c) that Leland fraudulently created it.

"Maddalena Talenti," who relayed the contents to him in 1886. She claimed to be from a traditional Italian witchcraft family. According to Maddalena, it was part of an older manuscript called *Il Vangelo* ("Gospel"). The resultant manuscript, which Leland published as *Aradia* in 1889, also included his own researched material. Regardless of its origin, one cannot ignore the effective incorporation of Leland's work into the modern practise of Drawing Down the Moon, particularly the Wiccan Charge, but there is little in it that can be used in the reconstruction of the ancient technique.

Traditional Techniques: Using the Mirror

In 1996 at an event in Wisconsin, we decided, for the first time, to publically reenact Drawing Down the Moon using a traditional technique. On a full moon evening with a gathering of over 150 people in the circle, Janet stood arms raised, with the moon high and behind her head. Gavin kneeled before her and invoked the Goddess Diana into her using a silver bowl to reflect the light of the moon into Janet's face. He tilted the bowl up and down, effectively "strobing" the moonlight into her eyes. This was, of course, a hypnotic induction technique, and was dramatically effective. Janet was and is very familiar with Drawing Down the Moon from her experience over the years of using the Wiccan ritual, but this was far more powerful. Diana manifested within Janet; there was no Charge spoken but a few well-spoken words before Diana insisted on walking around all of those gathered in the ritual circle, so that she could personally prophesize to them. In nearly all cases, she (Diana) spoke in rhyming meter, rather than in a normal fashion. As we discovered later, her prophecies were about 95 percent accurate. Gavin was very concerned for Janet's well-being during this possession, and he had good reason. After Gavin asked Diana politely to leave Janet's body, she collapsed like a rag doll. Clearly this was a different experience to what we, and many of those present, had come to expect with Drawing Down the Moon. Janet had previously been used to "withdrawing" into the back of her head as the Goddess spoke through her, but in this ritual she not only withdrew but also completely tranced out. Afterwards, she had only fragmented memories of what had happened. It was clear to us after this that something was missing within the Wiccan ritual; what had happened to Janet as a priestess was more akin to the Vodoun experience of being "ridden," as several participants of the rite later pointed out, and fell outside of the normal training we had both received within the Western Tradition.

It was this experience that led us to examine contemporary traditions and the subject of trance states in more depth.

The origins of this particular ritual go back to Gavin's involvement with a group on the edge of the New Forest in the early 1990s, which was run by a gentleman named Ron Hill. He received an initiation from Sybil Leek when she was living in Ringwood. It was he who gave a polished silver bowl to Gavin and his magical partner, saying that one day he would understand what it was used for. This does suggest that perhaps the use of the mirror or silver bowl for Drawing Down the Moon was not unknown to the Witches of the 1950s and 1960s who worked in the area of the New Forest. The use of the mirror to Draw Down the Moon, as we have previously mentioned, is ancient and probably originated from the trance-inducing effect of looking at the full moon reflected in a pool of water or a well. The myths of prophetic priestesses who dwell at wells acting as oracles is well known throughout ancient Europe, the most prominent example being the holy well at Glastonbury, associated with Morgan le Fay. In Ireland, holy wells are still venerated as places of prophecy and manifestation of the Female Divine in the form of the Madonna. The use of wells to trance and find hidden knowledge is prominent in Norse myth when Odin hangs from the World Tree (Yggdrasil) in search of the runes and spies them in the Well of Urd (Wyrd), the Norse sacred spring of fate.[10] The runes are, of course, a system of divination in their own right, so there is a divine symmetry in the runes being found in a well of prophecy. While in Northern Europe it seemed to rely on natural phenomena, in the ancient world of the Mediterranean, reflective surfaces such as mirrors seemed to be preferred. The connection between them and Drawing Down the Moon is well recorded, as we have shown with the previous quote by Aristophanes at the beginning of this chapter. Although we and others believe that the Goddess was historically invoked in this way, whether that is correct is irrelevant when it comes to the actual technique, which can be reconstructed. What is indisputable is that as a technique of trance and method of manifesting deities, it is highly effective.

The use of a reflective surface to invoke visions or deity is a form of trance-induction. In method it differs very little from the use of a swinging shiny object, such as a traditional pocket watch, often used in movies with hypnosis scenes. The technique we describe here is really for more advanced practitioners, as it relies on the priestess being susceptible to hypnotic induction. This does, of course, develop naturally and is a side effect of regular use of trance techniques (see chapter 6, "Long- and Short-Term Side Effects of Trance States"). The technique combines both ritual and trance induction, although the emphasis is obviously on the latter, with the ritual purpose being to invoke deity into the priestess, just as in the Wiccan Drawing Down the Moon (see chapter 12). This technique not only requires the use of moonlight for it to work but also has strong associations with the moon historically. That means that it can only be done at specific times of the month, hence the statement "better it be when the Moon is full" in the Wiccan "Charge of the Goddess" (see Appendix I). It would also make it very inappropriate to invoke anything other than a lunar deity, such as Diana, Selene, Aradia, Hekate, and Proserpina, as is done in the Wiccan Drawing Down the Moon, which is used to invoke any specific goddess with which the high priestess connects.

The invocation, as we explain later, makes it specifically suitable to bring through Diana Triformis. Many neo-Pagans are familiar with this goddess through Robert Graves' White Goddess. She is the blueprint for the neo-Pagan concept of the Maid, Mother, and Crone Goddess, with Diana Triformis being historically the only true Triple Goddess who takes these forms. Her origins are with Diana of Nemi, or Diana of the Woods, who although being of Etruscan origin was merged with the Hellenic Artemis by the Romans, and later with Hekate, according to Andreas Alföld:

> The Latin Diana was conceived as a threefold unity of the divine huntress, the Moon goddess, and the goddess of the nether world, Hekate. This mixture was not a contamination of later imperial syncretism . . . The mighty goddess of the dead, Hekate is invoked by Vergil as tergemina Hekate, tria virginis ora Dianae[11] . . . is addressed by Horace as diva triformis (triple goddess). Vergil calls Diana as well as Hekate the Trivia.[12]

The works of Horace suggest that Diva Triformis, the Triple Goddess, was not unknown to the Greeks who had settled on the Italian peninsula centuries earlier, making her possibly pre-Roman in origin. The fusion of Persephone and Proserpina was inevitable due to the cross-cultural exchange between the Latin tribes and the Greek colonists, creating a spring goddess who ascends from the underworld every year. The same was true of the fusion of the Greek Artemis, the Etruscan Diana, and the ancient Latin Selene, which created the lunar Mother Goddess. Combined with Hekate, these fusions created Diana Triformis. All the necessary cultural elements were present to create the archetypal Maid/ Mother/Crone Goddess, which became dominant in later Roman culture and was later adopted into modern Paganism via Robert Graves.

The invocation we use in our reconstruction of the ancient Drawing Down the Moon ritual is based on a traditional prayer to Selene found in a pre-fourth century CE text.[13] It has been edited here for use as an invocation to the previously mentioned Diana Triformis—Prosperina, Selene, and Hekate—as all three are mentioned in the prayer. It is, therefore, important to remember that any of these deities could manifest during the trance-induction. As we mentioned (in chapter 12), some elements of this prayer were clearly incorporated into the original Wiccan Drawing Down the Moon. Unlike the Wiccan Charge, the words are spoken by the priest or priestess as trance guide, rather than by the person who is having the Moon drawn down upon them.

Unlike Wiccan Drawing Down the Moon, which requires a polarity of male and female in the ritual process, this is not really required in the traditional form. There are plenty of references from ancient Greece where trance techniques only involved women (Illustration 4), so there is no reason why a priestess should not invoke the Moon down on another acting as the trance guide. All that is important is that the person assuming this role is aware of what they are doing. As we have previously mentioned, other techniques can also be incorporated, such as drumming and chanting (see chapter 9). In the ritual, we decided to use the "Dark Mother Phantom Queen Chant" to both invoke the deity (Hekate) and encourage the priestess to go into trance, but this chant can be used for any goddess with dark or underworld aspects. When it comes to drumming, we would recommend only one drummer, keeping a steady hypnotic beat.

Drawing Down the Moon Using Traditional Techniques

The first requirement of this ritual is that it should be done on the night of a full moon, outside, and in clear weather. It requires a minimum of two people to perform the rite—one to act as the invoker—either a priestess or a priest (taking the role of the trance guide, see page 94)—and the other to have Diana Triformis invoked upon them—a priestess (taking the role of the seer, see page 84). At least two torches or garden flares and a fire, contained in a brazier (traditionally three-legged) or similar will also be needed. The whole ritual should be performed so that the priestess who is to have the Goddess invoked upon her is standing with the moon above her head. The two torches should be set up on either side of where the priestess will be standing, for safety reasons, at least three feet on either side of her. The fire/brazier should be in front of her—again, for safety reasons, at least three feet from her.

The traditional offerings, which are to be placed on the fire/brazier toward the end of the rite, consist of storax, frankincense, and myrrh. Fruit is also a traditional offering and should be placed in a basket next to the fire/brazier at the appropriate moment during the rite. One ritual tool that is of vital importance is, of course, the bowl. Some experimentation should be done to find the most suitable one to use. We have found that a large steel mixing bowl that has been highly polished is just as effective as an ornate silver one. The concave nature of the bowl is important—it must be able to collect and focus the light of the moon into the face of the priestess. A large round mirror can also be used and is just as effective as a polished metal bowl.

All those attending the rite (including the participants) should, if possible, wear white robes. The exception may be the priestess, who may want to consider an appropriate colour for her robe; if invoking a specific aspect of Diana Triformis: red for Proserpina, white for Selene, and black for Hekate (another option may be green for Proserpina and red for Hekate depending on how you use Goddess correspondences).

The rite should start with the casting of the circle and calling of the quarters. This can be done either in Wiccan fashion or traditional Greek. It should be performed by the invoking priest or priestess in their role as trance guide.

The Rite

(For the benefit of the reader and to prevent confusion, we are using the term "priest" to define the role of trance guide in this rite.)

The priestess stands between the two lit torches, ensuring the moon is centrally placed above her head. The priest stands before her, holding the polished bowl, the fire/brazier between them.

The priestess raises her arms and says:

> *We stand at the crossroads, at the triple way, three paths before us woven by the Moerai since the beginning of time.*
> *We stand at the gates of choice and ask for the guidance of you the three faced, three-aspected Goddess*

who has walked these paths from time immemorial.
I am prepared for you. I call upon you.
I am waiting for you, my Great Goddess.

The priest kneels, raises the bowl to collect the light of the moon, and reflects it into the face of the priestess. He gently tilts the bowl backwards and forwards so that the light strobes into her eyes. (At this stage the priestess may wish to open her chakras; see page 128). As the moonlight begins to affect the priestess and place her in trance, the priest begins the invocation to the Goddess:

Come to me, O beloved mistress, three-faced
Hekate, Selene, Persephone; kindly hear my sacred chants;
Night's ornament, young, bringing light to mortals,
O Child of Morn who ride upon the Fierce Bulls,
O Queen who drive your chariot on equal course with Helios.
Who with the Triple Forms of Triple Graces dance and revels with
    the Stars.

You are Justice and the Moirai's threads: Klotho, Lachesis and Atropos.
Three-headed, you are Persephone, Megaira, and Alleketo.
Multiformed, you carry in your hands the dreaded, murky lamps.
You shake your fearful serpent locks, while from your mouth comes
    the sound of the roar of bulls.

With the eyes of bulls, the voice of dogs;
You hide in the form of a lion, a wolf.
You are surrounded by the fierce dogs that are dear to you.
You are Hekate, Menae, Goddess of the lunar year.

You cleave the air with your arrows like Artemis; Persephone,
the shooter of Deer.
Shining in the night and triple named, triple-faced, triple-voiced
Goddess of the triple Ways; Selene.
In triple baskets your eternal sacred flames burn,
lighting the triple way that you so oft frequent,
ruling the years of man and god.

We ask you to be gracious and kind.

Photograph 10: Drawing Down the Moon in Wicca. Janet and Stewart (Farrar) with their coven in Drogheda, Ireland 1984.

Listen to our requests, you who protect the three realms;
the spirits of the night quake in fear before your power;
even the immortal gods tremble before your many names;
you are the goddess who raises men to their heights.

You are the mother of gods and men. Of nature and all things.
You travel between all three realms; of man, of god, and of the dead.
You [are] the Alpha and the Omega;
from you all things come, and from you all things return.
You are eternity manifest; holder of Great Kronos' scepter.
You balance both order and chaos, in your great scales.

The priest pauses, lays down the bowl. He then makes the offering of fruit next to the fire and sprinkles the incense onto it. He signals to those gathered together in the circle to start drumming and chanting, while circling himself and the Priestess: "the Dark Mother, Phantom Queen Chant (*Dark Mother, Phantom Queen, Hear us call you*)." They continue to drum and chant as the priest again kneels and continues the invocation:

O child of Zeus; Persephone, Selene, Hekate,
accept this offering of spice, O heavenly one, O goddess of crossroads.
Come down from the mountains; come to us from the three realms;
Goddess of order and chaos, goddess of day and night.
Accept our sacrifices, quell vicious Cerberus and meet us, your children
at the crossroads on this moonlit night.

The priest, still kneeling, signals the group to stop circling and chanting and allow the Goddess to speak through the priestess. If she wishes to walk around the circle, he should stand and dutifully accompany her, holding her hand. He should stay by her side until she has finished speaking. If in his role as a trance guide the priest believes that she is staying too long in the priestess, he may politely point this out to the goddess (it is very likely that she will insist on finishing what she is doing before leaving). After the goddess leaves, it is important the priestess grounds and closes down; the priest should ensure that this is done. He should also check all of the other participants of the ritual. In our experience, a successful Drawing Down using this method releases a great deal of energy, and the circle can become highly charged emotionally due to the impact of the goddess' messages. (For more on closing and grounding, see page 129.)

NOTES

1 Levi is actually sourcing Herodotus (V.6) who said: "It was in special favour with the women, and the more nobly born they were, the richer and brighter coloured were the designs they used. Agathyrsi painted both their faces and their limbs with indelible designs (distinctive tribal marks), while the nobles also died their hair blue."

2 Lewis Richard Farnell, *The Cults of the Greek States* (Oxford: Clarendon Press, 1896).

3 Carol M. Mooney, *Hekate: Her Role and Character in Greek Literature from before the Fifth Century* (McMaster University, 1971), 8.

4 In all editions, the illustration can be found on the opening pages of the book with the following description: "Drawing down the moon: one of the few known depictions of this ancient ritual, from a Greek vase probably of the second century b.c.e. (New York Public Library)."

5 Drawing Down the Moon, from www.aradiagoddess.com.

6 From his comedy *The Clouds*. Aristophanes (446 BCE–386 BCE) was a playwright known as the "father of comedy."

7 From *The Fayum Papyri, A Papyrus Describing Magical Powers* (University of Michigan). Also known as the *Rainer Papyri*, a collection of pagan, Christian, and Arabic manuscripts found in Egypt in 1880. Material in the documents dates back as far as 250 BCE.

8 Horace, *Epode V: The Witch's Incantations.*

9 Plutarch, *De Defecto Oraculorum,* Section 13F, vol. 5, Loeb Classical Library Edition (1936).

10 From "Lay of the High One," the Prose Edda, stanzas 138–141.

11 *The Aeneid*, 4.511.

12 Andreas Alfodi, "Diana Nemorensis," *American Journal of Archaeology*, vol. 64, no. 2 (1960), 140. Originally translated from the Greek by E. N. O'Neil from the *Papyri Graccae Magicae*, 2785–2890. Published in book form by Hans Dieter Betz as *The Greek Magical Papyri in Translation* (University of Chicago, 1985).

13 Hans Dieter Betz, trans., *The Greek Magical Papyri in Translation* (University of Chicago, 1985).

Chapter 14

Ecstatic Ritual and the Sacred Procession: The Gods Entering through Dance, Drumming, and Singing

Ecstatic ritual involving dancing and drumming has always been an essential part of the magical practises of pagan and earth-based traditions, not just in Europe but also throughout the world. We have been lucky to be present at such ceremonies held by the *sangoma*, the traditional healers of South Africa; various Native American tribes; and the Cori (aborigines) of Australia. The patterns of their practises, as is common with all ecstatic rituals, probably date back well before humans left Africa. In modern traditions such as Vodoun and Santeria, these core elements are still present, just as they were among the Bacchanalian and Dionysian cults of Greece and Rome. They can also be found in some of the rituals of modern Witchcraft, as many practitioners seek to incorporate such traditional methods.

Ritual, which focuses on using dancing, drumming, and even intoxicants to encourage the connection to the divine by entering into an ecstatic or changed mental state, is commonly referred to as *Dionysian*. This term has a usage going back to classical times, but its use was first popularised by J. J. Bachofen, a Swiss anthropologist, and later on by Friedrich Nietzsche, whom we discuss more fully later. Several Pagan authors have introduced the term into common use in connection to ritual. Most prominent has been Wiccan high priestess Vivianne Crowley in her book *Wicca: The Old Religion in the New Age*. In the introduction she states: "The World of Wicca is the world of what Bachofen and later Nietzsche called 'Dionysiac truth'; truth which is intuitive and non-verbal; truth which is communicated through symbols and myth."[1]

Ecstatic ritual, which induces a change in mental state through drumming, dancing, and intoxicants, becomes the ultimate expression of this "Dionysiac truth."[2] These techniques take the participant directly to the divine root of these nonverbal symbols through the ecstatic experience of trance and, in some cases, result in possession by divinity itself. With the exception of a few groups, most Wiccan covens only use dancing in the form of the traditional circle dance to "The Witches' Rune," which is only used to raise energy rather than to allow its participants to enter a trance state. This ecstatic state is often reserved for the high priestess during the ritual of Drawing Down the Moon (see chapter 12). This is not the case in many native traditions, such as those of the Indian subcontinent, or the African diaspora traditions, such as Vodoun, where many of the Vodouisants (participants), may be ridden (possessed) by the loa. Any modern practitioner who wishes to understand ecstatic ritual can learn much from studying such contemporary traditions.

A good example of contemporary ecstatic practise that combines several techniques can be found among the Harasiddhi priests of Kathmandu in Nepal. Here a *puja* (festival) to the goddess Durga, one of the Indian mother goddesses, takes place every year on the April full moon, as it has for centuries. It is even recorded in the ancient chronicles of Nepal. To quote an article by Hamid Sadar on the website Asian Art: "Manifestations of the Mother Goddess and her retinue of deities possess the dancers, intoxicated on sacrificial blood and alcohol. A hypnotic musical score, punctuated by symbolic gestures accompanies the spectacle whose secret meanings remain closed to the non-initiate."[3]

Apart from the obvious use of music, dancing, and alcohol, several other methods are also incorporated into the ritual to prepare for and induce trance. The priests go through a prolonged period of abstinence and fasting, before donning the large hypnotic-eyed sacred masks and commencing a period of prayer and chanting. This is all done collectively while sitting in a circle surrounding a large clay pot filled with water, which is adorned by a silver headdress believed to contain the essence of the goddess Durga. At midnight, the pot is taken into the center of the village, ready for the ceremony to begin in earnest. It commences with ten of the masked priests emerging to the sound of drums and pipes into the courtyard carrying swords, and dancing as if possessed by the spirits of the ten directions, which they represent. They pound the earth with their feet, while whirling around brandishing their swords in a ritual to subdue the earth. The music steadily increases in tempo and reaches a beat that induces trance in the masked participants, who emerge from the temple and commence to dance down the streets of the village. Each masked priest in this drama represents a god or goddess, and during the processional ritual each is offered *ayla,* a powerful liquor made of grain and sacred herbs, which clearly has trance-inducing effects.* According to Hamid Sadar, "the concoction has a sweet flowery taste and after several bowls I feel a strong burning energy rising in my navel. A few more, and I feel invincible enough to try the raw buffalo meat and jellied blood . . ."

At different times along the route, the procession stops as the masked priests each reach the dedicated altars belonging to their possessing god or goddess. Here the villagers venerate the deity by making offerings of rice, money, and *sindhura* (a red powder representing menstrual blood of the Goddess), sprinkled over each possessed priest. This ritual continues through the early hours of the morning until midday, at which point the priests stop for a break. They then continue on into the evening, as the revellers begin to also partake of the ayla. It might seem strange that we used a practise from Nepal as an example in a book on European ecstatic tradition, but similar ecstatic processional practises not only exist throughout the world, but once also existed throughout Europe. The memory of such practises can still be found in processions of the Madonna in the Roman Catholic culture of the Mediterranean, and in the traditional folk processions found in the British Isles.

Sacred Procession as an Intrinsic Part of Traditional Ecstatic Ritual

Many of the old ecstatic festivals of Europe, such as Madonna processions, were tamed under Christianity, thus losing their more ecstatic aspects. The church continued such traditions in order to maintain control and rid them of their pagan origins. Good examples of this can be found in English folk traditions such as the Abbotts Bromley Horn Dance in Staffordshire, where the horns hang in the church to this day. New myths were even created to separate those traditions from their ecstatic pagan origins, and they were often connected with royalty or the establishment of rights given by them. For example, the previously mentioned Horn Dance is now said to mark the hunting rights granted to local families

---

* The inclusion of ayla in this section is incidental and given purely for anthropological reasons. We highly recommend those practising ecstatic ritual avoid the use of hallucinogens and psychedelics, as their effects, apart from being unpredictable, can also affect the participant negatively both in the short and longer term (see the introduction and chapter 9).

in the sixteenth century. In recent years, many of these festivals have begun to reclaim their pagan heritage. This is certainly true of annual Beltane Jack-in-the-Green Festival in Hastings, which is said historically to mark the restoration of King Charles II. We have been lucky enough to participate in this festival and watch as it reclaims its ecstatic nature (see Photograph 11). This festival follows a very similar pattern to the rites that take place in Kathmandu as the processional winds through the small streets of the seaside town. Drumming, the compulsory wearing of masks, chanting, and singing are all part of this sacred journey of the sacrificial "Jack," a crowned figure made of leaves. The procession even includes stopping to imbibe intoxicants, although in the case of this rite, drinking consists of nothing more than downing copious amount of ale rather than anything hallucinogenic. Upon reaching the altar—the stage in the grounds of Hastings Castle, "Jack" takes his final dance before being torn apart in frenzied mock sacrifice. His leaves are then distributed amongst the crowd to bring luck. Such sacred processions are, in fact, an essential part of ecstatic ritual, as we unexpectedly discovered while researching this chapter, possibly because they have truly ancient origins.

By its very nature, the sacred ecstatic procession is archetypal, part of the common shared human experience. They can be found in almost every culture around the world. In the Hindu-Tamil Thaipusam Festival found in Thailand, Singapore, Malaysia, and Myanamar, the participants practise the *Kavadi* trance tradition.* During the sacred procession, the participants skewer their bodies so that they can hold weights (see Photograph 12), thus inducing trance through pain. A similar practise that uses pain can be found in Spain among the Roman Catholic penitents taking part in the Easter week Los Picaos procession in San Vicente de la Sonsierra, where flagellation and skin cutting are common practises amongst the masked *disciplinante*. Both of these are, of course, extreme practises, but less extreme ones exist throughout the world and throughout time.

---

* Also known as Thai-Pusa, this festival takes place on the full moon month of Thai (January/February). *Pusa* or *Pusam* refers to a particular star, which reaches its highest point during this time. The celebration commemorates the giving of a spear by Parvati (a trance goddess) to the hero Murugan to vanquish the demon Soorapadman.

Photo by Thomas Smith

Photograph 11: The traditional Hastings Jack-in-the Green Festival, which takes place every Beltane (May 1), has all the hallmarks of a surviving ecstatic ritual, including a mock sacrifice of "Jack."
(Courtesy www.dreamstime.com)

In ancient Europe, similar processions can be found among the adherents of the Great Mother cults—the cults of Cybele, Isis, and Artemis—which took place throughout the Roman Empire; the origins of the previously mentioned processions of the Madonna. There may have even been a ritual procession to the sacred cave at Lykorei, the memory of which has now been lost. In Meso-America, there is evidence of processional routes at Nazca, famous for its pictograms, which can only be viewed properly from the air. The more recent routes in Mexico and Central America, which have origins with the Mayans and Aztecs, are still in use to this day by local shamans. Archaeologists have discovered processional routes going back thousands of years throughout the world. In England, they can be found at Stonehenge and Avebury, and in Ireland going from Rathcroghan,* in County Roscommon, to Uisneach in Westmeath, all of which probably hosted similar ecstatic processions before falling into

---

* Tulsk, County Roscommon, is a complex of sites including Oweynagat ("Cave of the Cat"), Cashel Mannannan, and Cruachan, dating back more than five thousand years. Archaeologists discovered a wooden pathway between these sites and Uisneach approximately 55 kilometres to the east.

disuse thousands of years ago.* Memories of such processions survived
into the Middle Ages and beyond in the Christian pilgrimages to the Holy
Land, and to the shrines of saints, so vividly described by Geoffrey Chau-
cer in his *Canterbury Tales*. Some processions continue today, such as the
annual pilgrimage to Croag Patrick in Ireland[†] and Lourdes in France,[‡]
which follow this same sacred pattern.

The abundance of sacred processional routes and the traditions associated with them can be rationalized with several possible explanations:
they represent the journey of life, the journey of the seasons through the
Wheel of the Year, or even the movement of the sun, moon, and stars
across the heavens. But what is often missed in such explanations is their
psychological effect. What struck us more than anything else when we
attended the Jack-in-the-Green Festival in Hastings was the atmosphere—
the smiling faces and a noticeable ecstatic feel in the air. This was not necessarily due to the constant drumming or downing several pints of beer,
but because shared experience of the journey itself has a psychological
effect on the individual. He becomes part of the group, the crowd, driven
by the excitement for the journey. We all feel this excitement when we
are young, whether it is the promised visit to Disneyland or somewhere
more exotic. Our heart pumps faster, and our senses become more acute
as we start our quest. This reaction comes from somewhere deeper, a
past memory in our shared collective consciousness. Perhaps it goes back
to the first journeys of humankind, the first migrations of humans out of
Africa, crossing the land bridge into the Americans, or the journey northwest into Europe. This psychological need to make the Sacred Journey
resulted in creation of myths because its pull is so strong. Many revolve
around the concept of the archetypal hero figure: Odysseus in Homer's
The Odyssey, Galahad in *The Quest for the Holy Grail*, and in contemporary culture the heroes and heroines of *Star Trek* and *Star Wars*. Such individual journeys result in a change in consciousness and spiritual growth:

---

* In myths, Uisneach in Westmeath is considered to be the center of Ireland. It is associated with the festival of Bealtaine, and consists of a set of Bronze Age monuments
and earthworks spread over two square kilometres.

† Procession to the top of Croagh Patrick Mountain, County Mayo, began at least
five thousand years and was originally sacred to the sacrificial corn god Crom Dubh.
St. Patrick is said to have fasted for forty days in 441 CE. His annual procession takes
place on Reek Sunday, the last Sunday in July.

‡ Sacred pilgrimages to Lourdes in the mid-Pyrenees go back the apparition of the
Virgin Mary in 1858. It is well known for its miraculous cures.

Photograph 12: Thaipusa devotees allow themselves to be skewered and hooked so they can hold not only fruit and weights but also elaborate bamboo designs. Taken at the Thaimpusam Festival, Little India, Singapore.
(Courtesy www.dreamstime.com)

we become our own hero or heroine as we become part of our own *monomyth* story.[4] This is typified by the Journey of the Fool in the Tarot.*

Many modern Pagans go on such sacred journeys or quests as part of their practise.† Sometimes this can be to an ancient site they have never visited, or a site specific to a deity they worship. Many we have talked to describe the anticipation before they leave, and a small group describe having synchronistic experiences resulting in a feeling of being "high"—they enter an ecstatic state. This is perhaps the reason for the development of the sacred procession, to relive this experience of gnosis—connection to the divine through the ecstatic state.

This experience is aptly described by one of our own initiate's experiences after she went on a sacred pilgrimage to connect with her patron goddess:

> When embarking on my own personal pilgrimage, to trace the footsteps of my goddess, I became aware, almost from the moment I left home, that I had stepped foot into the otherworld.

* The Journey of the Fool is the cycle through the Major Arcana starting with card 0, The Fool, and ending with card XXI, The World. It is the sacred journey of life itself.

† See M. Macha NightMare, *Pagan Pride: Honoring the Craft of Earth and Goddess* (Citadel: 2004).

Signs, symbols, and omens so littered my sacred landscape that it
became easy to take them for granted. Every soul that I spoke to,
spoke with the voices of the gods and the fae. I ate, drank, and
sang with them, immersing myself further and further in to the
euphoria of the journey. The hardest part was returning back to
this reality, one week and two thousand miles later. It was like
experiencing a grieving process. In truth, there is a part of me
that will never return.[5]

It is this type of quest and the ecstatic effect that it has on the individual that could perhaps be relived through the sacred procession and
ecstatic ritual in general.

The Swing Between Nietzsche's Concepts of Dionysian and Apollonian

As we have shown, the combined use of music, dancing, fasting, and intoxicants is clearly a major factor in creating and working ecstatic ritual.
This also seemed to be the case in ancient times in the rites of (the god)
Dionysus, which we explore later in this chapter. As Vivianne Crowley
states, Wicca (and modern Witchcraft in general) is a *Dionysian* religion,[6]
although we would argue that there has been more of a swing in recent
years toward Dionysian from Wicca's more *Apollonian*-structured aspects.
It is important to really look at Nietzsche and the history of Wicca to understand why this move from Apollonian to Dionysian ritual is occurring
in modern Witchcraft. Nietzsche is most often credited with expanding
the meaning of the terms Apollonian and Dionysian, even though this polar concept can be traced as far back as Plutarch. Nietzsche first uses the
terms in his work *The Birth of Tragedy*.[7] In his classic work, he explores
the two concepts as they evolved in Greek theatre, specifically tragedy,
ritual, and music. He also points out that in any culture, the two were
always in conflict, but never able to completely subdue the other. This
marks a swing between them, resulting in a natural balance: "Wherever
the Dionysian prevailed, the Apollonian was checked and destroyed. . . .
[W]herever the first Dionysian onslaught was successfully withstood, the
authority and majesty of the Delphic god Apollo exhibited itself as more
rigid and menacing than ever."[8]

He believed it was this conflict within any culture, and their natural
balancing of each other, that results in the creation of the dramatic arts.
They were principally religious in nature, and resulted in the eventual
creation of theatre as we know it today. He particularly points to the

works of Aeschylus and Sophocles, which seem to be the bedrock of his theory.

Named after Apollo, the god of social order, art, music, and the sun, Nietzsche's concept of the Apollonian governs thinking, self-control, the rational and the logical, social order and culture, personal appearance, etc. In Apollonian, it is the individual who is the artist, and who creates visible art for all to see, and who celebrates man's creation of art and culture. Nietzsche's Dionysian principle is named after the god of wine and intoxication, Dionysus, who holds the juxtaposition, representing feeling, passion, emotion, the instinctual and, obviously, the psychic; chaos opposed to the Apollonian order; intoxication; the wholeness of existence; and the celebration of nature, which includes both its wildness and brutality. In the Dionysian, man is the work of art, created by nature.

This balance of the two and the swing between them can be seen in the types of magic found both in ancient and modern Pagan practise (see Illustration 5: The Nietzchian Ritual Scale). Apollonian and Dionysian can be seen as two polarities that magical practise swings between, often portrayed symbolically in neo-Pagan ritual as the balance between masculine and feminine, or Sun God and Moon Goddess. Modern ceremonial ritual magic is structured with a system of degrees, a hierarchy, and an ordered and established methodology to ritual. This clearly makes ceremonial ritual magic principally Apollonian, although for the magic

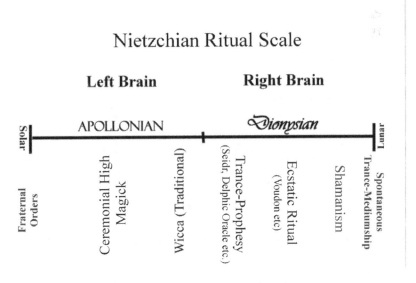

Illustration 5: Nietzchian Ritual Scale

to be fruitful, elements of the Dionysian must also be present. This is clearly something Aleister Crowley realised and imported in the rites of the OTO, specifically his sexual rites. There are very few magical traditions that are purely Apollonian or Dionysian, with the exception of the exclusively Apollonian rites of such organisations as Freemasonry, which yield no magical energy as a result. The opposite on the scale is *Dionysia*—spontaneous ecstatic trance such as in the case of solitary mediumship or trance-possession.

Just as Aleister Crowley realised this element is necessary in ceremonial magic, ancient Dionysian traditions realised a certain degree of Apollonian structure is necessary. In the ancient revelries of the Bacchanalia and the rites of Dionysus, this is demonstrated by the need for a priesthood (such as the Maenads) to conduct the rituals even though it is a Dionysian ritual in the Nietzschian sense. The Maenads create a ritual structure, with specific chants, invocations, and dances that allow the ecstatic elements to function unhindered, without which it ceases to be a ritual and deteriorates into intoxicated chaos.

Modern Witchcraft (Wicca), with its ritual origins in high magic, was principally Apollonian when it started, but even in the 1950s it carried more elements of the Dionysian than Crowley's OTO, which many of its rituals certainly derived from historically. The cultural taboos, norms, and values of that period prevented a full swing toward the Dionysian principle, which is inherent in a nature-based religion such as Witchcraft. Certainly, there was ritual nudity, open sex within covens, dancing, and revelry, but these seem to have been short-lived, and by the 1960s it had begun to swing back more toward the Apollonian. An example of this can be seen in the rise of the Alexandrian Tradition, which based nearly all its magical practise on ceremonial high magic. Changes occurred again by the end of the 1960s and beginning of the 1970s when feminist and Dionysian influences began to rise. We have attended at least one ritual by a well-known high priestess of that time period; she performed a Dionysian-style ritual using drumming and dancing without any structure. The result was a total inability to control or direct any raised magical energy whatsoever.

Camille Paglia is another writer who uses the terms in her book *Sexual Personae* (1981). Her book was so controversial that she failed to get published until 1990. For Paglia, the Dionysian is dark and chthonic; by nature feminine, it is a force of chaos; wild, unbridled lust; and procreation. The Apollonian is reality, clarity, reason, etc. Although principally no different from Nietzsche's viewpoint, she sees them as being the basis of the "battle of the sexes," the male Apollonian need to control nature and, therefore, woman—the archetype of the Apollonian priesthood. The Dionysian is the revolutionary nature of femininity and Nature, which refuses to be controlled—the archetype of the wild Maenads. Modern Witchcraft presently finds itself at crossroads as it swings between Nietzsche's and Paglia's concepts of Apollonian and Dionysian.

Energy Waves in Ecstatic Ritual

Anyone who has attended a full ecstatic ritual will tell you that an interesting phenomena regarding the energy occurs. What is noticeable is that energy rises and falls in waves, with drumming, dancing, and singing reaching a crescendo, tailing off for a period, and then building to a crescendo again. Each time, it is noticeable that the tailing off of energy lessens. This can be likened to the waves that occur in *ultradian rhythms* (see page 135), with the periods of slow drumming and dancing occurring during the same time as the alpha cycle in the human brain. In traditional Vodoun rituals, these periods are seen as opportunities to invoke or recognise any loa or deities who have manifested in the dancers. The same can be applied to the ecstatic ritual we describe here. Like trance-prophecy, we have seen participants possessed by European deities they work with during such rites. Much like a Vodoun ceremony, it is important not to interrupt the main ritual. The drumming should continue unbroken except in real emergencies. If participants do get into trouble, which is not uncommon, as these are intense rituals, it is the role of the priesthood to deal with it. For this reason, we recommend that there be appointed guardians or vibes watchers to deal with any emergencies such as the potential negative side effects from trance.[9]

The Dionysian Feast—Creating an Ecstatic Trance Ritual

We conducted the following ritual in July 2010 in Tuscany with our Italian Wiccan Study Group. It was created to give the group an experience of Dionysian, as opposed to Apollonian, ritual, which they were used to. It is given here as an example of how to create and conduct such a ritual. Because this ritual was created for an Italian group, it was natural to give it a Mediterranean flavour, particularly as it was being performed in a wine-producing area. For this reason, we decided to perform a ritual to the god Dionysus, the god of the grape, but this ritual could just as easily be converted to be a feast of another god of death and rebirth, such as John Barleycorn.

Preparation

The location for this ritual should be outside, preferably in the summer months. Rites for Dionysus started in March and continued until
the grape harvest in October. Likewise, any ritual should be orientated
toward the season of the god/goddess invoked. The ritual should start
approximately half an hour before sunset. A circle of torches or garden
flares should be set up in a circle around the ritual area. The central altar
should be decorated appropriately, with plenty of ivy and vine leaves (as
later on they become an important part of the ritual). Magical tools on
the altar should include the *thyrsus*, a wand with a pinecone on the end,
which is a traditional tool of Dionysus. While the other traditional Wiccan
ritual tools of the pentacle and sword may also be included, the chalice
is of particular importance. It should be large and contain red wine. If
possible, a statue representing an earth goddess should also be present
on the altar.

It is preferable to set the feast up before the ritual begins. This may be
placed on the floor on the edge of the ritual area or on a table. The food
and wine should be easily accessible during the ritual, as it is an intrinsic part. These should be simple foods: bread, cheese, cold meats, fruit,
including plenty of grapes, and plenty of wine. The last is, of course, the
most controversial aspect of this ritual. Many rituals in the US are "dry";
this one certainly isn't. Wine is an intrinsic part of ritual, and part of the
ecstatic process. Awareness of the potential for things to get out of hand
due to the overdrinking of alcohol should be taken into account when
roles are defined for the ritual feast.

Roles

Like most neo-Pagan circles, there is a high priestess and a high priest.
Their responsibility is to conduct the initial opening of the ritual feast,
and appropriate invocations. Unlike Wiccan circles, the high priest does
not take on the god form during Drawing Down. A separate individual
is appointed to manifest Dionysus during the ritual. He is prepared and
kept separate from the ritual until the Maenads invoke Dionysus—three
women are appointed to take on this role. They have to be chosen carefully as they must be willing to let go of all their inhibitions during the
rite and literally become "wild women." They must be willing to act flir-
tatiously and quite outrageously. They need to be briefed beforehand on
the nature of the ritual and what is expected of them.

The high priest (or another member of the circle) can assume the
role of the Vibe Watcher or Ritual Guardian. Depending on the size of

the group participating, there may be a need for more than one. They
need to refrain from alcohol and any ecstatic participation. Their job is to
maintain safety and to ensure that things do not go too far. They should
have some training in magical energy work (see chapter 8) and the ability
to ground and center people if they get into trouble due to heightened
emotion.

Dress

As the ritual is to have a Greek/Roman feel, dress for the majority of
the participants—the *bacchante*—can be simple togas, which are easily
made out of single white sheets. They should have headdresses made of
ivy or vines. Dionysus traditionally wore a leopard skin. In lieu of this,
leopard-print material from a drapery store can be brought to make his
toga. Likewise, he should have a headdress of ivy or vines. The Maenads
and the high priestess can be dressed either as the other participants or
in red togas, which traditionally defined a prophetic priestess. They may
also carry the previously mentioned thyrsus, which was one of their traditional magical tools.

Music and Drumming

Musical instruments are also an essential part of this rite. These can include drums such as the Irish bodhran or African djembé style, shakers,
and bells. They are used sparingly at the beginning of the ritual and more
frenetically after the invocation of Dionysus. The dancing itself may initially take a free-flow form, but should be encouraged, as it progresses,
to take the form of a snake—a serpentine dance by the participants. This
dance causes connection to the earth via the root chakra (see chapter
8). Dionysus was an earth god, with the snake being one of his symbols.
This snake is, of course, also the symbol of the earth goddess Gaea, who
is strongly associated with trance. As the dancing continues, energy will
come up through the root chakra and open the other chakras as it rises.
It is important to point out that this is NOT kundalini, although it will
open the participants' other energy centers and expand their aura in a
similar way. Traditionally, the snake represents the energy flow up the
body, which is symbolised in the dance. If successful, it will culminate in
the opening of the crown center, causing the participant to enter into an
ecstatic state, if not an experience of gnosis.

Including the Sacred Procession

Linked to the drumming and dancing is the inclusion of the previously mentioned sacred procession. This should be incorporated wherever possible before the start of the main ritual if there is a suitable site available. The route should be chosen carefully beforehand, but it should not be too far away from the ritual site. Drumming, singing, and chanting should start at the meeting point of the procession as the participants gather. When all are present, the drummers should lead the procession off on a winding path, stopping occasionally to make offerings or invocations if participants so wish. At this point, the drumming should be light and not induce full trance, although it should encourage a euphoric state. It should build up until the procession reaches the ritual site, where the circle and quarters are going to be invoked.

Circle Casting and Traditional Offerings

Unlike Wiccan and neo-Pagan rites, a circle was not traditionally cast in Greek ritual, although quarters were called. Some groups may feel more comfortable with the circle being cast beforehand. If so, it should be done in a style appropriate to the ritual, in this case the *Anemoi*, the Greek gods of the four winds, are invoked rather than the usual Watchtowers. This is done with arms raised, but if the invoker feels more comfortable using the traditional Invoking Pentagram of Earth, there is no reason why they shouldn't. The spirits of the ancestors and the land are also invoked, which is not a normal part of Wiccan traditional circle-casting. But this is done because it is an earth-based ritual about connection to the land, as much as connection to the gods. The offerings used in this ritual are milk, honey, and bread, but substitutes may be used. The Maenads make the offerings, which are kept on the altar until they are needed.

Ritual Flow

Because this is a Dionysian ritual, it is a great deal more free-flowing than Apollonian rituals. The words used in the ritual script are for guidance, and the high priestess and Maenads should be allowed to adapt and adlib according to the natural flow that the ritual takes. When Semele is invoked into the high priestess, she should be allowed control of the ritual as much as possible, with the high priest ensuring that the flow of the ritual stays on track. With this in mind, there should be predetermined signals between the high priest and the Maenads, particularly in regard to the tying of Dionysus and his symbolic sacrifice.

The Rite

Calling of the Quarters, the Anemoi

The high priest stands in the east and, with arms raised, calls the Guardian of the East:

> "Hail to thee, Eurus, Guardian of the Eastern Wind, Lord of Spring.
> We call on you, who brings forth the gentle rains and warm breeze,
> to witness this rite and guard this circle. So mote it be."

High priest then stands in the south and, with arms raised, calls the Guardian of the South:

> "Hail to thee, Notus, Guardian of the Southern Wind, Lord of Summer.
> We call on you, who brings forth the hot and dry winds,
> to witness this rite and guard this circle. So mote it be."

The high priest then stands in the west and, with arms raised, calls the Guardian of the West:

> "Hail to thee, Zephyrus, Guardian of the Western Wind, Lord of
> Autumn.
> We call on you, who brings forth the gentlest of breezes,
> to witness this rite and guard this circle. So mote it be."

The high priest then stands in the north and, with arms raised, calls the Guardian of the North:

> "Hail to thee, Boreas, Guardian of the Northern Wind, Lord of
> Winter.
> We call on you, who brings forth the coldness of the winter wind,
> to witness this rite and guard this circle. So mote it be."

Offerings to the Spirits of the Land

The high priest directs the Maenads to collect the offerings from the altar.

> "O spirits of the land, spirits of our ancestors, who provide us with
> sustenance
> accept these offerings, in the many names of Dionysus.
> He who causes the crops to grow, and the grape to hang on the
> vine.

He who is the wildness of nature, and the joy of desire. So mote it
be.' *(All repeat.)*

Each Maenad makes an offering on the ground. First the milk, then
the honey, then the bread. The First Maenad offers milk, pouring it on
to the ground, saying:

"Spirits of the land, spirits of our ancestors,
accept this offering of milk, which sustains us at birth.
So mote it be." *(All repeat.)*

The Second Maenad offers honey, pouring it on to the ground, saying:

"Spirits of the land, spirits of our ancestors,
accept this offering of honey,
which gives us sweetness in our life. So mote it be. *(All repeat.)*

The Third Maenad breaks the bread and sprinkles it on to the ground,
saying:

"Spirits of the land, spirits of our ancestors,
accept this gift of bread,
which gives us life itself. So mote it be." *(All repeat.)*

Invocation of Semele, Mother of Dionysus
The high priestess and high priest stand in circle facing each other. The
drummers in the circle begin drumming a fast but gentle beat. The high
priest kneels in front of the priestess and, with arms raised, says:

"Hail to Thee, Semele, Mother of Dionysus.
Who as a mortal rose to Olympus as the goddess Thyone.
O raging Queen, daughter of Kadmos, Goddess universal,
I call, O, beauteous one; deep-bosomed of the lovely flowing locks,
joyful and divine, who bore the mighty offspring Dionysus,
whom Zeus' thunder bright forced immature, and frightened into
    light.
Born from the deathless counsels, secret, high,
of Kronion Zeus, regent of the sky;
whom Persephone permits to view the light,
and visit mortals from the realms of night.
Constant attending on the sacred rites,

and feasts of your son, which Thy soul delights;
when Thy son's wondrous birth mankind relate,
and secrets pure and holy celebrate.
Now I invoke Thee, great Queen Kadmeis,
to bless Thy mystics, lenient and serene,
to descend into this your priestess.
Bring her your gifts of joy and ecstasy,
that she may share with your son's devotees."[10]

The high priest kisses the feet of the high priestess.

The high priestess speaks as Semele, either channelling her or speaking in her own words.

The high priest brings the chalice of wine to the high priestess and says:

"Thrice-blessed Semele, goddess Thyone,
bless this wine, and consecrate us, with this, the blood of your son."

The high priestess, as Semele, now walks around the circle of the gathered bacchante. She sprinkles each with wine, and may prophesy to each in turn. When almost all have been blessed with wine, the high priest directs the Maenads to start to chant with the drumming, slowly, in the background:

"Dythram, Dythrambus. Dythram, Dythrambus. Dythram, Dythrambus."

The Invocation of Dionysus

The high priestess as Semele joins the Maenads, and they begin to dance around the circle, holding hands and chanting. With arms raised, the high priest begins the invocation of Dionysus:

"Hear me, Zeus' son, blessed Dionysos, god of wine,
born of two mothers, honoured and divine.
Lysios, Euios, Bacchus, various-named,
of gods the offspring, secret, holy, famed.
Fertile and nourishing, whose liberal care
augments the fruit that banishes despair.
Sounding, magnanimous, Lenaios power,
of various-formed, medicinal, holy flower:

mortals in Thee repose from labour find,
delightful charm, desired by all mankind.
Fair-haired Euion, Bromios, joyful god,
Lysios, insanely raging with the leafy rod.
To these our rites, benignant power, incline,
when favouring men, or when on gods you shine;
be present to thy mystics' suppliant prayer,
rejoicing come, and fruits abundant bear."[11]

The high priestess and Maenads leave the circle to collect "Dionysus" from outside the circle. The high priest continues the invocation:

"Dionysos, bearer of the vine,
Thee I invoke to bless these rites divine:
florid and gay, of Nymphai the blossom bright,
and of fair Aphrodite, Goddess of delight.
'Tis thine mad footsteps with mad Nymphai to beat,
dancing through groves with lightly leaping feet.
From Zeus' high counsels nursed by Persephone,
and born the dread of all the powers divine.
Come, blessed God, regard Thy suppliant's voice,
propitious come, and in these rites rejoice."[12]

The bacchante chant as the high priestess and the Maenads go to fetch the concealed "Dionysus":

"Hail the God that comes, hail the God that comes, hail the God that comes . . .!" (*Repeated until Dionysus arrives.*)

The high priestess and the Maenads return, with Dionysus dancing into the circle, chanting as before. The bacchante cheer at his arrival and join in, and the Maenads encourage the participants to drink wine and dance. The drummers increase their drum beat with the dance, led by the Dionysus, the high priestess, and the Maenads. They use a fast drum beat to encourage trance.

When the high priest is satisfied that the drumming is beginning to reach a crescendo, he signals to the Maenads to lead Dionysus to where he is to be tied. The high priest signals to the drummers to slow the beat, as the Maenads loosely tie Dionysus, standing, to a tree or other upright structure. They cover him in ivy, grape vines, and grapes.

The high priest then signals the drummers to increase the drum beat as before, and the Maenads feed Dionysus wine and grapes, and encourage the bacchante to do the same. The bacchante may even flirt with him, and rub grapes into his skin as part of the revelries. Meanwhile, the drinking of wine and dancing continues, along with the fast trance beat of the drums. The participants continue to feed Dionysus with wine and grapes.

During this portion of the ritual, the priest chosen to represent Dionysus may trance and be possessed by the spirit of the god, which is normally signalled by his roaring. If this happens, the high priest should signal to lower the drum beat and allow Dionysus to speak. Offerings may also be made to him at this time, after which the drumming and dancing should be allowed to continue.

As the drumming and dancing again reaches a crescendo, the high priest signals to the Maenads to mock 'sacrifice' Dionysus. They 'charge' at him screaming, ripping off the ivy, vines, and grapes. They may also cover him in the remains of any wine and rip off his clothing, if appropriate.

The Feast and Ecstatic Ritual

After Dionysus' 'sacrifice,' the drumming and dancing should continue and the feast should begin with participants helping themselves to food and wine. This serves two purposes: it both reenergises and grounds the participants. The ritual should now become free-flowing, giving the opportunity for those wish to enter into trance and possibly bring through the deities they work with. They may wish to use the Underworld Descent Technique (see chapter 11) during the dancing to do this. The high priestess, priest, and ritual guardians should be vigilant at this stage, stepping in if necessary to assist anyone in trance, particularly someone possessed by a deity. If this occurs, the drumming and dancing should cease, and the priest or guardians act as trance guides for the possessed participant until the deity has left. They should then signal for dancing and drumming to continue.

Closing the Rite: Grounding

The dancing and drumming may continue for some time (in some cases all night), but will reach a natural conclusion as the drumming and dancing slows and the evening progresses. This gives the opportunity for the high priestess and priest to close the ritual, signaling for the dancing and drumming to stop. The first stage of closing the ritual should be for the priesthood to thank Dionysus and any other deities for their presence. This is then followed by the banishing of the Anemoi, the quarter Guardians, by simply thanking them to leave in the same fashion they were called, for example:

> "Hail to thee, Eurus, Guardian of the Eastern Wind, Lord of Spring.
> We thank you for attending this rite
> And ask you now to leave and return to your realm,
> Hail and farewell. So mote it be."

Finally, both the priesthood and ritual guardians should make sure all the participants are grounded appropriately (see page 129). They can initially do this by encouraging the participants to close their own chakras and ground themselves, but they should also take time to assist any who may need further help with grounding.

NOTES

1 Vivianne Crowley, *Wicca: The Old Religion in the New Age* (Wellingborough, UK: The Aquarian Press, 1989), 18.

2 Nietzsche, *The Birth of Tragedy* (1872), 5.

3 Sadar, Hamid. Asian Art. http://www.asianart.com/articles/hamid/index.html.

4 Joseph Campbell coined the term *monomyth* in his book *The Hero with a Thousand Faces* (1949), which explains the commonalities in the myths that exist throughout the world's cultures. A *monomyth* is a common myth.

5 Gemma McGowan, high priestess of Keepers of the Well, on her Brigid pilgrimage through Wales and England.

6 Vivianne Crowley, *Wicca*.

7 First published in 1872 as *Die Geburt der Tragödie aus dem Geiste der Musik*. This is a work of philosophical theory, which analyzes the nature of ancient Greek theatre and its ability to balance the Apollonian and Dionysian ritual forms.

8 Nietzsche, *The Birth of Tragedy*, 12.

9 See Starhawk, *Truth or Dare*.

10 Adapted from the Orphic "Hymn to Semele-Thyone," hymn 44 to Semele, by Orpheus.

11 Adapted from Orphic hymn 50, to Lysius Lenaeus, by Orpheus.

12 Adapted from Orphic hymn 46, to Licnitus, by Orpheus.

Chapter 15

Divine Mysteries: Sex With the Gods

Humankind has always sought to achieve ultimate union with the divine in one form or another. In many cultures, particularly those with goddess-oriented fertility cults such as witchcraft, it is not surprising that sexual union was considered the most sublime expression of that need. Either one or both parties involved were seen as manifestations of the divine incarnate. Initially such manifestation of the deity in the physical body of a priest, priestess, or adherent took the form of possession through trance, but as time progressed and taboos against sex were enforced, the divine presence took more symbolic forms. Even in the spiritually diverse cultures of the Indian subcontinent, these sexual cults are disapproved of or their devotees and their practises are feared and considered taboo, even though tantric practises survive and are still performed by sacred prostitutes in certain temples in modern India.

In the West we live in a culture where, since the late 1960s, many of the taboos against sex have been lifted. But even though we communicate more openly about eros more than we ever have, we still find the idea of sexuality as being spiritual, as a way of communing with the divine, to be abhorrent, because beneath the apparent openness of our societies' attitudes about sex, we still unconsciously cling to that Judeo-Christian hang-up: the doctrine of original sin, which still lurks just below the surface of our seemingly permissive society.

Judeo-Christian culture has for centuries seen sex as something spiritually impure, and claimed that by giving in to our physical natural needs and desires, we distance ourselves even further from the divine. This is, of course, a dualistic viewpoint, from a religious philosophy that believes

239

the material world is corrupt and only by transcending our physicality completely can we connect to the divine and the world of the spirit. Of course, the traditional pagan viewpoint is very different, believing that our spiritual and physical selves are intimately linked, but even so, 2,000 years of the Judeo-Christian attitude pervaded Western tradition magical practises until recent years. It is not surprising that when sex magic was revived in the early twentieth century, it was inevitably regarded as one of the ultimate degrading practises of 'black' magic, as was any magical technique connected to it. Even the spiritualist mediums of the late nineteenth and twentieth centuries found themselves accused of sexual improprieties during the darkness of a séance. Magic, psychism, and trance became unconsciously linked in the Victorian and Edwardian mind with wanton sexuality.

We remember when this attitude toward sex still pervaded Western occultism, with sex magic often being referred to as a "left-hand path," the belief that it was in some way wrong or evil. The fact is that many of the teachings in this book, including the Underworld Descent Technique, could be construed as being "left-hand path." After all, it is a technique for accessing the Shadow.

Prior to the Christian concept of original sin, in most ancient cultures, sex had always been revered as a way of connecting with divinity through union in the great act of universal creation. This is what is often referred to in Eastern Mysticism as tantra, although to call tantra just "sex magic" would be simplistic, to say the least. Tantra was originally the indigenous system of magic in India before the arrival of the Aryans, and under the Moghuls developed into a tradition of rebellion, a reaction against the restrictive religious laws of that empire, just as medieval witchcraft did in Christian Europe. Both cultures instituted laws that restricted the sexual practices of the older pagan religions, so the traditions went underground to maintain their survival. The same occurred within the sexual seidr/seith practises of the Northern European peoples.

Unfortunately, little is known of the magical sexual practises of the Western European peoples, although some fragments survived in the Norse traditions. From these we can surmise several things. First of all, there was possibly some philosophy regarding polarity practise. The mythology of Northern Europe includes the concepts of Fire and Ice, which can be seen as polarizing forces both externally and internally (macrocosm and microcosm respectively). They can also be seen as sexual forces—the concepts of yin and yang, Shiva and Shakti, the masculine and feminine forces, which are the basis of sex magic practise. In fact, male seidr/seith practitioners were often accused of being effeminate. In a culture based on warrior values this is quite a slur, and has often been interpreted as the seidr/seith practitioner being homosexual. Diana Paxson suggests that these attitudes in Norse culture were not present originally, but were introduced by Christianity:

> Most of Old Norse literature was written down after the intro-duction of Christianity (in the 10-11th centuries), however much of its content is older. The surviving examples include some striking examples of homophobic speech and behavior. In the Icelandic sagas, wearing the clothing of the opposite sex was grounds for divorce, and giving a man a gift which could be interpreted as feminine was an insult.[1]

Although such accusations made about seidr/seith practitioners may have in some cases been correct, it may also be an overly simplistic inter-pretation of something else that was happening. In traditional tantra, the male participant becomes the passive (submissive) partner in shaktiism (sex magic), while in contrast, the female takes on the active (dominant) role. This suggests that there is a common Indo-European origin in both traditions. Training in seidr/seith for both sexes includes balancing the aforementioned forces of Fire (in tantra, Shiva) and Ice (in tantra, Shakti) within themselves. From the viewpoint of Jungian psychology, we are, of course, talking about the balance of the personality, the anima within the male and the animus within the female. This is common practise in many forms of shamanism, where in some cases the male apprentice shaman may be expected to dress as a woman for a period of time[2] or enter into a sexual relationship with his own contrasexual self (more on this at the end of the chapter). Within sex magic, the balance of this internal polar-ity is essential to make any energy flow, as well as the basis for modern Wiccan practises related to sex magic.

The concept of Polarity, of two complementary but opposing forces, has always been an important part of Wiccan teaching, symbolised by the union of the God and Goddess. But the concept of cross-polariza-tion, where a couple polarized with their partner's anima or animus, was ignored until recent times except by a few authors, including our-selves and Vivianne and Chris Crowley, to name a few. From the 1980s onward, the concept of magical cross-polarization through the couple's contra-sexual selves became an important part of Wiccan philosophy.

The practise of consecrating the wine was adapted to symbolise this. Previously, the male partner held the athame and the female partner the chalice. These were swapped; the male Witch now holding the chalice, representing his own anima, while the female Witch is holding the athame, representing her animus. Of course, the dipping of the phallic athame into the womb-like chalice is a symbolic act of sexual union on several levels; however, it can be a powerful reenactment of The Great Rite on its own (which we discuss later) if a correct understanding of magical energy flow is applied.

Nearly all modern sex magic practises have their origin in Vedic tantra. Returning British officers brought knowledge of these practises back to Britain during the time of the British colonization of India in the eighteenth and nineteenth centuries. The most obvious aspect of this was the incorporation of the chakra system into Western mysticism, specifically into Theosophy, and from there into the Western tradition of magic. It was the flamboyant Aleister Crowley who really brought tantric sex magic to the attention of the public, although its incorporation into OTO practises came from its founders Theodor Reuss and Karl Kellner.[3] The most open sexual practise within neo-Paganism today, is, of course, The Great Rite, which is part of the Third Degree sexual initiation (actual or otherwise) in Wicca, or as an act of communion with the God and Goddess, or for the purpose of energy-raising.

The use of sexual magic in Wicca probably derives from two sources. The first is from Gerald Gardner, who (as we previously mentioned in chapter 3), spent much of his life in the shadow of several ancient temples in Ceylon (Sri Lanka) and immersed himself into the spirituality of that culture.* The other source is Aleister Crowley and the OTO, as much of the original Wiccan Book of Shadows (*Ye Bok of Ye Art Magical*) derived from Crowley's work. The Third Degree Rite in Wicca was originally intended by Gardner to make this type of connection to the divine as part of the initiation rite. This would have resulted in the opening of the initiate's crown chakra. Once this is achieved, it is possible to channel that energy at any time. It was not an uncommon practise in Gardnerian Wicca for magical energy to be raised in this way for a particular purpose, with the cone of power centering on a couple doing The Great Rite in actuality, or for a group of Third Degree Witches to perform the act

---

* We own two tourist souvenirs from the Gerald Gardner collection, which he brought from these temples. Both are copies of the tantric poses found decorating the walls of the temples.

in circle simultaneously. This has been discussed publically by various members of the Craft.*

Generally sex magic falls into two categories, as we previously mentioned. The first is raising energy for magical purposes, as in the cone of power. The second is connection to the divine as in The Great Rite. This can include deities manifesting in the practitioners during the rite. The latter reason is what we are really discussing here: the bringing through of the divine through sexual energy. As we mentioned earlier, much of Wicca's sexual practices can be traced back to the introduction of tantra into the Western Tradition, specifically the final part of the tantric Pancha-Makara rite, Maithuna.† In the final part of this rite, as in Wicca, the priestess is believed to be the embodiment of the divine, in this case the goddess Shakti, who manifests in physical form, while the priest becomes the embodiment of the god Shiva. This is no different from The Great Rite where the priestess manifests the Lunar Goddess and the priest, the Horned God.

Unlike the other techniques mentioned in this book, the act of communion with divinity through sex focuses almost completely on the body's energy system, the chakras and the aura (see chapter 8, "The Second Key: Energy"), while trance techniques such as breathing patterns take a secondary role. The roles also change, as the participants perform both roles simultaneously. They are both trance-guide and seer to each other (see chapter 6). This means that sex magic used for deity possession is, by its very definition, an advanced form of practise. Anyone doing this work should be fully familiar with their own chakra systems, having worked through their own chakra "blockages." This means that they must have done a great deal of personal work on their own centers. We cannot understate the dangers of performing this form of magic unless properly trained and adequately prepared in this way. It can easily result in what is often referred to as a blown crown chakra: the expansion of the chakra before it is ready, resulting in an inability to close it. Physically, it can result in problems of a metabolic nature, with the inability to regulate body's energy, causing fatigue. Mentally, it can result in severe problems,

---

* High Priest Frederic Lamond, who hived off Gardner's coven, has discussed this openly for many years, and covers the ritual aspect of sex in his book *Fifty Years of Wicca*. Maxine Sanders has also discussed it.

† Consisting of what is called "the five M's": Madya (wine or blood), Mamsa (flesh or muscles), Matsya (fish or fat), Mudra (wafer, bone or marrow), and Maithuna (holy communion with the divine).

with symptoms similar to a bipolar disorder or schizophrenia, which includes manic behaviour and depression.

The Great Rite as a Tantric Technique: Communing With the Gods

As with Drawing Down the Moon, very little internal technique was taught to either of us regarding The Great Rite. The following technique we developed originally to give the symbolic Great Rite, performed at Third Degree initiations in our coven, as much power as if performed in actuality. As deity connection is one of the most important aspects in our current system of training, our students are also encouraged to bring deity through during this process. We've found that it is not unusual for the initiate to experience changes in consciousness during this rite as they commune with their personal deity, and even those that don't trance find that it has a profound effect on them, causing ecstatic changes both physically and mentally. This technique can be combined with full sexual intercourse between consenting partners if they so wish.

Obviously, this is a two-person technique. Although the participants do not have to be in a physical relationship, they must be in a relationship where there is a high level of trust. The exception to this is when it includes full sexual contact, in which case we recommend that this is ONLY done between partners where there is an existing, loving relationship.* This rite can be performed as part of an initiation ritual, to raise magical energy, or as an act of communing with the gods, either privately or semi-publically in a trusted magical group (e.g., a coven or a grove). Either way, it should be done in the right atmosphere, with the place being sanctified in some way, such as circle-casting, even if it is done informally in a bedroom. Music may also be incorporated, such as drumming or chanting to encourage the change in consciousness of the participants. In a group, live chanting and drumming the appropriate beats can be practised, but if performed privately the music may be played on a CD or MP3. Both shamanic drumming and chanting CDs are easily available on the Internet, which would be suitable for such work. The technique, apart from requiring an understanding of magical energy, also requires

---

* In traditional Indian tantra, it is often stated that it should not take place "between husband and wife" but with a temple priestess. It must be understood that this is because marriages were arranged in India and were not based on an emotional connection.

the use of controlled breathing (see below). This is an essential part of traditional tantra, where the use of pranayama (etheric) breath is exchanged between partners.

Breathing Patterns

There are several breathing techniques that can be used in sex magic. Nearly all affect the metabolism of carbon dioxide within the body (see page 149). Some have their origins in traditional tantric practise, while others have more modern origins.

- **Bhramari or Hummingbird Breath:** This is a traditional tantra breathing pattern, which is a good one to use before starting on one of the more complex patterns. Its purpose is to help shut down the senses. This can be assisted by placing your thumbs in your ears, small fingers on the mouth, second fingers ringing under the nostrils, middle finger on the bridge of the nose, and the index fingers on the closed eyes. Start sitting in the "lotus" or cross-legged position and exhaling all the breath from your lungs. Contract the abdominal muscles to get all of the air out. Now inhale through nose rapidly, making a snoring sound. Now pause and retain the breath for seven seconds, focusing on your Manipura chakra and the stored pranic energy there. Next, as you exhale, do so out of your mouth with your lips closed, making a humming noise. The sound should be as loud and continuous as possible. Focus on this sound while you exhale. Start with seven cycles of breath, building it up over ten minutes.

- **Seven Second (Trapezoidal) Breath:** This breathing pattern consists of inhaling for a count of seven (yogic breath), holding for seven, exhaling for seven, and then again, holding for seven. This cycle of breathing lasts for a count of twenty-eight overall. It is sometimes called trapezoidal, as it can be visualized as this shape. It is both relaxing and energizing, as it oxygenates the vital organs of the body. It is a good precursor breath before any magical work. When inhaling, the breath should be drawn deeply into the abdomen, and then into the rib cage. When inhaling, visualize the breath filling you with blue pranic (etheric) energy. While retaining the breath, you should also tighten your pelvic floor muscles (the muscles between the genitalia and the anus). Inhale slowly and gently for the count of seven, while releasing all the tension in your body. You should then relax for the following count of seven, with your lungs empty until repeating the breath. This breathing should initially be done for ten cycles and slowly built up until it can be performed for ten minutes.

- **Circular or Holotropic Breath:** Leonard Orr popularized this technique within the New Age movement in the 1980s, and it is used extensively in Rebirthing (a method of dealing with repressed emotions) as well as some modern schools of shamanism. It is quite capable, in our experience, of inducing a trance state on its own. The technique consists of visualizing a circle as you breathe fully into your abdomen (Manipura chakra) for a count of seven, and then out again for a count of seven. The breathing rate should be increased after about twenty minutes, so that eventually after an hour you are taking only two seconds to breathe in and two seconds to breathe out. Breathing should be through the nose, and there should be no pause between breathing in and out.

- **Kapalabhathi (Kundalini) or Fire Breath:** Kapalabhathi translates as "shining forehead." It is a form of power breathing; it energizes the body, literally bringing a glow to the face (hence its Vedic name). Unlike other breathing exercises, this one can be done standing. Breathe in with short breaths then out rapidly, inhaling and exhaling as quickly as possible. This should be done only using the muscles of the diaphragm. Because this breathing technique can cause light-headedness and even, in some cases, loss of consciousness, start slowly by doing it for two minutes initially and then building up to ten minutes over time. If you are using this breathing technique during intercourse for sex magic, tighten up the pelvic floor muscles while exhaling. Traditionally, this technique is followed by alternative nostril breathing (Nadi Shodhan Pranayama).

- **Pranavayua Rasa:** This breathing technique is the most complicated and active of the ones we have mentioned so far, as it includes six distinct actions performed at the same time. Its purpose is to recharge the body with pranayama, which results in the linking of the personal life force (prana) with that of the universe. This results in the linking of the practitioner directly with his or her divinity.

  1. Initially, you should stand with your eyes closed or looking up toward your brow chakra (forehead). Start by inhaling deeply, with your hands grasped in front of you at chest height. As you breathe in, swing your arms forward, level with your chest, then backward twice before exhaling.

2. Now repeat above, but this time stretch your arms out directly at shoulder level in front of you and swing them forward and backward twice as you inhale. When you exhale, drop your arms to your sides.

3. Now as you inhale, swing your arms up and down twice, parallel to your sides, arching your back slightly as you do so. Then exhale.

4. Inhale again, keeping the breath in as you stretch your arms slowly forward. When fully stretched, clench your firsts and bring them back to your chest. Shake your whole body as you do this, then exhale.

5. Inhale again and bring your arms up above your head while swinging your body to the right at the waist, holding the breath within your lungs. Focus on the parts of your body being stretched. Exhale as you straighten, then repeat, but this time bending to the left.

6. Finally, inhale again. While holding the breath in your lungs, massage your rib cage. Exhale, then repeat, but this time massage your breast and chest muscles.

• **Prana Sukha (Joyous Life Force) Breath:** This pattern is considered to be very healing, as it pulls vital etheric energy from the atmosphere and converts it to healing energy. This breathing pattern consists of three cycles: inhale for a count of one, hold for a count of four, exhale for a count of two. While most counts last a second, these counts can be extended over time. The rhythm of the breath is what's important. Start by inhaling just slightly longer than you normally would. This will mark your base count of one. Afterwards adjust the rest of the breathing exercise appropriately; you will hold your breath four times longer than when you inhaled. As you increase the length of the counts over time, you should not allow them to become uncomfortable, but let the process develop naturally. This breathing pattern naturally slows down the breathing process. After initially focusing on the counts of breathing, you should allow it occur unconsciously, so it does not interfere with the meditative process.

We recommend that couples experiment with different breathing patterns before doing any sexual magic work. The Pranavayua Rasa breath is a good pattern to limber up with before starting energy work, followed by the Bhramari breath, which is an excellent way of starting any breathing work. The Prana Sukha is the easiest for both couples to synchronize their breathing patterns. Traditionally in tantra, each partner alternates their breath; as one breaths in, the other breaths out. The theory being that each partner will inhale the other's prana, resulting in an energetic connection between them. While this will work well with a couple doing this rite sexually in its fullness, with a couple not in a physical and emotional relationship, it could result in emotional complications. If there is a concern regarding this process, we recommend the couple synchronize their breaths.

The Polarity Energy Exercise

We highly recommend that couples refrain from using alcohol and recreational drugs when performing the following exercise and rite. When combined with the energy practises we discuss here, these substances can result in harmful physical and psychological side effects (see "Blown Crown Chakra," page 88). Because of the complexity of the energy work and the breathing patterns, we generally teach any couple who is going to perform this rite the polarity energy work first. It is a useful exercise for any couple working with polarity energy, even if they are not planning to do The Great Rite, as it will cause a greater magical connection between partners and, therefore, increase the magical energy they can generate. We would recommend any couple planning to do The Great Rite, as we describe further on in this chapter, to practise this exercise several times before performing the ritual. Four flows of energy have to be visualized, and more importantly, actually felt. After practising this exercise several times, the flow of energy will become natural with very little need to concentrate or visualize the energy, as they will feel it automatically begin flowing the moment they commence the exercise.

A quiet room is required for this exercise, although unlike the full Great Rite, there is no need for drumming, chanting, or any other technique to induce trance at this stage. Breathing is important, however, and the previously mentioned breathing patterns can be used, along with synchronization of the exhalation and inhalation of breath. The couple face each other, sitting cross-legged, with their hands on their own knees.

1. They start by opening their own chakras (see page 128 for Chakra Opening) and commencing one of the simple breathing patterns. It is important that they regulate their own breathing patterns. The previously described breathing pattern should be used, but at this stage just regulating and synchronizing breathing will be effective.

2. Both partners now visualize the energy flowing in their bodies, one up and one down. From crown to root, and from root to crown. When

they are confident that they have the energy flowing, they clasp their own hands in front of them. They visualize the energy from their own crowns (silver or white energy) coming down to their heart centers and down their left arm, into their right arm, back to their heart centers, and then down their body until it grounds through their root chakras. They should repeat this several times before moving on to the next stage.

3. This time they include the other flow of energy: from beneath their root centers to their crown chakras. This energy (visualized again as silver or white energy*) comes up their body until it reaches their heart centers, where the energy circles before it then goes down their right arm, into their left arm, and then back to their heart centers. It is then visualized going up through their throat, brow, and finally reaching their crown centers.

4. When both partners are confident that they have mastered this part of the exercise, they can let go of their own hand and hold the hands of their partner, right hand holding partner's left.

5. They now exchange their energy with each other by visualizing the energy coming down from through their crown to their heart, passing down their left hand into their partner's right hand. Likewise, they will receive energy down their right hand from their partner, which they now ground through their lower chakras to their roots.

6. While maintaining the crown to root flow, each partner now visualizes the energy coming up from their root centers (the same silver or white energy), going to their hearts and passing down their right arm and into their partner's left arm. Likewise, they will receive energy down their left arm from their partner, which should now be visualized as flowing up to their crowns.

7. After allowing the energy flow for several minutes, the couple now separate their hands and begin the grounding process. They start by visualizing the energy flows within themselves decreasing and then go through the process of closing their chakras (see page 129).

---

* This is an amended version of the technique for raising kundalini, where root energy is brought up rather than the recycling of the silver/white crown energy, which we use here. This has been done for safety reasons (see "Blown Crown Chakra," page 248 in this chapter).

The Great Rite Using Energy

Like the above energy exercise, the couple initially face each other. This is very different compared with the traditional Wiccan Great Rite. In the traditional rite, the couple is positioned with the female partner laying in the star position, and the male partner kneeling between her legs as they do the rite. In the Great Rite energy method, the partners first face each other cross-legged (as above) before adopting the Yab Yum tantric position to invoke their personal deities and consecrate the wine using the athame and chalice. This does not mean that the traditional positions cannot be incorporated, particularly in third-degree initiations, but before the wine is consecrated the female/passive partner sits on the lap of the male/dominant partner facing him (see Illustration 6). They then pick up (or are passed) the athame and the chalice to perform the climax of the rite. This has the effect of bringing each partner's chakra center in alignment with each other, and causes a spiritual, etheric, and a mental-emotional link between them. It is often portrayed as strands of auric energy connecting chakra to chakra—root center to root center, sacral center to sacral center, all the way up the body and finishing at the crown.

Although in the above Great Rite Using Energy Exercise, and the preceding energy exercise, we are principally talking about a male/female polarity, it will work just as well with male/male or female/female couples. What is important beforehand is to determine who is the dominant and who is the passive personality. In an initiatory situation, the initiate would take the dominant role (for reasons we mention below). The couple may wish to do this privately if they wish to go one stage further by including coitus, but we do recommend that they first practise and master the Polarity Energy Exercise.

This repeats the four flows of energy found in the Polarity Energy Exercise.

1. The couple face each other in a lotus- or cross-legged position as in the Polarity Exercise. A chalice is placed to the left of the passive/female partner. An athame is placed to the left of the male/dominant partner.

2. They each open their chakras, looking directly into each other's eyes. Once their chakras are open, they start to regulate and synchronize their breathing using the breathing pattern as previously described.

3. After several minutes, when both feel that a strong connection has been made, the passive partner moves and sits on the lap of the

dominant partner facing him/her (the Yab Yum position). Eye contact and breathing pattern should be maintained as much as possible.

4. Both partners now visualize the two paths of energy in their bodies (as described in the Polarity Energy Exercise), so that four flows of energy are flowing between them.

5. They simultaneously pick up the chalice and the athame, the male/ dominant partner holding the chalice in both hands, and the female/ submissive partner holding the athame in both hands.

6. They now alter the paths of energy that they have been visualizing, continuing with the breathing pattern. The path of energy from their

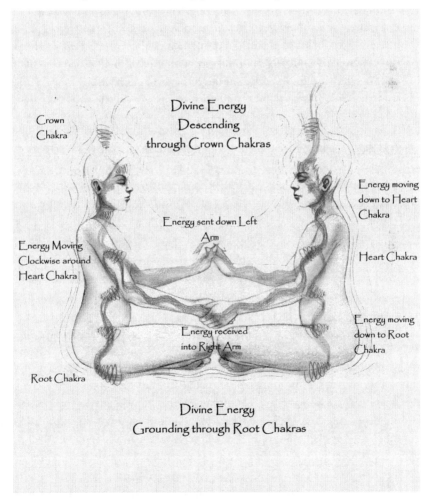

Illustration 6: Energy Exercise

crown centers now comes down through their heart centers, passing down their left arms, through the athame or chalice, and goes back to their heart centers, and then down their body, grounding at the root centers.

7. They also alter the path of energy coming up from their root to their crown centers. This energy comes up to their heart centers, goes down their right arms through the chalice or athame, and then back to their heart centers before proceeding up to their crown centers.

8. At the point where they feel the energy is flowing well, the couple may wish to invoke their own personal deities into themselves, visualizing them at their crown centers.

9. Once invoked, the couple bring the athame and the chalice together, inserting the point of the athame into the chalice. During this process they exchange both flows of energy with each other (as described in the Polarity Energy Exercise), though the magical tools. If they are in a romantic relationship, they may wish to engage in the full sexual act.

After the rite, full closing down and grounding is essential. Couples often describe being in an ecstatic state and full of energy. This energy either needs to be grounded or used and disposed of magically. Failure to expel this energy from the body can result in a "blown" crown chakra. Particular emphasis should, therefore, be placed on making sure the crown center is closed fully, while the root center is grounding the energy correctly. It may be necessary to use the Trap Door Technique (as described on page 130) to make sure the crown is fully closed. Eating some food particularly helps in closing the crown center.

The Bright Shadow Self: Anima/Animus as Manifestation of Divinity and Past Lives

As we mentioned previously in this chapter, one of the practises of traditional tantra is for the partners involved to take on contrasexual roles: the female taking the active (dominant) role and the male the passive (submissive) role. This allows them to access their own anima/animus complex. Accessing this area of the unconscious mind may also allow them to connect with divinity as well as past lives. Theoretically, this may be possible because we may repress our natural ability to connect with the divine (often referred to as the Higher Self) and knowledge of past lives. In both cases these abilities—to remember past lives and to connect with divinity—are repressed into the Bright Shadow, the positive aspect of Jung's Shadow. While in traditional European cosmology the Shadow is analogous with the underworld, the Bright Shadow is rarely mentioned as a separate realm within it. In Harner's core shamanism, it is none other than the Lower World, as it is called in his system of teaching, from where the soul must be retrieved.

The Bright Shadow is also where the contrasexual aspects (the anima/animus) are suppressed. The result is that all three may, under certain circumstances, manifest as one entity. We have termed this The Bright Shadow Self,* which can be seen as the opposite of the Shadow Self. There is a historical precedent for this in the ancient Norse concept of the flygja or hamingja,[4] which was believed to be the soul of, as well as the tutelary goddess of, particularly gifted individuals, a more elaborate and divinely connected form of the Muse. Most people are more familiar with the Shadow Self, as it often appears in stories as the dark side of our nature, such as Mr. Hyde in Robert Louis Stevenson's novel. The Bright Shadow Self is best illustrated in the much older story of Beauty and the Beast,[5] where it manifests as Beauty in the story, able to transform the Beast back into the Handsome Prince, who is the ego/persona—the balance between both the Shadow and the Bright Shadow. It also manifests in ancient cultures of Europe as deities, which seem to take on contrasexual roles. For example war goddesses, such as the Macha in Irish mythology and later Freya in Norse, are manifestations of the warrior's anima. In many cases, this is balanced by connection with a deity of the opposite sex, which can manifest through the ego/persona; in case of the Macha (Morrigan) by also connecting with the God Lugh or a similar Irish male deity.

These connections with deity through the Bright Shadow are, of course, much deeper than those made through the ego/persona, and are often made much later by magical practitioners, and in traditional Wicca does not normally occur until sometime between the second and third degree initiations. Such connection is essential in serious shamanic practise and in seidr/seith, as we have previously mentioned, as well as in all forms of sex magic. Sex magic is generally seen as being a two (or more)

---

* We coined this term to describe the results of this process. It is a metaphysical term rather than one that applies to orthodox psychology. The concept of the neo-Jungian Bright Shadow does not include this concept of a Bright Shadow Self as we describe here.

person affair, requiring physical sexual intercourse to take place between the participants.

In her book *Dreaming The Dark: Magic, Sex and Politics*, Starhawk includes a series of exercises that culminate in an act of solo sex magic, by using a mirror to reflect the "twin," or "Companion Self" (the anima/animus).[6] Such exercises, although valid for a single magical practitioner, may not necessarily be as intense as meeting and having sexual relations with your own deity on a different level of consciousness obtained through trance. This is brow chakra/"third eye" work, rather than a technique that involves trance-possession. Regardless, it is a useful exercise for starting the process of connection with the Bright Shadow.

While the Underworld Descent Technique (see chapter 11) is the method we recommend for meeting with deity in trance-prophecy, for the purposes of solo sexual encounters with deities, we recommend a different route, which takes the individual to meet the combined anima/animus and deity. This route uses a similar tree and cave path taken to obtain the individual's power animal, but takes it a stage further.

The Descent to the Soul

In shamanic practise it is believed that the soul or fragments of it can be 'lost,' in other words repressed into the unconscious area of the mind that neo-Jungians call the Bright Shadow (see page 110). We are not going to describe a full pathworking as an exercise to retrieve the soul or parts of it. The reason is that anyone who is going to take this journey should already have the knowledge to construct their own journey. If they don't, then they simply aren't ready to do it! It is important to have an understanding of spiritual cosmology (see chapter 7) to do this journey. It should also be combined with other trance techniques, such as drumming or rattling.

Many who take the journey to connect with and recover their soul, the previously mentioned Bright Shadow Self, often describe this meeting as being of a sexual nature, and the merging of the personality with the soul as an act of sexual union. This is, of course, a spiritual initiation, which can cause considerable change in the individual's consciousness. This process is well known in traditional shamanism where the shaman takes this entity as his "celestial wife," or a tutelary spirit.[7]

In his novel about Anglo-Saxon shamanism, *The Way of Wyrd*, Brian Bates describes this intimate union occurring during a shamanic initiation of a young novice monk:

> Suddenly she rose from the water naked, her skin smooth and glistening. She seemed iridescent and it almost hurt my eyes to look

at her. We embraced . . . I rolled and glimpsed the side of the mountain towering above. The sight took my breath away; far above me on the mountainside loomed a gigantic face, the lustrous eyes fringed by a leather crown. It was the woman, in my arms and on the mountainside. Her mouth pouted and a shower of brilliant stars poured into the stream like a waterfall and covered me like drops of spray which blinded me with crystal radiance. The hissing sparkles filled my ears with an ecstatic sound like rushing wind . . ."[8]

Bates' description of the young monk's ecstatic meeting with his own Bright Shadow, although fictional, describes one of the most important truths when it comes to sexual magical practise. Ecstatic sexual union with the divine through trance, often denigrated by mainstream religion, is one of the most spiritual and deep life-changing experiences. It not only connects us with the deepest areas of our own soul, but also with the divine in the form of God/Goddess. In this chapter we have tried to give you an insight into the level of power that comes from these techniques, which not only help us make connection with deity but also to understand the mysteries of the soul. It is important to remember though that such techniques must be approached with care and patience if anything is to be gained from them. If this is done, then the results far outweigh the time and effort expended.

NOTES

1 Diana Paxson, *Sex, Status and Seidr: Homosexuality and Germanic Religion*. First published in Idunna 31, 1997.

2 Mircea Eliade, *Shamanism: Archaic Techniques of Ecstasy*, pp. 258, 351, and 461.

3 Reuss and Kellner founded the OTO in 1902.

4 *Flygja* translates as "attendant" or "fetch" when it takes an external form. *Hamingja* translates as "luck" and like the former translation of *Flylgja*, can take an external form as a spirit or deity of luck sent by an individual to accompany another. Karl Mortensen, *A Handbook of Norse Mythology*, 48.

5 First published in 1740 by Gabrielle-Suzanne Bardot de Villeneuve.

6 Chapter 8, "Sex and Politics," 146–149. Originated from Victor and Cora Anderson's Faery Tradition.

7 Mircea Eliade, *Shamanism: Archaic Techniques of Ecstasy*, 79–80.

8 Chapter 14, "A Sorcerer's Soul," 195–196.

Chapter 16

The Oracle of the Dead: Speaking with the Deceased

It is important to include this chapter for two very good reasons. First, historically there has always been a strong connection between trance states and the ability of the seer to talk to the dead. This is obvious by looking at the ancient history of such oracles as the Necromanteio at Ephyra, the Oracle of the Dead at Baia, the medieval history of magic and the necromancy of John Dee and Edward Kelly, but also in the development of the modern trance traditions with its connections to the Spiritualist movement (see chapter 2). Of course, going back into the mists of time, while also looking at comparative tribal practises from around the world, there is truly no difference between talking with the dead and traditional communing with the ancestors; it is all really a matter of semantics. Secondly and more importantly, from a practical viewpoint, if you practise trance-prophecy and ecstatic trance states, sooner or later you will find yourself having to deal with discarnate entities, with the souls of the dead. We have come to this conclusion not from an intellectual angle, but from experience. Over the years, we have found that anyone who goes into trance will at some point attract those who have had problems passing over to the other side. The concept of communicating with the deceased to ask for advice is not a recent invention of modern Spiritualism. An example of this as can be found in Homer's *Odyssey*.* Odysseus descends into Hades and invokes the spirit of the dead seer Teiresias after being told by the witch Circe that Teiresias will

---

* Homer completed this classic Greek poem toward the end of the eighth century. It is a sequel to his previous classic, *The Iliad*. It is the story of the adventures of the Greek hero Odysseus as he and his crew return home from the Trojan Wars.

guide him on his journey. Teiresias warns Odysseus that "he will never escape the one that shakes the earth," a reference to Poseidon, the Greek god of the sea, and Odysseus and his crew spend ten years at sea trying to return home.

What Happens at Death?

This is really the big question and some would say the question that causes all religions to come into being. Unlike other religious movements, neo-Paganism has never fully come to terms with the question. Generally, most modern Pagans will say that they believe in reincarnation, but what happens at the moment of death and immediately afterward has only been discussed in depth by a few Pagan authors.* This causes a problem, because it is absolutely essential to know all you can about the spirit if you are going to speak with the dead. Of course, our ancient ancestors had no such problems, as they had established theologies surrounding death that answered these questions.

Unlike modern neo-Pagans, the ancient Egyptians did not believe in reincarnation. Their concept of afterlife was, in fact, the forerunner to Christianity with its concept of judgement after death, and the belief that you would be united with your ancestors in the afterlife, with your *Ka*. The concept of Ka is important to anyone practising trance-prophecy, as is the other component of the individual spirituality—the *Ba*. The Ba was the personality of the individual, and was considered to be unique to the individual. It corresponds to the Mental-Emotional Body (see chapter 8 for information on the aura and its bodies). The Ka was considered to be life giving to the physical body. Egyptians believed it entered physical body at the moment of birth. This is best likened to the etheric and spiritual bodies in regard to the aura. In ancient Egyptian theology, it was believed that the two split at the moment of death. This ancient Egyptian concept is important, as it gives clues to what happens to us at the moment of death.

One theory is that at the moment of death the aura splits into its component pieces. The Etheric Body, the individual's life force, begins to naturally fade away at the moment of death. The Mental-Emotional Body, the individual personality, may continue earthbound or may follow

---

* Pagan authors who have discussed death include Sybil Leek (*The Complete Art of Witchcraft*, 1971), Victor Anderson ("The Psychic Structure of the Human Being," *Nemeton*, 1972, 1973), Raymond Buckland, Doreen Valiente (*The Rebirth of Witchcraft*, 1989), and Starhawk and M. Macha NightMare (*The Pagan Book of Living and Dying*, 1997).

the Akashic or Spiritual Body, the soul, "down the tunnel." This tunnel is often described by people who have had near-death experiences.* While working as a staff nurse, Gavin heard these stories on many occasions directly from patients who had experienced the phenomenon, or from other nurses who had heard the stories from their patients. Individuals who have had near-death experiences often describe an illuminated tunnel, bright white or hues of blue, and images of relatives waiting for them on the other side. Some occasionally describe a relative coming to meet them through the tunnel, letting them know that "it wasn't their time yet" and telling them to return back to their physical lives. At the moment of death, the individual's Mental-Emotional Body and Spiritual Body passes through the "tunnel" at the same time, but for several reasons this may not occur, as we explain later. But the question then becomes where do they go?

The following is, of course, hypothetical. Some would argue that this is true of all religious beliefs regarding what happens after death. The next stage is what is described in Wiccan terms as the "Summerlands," or what the ancient Greeks knew as Elysium fields. It is, in fact, where we expect to go after death. Doreen Valiente talks of this in *The Rebirth of Witchcraft*:

> But why should not each religion have its own paradise? The Moslems' idea of paradise bears little resemblance to the Christian one. The Spiritualists have their 'Summerland', and the Red Indians [Native Americans] their 'Happy Hunting-ground'. Is it not possible that these 'many mansions' may exist in other dimensions? One recalls the 'fair Elfland' of the old ballads, existing as an alternative to that road which leads to the Christian Heaven. (116)

If we are expecting to go to a heavenly place, well, that is where we will go. But, if we are guilt-ridden, if our conscience is heavy, the place we go to might not be as pleasant. Of course, it is an illusion. It is of our own creation. Over time, if the time exists in this place, we will come to realise this, and the illusion will break down. We may decide to prolong this illusionary world and stay there longer, or we may find ourselves at a stage where we are ready to reincarnate, after deciding how to deal with the karma we have accumulated from the previous lifetimes, both negative and positive. This is the "weighing of the scales" in Egyptian

* Dr. Raymond Moody Jr. coined the term near-death experience (NDE) in his seminal work *Life After Life* (1977).

cosmology, or the facing of the "Lords of Karma." Before returning into another incarnation, it is necessary to balance our karma, a decision that our soul is given and no other entity. One of the best descriptions we have come across was in a movie called *What Dreams May Come*,[1] where a newly deceased doctor is given a chance to save the soul of his wife from her self-induced form of purgatory, after she committed suicide several years earlier.

The Ancient Pagan Origins of Spiritualism

As we said at the beginning of this chapter, if you practise trance-prophecy, unavoidably you will start getting in close contact with the souls of the deceased. It isn't that you will have to look for discarnate entities, the dead will find you! This has been our experience now for over twenty years, and in one out of three practical workshops where we have taught the techniques described in this book, someone has had an encounter with a deceased relative or friend. The primary reason for the existence of the Spiritualist movement in the nineteenth and early twentieth centuries was to allow closure, that is, to allow relatives to say good-bye to their loved ones one last time. There is a historical precedence for this in the religio-magical practises of the ancient Greeks, known as *Nekyia*. These rites were particularly associated with the ancient temples at Baia in Italy, and Ephyra in Greece (see Photograph 14). We were lucky enough to visit the older of the two sites, Baia, in 2006. Baia is west of Naples, on the south-facing coast just before you reach the Bacoli Peninsula. It is an area of volcanic activity known as Campi Flegria ("The Fields of Fire"), being less than twenty miles from Mount Vesuvius. It is one of those ancient sites that was almost forgotten, probably due to most visitors being more interested in the nearby remains at Pompeii, Herculaneum, and Cuma (mentioned in chapter 1).

Photograph 13: The Nekromanteion, or Oracle of the Dead, at Ephyra, Greece, was one of the most intense sites of ritual for connection with the souls of the dead in the ancient world.
(Courtesy www.dreamstime.com)

Baia appears in Virgil's *The Aeneid*,* as well as Strabo.[2] According to Virgil, Aeneas had once visited Baia to contact the spirit of his father; he gave a full description of the ritual practises he had to go through and documented his visit to the sibyl at Cuma. According to Virgil's account, an inquirer had to first spend three days in a room decorated with murals depicting the afterlife. Most likely, the inquirer was then encouraged by the priests to go through a regime of meditation and fasting. At the end of the third day, he or she was expected to make a sacrificial offering of a sheep, whose entrails would then be read by the priesthood. From this reading, the priests would decide whether the inquirer should continue on their journey. If a positive outcome were forecast, the inquirer would then be lead deeper into the labyrinth of tunnels cut into the hillside, which recreated the mythical Greek underworld, ready to start on the next phase of their journey.

Following two baths and a period of meditation in between, the querent would then be dressed in a white robe (symbolizing purity), before descending a ladder into a round antechamber and commencing down a

---

* Virgil wrote *The Aeneid* between 29 and 19 BCE. It is the story of Aeneas, a Trojan who travels to Italy. It consists of twelve books that chart his and his followers' progress as they become the ancestors of the modern Romans.

long tunnel, dimly lit by oil lamps, surrounded by the sounds of the dead. After a long and disorientating journey down this tunnel, the inquirer arrived at an underground river, which he was told was the river Styx. Here the inquirer met the ghostly figure of a priest dressed as Charon, the ferryman of the dead. After being steered down the Styx by the ferryman, the inquirer disembarked and was confronted by three barking dogs chained to the wall. This was done by the priesthood to recreate the guardian of the dead, the three-headed dog Cerberus. The inquirer proceeded through the next tunnel to the pillared inner sanctuary, where the querent offered mistletoe to Persephone before talking with the spirits of the dead.[3] At this point, no one really knows what form the séance took; we can only surmise that the spirit of the relative manifested within the sanctuary. There the inquirer encountered a seeress who channelled or even became possessed by Persephone. If this is the case, the séance differed very little from the practise of modern Spiritualism, albeit the inquirer was also in an altered state of consciousness.

The Nekromanteion at Ephyra is mentioned by Herodotus in his account of Periander's encounter with his deceased wife, Melissa. This is the younger of the two sites. Some believe that it was actually based on the Oracle of the Dead at Baia, as it is not mentioned before 800 BCE. It can be found on the river Acheron (rivers play an important symbolic part in the passage of the dead, see page 112), in the Greek province of Epirius. It is said that it was built at the gates of Hades. While it was a place of closure for many, it was also a place where one sought advice from their dead relatives—again a practise no different to the practices of nineteenth century Spiritualism, and in the twentieth century it inspired Dr. Raymond Moody Jr. to recreate the Nekromanteion in the form of a "psychomanteum."* Just like at Baia, there were elaborate rituals that had to be undergone before meeting with the deceased spirits, as it was believed any such meeting was considered to be potentially dangerous. The priesthood conducted purification rituals on the site, including dieting, fasting, meditation, and isolation, similar to those performed in Baia. These rituals went on over several days, and when completed, the adherent was ready to enter the realm of the dead and meet his ancestors. The adherent would enter the east passage of the Nekromanteion and make

---

* Dr. Raymond A. Moody Jr. is an author, lecturer, and counsellor specializing in the grieving process. He created the psychomanteum in 1993 and popularized its use through his book *Reunions*. It consists of a small, dimly lit chamber, with a central chair and an angled mirror. Similar to the practises in the Nekromanteion, participants are expected to lightly fast.

the appropriate offerings and libations, which would normally consist of sacrificing a sheep into a pit. He would then pass into the labyrinth, a maze of dark passages, while the accompanying priest invoked the spirits of the dead, as well as the goddesses Hecate and Persephone. This undoubtedly increased the depth of his trance state as he wandered the tunnels under the illusion that he was passing through the streets of Hades. He finally approached the three arched doors that led to the central hall. It was here that he made his final offering of a barley meal in a bowl, cast an *apotropaic stone*,* and poured the final offering of barley meal onto the floor of the chamber to the gods of the underworld, Aidoneus (Hades) and Persephone.

In his book *Netherworld*, Robert Temple suggests that it was the whole procedure leading to the adherents decent into Hades that was responsible for his ability to encounter the dead:

> The physical and spiritual trials during the sojourns, which lasted for many days in the dark chambers of the Necromanteion, together with the isolation, the magic rituals, prayers and invocations, the perambulation through the dark passages and the common belief in the manifestation of the dead spirits created the proper psychological state of mind in the pilgrim. This was greatly assisted by the special diet he was given. In the course of the excavations large jars full of carbonised fruits, wheat, barley and broadbeans were found, of a small variety similar to the Egyptian "fool" (*Vicia faba equina*) and quantities of lupine seeds. Broadbeans possess toxic qualities, and when eaten green cause wind, indigestion and a relaxation of the senses to the point of giddiness and hallucination and allergic syndromes (*cyamisasis*). The same effects were produced by lupines (*lathyrism*). Thus, with the relaxation of the senses, often approaching the point of vertigo and loss of understanding, the necessary condition of mind was achieved for communication with the spirits of the dead.[4]

What is described here are several trance-inducing techniques that we explained earlier in this book (see chapter 9), which are familiar to anyone who has studied traditional forms of shamanic trance practise. At Ephyra, these techniques appeared to be more intensely used than at Baia, which relied on the nature of the architecture of the temple

---

* *Apotropaic magic* was intended to ward off evil or harmful influences. An *apotropaic stone* was therefore decorated with symbols that allowed it to act as an amulet.

complex. These are not techniques we necessarily recommend, as several writers of the period point out—many of those who decided to take the journey into the oracle of the dead never returned, having been claimed by the realm itself as permanent residents. Like Baia, we can only surmise that those who contacted the dead did so in a similar fashion to Baia with a seeress representing Persephone present and acting as a medium for the deceased spirit.

Negative Possession, Exorcism, and Spirit Attachment

While most spirits of the deceased pass over when made aware of their mortality, some may not pass over for other reasons, both positive and negative. This can range from fear of what they will face when they pass over (judgment), to being concerned about what will happen to their relatives or loved ones. In the latter case, the duration can be quite short. When Gavin's first niece was born, his sister saw their deceased grandfather standing at the end of the bed. He had passed over about a year earlier and made his presence felt on several occasions. After this instance, he was not seen or felt again. This is, of course, a positive example. The problems occur when the spirit stays much longer because of negative reasons, such as the aforementioned fear. It usually means that the spirit feeds off of the living. When this occurs, it is described as an "attachment," rather than a possession. Possessions are, in fact, incredibly rare and only occur in individuals with mental illness. A deceased spirit who attaches will feed off of the etheric body of an individual to whom it is close. While it may not consider its motives as negative, the spirit may attempt to influence the living, trying to live its old life through that individual. In other cases, it may become overprotective and damage the individual whom the spirit is trying to protect. Janet witnessed this on one occasion when the spirit of a friend, a mother who had died of cancer, attached itself to her four children. The three older children described seeing their mother coming into the bedroom and claimed she would "bite them" (she was, in fact, draining etheric energy from them). All three of them were frightened and continually tired due to their energy being drained. The spirit of the mother was simply overprotective, but required the etheric energy to manifest. To resolve the situation, Janet, Stewart, and the coven did a Passing Over Ritual for her using personal items from her wedding. She was made aware that the children would be safe, and after the ritual she never bothered the children again. Of course, this is an extreme occurrence and the only one we have come across where a form of classic energy "vampirism" took place.

What we have described above is actually well-recognised both today and in antiquity. The ancient Greeks used the term barathēkē to describe a spirit attachment that, although symbiotic between the host and the spirit, almost always has negative effects on the living individual.[5] The recognition of this form is now recognised not just in the metaphysical/occult communities but also by some psychiatrists who have realised that orthodox psychiatry does not necessarily provide all the answers. In 1987 Edith Fiore published *The Unquiet Dead,* which described the use of trance-induction (hypnosis) in the treatment of "possessed" patients. This book influenced William Baldwin who coined the term "spirit attachment" in his book *Spirit Releasement Therapy* (1992). He defined the different type of entities, creating clinical procedures for dealing with attachments in a secular pragmatic fashion. The biggest exponent of the concept of spirit attachment and William Baldwin's work is Dr. Alan Sanderson, MB, BS (London), MRCP, DPM, MRC Psych. We have included all his qualifications to show that he is somebody with an impeccable background in the subject of psychiatry. There are clearly strong Spiritualist practises involved in his work, and in an article he wrote for the *Spirit Release Foundation*, he states:

> Spirit release developed from spiritualism in the second half of the 19th century. The writings of Allan Kardec, a prominent French scholar, who compiled *The Spirits' Book* (1857) and *The Book of Mediums* (1874) both still in print, have been influential, leading to the development of the Spiritist movement, worldwide, with many adherents, especially in Brazil.
>
> An American psychiatrist, Carl Wickland, and his wife, Anna, a spirit medium, were the pioneers of depossession, as it was then called, in North America. His classic, "Thirty Years Among the Dead", first published in 1924, tells how static electricity was applied to the patient's head and back, in order to drive out possessing spirits. The spirits then entered Anna, through whom they spoke with Carl, who persuaded them to leave. This was an effective, but dangerous, procedure.[6]

Again, we would like to point out that this is not possession, something that we are in agreement with Dr. Sanderson about, and like Sanderson, we do not support the use of exorcism as it is and has been carried out by the Roman Catholic and subsequent other Christian churches since the Middle Ages. To quote Sanderson: "Expelling the attached entity in this way is an adversarial procedure, far removed from contemporary spirit release, which aims to help both host and entity."

We would go one step further by saying that exorcism is, in fact, a violent act that damages both the individual and the spirit concerned. Of course, exorcism in Christianity was not originally aimed at removing discarnate spirits, but demons. The origins of exorcism, as we see it today in the Christian Church, are in fact dubious to say the least, originating in the Catholic Church's use of exorcism to prove the existence of demons which is then used as propaganda against Protestantism.[7] This violent form of exorcism therefore has its origins no further back than the sixteenth century, the most notable and first use of this form being recorded in Laon, France in 1566.* The practice of exorcism in Christianity actually originated from Judaism, and probably goes back even further to Mesopotamia, where the belief in demons, in the Judeo-Christian sense, originated. In Babylonian culture, the priesthood also served as exorcists, but rather than taking the hands-on approach, this was normally done ritually by driving the evil spirit into a clay tablet or effigy and then destroying it, thus destroying the invading spirit. It was not the invasive and violent method that is currently employed by some modern Christian exorcists. With this belief in demons and spirits as part of his cultural background, it is not surprising that Jesus was known principally during his time as an exorcist. There are numerous references of Jesus banishing demons from the sick, and it was one of the principle teachings that he passed on to his disciples as noted by Matthew 10.1: "And when he had called unto him his twelve disciples, he gave them power against unclean spirits, to cast them out" (KJV).

In Judaism, a possessing spirit was referred to as a *dybukk* and was believed to cause mental illness. It was believed that this spirit could be drawn out through the small toe of the victim.[8] The purpose was not necessarily to banish the spirit back to the hell, but to redeem it. This suggests a *discarnate entity*, the spirit of a deceased person rather than a demon in the Christian sense. This is undoubtedly what Jesus was originally practising and teaching, which is in stark contrast to the medieval and modern Christian viewpoint, where the only purpose in banishing it is to send the spirit back to the infernal regions that it came from. At some

---

* The exorcism of Nicole Aubrey lasted over three months, from November 1566 to January 1567. She initially claimed that she was possessed by the spirit of her deceased grandfather. During the exorcism by Dominican Priest Pierre de la Motte, the entity claimed conveniently to be Beelzebub himself. Bishop Jean de Bours finally "drove him out" on January 4.

point, the practise of exorcism became twisted by the politics of medieval
Christianity, instilling fear in the population by convincing them that the
legions of hell were just waiting to take control and consume the souls
of anyone who sinned against the church and established feudal order.

The methods of exorcism within modern Christianity seem to
have developed in the ethos of the Middle Ages rather than the earlier
practises found in the Middle East and even earlier shamanic practises of
banishing malevolent spirits from ill people. Most traditional and modern
shamans would argue that they do not actually practise exorcism. They
would define their methods as "retrieving the soul" of the individual, thus
replacing the offending spirit that slipped into the vacuum created by
the loss of the person's soul. Modern shamans specifically using the term
soul retrieval for this reason.[9] In Judeo-Christian exorcism, the objective is
the reverse: to banish the spirit. This implies that the soul is the weaker
of the two forces, and presupposes that original sin exists. This concept,
of course, does not exist in shamanic or native pagan cultures. The neo-
Pagan approach to dealing with discarnate spirits must, therefore, be
more in keeping with the practises of shamanism rather than that of the
Christian churches.

The Séance, Passing Over, and the Ethics of Contacting the Dead

We believe that the most ethical reason for a séance must be to assist the
dead in passing over to the other side. Both of us found ourselves performing this role on several occasions. For Gavin it started when he was a
registered nurse and discovered he was sensitive to the spirits of patients
who had failed to pass over at the moment of death. He found that this
was common with individuals who had sudden deaths, such as myocar-
dial infarctions (heart attacks) or fatal strokes. The spirit of the individual
simply didn't know they were dead, as it happened so fast. Gavin often
found himself having to simply tell them what happened, reassure them
that their relatives were okay, and then encourage them to "find the tunnel" and finally pass over. He found that many of the nurses he met and
had a spiritual practise did the same thing; this became a natural part of
his job. Of course, it is not just sudden death due to medical conditions
that can leave a deceased spirit stranded. It is also common with fatal
road accidents and disasters, natural or otherwise. This occurred after
9/11 and many Pagans and Witches in New York City found themselves

working alongside other spiritual groups to pass over the spirits of the dead from the site of the Twin Towers. Even today there are still shrines to those who died there. Although there may be minor cultural differences, this practise is common in nearly every culture: from Christianity to Buddhism, from Hinduism to Shintoism. It is common everywhere in the world to leave flowers or religious symbols at sites of sudden death. Most relatives and friends leave remembrances at the sites to inform the earthbound spirit of its mortality, and that the spirit is loved and remembered and can now pass over.

When it comes to initiating contact with the dead, we feel it is only ethical if the discarnate spirit already attempted to make contact with the living—in which case holding a séance or an Oracle of the Dead is quite fitting. We certainly do not believe it is right to summon the dead if they do not wish to come. It is better to leave them to find you, and we feel very strongly that they should not be seen as a form of entertainment or a method of obtaining self-gain. The dead need to be treated in the same way the living are treated—with respect. Contact with the dead should be seen as much an act of healing as practising any forms of conventional or complementary healing practise. This is particularly true when it comes to bereaved relatives who are seeking closure, which is another ethical reason for holding a séance. Again, this should only be done if the person feels the spirit of their lost loved one has been trying to make contact. We should warn you that holding a séance and performing a Passing Over ritual for the wrong reasons and without knowing what you are doing is to invite more problems than good. It can, in fact, result in a haunting or, worse, a spirit attachment.

The Traditional Séance

The traditional séance takes place in a room dimly lit with either candles or veils over electric lamps. The attendees, usually relatives seeking questions from deceased loved ones, sit at a round or oval table. Everyone present forms a circle by touching their hands, little finger to little finger, focusing on the medium. The auras of the participants and the medium now create "the circle," allowing movement of etheric energy. The medium may or may not be veiled, depending on his or her method of working. The Underworld Decent Technique (see chapter 11) may be used by the modern medium to make this connection at the gates of death (Realm of the Ancestors). Deities may be invoked to help a discarnate spirit pass over to the other side, but it should be appropriate to that spirit's belief system. (During the Indonesian Tsunami in 2006, our own group *Teampal*

Na Callaighe invoked Kwan Yin, Buddha, and Ganesha to help the souls of the dead pass over to the other side.)

The Witches' Table or Board

The use of polished tables as a tool to conduct séances first appeared in the 1960s and quickly became beloved of horror movie script writers. The concept derived from the Ouija Board™ (see page 25). Unlike the traditional séance (above), it does not rely on a central medium, but a minimum of four people. Three are seated around a smooth table acting as mediums by creating a *gestalt mind*—a psychic connection among the participants on an astral level. One participant needs to have a notebook and pen to record the conversation. This is essential, as messages from the world of spirit can be received rapidly, and the spelling may not necessarily be coherent. It is common for spirits to use abbreviated messages, so writing it down helps to decipher more cryptic conversations that may be received.

The table should be waxed so the surface is slippery (glass-top tables are excellent for this). On the table are placed twenty-six white cards cut to about 10 centimetres by 10 centimetres (4 inches by 4 inches), with letters of the alphabet, plus "Yes" and "No" written on them. The letters are placed around the outer edge of the table, with Yes and No in the center. A drinking glass or a smooth round tablemat is needed to act as a pointer or *planchette*.

It is vitally important that a circle is cast when using a Witches' table. This is the commonest mistake when people use the Ouija Board™; not having a consecrated, protected space allows lower spirits forms to interfere. This is the problem when it comes to urban myths regarding Ouija boards, which is what Hollywood horror film directors love so much. It does not matter how you put up a protective circle. It can be as simple as holding hands, passing energy around and visualizing a blue sphere expanding outward (see page 175), or it can be a full Wiccan ritual with incense, candles, etc. The important thing is that the space is consecrated. We also suggest calling your own guides, or the god or goddess you personally work with, to act as a psychopomp. This is important, as they will filter and protect you from anything negative out there and allow you to only communicate with the spirits with whom you wish to communicate. Fear and negative emotion is the main problem when you are practising spirit communication or Passing Over séances. It is this kind of emotion that will attract negative spirit forms, which is why a group must discuss and air any problems before commencing a séance. It is also important to decide who will ask the questions.

The next stage is to call and identify the spirit you are dealing with. This is done by everyone placing the index finger of their left hand onto the glass or planchette placed in the middle of the table. The person chosen will then begin to ask the questions, the first being: "We ask any spirits present to identify themselves—is anybody there?" The glass should then begin to move of its own accord and hopefully will go to the Yes card. Of course, what is really happening is that one or maybe more people in the group are acting as mediums. The effect of having a group of people create a gestalt is to increase any psychic energy used to further attract any discarnate spirit. After this, hopefully the glass will move and spell out the name of the individual spirit. It must give its name, and if there is any doubt about its intent, this should also be questioned by asking, "What if your purpose here?"

The spirit that initially starts to communicate may be a discarnate entity, or it could just as easily be one of the participant's guides. If it is their guide, this is a good indication that they have a primary medium present. The guide can then be asked to search for the spirit that the group intends to communicate with or pass over. It is best to keep questions during this stage simple, so that the reply consists of a yes or no answer. Once the guide finds the individual spirit, the group can start communicating with it. Of course, they may find the spirit they are looking for immediately, in which case they can go straight to this stage. Again, name has to be asked, and if there are any concerns, its intention. Once this has been established, the group can start gathering information about the spirit.

The next question after name and intention has to be "Why are you here?" Obviously, this should inform the group whether the spirit is aware that it passed on to the otherworld. If it is not aware, then it needs to be made aware of its situation. This can result in a flurry of activity on the board, as the glass moves backward and forward. It will be particularly frenetic for a spirit that has not yet come to terms with its situation. Of course, it could be that the spirit is simply there to communicate, in which case the activity will be noticeably calmer. It may have come from the Realm of the Divine, or it may not be ready to pass over just yet. In that case, it should be allowed to communicate before being thanked and asked to leave. But if it is a spirit who is unaware of its death, it needs to be reassured, just as you would reassure a person. This is essential until the spirit and the subsequent movement on the board calms down. If the spirit is aware of its situation, then the group needs to ascertain why it has not moved on. The reasons can be numerous, but commonly it is concern about relatives. The spirit may stay behind because it feels that there has not been a resolution in a situation, and it cannot pass over until this has taken place. Whatever the reason, the spirit now needs to be reassured that it does not need to stay. For example, one could say: "Your wife is okay. She is happy, and you don't need to worry about her. The rest of the family is looking after her, and it is okay to leave now." At this point, it is important to ask the spirit whether it is happy to leave. It should reply firmly with a "Yes," but if it doesn't, then there is little you can do until it is ready to move on. A yes reply leads on to the next stage, calling a guide to pass it over.

Generally, your own guide will not be able to pass the person's spirit over to the other side unless it is a deity to which the spirit has a connection as well. If there is no connection with a mutual deity, you will need to call a personal guide to take the spirit over, which can take several forms. If the person was particularly religious, you may wish to call a spirit from that person's religious ideology, such as an angel, or you might want to call forth a loved one who passed on. The spirit should be asked to look for the light, and then the guide who will emerge from it. It should be encouraged to follow the guide back into the light. If it has passed over successfully, there will be a particular feeling that fills the room. Some people often describe the smell of flowers, particularly roses.

Dealing with Negative Possessions in Trance-Prophecy Work

At different times we have been approached by individuals who were concerned that the work we were doing in trance-prophecy was 'dangerous.' They hold onto a fear that in some way those participating in trance states may be affected adversely. It is true there are potentially some side effects to doing trance work, which you may not necessarily wish to open yourself up to, but this is no different from the fact that you open yourself up to adverse side effects in almost everything you do in life. When you walk down the street, you inhale car fumes; when you drink alcohol; you risk damaging your liver. There are risks in everything, so in that respect trance-prophecy is no different. Of course, what they were really asking was: "Don't you risk the seer becoming schizophrenic or being possessed by an evil spirit?" Such statements really say more about the individual asking than the work being undertaken. You noticed we said "schizophrenic or being possessed"—that is because some will refuse to accept that they still hold onto fears of demons and evil spirits they were brought up with, and will clothe them in rational explanations.

Most of us were brought up in a culture with an underlying belief that spirits we could communicate with were evil. Initially, this was a doctrine of the church, that such spirits were earthbound as they had "fallen from grace" and therefore did the work of the devil. Without realising it, this has affected the way we work magically within Wicca and other pagan traditions. We cast a circle for protection from such spirits, even though our ancestors did not, a legacy of monotheistic, ceremonial ritual magick. One would think that such a myth would fade away considering the waning of the church's power in the twentieth century. But since the advent of film and television, various lurid horror films, such as *The Exorcist*, perpetuated this myth. The fact that they were fiction was beside the point; the myth continued, as do the various stories of bad experiences with Ouija Boards™.

Over the years we have had to deal with several situations relating to spirit attachment, either with discarnate entities or with lower forms. In most cases, it is either due to a mental instability of some form, or a lack of knowledge in dealing with spirits, such as dabbling with Ouija Boards™, ghost hunting, etc. While writing this chapter, we had to deal with a young man who had a lower spirit attached to himself. He had gone out "ghost hunting" on Halloween night purely for fun. He was, in fact, quite cynical about the occult, but had had several near-death experiences due to his passion for motor sports. This made him susceptible to psychic experiences, opening both his brow and crown chakra centers. While his cynicism held during the ghost hunt around the old convent in our hometown of Kells, it quickly changed when he started experiencing things the following nights after going to bed. He saw red eyes watching him, heard sounds, and woke up when he felt pressure on his body. He had never experienced these things before. He picked up a lower entity form, which attached itself to his aura. It was attracted to the energy given off because of his abilities. The problem was easily resolved by having Gavin do a full aura cleansing on him, which removed the entity and taught the young man how to close the brow and chakras centers. There is an old saying: "The only thing we have to fear is fear itself,"[10] and this is certainly true when you work with trance-prophecy and mediumship, as it is negative emotion that is the biggest danger when working in the world of spirit.

NOTES

1 Polygram Film Entertainment (1988). Based on the novel by Richard Matheson. The title originates from William Shakespeare's *Hamlet.*

2 Strabo (64 BCE–24 CE), a Greek geographer who lived at the turn of the first millennium, describes the practises of Baia in Book 5 of his *Geography.*

3 Robert Temple, chap. 2 in *Netherworld: Discovering the Oracle of the Dead.*

4 Chapter 1 in *Discovery of the Underworld,* page 42.

5 Monte Plaisance, *Scrolls of Manetho,* Scroll 1, page 54. Sourced from Daniel Ogden's *Greek and Roman Necromancy* (Princeton, 2001). *Barathēkē* (ancient Greek) means "to be struck."

6 Dr. Alan Sanderson, "Spirit Attachment and Human Health," Spirit Release Foundation. http://www.spiritrelease.com/cases/review_spiritrelease.htm.

7 Johnathan L. Pearl, *The Crime of Crimes: Criminology and Politics in France, 1560 to 1620,* page 43.

8 R. E. Guiley, *Harper's Encyclopaedia of Mystical & Paranormal Experience* (New York: Harper Collins, 1991).

9 A term derived from and used in Michael Harner's core shamanism.

10 Franklin D. Roosevelt, from his first Inaugural Address, 1932.

Chapter 17

And Now a Word from Our Sponsors: The Gods Speak

We have always felt that it was rude to talk about someone in a conversation but then not allow him or her to have their "penny's worth," to use the English phrase. For a long time we have felt that the wishes of the goddesses and gods have been ignored within the neo-Paganism. With this in mind, we decided it was time to bring them into the debate on the direction of the neo-Pagan movement, to give them a public voice; after all, who wouldn't like the chance to voice their views and opinions to a large audience through the medium of a book? So the next question for us was what questions do we ask a god or goddess? The questions had to be broad, and the answers had to be easily interpretable. It came down to just three:

- Who are you?
- What future do you see, and what advice do you wish to give to the neo-Pagan movement as a whole?
- Is there anything else you wish to say?

The next thing was to choose which gods and goddesses to ask. Not a choice you would think would be an easy task, but it was already made for us due to the work we have been doing over the years in trance-prophecy. All the seers chosen are experienced in trance-prophecy and have worked with specific deities for several years: Aphrodite, Apollo, Bríd, Freya, Hekate, and The Morrigan. When we first approached the seers, we asked them to go into trance, approach the deity they were dedicated to, and then ask him of her if they would like to answer some questions for this chapter. There were no refusals; in fact, most seers reported enthusiastic replies. The next stage was for the seer to ask the questions; sometimes this was during the same trance-prophecy session, sometimes a later session. The seers sent the following transcripts to us. We have tried to keep the editing to a minimum, although we have removed personal messages given to some of those present.

Aphrodite

This eternal love goddess has stood the test of time, and has never been forgotten. She retained her image and power, through art, poetry, and even modern media; nothing in human history has ever had the ability to repress human love. Hollywood revelled, monopolized, and exploited her sensuality. Films were made about her, while stars were compared in beauty to her and, someone would say, paid the price for it. In modern imagery she is as much Marilyn Monroe as she is Botticelli's Venus emerging from the sea in a clamshell. She is everything that constitutes sensual love: sexuality, fickleness, and even unpredictability, but her message today is the same as it has always been: one of love and healing.

The seer Anthea (34) is a priestess of Aphrodite, living in Belgium. She works as a psychotherapist, which she considers to be as much a part of her being a priestess as doing seership or ritual. In 2000, Anthea took her first steps on the path of modern Witchcraft as a solitary practitioner. Not long after, signs started to appear, although she was not aware of their true meaning. They eventually lead her to Aphrodite, the Greek goddess of love, beauty, and fertility. At Pagan Gathering Europe (PaGE) 2004,* during a very intense trance-prophecy workshop, she finally came face to face with Aphrodite while in trance, and everything fell into place for her. From 2004 onward, Anthea received her training in eclectic Witchcraft from Arcadia Coven, and was for several years given responsibility for new trainees within that group. During that time she developed a very special bond with Aphrodite, who she realizes now was slowly preparing her for priestesshood. In 2006, she went to Greece for a pilgrimage to the old temples and places of power of the ancient gods: to the Acrokorinthos in Corinth, where once the famous holy temple of Aphrodite stood. In that place and at that time, Anthea got the confirmation that she was indeed a priestess of Aphrodite, and she dedicated her life in service to the goddess of love, and as her priestess, in 2007. Anthea is now the high priestess of the Temple of Aphrodite, a daughter coven of Arcadia, where she is a mentor to anyone who wants to become a priest

* PaGE is a festival held in Belgium every three years by Arcadia.

or priestess for a specific god or goddess. She's also a member of the Magna Dea Coven, also a daughter coven of Arcadia focusing on trance work and a deeper level of spiritual knowing and experience.

This trance-prophecy session was conducted and recorded in her group, Arcadia, on July 20, 2013. It was originally performed in Flemish then transcribed and translated into English. Several members were present and took part in the ritual, including Fjierra who acted as trance guide, and Eirinn, who also put questions to Aphrodite. It commenced with the use of the Underworld Decent Technique aided with a chant to Aphrodite to enable her to fully possess Anthea. Ellipses indicate pauses:

Photograph 14: Priestess Anthea possessed by Aphrodite during trance-prophecy ritual
(Courtesy Michel De Groot)

Trance guide (TG): *"Lady Aphrodite, welcome!"*

Eírinn (Arcadia member): *"Lady Aphrodite, welcome!"*

TG: *"Aphrodite, golden lady of beauty and of love. Did your Priestess Anthea tell you why we have gathered here tonight with our coven, Magna Dea?"*

Aphrodite: "Yes, she told me about a book."

TG: *"That is correct. A priestess and priest living in Ireland are working on a new book, and they want to give the gods their say. So today we gathered here in the temple of your Priestess Anthea, in order to write down and record your words, so that they can be admitted in this book. Would that be okay, my Lady?"*

Aphrodite: *(Nods in agreement.)*

TG: *"I have three questions for you tonight. These questions are not mine, but Janet and Gavin's. The first question is 'Who are you?'"*

Aphrodite: *(Laughs)* "I am rather surprised that they ask me this question. They do know who I am? I am the sister of Freya."

TG: *"They certainly know who you are, my Lady, but I presume it is their intention to add this in the book, perhaps for people who don't know yet who you are."*

Aphrodite: "I am love . . . and connection . . . I am that what lives in the heart of mother and child, of loved ones . . . I am that what moves the universe . . . what makes that everything grows and procreates."

TG: *"The next questions, Aphrodite, are what future can you see, and what advice do you wish to give to the neo-Pagan movement as a whole? How do you see it evolving?"*

Aphrodite: "I am very disappointed . . . Although your goals as such are good, I see that too few people actually act according to those goals . . . There is a lot of good will, but there are few true priests and priestesses . . . who listen to the words that we have been trying to say to you . . . Times will change . . . It is too late now to turn those things around . . . The Great Mother will change . . . She looks for ways to become herself again, to become free of ballast . . . and the greed . . . that human nature has caused . . . And it will be for you . . . a time of survival, of learning to survive. Still too few people . . . know what is really important. Or they think they know what is important, but in reality they don't know anything. We have consigned you with this task . . . to help those people . . . (starts to cry) but there are too few . . . who have answered . . . and that deeply saddens me."

TG: *"What is your advice, my Lady? What can, not just us but the entire Pagan community as a whole, do? What should we do?"*

Aphrodite: "Search and look. Look . . . for who you truly are. Look and search for the things you really believe in . . . and disseminate this. Don't hide behind . . . behind words, but act in deeds. Modern priests and priestesses have long lost their sole responsibilities in guiding people

through rituals and prayers . . . It is your task to affect and touch people
. . . to change people."

TG: *(whispers) "Thank you, my Lady. This is the last question: is there
anything else you wish to say?"*

Aphrodite: "All my brothers and sisters are trying to work together . . .
For a long time now, we haven't been . . . each separate from one another
. . . We go beyond and transcend our boundaries. Let yourself go beyond
and transcend your boundaries now."

TG: *"Thank you, my lady."*

(What followed was a personal question from the trance guide, which
Aphrodite answered. It is removed for reasons of privacy.)

TG: *"We thank you for being with us here today, my lady. We greet you,
and always carry you in our hearts. We now ask you to leave the body of
your priestess, so that our sister Anthea can return to us."*

Anthea pointed out something quite interesting in the cover letter of
the transcript, which is worth noting:

> When I was typing the transcript out later on, I also noticed
> that the words coming out of my mouth do not always cover the
> full scope of what Aphrodite is saying. My sense is that there's a
> lot more meaning to it, unable to be expressed in the words she is
> saying at that moment, like there is some kind of obstruction in the
> process there. When I'm in trance, I really feel her feelings, hear
> her thoughts, observe everything from in the back of my head, and
> it is also clear. But when I compare it to what she has actually said,
> to me it feels like something has gone missing and it's not clear at
> all anymore. It's like there's is another dimension to it that can't
> come across and afterward, also to me, this dimension becomes
> vague again. I only noticed it now, because it was the first time
> we've recorded and transcribed it.

This feeling is not unusual in our experience, and often those receiving a message from a deity possessing a seer say they also feel that they
have received more than a verbal message, that it is was almost as if
there was a telepathic connection and unconscious information was being
passed between them.

Apollo

One of the most popular deities of Greece and later Rome, this Sun God was the god of music, art, philosophy, inspiration, and healing. He was the counterpart to his older lunar sister, Artemis. With the coming of the patriarchal period, he absorbed the aspects of several goddesses. It is said that he defeated the python goddess Gaia at Mount Parnassus and absorbed her prophetic aspects. This allowed the male priesthood to take control of the Oracle at Delphi. His prophetic role continued until the coming of Christianity, but even then it was not forgotten. Remembrance of his role as the god of prophecy reemerged during the Renaissance in the works of the great artistic masters, which has made him a particularly powerful deity to invoke in modern practise. It is for this reason, along with Hekate, that he continues as one of the primary gods invoked in the modern recreations of the sibylline oracle.

For more than twenty years, Monte and Jamie Plaisance have served as elders, clergy, religious freedom activists, and public media spokespersons for the Hellenic religion and related forms of contemporary Paganism and alternative religions nationwide.* Monte holds a BA in psychology and is in his second year of college for environmental science. Jamie is a certified medic and holds other degrees in the medical field. Together they are the owners and operators of Lucky 13 Curio, an occult and mystical shop, as well as being published authors. In addition, they speak at book stores, festivals, and other venues. Their books include Reclaim the Power of the Witch, Scrolls of Manetho, Oracle of Olympus, A Treasury of Hellenic Prayers, and A New Traveler on an Ancient Path. Their writings have been published in a variety of other books and periodicals, as well as on the web.

This oracular consultation was performed on July 21, 2013 by ancient rite, which took the form of Apollo's possession of a *pythia* (seeress). Gypsy performed the duties of the pythia and prepared herself through fasting and meditation for nearly two weeks. A member of their group, Richard, took the role of Hierophant—the role of trance guide as we describe it in this book. The "Hymn to Apollo" was intoned and sung by all the students and *neokori* (temple wards) during the rite. Over six pounds of frankincense and bay laurel were burned throughout the ceremony, and all in attendance wore white and gold. The actual ritual took nearly

---

* Monte and Jamie Plaisance are the senior instructors and the Hierophant and Hierophantissa of Thessaly Temenos, a Hellenic religious center and academy that includes networking, publishing, education, spiritual counseling, and ritual therapy.

three hours of singing and chanting before *katoché* (possession) commenced. Once the deity's presence was obvious, they began the questioning. Below is the verbatim conversation as it was recorded.

TG: "*Who are you?*"

Apollo: "I am he who can count the grains of sand and knows the measure of the oceans, and I am conscious of the mute and hear the ones who cannot speak."

TG: "*To onoma sou enai?*" (What is your name?)

Apollo: "Emai Apollon." (I am Apollo.)

TG: "*Kalosorizo, Apollon! Boro na sas kano merikes erotiseis?*" (*Welcome, Apollo! May I ask you some questions?*)

Apollo: "Nai." (Yes.)

TG: *What future do you see and what advice do you give to the neo-Pagan movement as a whole?*

Apollo: (pause and deep breath) "The single river has now divided its waters, and the once raging waters have weakened to a thousand trickling streams. The stream can bring fertility and growth, but it cannot carve nor create. What was once powerful has weakened through division. Now your images and statues shiver with sweat and dread, for they see the evil that lurks still behind in the shadows. Stand now at the midship, for you are the pilots of this future. Take the helm into your hands and know that there are but two rivers to navigate. One you travel by courage, for it still runs strong and fast, yet it does not divide and takes you home to loving accord. The other river is traveled through hateful strife and cowardly pettiness. It branches out into many smaller streams, easy to navigate, but leading to no place of importance. Shun this cowardly river at all costs and lead your people to the river of courage. All glory comes by way of trials, never by luxury and comfort."

TG: "*Is there anything else you would like to say?*"

Apollo: "Let your own soul be your guide in life, not the opinions of mortals."

Gypsy and Monte's oracular practise gives an example of what can be achieved by studying historical sources. It is important to note the way Apollo uses language; it is common for deities to speak heavily in metaphor and analogy. It also shows that gender is irrelevant in traditional practice, as Apollo fully possessed the female seer.

Bríd

The Irish Goddess Bríd survived the coming of Christianity in Ireland by merging with Saint Brídget, herself originally a priestess of Bríd.* She is said to be "three sisters of the same name," a reference to her original triple form.[1] She also has two other aspects related to fire and water. In her fire aspect, she is the Lady of the Forge, a goddess of initiation and transformation; and in her water aspect, she is the goddess of the well, a goddess of healing and compassion. She is also the goddess of the sovereignty of the land, and this connection comes through very strongly when she possesses Miriam as forthright goddess of the land.

With Irish and Italian heritage, Miriam DeFehr has lived all over Europe, as well as India, where she studied the spiritual practises of Bengal and Northern India. It is here she learned the Vedic spiritual traditions, including Ayurveda, traditional Indian music, and the Vedic forms of palmistry and Eastern astrology. She also has a background in psychology and fine arts, an interesting combination which she utilizes daily. She is also a certified herbalist and a spiritual healer. She is a third-degree initiate of Janet Farrar and Gavin Bone and considers herself a progressive Witch, one who is open to new ideas and loves to learn from everyone. But most importantly, she considers herself a priestess of Bríd, to whom she dedicated her life.†

This trance-prophecy session was carried out by Miriam's coven, the Forge of Fire, on the full moon Esbat ritual of March 2014. During the

---

* There is little doubt historically that the original Brídget was a Druidic priestess at a time when both traditions merged in Ireland. She is strongly associated with Druidism in all the ancient Irish texts (James Bonwick, *Irish Druids and Old Irish Religions* [1986], 200). The tradition of her sacred fire at Kildare is a remnant of the same European tradition of fire-keeping priestesses found throughout Europe and typified by the vestal virgins of Rome.

† Miriam lives with her high priestess and wife, Carolyn, in Harrisburg, Pennsylvania, where they run The Forge of Fire, a progressive Wiccan coven, which has initiates all over the USA, as well as few in other parts of the world. It has an active online community as well, with classes, chats, and forums. The main focus of the group is introspective, with students learning about themselves and their connection with the divine.

ritual, Carolyn acted as the trance guide. The five coven members who attended the ritual all responded to Bríd's messages. There were several personal messages and exchanges with the coven members, which are excluded from the transcription.

The coven began to chant: *"Bríd has come, Bríd is welcome! Bríd has come, Bríd is welcome . . ."* As the coven chanted louder and louder, building the energy in the room, Bríd came through.

TG: *"Welcome, my Lady. We have a few questions tonight, if you don't mind answering them."*

(Bríd nodded yes, after addressing a newcomer.)

TG: *"Who are you?"*

Bríd: "Who am I? I am the hills, the mountains, the lakes, the trees, the ocean, the land, the earth itself. And what are you doing with the earth? What are you doing to me? You are raping me! You are destroying me! All of you! All of you! I don't care about the altar . . . decorated altar! I want ME decorated! I want ME worshiped! Who am I? I am not on the altar! I am in the land—worship me there!"

TG: *"What future do you see, and what advice do you wish to give to the neo-Pagan movement?"*

Bríd: "Worship me. I am the earth, the movement. And what is the movement about?"

Pat (Forge of Fire member): *"It should be reconnecting with the earth."*

Bríd: "And who is the *earth*?"

Sharon (Forge of Fire member): *"All of us—people, animals, plants, forests, trees, the land, the water."*

Bríd: "So why are all the impurities, all the contamination going in to the water? Going into the earth?"

TG: *"Because of people's ignorance."*

Bríd: "What will you do? What will go into your books? What will be read? What will be learned? Theory! Theory! Theory! Who cares? What is your book made out of? What?"

TG: *"Trees."*

Bríd: "Trees! You are raping me! How will you survive? How will you survive?"

TG: *"By healing the land and caring for our environment. By changing—starting with ourselves."*

Bríd: "Yes, that is what you can do. What else?"

Pat: *"By putting your message in the book for everyone to read."*

TG: *"Decorate you, restoring beauty to the land."*

Bríd: "Yes. Beauty is in clean water. And clean air. And clean soil. Not chemicals, not pollution, and poison. Because all that is ME that is being poisoned. All that is me: animals, trees."

Coven: *"Thank you, Bríd."*

TG: *"Is there anything else you wish to say tonight?"*

Bríd: "Everything is changing. Even my seasons are changing. Everything is being destroyed. It very much saddens me."

TG: *"There are people who care and who are fighting for those positive changes."*

Bríd: "More should fight. Words are not fighting. Actions and deeds are what matters.

What do you have for me?"

Pat: *"Cake and wine."*

Bríd: "Very good. Remember, no words—actions and deeds."

TG: "That is what we will bring you. Thank you for your visit and your messages, Bríd!"

What comes through clearly in this message is Bríd's passion for the world. She has not come through just to give a prophecy but to inspire those present to act on her behalf. You would, of course, expect no less from an Irish goddess of the land.

Freya

Often portrayed as a deity of love and sexuality, or of the Valkyrie goddess who takes the slain to Valhalla, these descriptions really do not do justice to the complexity of this goddess. Of all the Northern goddesses, she is the most multifaceted, which has earned her the title "the Isis of the North." Her name means "Mistress" or "Lady," titles rather than names. She was not originally a member of the Norse pantheon, the Asatru, but of a people known in the Eddas (the stories of the Northern peoples) as the Vanir.

Freya in her true, original form is the mistress of magic—Freya-Vanadis, the mistress of the Vanir goddesses and the Lady of Seidr, the dark feminine magic of the Northern peoples, which in medieval times became known as witchcraft. Although portrayed in later Norse myths as a fickle love goddess, she is more correctly a goddess of sacred sexuality. Her followers practise ecstatic magical rites akin to Vedic tantra. Accompanied by her two cats, and wearing her feathered cloak, she is able to travel between the worlds, pointing to her ancient roots as a goddess of shamanic practise. It is for this reason that as Freya-Vanadis, she is also the Lady of Spaework, of seership, a natural development of shamanism. She is therefore patron goddess of the *vala* or *volva*, the oracles and seers of northern Europe, so it is not surprising, then, that this is the form she takes when she possesses Sagadis Duncansdottir.

Sagadis (Melodi Grundy) was born in Long Beach, California, and grew up on the rural central coast before moving to Mississippi, where she got a BA in anthropology and history from the University of Southern Mississippi. She has been involved with various Pagan and alternative spiritual practices since the early 1980s; she studied Wicca while living in Colorado, and later joined The Fellowship of the Spiral Path and the Hrafnir Asatru Kindred in the early 1990s, in Northern California. She trained as a Norse trance seeress with Diana L. Paxson and was one of the early Hrafnir "high seat" spae-trance workers. She is legal clergy in the Fellowship of the Spiral Path and a God-woman (priestess) in the Troth Asatru Clergy Program. She has primarily concentrated on a Norse/Heathen path since marrying Kveldulfr Gundarsson (Stephan Grundy) and followed him on his adventures in England, Sweden, and Ireland for the last twenty years. The recording of this seith took place in Ireland and was recorded on the February 28, 2015. Skirnir Freyasson acted as the trance guide for this session. A member of the group sung Sagadis down into Helheim (the underworld) using the song used by

Hrafnir (see page 42). After the first three questions were asked, members of the circle were able to ask personal questions, which have been excluded for reasons of privacy.

Freya: "Who calls me?"

TG: *"I call you my Lady, Skirnir your priest."*

Freya: "I recognize thee."

TG: *"I recognize you, my Lady. I ask you now if you will answer three questions?"*

Freya: "Yes, I will."

TG: *"The first question if not for me, for I know who you are and I recognize you, my Lady. This question is for others. And I ask the simple question: who are you?"*

Freya: "I am the Lady. I am the Lady who was, who is, and who shall be. I am the one who dances, I am the one who sings, I am the one who brings joy, but I can also bring wrath. Call me in joy and hear me laugh, but take me not seriously and you will regret it. I am Freya, the Lady."

TG: *"My Lady, I thank you, the question was well answered. I now ask you a second question. What advice do you give to the neo-Pagan community; what guidance can you give them?"*

Freya: "There has been a great scattering. I cannot speak for all, but I can speak for those who are mine. And I wish for them . . . I wish them to seek me more in all of my aspects. I am one, but I am also many. There is more to me than simply a necklace or a shape, or the joys of the body. I wish for everyone to truly know me and my brother and all of thy kin. We have been nearly forgotten. You have already lost my name; I wish you to find it. But no, I will not speak it—you must find it! Seek and it will come, as will my other aspects, some of which you will find great pleasure in; others you will find disturbing. My magic must also be explored; my knowledge and wisdom must be shared, and freedom. Freedom especially for both men and women, but especially for women must be respected, and it must learned what freedom actually is. Do not . . . do not take on chains. Do not allow those around you to bind you further with chains. See me for who I really am and my brother for who he truly is. That is what I have to say."

TG: *"Thank you, my Lady, the question was well answered. The last thing I ask of you is if there is anything else you wish to say? Anything you feel that needs to be said?"*

Freya: "There is a day coming . . . it is not the end, but it is a time period that will be difficult. My brother, you see, is angry. I am not sure why; he does not confide everything in me. But I have seen great stirrings and great strife, as well as great joy. Many, many are coming back to the old ways, but they are confused in some ways, as well. It is easy for mortals to become confused. But you must not let this confusion blind you to what is coming, and you must be careful of others. Walk with them, who will walk with you in respect, but it does no good to walk with those who would disdain you. Join where you can because there is power in kindred. There is power in the community. There is power when we are together, but not even this shall be totally enough for what is to come. But be brave, be aware and meet your wyrd because surely it will come anyway. But that which comes, is what is, and that which will be is what will be at the end. As I have said, you will remember."

TG: *"Thank you my Lady for those words of wisdom. This work is done and I ask you now if you will take personal questions."*

Sagadis interpreted Freya's last statement after the she listened to the recording. She had no memory of Freya's possession, which is not unusual, but she believes that Freya's warning about her brother is about a plague or disease, something which she has experienced before. Her advice is to cooperate with those you trust and respect. These sort of warnings are not unusual in trance-prophecy, as we discuss in chapter 5.

Hekate

Hekate is a complex goddess with a long history, having been adopted by multiple cultures over the centuries. She is referred to as the goddess of ancient Colchis (550–164 BCE) in the classic poem "Argonautica (Jason and the Golden Fleece)."[2] She was later absorbed into Diva Triformis with the goddess Luna and Persephone, and eventually as that triple-form goddess made her way to ancient Rome as Diane Triformis (Diane/Selene, Proserpina/Persephone, and Hekate). The modern concept of the Wiccan Triple Goddess, in fact, derives from this later Roman evolution of Hekate. This has resulted in the modern Hekate manifesting in contemporary gothic garb on occasion, as the younger Proserpina/Persephone Maiden rather than the Wiccan Crone figure. Because of this merging of both older and younger aspects, there is no doubt in anyone's mind who has experienced her that she is the personification of Wisdom; she encourages us to explore all aspects of our self, including our darker aspects, in search of wisdom. She truly is the goddess who carries the torches in her hands encouraging us to explore ourselves. It is for this reason that she seems, in our experience, to have taken on the role as the goddess of modern trance-prophecy practise.

This trance-prophecy session was recorded on July 13, 2013 in Indianapolis, Indiana (USA). Tamrha Richardson acted as seer for this invocation of Hekate, with one of her group members, Rebekah, acting as trance guide. Tamrha notes: "I got in trouble in the beginning for not having a chant offering for her. Nice move right? Ugh. We did do it when she wouldn't come to the gate, and (when) I knew she wanted the chant that I thought we didn't need. At first, I got reprimanded." It's important to realize that like orishas and loa, Western deities also like specific offerings, although they rarely refuse to make an appearance if they aren't offered.

TG: *"Thank you for coming. We appreciate it. Can you tell us who you are?"*

Hekate: "I know who you are recording this for. I am that whom you seek. The Goddess of the Crossroads, the Guardian of the Underworld, Torchbearer, World Soul. One who is so ancient that most who say to follow me have not but a clue. They like to make me a Crone, and while I don't have a problem with age and the visible signs of age, that shows wisdom, I have never been depicted as old, until recently. And I might adapt to an image such as that, but I am no hag. Now what would they like to know?"

TG: *"What future do you see, and what advice do you wish to give to the neo-Pagan community as a whole?"*

Hekate: "The answer is different for every area of this movement. The different areas have different jobs and responsibilities. Some are miles ahead of others; some are just beginning to find their roots, to hear the calling, to find their purpose. There is a purity in those new groups, in those new sparks of this movement. And there is a strength in the ones that are established, but all need to be leery, all need to be careful not to be caught up in their own egos, not to argue over petty differences or different ways of doing things. If we wanted you all the same, you would be. You are not. So there is no one message.

More established groups need to look out into their communities and serve their communities, be it Pagan, secular, or whatever other spiritualties under the sun, but also to not forget to take care of their own as well. New groups need to come together to build structure, because that is what it's all about—it's about structure. You are going to need that structure. For this movement is not going away, even when times seem dark, it is this movement is what will get the people through.

It's a time of change for the Pagan community. Look to your gods. Do not look to your egos. It's a give-and-take relationship. Serve your gods and your gods will serve you, sometimes in ways you don't particularly appreciate, but it's not all about the cozy, what you want. Sometimes what you need is not what you want, and those that hear this message will know exactly what I am talking about. What else?"

TG: "*What else would you like to share?*"

Hekate: "You are skating on thin, thin ice. Not you particularly dear, but you (the human race) as a whole. Whether that ice cracks is up to you. This planet will survive; it always does. The gods will survive; we always do. Some of us may sleep while some of us are more active. The world is on thin ice, but all hope is not lost. I feel the ice strengthening. The not too past, the not too . . . oh the words . . . the ice was once thinner. But as you all start to wake up . . . wake up to this change of paradigm, this change of humanity . . . as the old ways go through their death throes and grasp as power, the ice thickens. Do not be afraid when it cracks; it can be repaired. It's in your hands."

TG: "*You mentioned the other gods and goddesses, that some of them sleep and some are up. Are there others that you are with more often?*"

Hekate: "I've dated others, but often times I am alone. I don't think I'm the only one as some others might, but I like to hang out on the fringe with the people who live on the fringe. I play well with others, if they play well with me. There is no time for petty bullshit. And as much as I may love my sisters and brothers who like to get caught up in drama, it's never been my bag. The Lady Isis is a dear friend. Persephone is me, and I am her. Demeter is a sister of my heart. Anubis, loyal and kind. He is a strong, strong deity for those who are strong enough to follow Him. And I recently got to know Tlachtga, who remains an ancient goddess in her own right, a goddess that not many new—or 'neo,' as you might call them—Pagans know anything about."

TG: "*Do you have anything left to say?*"

Hekate: "The next time that you do this, make sure that I have something to eat. Because I don't get to do this very often and I like to eat!"

TG: "*What is your favorite?*"

Hekate: "Chicken and chocolate!"

TG: "*Thank you for coming, in spite of the lack of food.*"

Hekate: "It's time to go."

Over the years we have developed a relationship with Hekate through our trance-prophecy work, even though she is not the principal deity that we work with. She has often appeared during workshops on trance-prophecy and the private group work we have been doing. It is our opinion that she has, in fact, taken on the principal role as a teacher of trance among neo-Pagans. It is one of the reasons she pre-empted the first question—she already knew who we were and what we wanted to be asked of her. We have had this situation repeat on several occasions during trance-prophecy sessions with several different deities.

The Morrigan
One of the principal mother goddesses of the Irish, the earliest entries about her being found in the Táin Bó Regamna and the Táin Bó Cuailnge.[3] As the goddess of war, The Morrigan is often described as hovering above the battlefield in the form of a crow. The word morrigan is often translated from the Irish as "Great Queen" or "Phantom Queen," and she is often described as being three sisters: Badh, Macha and Nemain or Anand. She is a resolute and strong goddess, and this confidence of spirit comes through in her priestesses.

Lora O'Brien is an Irish woman with a strong interest and experience in Irish history, heritage, archaeology, mythology, and pre-Christian Irish spirituality. You could call her Pagan, Witch, Druid, priestess, or shaman, and you wouldn't be wrong, although she doesn't call herself anything but bean draoí, a female user of magic. She is a guide, a teacher, and writes Irish heritage articles and books, including *Irish Witchcraft from an Irish Witch* and her latest *A Practical Guide to Irish Spirituality*, which combines her psychology studies with very accessible information and technique, to provide a clear pathway for connection to Ireland. Called to work for The Morrigan a long time ago, Lora combines her day-to-day work life, her writing and teaching, and her on the ground (and under ground!) access, to facilitate communication and authentic experience of this Irish goddess.

This session took place in February 2014 within Uaimh na gCait (the "Cave of the Cat") in Rathcrogan, County Roscommon, Ireland.* Lora travelled into the earth alone, with the questions in mind and a recording device in hand. As Lora points out: "Technology doesn't always survive the cave intact, but thankfully this time the sídhe (fairy folk) seemed to want no part in interference with the queen's message, so everything worked as it should." Unlike the previous possessions by deities, there was no trance guide involved. Instead, Lora placed herself in trance and recorded the resulting message once she had contacted The Morrigan. Lora writes that there was a period of three minutes of silence before The Morrigan spoke, and a minute after.

> "I feel the kiss of feathers.
> The brush of crow's wing – touches the sky.
> I find my way to the world – through the gateway.
> Dark in the depths of earth. I find my way.
> I push forth.
> I am birthed in mud and blood. I find my way.
> I am in your world. I find my way.

> "Who. Am I.
> I am She by brush of raven – crow in this land.
> I am She. She of the wolf. She of the eel. She of the heifer, the sacred cow.
> I am She of red. Of blood. Of battle and power and prophecy and fury.
> I am She of terror.
> I am She who finds her way – through your heart, through your head.

---

* Uaimh na gCait, also known as Oweynagat, is a subterranean passage leading to a limestone cave close to Lusk, County Roscommon. Its name, which means "the Cave of the Cat," refers to the large wild cats that Ulster champions must fight in the tale of the Bricrus Feast. It is also believed to be the birth place of The Morrigan, who is said to emerge from the cave at Samhain.

I am She who speaks – who tells the world.
I am the truth. I am the right, and the light. I am the endless
    depths of night.
I. Am. She.'

"Great Queen you have called me. I am She.
Mother you have called me. I am She.
I am the one who births.
I am the one who bleeds. And screams.
I am the one who protects. And strengthens.
I. Am. She.

"And you. You who seek for me now, in this world.
You who are disconnected – who are free of responsibility.

"You seek the power – without the pain.
You seek the knowledge – without the work.
You seek the gain – without the understanding.

"You. You who are Pagan. You who are shaman—where is your
    tribe?
Where are your people?
Where is your language and your spirit?
Where is your connection to this land?
This Ire-Land. Our Land.
Do you walk? Do you feel the Irish grass beneath your feet?
Do you speak the tongue of the ancient people?
Do you seek the knowledge that remains to us now?
For all that is left is bits and broken, is misremembered.
All that is left is unclear, uncertain.
Do you seek to put this together?
Do you seek the draoi? Do you seek the ancient knowledge, the
    spirit that remains?
And what do ya find when you do?
Who. Are. You.

"Speak your truth.
Listen. Listen to the land.
Find the questions. Find your path.

Be guided by what has gone before. The truth. The real knowl-
edge – the real power.
Find your way. Come home.
I. I am She. I who speak.
I who give you real knowledge. Real experience.
Truth – and pain.
Power.
Community. Responsibility.
I am She.
I am the queen, and I am the servant.
I give – and I expect.
If you seek me – find your way home.

"They say . . . they say (light laugh) – I sought love of an Ulster
boy.
They say I sought to give him my power, my sacred cattle.
Misremembered.
I offer help.
I take – what I need – in return.
If you give – I give.
Find me in the land.
Find me under the land.
Find me in the darkness – but – beware.
I am change. I am pain.
I am growth that pushes. That flows on waves of blood.
I am life – and death.
I am reborn.
I am She."

While some seers entered into full trance and were possessed, others
just channeled the information. The last entry is a good example of this,
where Lora O'Brien brings through The Morrigan. She speaks in prose
and rhyme, an act which is not uncommon when a seer has made a genuine connection. This made the results as powerful as any full possession.
Her replies are unique for another reason in that she is one of the few
who was brought through in her own land and inside one of her own
sacred sites. It meant that her replies were more localized and concerned
with her own people and her own land (Ireland). When it came to replies,

although there were often similarities in answers, like The Morrigan's, each was unique. What does come across is that every individual god or goddess has its own distinct personality, interests, and personal point of view. Often a sense of humor showed through, such as in the case of Hekate's passion for chocolate and cheese!* Deities are, of course, true to their own natures in how they reply to questions, but many replied with concern about the divisions of the neo-Pagan movement. Among all the gods, there was concern about the direction the Pagan movement is going, concerned that it has become egocentric, and rife with squabbling because, to quote Apollo, people are taking "the smaller streams, more easy to navigate," with the blame being clearly laid on the ego.

The most interesting replies, though, came through when the deities were asked what else they would like to say. Many, such as Bríd and Hekate gave warnings about our impact on the environment, that we were "skating on thin ice," and that unless we change our ways, we face destruction because of our own actions. It is with that thought that we conclude this book. The gods and goddesses of any culture cannot change the world around us directly. They have to work through us, through the priestesses and priests who freely give over their bodies and mouths to allow them to speak. The purpose of the oracle, seer, or the high priestess who has the moon drawn down upon herself is to serve the gods, to be the conduit for the message they give. The gods are here to guide us; which divinity it is, is really unimportant, as it is only the message that is important, not the messenger, and we ignore this message at our peril.

NOTES

1   Janet and Stewart Farrar, *The Witches' Goddess: The Feminine Principle of Divinity* (Phoenix Publishing, 1987), 33.
2   Written by Apollonius Rhodius, 3 BCE, it is the only surviving Hellenistic epic.
3   Both of these stories are found in the Ulster Cycle.

---

* While in some cases where the ego/persona is not fully repressed, aspects of the individual can come through (see page 108). We do not believe this is the case here, as we know this has occurred on several occasions in this working, including to a seer was who is vegan and has no objection or problems after eating chicken while possessed.

Appendices

Appendix 1

Leviter Veslis

[This version originates from a manuscript from Doreen Valiente via the authors.]

Listen to the words of the Great mother, who of old was also called among men Artemis, Astarte, Dione, Melusine, Aphrodite, Cerridwen, Diana, Arianrhod, Bride, and by many other names.

At mine Altars the youth of Lacedaemon in Sparta made due sacrifice.

Whenever ye have need of anything, once in the month, and better it be when the moon is full, ye shall assemble in some secret place and adore the spirit of Me who am Queen of all Witcheries and magics.

There ye shall assemble, ye who are fain to learn all sorcery, yet have not won its deepest secrets. To these will I teach things that are yet unknown.

And ye shall be free from slavery, and as a sign that ye be really free, ye shall be naked in your rites, both men and women, and ye shall dance, sing, feast, make music, and love, all in my praise.

There is a Secret Door that I have made to establish the way to taste even on earth the elixir of immortality. Say, 'Let ecstasy be mine, and joy on earth even to me, To Me,'

For I am a gracious Goddess. I give unimaginable joys on earth, certainty, not faith, while in life! And upon death, peace unutterable, rest, and ecstasy, nor do I demand aught in sacrifice.

Hear ye the words of the Star Goddess.

I love you: I yearn for you: pale or purple, veiled or voluptuous.

I who am all pleasure, and purple and drunkenness of the innermost senses, desire you. Put on the wings, arouse the coiled splendor within you, 'Come unto me.'

For I am the flame that burns in the heart of every man, and the core of every Star. Lo, thou wast with me from the beginning, for they that ever desired me shall ever attain me, even to the end of all desire

Let it be your inmost divine self who art lost in the constant rapture of infinite joy.

Let the rituals be rightly performed with joy and beauty. Remember that all acts of love and pleasure are my rituals. So let there be beauty and strength, leaping laughter, force and fire by [sic] within you.

And if thou sayest, 'I have journeyed unto thee, and it availed me not,' rather shalt thou say, 'I called upon thee, and I waited patiently, and Lo, thou wast with me from the beginning,' for they that ever desired me shall ever attain me, even to the end of all desire.

Appendix 2

The Rite of Drawing Down the Moon and The Charge of the Goddess

The high priestess stands in the "Osiris-Slain" (arms across chest) position in the north before the altar, holding scourge and athame. Coven members stand in the south facing the altar.

The high priest kneels before the high priestess and salutes her with the Fivefold Kiss. As he kisses her womb, she opens into the "Osiris-Risen" (arms open and raised) position. He says:

> Blessed be thy feet, which have brought thee in these ways (*high priest kisses right, then left foot*).
> Blessed be thy knees, that shall kneel at the sacred altar (*high priest kisses right, then left knee*].
> Blessed be thy womb, without which we would not be (*high priest kisses above pubes*).
> Blessed be thy breasts formed in beauty (*high priest kisses right, then left breast*).
> Blessed be thy lips, that shall utter the sacred names (*high priest kisses the lips of the high priestess and then rises*).

The high priest again kneels before the high priestess, who now stands in the same position but with right foot slightly forward.

The high priest now invokes the Goddess into the high priestess using the Invoking Triangle of Water: As he invokes, the high priest touches the high priestess gently with wand upon her right breast, left breast, womb, and upon the same three places again, saying:

I invoke Thee and call upon Thee,
Mighty Mother of us all (*high priest touches her right breast*),
Bringer of all fruitfulness (*high priest touches her left breast*),
By seed and root (*high priest touches her womb*)
By stem and bud (*touches her right breast*)
By leaf and flower and fruit,
By life and love (*high priest touches her womb*)
Do I invoke (*high priest raises wand*)
Thee to descend upon the body
Of this Thy servant and priestess here.
Speak with her tongue,
Touch with her hands,
Kiss with her lips,
That Thy servants may be fulfilled.

As the high priest finishes the invocation, he spreads his arms, while kneeling in adoration, and says:

Hail, Aradia! From the Amalthean Horn
Pour forth thy store of love; I lowly bend
Before thee, I adore thee to the end,
With loving sacrifice thy shrine adorn.
Thy foot is to my lip [*kiss*], my prayers upborne
Upon the rising incense smoke; then spend
Thine ancient love, O Mighty One, descend
To aid me, who without thee am forlorn.

The high priest now stands and takes a step back and puts himself into the Osiris-Slain position again. The high priestess traces an Invoking Earth Pentagram in the air before them with her athame, saying:

Of the Mother, darksome and divine,
Mine the scourge, and mine the kiss,
The five-point star of love and bliss
Here I charge you, in this sign.

The high priest opens up his arms in the Osiris-Risen position. Facing the high priestess, he commences the invocation to the Great Mother:*

* "Our version has one or two tiny differences from Doreen's (such as 'witches' for 'witcheries'), but we have let them stand, with apologies to her" (Farrar/Farrar, *A Witches' Bible*). We have also formatted this new version of The Charge in sense lines for ease of recitation.

Listen to the words of the Great Mother;
She who of old was also called among men
Artemis, Astarte, Athene, Dione, Melusine,
Aphrodite, Cerridwen, Cybele, Arianrhod, Isis,
Dana, Bride,* and by many other names.†

This is then followed by the high priestess reciting the first part of
The Charge:

Whenever ye have need of anything, once in the month,
and better it be when the moon is full,
then shall ye assemble in some secret place and adore the spirit of me,
who am Queen of all the witches.
There shall ye assemble, ye who are fain to learn all sorcery,
yet have not won its deepest secrets;
to these will I teach things that are yet unknown.
And ye shall be free from slavery;
and as a sign that ye be really free, ye shall be naked in your rites;
and ye shall dance, sing, feast, make music and love, all in my praise.
For mine is the ecstasy of the spirit, and mine also is joy on earth;
for my law is love unto all beings.
Keep pure your highest ideal; strive ever towards it;
let naught stop you or turn you aside.
For mine is the secret door which opens upon the Land of Youth,
and mine is the cup of the wine of life, and the Cauldron of Cerridwen,
which is the Holy Grail of immortality.
I am the Gracious Goddess,
who gives the gift of joy unto the heart of man.
Upon earth, I give the knowledge of the spirit eternal;
and beyond death, I give peace and freedom
and reunion with those who have gone before.

---

* "If you have a local Goddess-name, by all means add it to the list" (*A Witches' Bible*).

† Deleted from this version is a line at the end: "At her altars the youth of Lacedaemon in Sparta made due sacrifice." Janet and Stewart comment: "The sentence originated from Gardner, not Valiente. Like many covens, we omit it. The Spartan sacrifice
. . . was certainly a gruesome business . . . and out of keeping with the Charge's later
statement 'Nor do I demand aught of sacrifice.' By the way, the sentence is also inac-
curately worded; Sparta was in Lacedaemon, not Lacedaemon in Sparta" (*A Witches'
Bible*).

Nor do I demand aught in sacrifice;
for behold, I am the Mother of all living,
and my love is poured out upon the earth."

The high priest then says:

Hear ye the words of the Star Goddess;
She in the dust of whose feet are the hosts of heaven,
and whose body encircles the Universe.

The high priestess recites the final part of The Charge:

I who am the beauty of the green earth, and the white Moon among
     the stars,
and the mystery of the waters, and the desire of the heart of man,
call unto thy soul. Arise, and come unto me.
For I am the soul of nature, who gives life to the universe.
From me all things proceed, and unto me all things must return;
and before my face, beloved of Gods and of men,
let thine innermost divine self be enfolded in the rapture of the
     infinite.
Let my worship be within the heart that rejoiceth;
for behold, all acts of love and pleasure are my rituals.
And therefore let there be beauty and strength, power and compassion,
honour and humility, mirth and reverence within you.
And thou who thinkest to seek for me,
know thy seeking and yearning shall avail thee not
unless thou knowest the mystery:
that if that which thou seekest thee findest not within thee,
thou wilt never find it without thee.
For behold, I have been with thee from the beginning;
and I am that which is attained at the end of desire.

Appendix 3

Prayer to Selene: from the Papyri Graece Magicae

This invocation was first written down between the second century BCE to fifth century CE in the *Papyri Graece Magicae* (*PGM*) and is of Ptolemic (Graeco-Egyptian) origin. There is no indication of how long it predated this first record of it. It is a general prayer to Selene, a multipurpose invocation. The first modern publications of the prayer within the *PGM* occur in the nineteenth century, first in Greek (1843) and then in a Latin translation (1885). Between 1928–1931 it was published as first edition by Priesendanz and became freely available in this edition to the magical community. The latest English edition was published in 1985 by Hans Betz (University of Chicago Press) as *The Greek Magical Papyri in Translation. Including the Demotic Texts.* Several versions of this text are available on the World Wide Web.

> Come to me, O Beloved Mistress, Three-faced
> Selene; kindly hear my Sacred Chants;
> Night's Ornament, young, bringing Light to Mortals,
> O Child of Morn who ride upon the Fierce Bulls,
> O Queen who drive Your Car on Equal Course
> With Helios, who with the Triple Forms
> Of Triple Graces dance in Revel with
> The Stars. You're Justice and the Moira's Threads:
> Klotho and Lachesis and Atropos
> Three-headed, You are Persephone, Megaira,
> Allekto, Many-Formed, who arm Your Hands
> With Dreaded, Murky Lamps, who shake Your Locks

Of fearful Serpents on Your Brow, who sound
The Roar of Bulls out from Your Mouths, whose Womb
Is decked out with the Scales of Creeping Things,
With Pois'nous Rows of Serpents down the Back,
Bound down Your Backs with Horrifying Chains
Night-Crier, Bull-faced, loving Solitude,
Bull-headed, You have Eyes of Bulls, the Voice
Of Dogs; You hide Your Forms in Shanks of Lions,
Your Ankle is Wolf-shaped, Fierce Dogs are dear
To You, wherefore they call You Hekate,
Many-named, Mene, cleaving Air just like
Dart-shooter Artemis, Persephone,
Shooter of Deer, night shining, triple-sounding,
Triple-headed, triple-voiced Selene
Triple-pointed, triple-faced, triple-necked,
And Goddess of the Triple Ways, who hold
Untiring Flaming Fire in Triple Baskets,
And You who oft frequent the Triple Way
And rule the Triple Decades, unto me
Who'm calling You be gracious and with Kindness
Give Heed, You who protect the Spacious World
At night, before whom Daimons quake in Fear
And Gods Immortal tremble, Goddess who
Exalt Men, You of Many Names, who bear
Fair Offspring, Bull-eyed, Horned, Mother of Gods
And Men, and Nature, Mother of All Things,
For You frequent Olympos, and the broad
And boundless Chasm You traverse. Beginning
And End are You, and You Alone rule All.
For All Things are from You, and in You do
All Things, Eternal One, come to their End.
As Everlasting Band around Your Temples
You wear Great Kronos' Chains, unbreakable
And unremovable, and You hold in
Your Hands a Golden Scepter. Letters 'round
Your Scepter Kronos wrote Himself and gave
To You to wear that All Things stay steadfast:
Subduer and subdued, Mankind's Subduer,

And Force-subduer; Chaos, too, You rule.
Hail, Goddess, and attend Your Epithets,

I burn for You this Spice, O Child of Zeus,
Dart-shooter, Heav'nly One, Goddess of Harbors,
Who roam the Mountains, Goddess of Crossroads,
O Nether and Nocturnal, and Infernal,
Goddess of Dark, Quiet and Frightful One,
O You who have Your Meal amid the Graves,
Night, Darkness, Broad Chaos: Necessity
Hard to escape are You; You're Moira and
Erinys, Torment, Justice and Destroyer,
And You keep Kerberos in Chains, with Scales
Of Serpents are You dark, O You with Hair
Of Serpents, Serpent-girded, who drink Blood,
Who bring Death and Destruction, and who feast
On Hearts, Flesh Eater, who devour Those Dead
Untimely, and You who make Grief resound
And spread Madness, come to my Sacrifices,
And now for me do You fulfill this Matter."
  [Tr.: E. N. O'Neil]

Offering for The Rite: For doing Good, offer Storax,
Myrrh, Sage, Frankincense, a Fruit Pit. But for doing
Harm, offer Magical Material of a Dog and a Dappled Goat
(or in a similar way, of a Virgin Untimely Dead).

Protective Charm for The Rite: Take a Lodestone and on
it have carved a Three-faced Hekate. And let the Middle
Face be that of a Maiden wearing Horns, and the Left Face
that of a Dog, and the One on the Right that of a Goat.
After the Carving is done, clean with Natron and Water,
and dip in the Blood of One who has died a Violent Death.
Then make Food Offering to it and say the same Spell at
the time of the Ritual. [PGM IV.2785-2890]

Bibliography

Adler, Margot. *Drawing Down the Moon: Witches, Druids, Goddess Worshippers, and Other Pagans in American Today.* 2nd, rev. ed. Boston: Beacon Press, 1986.

Alfodi, Andreas. "Diana Nemorensis." *American Journal of Archaeology* 64, no. 2 (1960). Originally translated from the Greek by E. N. O'Neil from *The Papyri Graccae Magicae.* Published in book form by Hans Dieter Betz as *The Greek Magical Papyri in Translation.* University of Chicago, 1985.

Aristophanes. *The Clouds.* Translated by Theodor Kock. Boston: Ginn, Heath and Company, 1885.

Aune, David E. *Prophecy in Early Christianity and the Ancient Mediterranean World.* Grand Rapids, Michigan: Willam B. Eerdmans Publishing, 1983.

Aune, Michael Bjerknes, and Valerie M. DeMarinis, eds. *Religious and Social Ritual: Interdisciplinary Explorations.* Albany: State University of New York Press, 1996.

Bancroft, Mark. *The History and Psychology of Spirit Possession and Exorcism.* EnSpire Press (no longer available).

Bartlett, Sarah. *A Brief History of Angels and Demons.* London: Constable and Robinson, 2011.

Bates, Brian, *The Way of Wyrd.* London: Arrow Books, 1987.

de Villeneuve, Gabrielle-Suzanne Bardot. "Beauty and the Beast." First published 1740. English translation 1757. New York: Start Publishing LLC, 2014.

Bem, Daryl. *The Journal of Personality and Social Psychology* 100 (March 2011).

Betz, Hans. *The Greek Magical Papyri in Translation, Including the Demotic Texts.* University of Chicago Press, 1985.

Bonwick, James. *Irish Druids and Old Irish Religions.* New York: Dorset Press, 1986.

Braid, James. *The Discovery of Hypnosis: The Complete Writings of James Braid.* Edited by Donald Robertson. London: National Council of Hypnotherapy, 2008.

Bramwell, Dr. John Milne. *James Braid: His Work and Writings.* 1896.

Buckland, Raymond. *Buckland's Book of Spirit Communications.* St. Paul, MN: Llewellyn Publications, 2004.

———. *Dragons, Shamans and Spiritualists.* Buckland Books, 2007.

———. *Ouija - 'Yes! Yes!'* Fortuna, CA: Doorway Publications, 2006.

———. *The Spirit Book: The Encyclopedia of Clairvoyance, Channeling and Spirit Communication.* New York: Visible Ink Press, 2005.

———. *The Weiser Field Guide to Ghosts.* San Francisco: Red Wheel/Weiser, 2009.

Campbell, Joseph. *The Hero with a Thousand Faces.* New York: Pantheon Books, 1968.

Crowley, Aleister. *The Equinox* 3, no. 1. San Francisco: Red Wheel/Weiser, 1974, 1992.

———. *Liber XV: Ecclesiae Gnosticae Catholicae Canon Missae (The Gnostic Mass).* Berkeley, CA: Ordo Templi Orientis, 1978.

———. *Magick.* London: Routledge and Kegan Paul plc, 1986.

Crowley, Vivianne. *Wicca: The Old Religion in the New Age.* Wellingborough: Aquarian Press, 1989.

Eliade, Mircea. *Shamanism: Archaic Techniques of Ecstasy.* New Jersey: Princeton University Press, 1972.

d'Este, Sorita, ed. *Priestesses, Pythonesses, Sibyls: The Sacred Voices of Women Who Speak With and for the Gods.* London: Avalonia Press, 2008.

d'Este, Sorita, and David Rankine. *Wicca: Magickal Beginnings.* London: Avalonia Press, 2008.

Farnell, Lewis Richard. *The Cults of the Greek States*. Clarendon Press, Oxford, 1896.

Farrar, Janet, and Gavin Bone. *The Inner Mysteries*. Portland, OR: Acorn Guild Press, 2012.

Farrar, Janet and Stewart. *Eight Sabbats for Witches*. London: Robert Hale, 1981.

———. "Wicca transcriptions." Personal training notes, 1970.

———. *A Witches' Bible: The Complete Witches' Handbook*. Phoenix Publishing.

———. *The Witches' God*. London: Robert Hale, 1989.

———. *The Witches' Goddess: The Feminine Principle of Divinity*. Phoenix Publishing, 1987.

———. *The Witches' Way*. London: Robert Hale, 1984.

The Fayum Papyri. University of Michigan. Also known as the Rainer Papyri, 250 BCE, 1880 CE.

Fitch, Ed. *Magical Rites from the Crystal Well*. St. Paul, MN: Llewellyn Publications, 1984.

Geology (August 2001).

Graves, Robert. *The White Goddess*. London: Faber and Faber Limited, 1961.

Guiley, R. E. *Harper's Encyclopaedia of Mystical & Paranormal Experience*. New York: Harper Collins, 1991.

Hampden-Turner, Charles. *Gods, Voices, and the Bicarmeral Mind: The Theories of Julian Jaynes; Maps of the Mind: Charts and Concepts of the Mind and Its Labyrinths*. London: Mitchell Beazley Publishers, 1981.

Harner, Michael. *The Way of the Shaman*. New York: Harper and Row, 1980.

Heraclitus. *Fragments*. Translated by T. M. Robertson. University of Toronto Press, 1987, 1991.

Herodotus. Book I *of The Histories*. Translated by Robin Waterfield. Oxford University Press, 1998.

Heselton, Philip. *Gerald Gardner and the Cauldron of Inspiration*. Milverton, Somerset: Capall Bann Publishing, 2003.

———. *Gerald Gardner and the Witchcraft Revival*. I H O Books, 2001.

———. *Wiccan Roots: Gerald Gardner and the Modern Witchcraft Revival*. Milverton, Somerset: Capall Bann Publishing, 2000.

———. *Witchfather: A Life of Gerald Gardner*. 2 vols. Loughborough, Leicester: Thoth Publications, 2012.

Hesiod. *Works and Days*. Edited by T. A. Sinclair. New York: George Olms Verlag, 1985.

Homer. *The Odyssey*. London, England: Penguin Classics, 1991.

Horace, "Epode V: The Witch's Incantations." *The Epodes and Secular Odes of Horace*. Translated by F. Howes. Norwich, UK: Charles Muskett, Bridewell, 1841.

Hutton, Ronald. *The Triumph of the Moon*. Oxford University Press, 1999.

Joyce, Patrick Weston. Vol. 1 of *A Social History of Ancient Ireland*. University of Toronto Press, 1903.

Judith, Anodea. *The Truth About Chakras*. St. Paul, MN: Llewellyn Publications, 1994.

———. *Wheels of Life*. St. Paul, MN: Llewellyn Publications, 1994.

Kardec, Allan. *The Book on Mediums: Guide for Mediums and Invocators*. Cosimo Inc., 2007.

———. *The Spirits' Book*. New York: Cosimo Inc., 2006.

Kelly, Aidan. *Crafting the Art of Magic: A History of Modern Witchcraft: 1939–1964*. St. Paul, MN: Llewellyn Publications, 1991.

———. *The Original Gardnerian Documents of the Book of Shadows; The Bok of Ye Art Magical (BAM)*. San Francisco: Art Magickal Publications, 1993.

Knight, Gareth. *Spiritualism and Occultism*. Thoth Press, 1999.

Lamond, Frederic. *Fifty Years of Wicca*. Sutton Mallet: Green Magic, 2004.

Leadbeater, C. W. *The Chakras: A Monograph*. 8th reprint. Adyar: The Theosophical Publishing House, 1969.

Lebbon, Tim. *Mesmer*. Canton, OH: Prime Books, 2002.

Leek, Sybil. *The Complete Art of Witchcraft*. New York: Signet Books, 1971.

Leland, Charles, Godfrey. *Aradia: The Gospel of the Witches*. London: The C. W. Daniel Company, 1899, 1974.

Leonard, Todd Jay. *Talking to the Other Side: A History of Modern Spiritualism and Mediumship*. Lincoln, Nebraska: iUniverse Books, 2005.

Markale, Jean. *The Great Goddess: Reverence of the Divine Feminine from the Paleolithic to the Present*. Rochester, Vermont: Inner Traditions International, 1997.

Matheson, Richard. *What Dreams May Come*. Polygram Film Entertainment. 1988.

Moody, Dr. Raymond A. *Life after Life: Investigation of a Phenomenon - Survival of Bodily Death*. New York: Bantam Books, 1976.

———. *Reunions*. New York: Ivy Books, 1993.

Mooney, Carol M. *Hekate: Her Role and Character in Greek Literature from Before the Fifth Century*. McMaster University, 1971.

Mortensen, Karl. *A Handbook of Norse Mythology*. New York: Thomas Y. Crowell, 1913.

National Spiritualist Association of Churches, USA, "Declaration of Principles," https://www.nsac.org/principles.php (accessed May 25, 2015).

Nietzsche, Friedrich. *The Birth of Tragedy (Die Geburt der Tragödie aus dem Geiste der Musik)*. Originally published 1871. London: Dover Publications, 1995.

NightMare, M. Macha. *Pride: Honoring the Craft of Earth and Goddess*. Citadel, 2004.

Orpheus. *Orphic Hymns*. Translated by N. Athanassakis and B. M. Wolkow. Baltimore: John Hopkins University Press, 2013.

Osbourne, Carla. "A Short Detour to Delphi and the Sibyls." Chapter 6 in *The Amazon Nation*. 2000. New York: Dare 2 Dream Publishing, 2003.

Paxson, Diana. "The Return of the Volva: Recovering the Practice of Seidh." *Mountain Thunder* magazine (1993).

———. *Sex, Status and Seidr: Homosexuality and Germanic Religion*. *Idunna* magazine (1997).

———. *Trance-Portation: Learning to Navigate the Inner World*. San Francisco: Red Wheel/Weiser, 2008.

———. *The Way of the Oracle*. San Francisco: Red Wheel/Weiser, 2012.

Pearl, Johnathan L. *The Crime of Crimes: Demonology and Politics in France, 1560 to 1620.* Ontario, Canada: Wilfred Laurier University Press, 1999.

Philostorgius. *Church History 7.1c = The Passion of Artemius.*

Plaisance, Monte. *Scrolls of Manetho,* Scroll 1: 54. Sourced from Daniel Ogden's *Greek and Roman Necromancy.* Princeton, 2001.

Plutarch. Vol. 5 of *De Defecto Oraculorum.* Section 13F. Loeb Classical Library Edition, 1936.

Polona, M. M. "The Toronto Blessing." Edited by Stanley M. Burgess. *The New International Dictionary of Pentecostal and Charismatic Movements.* Grand Rapids, Michigan, USA.

Sturluson, Snorri. *The Prose Edda.* Translated by Arthur Brodeur. University of California, 1914.

Regardie, Israel. *The Middle Pillar.* Chicago: Aries Press, 1945.

Roosevelt, Franklin D. from his first Inaugural Address, 1932.

Roth, Gabrielle. *Connections: The Five Threads of Intuitive Wisdom.* Novato, CA: New World Library, 2004.

———. *Sweat Your Prayers: Movement As a Spiritual Practise.* Tarcher and Putnam/Penguin Books, 1997.

Roth, Gabrielle, with John Loudon. *Maps to Ecstasy: Teachings of an Urban Shaman.* Novato CA: New World Library, 1989.

Sadar, Hamid. Asian Art. http://www.asianart.com/articles/hamid/index.html.

Sanders, Maxine. *Firechild: The Life and Magic of Maxine Sanders.* Mandrake, Oxford, 2007.

Sanderson, Dr. Alan. "Spirit Attachment and Human Health," Spirit Release Foundation, 2010. http://www.spiritrelease.com/cases/review_spiritrelease.htm.

———. *Spirit Releasement Therapy.* 1992.

St. Clair, David. *David St. Clair's Lessons in Instant ESP.* New York: Signet Books, 1986.

Strabo. *Geography.* Riverside, California: Ulan Press, 2012.

Starhawk. *The Spiral Dance: A Rebirth of the Ancient Religion of the Great Goddess.* New York, London: Harper and Row, 1979.

————. *Dreaming the Dark: Magic, Sex and Politics*. London: Mandala, 1982.

————. *Truth or Dare: Encounters with Power, Authority, and Mystery*. New York: Harper Collins, 1989.

Stewart, R. J. *The Underworld Initiation*. Wellingborough, UK: The Aquarian Press, 1985. Mercury Press, 1990.

Stortz, Martha Ellen. *Ritual Power, Ritual Authority*. State University of New York Press, 1996.

The Táin (The Táin Bó Cuailnge). Translated by Thomas Kinsella. Oxford University Press, 1960.

The Táin Bó Regamna. Author unknown. From a corpus of electronic texts, http://www.ucc.ie/celt/online/G301005/.

Temple, Robert. *Netherworld: Discovering the Oracle of the Dead*. London: Century/Random House, 2001.

Tillyard, Eustace Mandevile Wetenhall. "A Cybele Altar in London." *Journal of Roman Studies*, 1918.

Valiente, Doreen. *An ABC of Witchcraft, Past and Present*. London: Robert Hale, 1973.

————. *The Rebirth of Witchcraft*. London: Robert Hale, 1989.

————. *Witchcraft for Tomorrow*. London: Robert Hale, 1978.

Virgil. *The Aeneid*. Translated by Patrick Dickinson. New York: New American Library, 1961.

Westwood, Richard. *Weaving the Web*. Birmingham, UK: Moonshine Publications, 1987.

Bell, Jesse Wicker (Lady Sheba). *Lady Sheba's Book of Shadows*. St. Paul, MN: Llewellyn, 1970.

Wilson, Colin. "A Seeker After the Truth." Chapter 1 in *The Unexplained File: Cult and Occult*. Edited by Peter Brookesmith. London: Orbis Publishing, 1985.

Witt, R. E. *Isis in the Graceo-Roman World*. London: Thames and Hudson, 1971.

Wosien, Maria-Gabriele. *Sacred Dance: Encounter with the Gods*. London: Thames and Hudson, 1986.

Recommended Reading

Bodgan, Henrik. *Western Esotericism and Rituals of Initiation*. State University of New York Press, 2008.

Davis, Andrew Jackson. *Principles of Nature, Her Divine Revelations and a Voice to Mankind*. Whitefish, Montana: Kessinger Publishing, 2010.

Dominguez, Ivo. *Spirit Speak: Knowing and Understanding Spirit Guides, Ancestors, Ghosts, Angels, and the Divine*. Wayne, NJ: New Page Books, 2008.

Ellis-Davidson, H. R. *Gods and Myths of Northern Europe*. Penguin Books, 1964.

Farrar, Janet and Stewart. *Eight Sabbats for Witches*. London: Robert Hale, 1981.

———. *Spells and How They Work*. London: Robert Hale, 1990.

———. *The Witches' God*. London: Robert Hale, 1989.

———. *The Witches' Goddess: The Feminine Principle of Divinity*. Index, WA: Phoenix Publishing, 1987.

———. *The Witches' Way*. London: Robert Hale, 1984.

Flaceliere, Robert. *Greek Oracles*. Paris: Press Universitaires de France, 1961.

Fontenrose, Joseph. *The Delphic Oracle: Its Responses and Operations*. University of California Press, 1978.

Fortune, Dion. *Spiritualism in the Light of Occult Science*. San Francisco: Red Wheel/Weiser, 2000.

———. *Through the Gates of Death*. San Francisco: Red Wheel/Weiser, 2000.

Fortune, Dion, with Gareth Knight. *Spiritualism and Occultism*. Leicestershire: Thoth Publications, 2000.

Hunter, Jennifer. *Rites of Pleasure: Sexuality in Wicca and Neopaganism*. New York: Citadel Press, 2004.

Iamblichus. *On the Mysteries of the Egyptians, Chaldeans, and Assyrians*. Edited by Thomas Taylor. London: Bertram Dobell, 1821.

———. *Theurgia, or the Egyptian Mysteries*. Edited by Alexander Wilder. Greenwich, CT: American School of Metaphysics, 1915.

Jacobi, Jolande. *The Psychology of C. G. Jung*. London: Routledge, 1962.

Jones, Evan John. *Sacred Mask, Sacred Dance*. St. Paul, MN: Llewellyn Publications, 1997.

Jung, Carl Gustav. *Four Archetypes*. London: Routledge, 1972.

———. *The Psychology of C. G. Jung*. London: Routledge and Kegan Paul, 1962.

———. *Synchronicity: An Acausal Connecting Principle*. London: Routledge and Kegan Paul, 1955.

Levi, Peter. *Atlas of the Greek World*. Facts on File. New York: Infobase Publishing, 1983.

Niemark, Philiph, John. *The Way of the Orisa*. San Francisco: Harper-Collins, 1993.

Ogden, Daniel. *Magic, Witchcraft and Ghosts in the Greek and Roman Worlds*. Oxford University Press, 2002.

Paglia, Camille. *Sexual Personae*. Yale University Press, 1990.

Powell, A. E. *The Astral Body*. London: The Theosophical Publishing House, 1927.

———. *The Etheric Double*. London: The Theosophical Publishing House, 1925.

———. *The Mental Body*. London: The Theosophical Publishing House, 1927.

Raine, Kathleen. *Yeats the Initiate: Essays on Certain Themes in the Work of W. B. Yeats*. Maryland: Barnes and Noble, 1990.

Rawson, Philip. *Tantra: The Indian Cult of Ecstasy*. London: Thames and Hudson, 1973.

Rhodius, Apollonius. "Argonautica (Jason and the Golden Fleece)." 3 BCE.

Robertson, James. *Spiritualism*. London: L. N. Fowle and Co., 1908.

Syme, Ronald. Vol. 1 of *Tacitus*. Oxford: Clarendon Press, 1958.

Westwood, Richard. *Banging the Drum*. Birmingham, UK: Moonshine Publications, 1989.

———. *Riding the Horse*. Birmingham, UK: Moonshine Publications, 1987.

Glossary

Anemoi: Greek for "winds." Often represented as four winged men or horses. Each was ascribed a cardinal point, but were also associated with the seasons and the weather. Boreas: the northern wind and the cold winter air; Zephyrus: the west wind, bringer of spring and early summer breezes; Notos: the south wind, associated with late summer and storms; and Eurus: the west wind, associated with the autumn.

aspecting: In aspecting (also called "embodiment"), the individual takes on, or aspects or embodies, an archetype rather than actually being in contact with or possessed by a spirit or deity. The participant may enter into a light trance state, or alpha state, but rarely do they enter into full trance. This reason is the process is not about the sublimation of the ego or personality.

ba: In Egyptian religion, the human soul was believed to be made up of five parts: the *ren*, the *ba*, the *ka*, the *sheut*, and the *ib*. The *ba* was considered to be the spirit manifest in the human body. Its equivalent in the Vedic tradition would be the Akashic or Spiritual Body.

bembé: A drum circle or celebration of the spirits or orishas in Santeria. The rhythms used during the bembé are important as they are considered to be a language that allows communication with the spirits. Dance is an important part of the ritual, which often results in participants entering ecstatic states and going into trance or being 'ridden' by the orisha. *See* djembé, djembe, or jembe, and ridden.

312

channeller: A medium, or intermediary, for a spirit. One who relays a message from a spirit. *See* channeling.

channelling: Channelling is the ability to relay information from an alleged spirit source (e.g., an angel or a mythological figure such as Merlin). The New Age movement often uses this term as a replacement for the older term mediumship. There is often confusion about the actual meaning of channelling. As yet, *Merriam-Webster's Dictionary* doesn't include a definition of the term from the occult viewpoint, although there is a general meaning given: "to serve as a channeller or intermediary." As a result, channelling has come to mean anything from simply relaying a message to intermediate possession. *See* mediumship.

circadian rhythm: This is a twenty-four-hour physiological cycle that affects our waking and sleeping patterns. It affects all living organisms, as it is dictated by the daily solar cycle. Sunlight and temperature affect this rhythm.

deity assumption: Possession by a god or goddess. *See* Drawing Down the Moon.

djembé, djembe, or jembe: A goblet-shaped hardwood drum, covered in skin that is tuned by the use of rope ties. It originates in West Africa and its name translates as "everyone gather together in peace." This defines its role as an important musical and magical tool in West African-derived religio-magical practices such as Ifa and Vodoun. Each drum is believed to have its own spirit.

Drawing Down the Moon (Wiccan): Drawing Down the Moon is a form of deity , assumption in which the high priest invokes the power of the Goddess into the body of the high priestess. How this ultimately manifests varies from priestess to priestess and from occasion to occasion. At its core, Drawing Down is a specific occult method that depends heavily on the rapport of the participants, who bring through the godlike dynamics of a deep polar relationship, mediating to all men and women via the group soul/collective. *See* deity assumption.

ecstasy: A state of sudden, intense, overpowering emotion, often euphoric. An overwhelming feeling of great happiness or joyful excitement. Also, an emotional or religious frenzy or trance-like state, originally involving an experience of mystic self-transcendence.

ecstatic ritual: Ecstatic ritual induces a change in the mental state through drumming, dancing, and intoxicants. These techniques take the participant directly to the divine root of the mysteries through the ecstatic experience of trance and, in some cases, result in possession by divinity.

ecstatic states: A heightened state of consciousness brought on by communion with an entity, such as a deity, and characterized by a feeling of euphoria. A person experiencing an ecstatic state often may receive visions and relay prophecies from the deity. A person in trance may commonly enter an ecstatic state after coming out of trance. Feeling or showing ecstasy. *See* ecstasy.

embodiment: *See* aspecting.

entheogen: "A chemical substance, typically of plant origin, that is ingested to produce a nonordinary state of consciousness for religious or spiritual purposes. Origin: 1970s: from Greek, literally 'becoming the divine within'" (*Oxford Dictionaries*). "A chemical substance used in a religious, shamanic, or spiritual context" (Brazillian Archives of Biology and Technology, Jurema-Preta, 2009).

guided visualisation: A meditation technique where the imagination of the participant is evoked and guided using words and images. In trance-prophecy it is often used as a pathworking to guide the participant into their own unconscious mind to make connection with deity. *See* pathworking.

horse: Within a Vodoun ritual, it is common for a participant to become possessed by a spirit or *loa*. The participant is often referred to as a 'horse,' as they are 'ridden' (i.e., possessed) by the spirit.

houngan: Haitian Vodoun word for a priest. There are two ranks, *houngan asogwe* (high priest) and *houngan sur pwen* (junior priest). Their role is to conduct and preserve the traditions of their community, as well as maintain its connection with the ancestral spirits.

hypoglycaemia: A metabolic condition where the individual's blood sugar levels drop dangerously low. It is most common in diabetics but can also affect individuals who are hyperactive or fasting. This condition can result in confusion, dysphoria, and even unconsciousness if the individual does not have an intake of sugar or carbohydrates in some form immediately.

ka: In Egyptian religion, this is one of the five components of the soul. The *ka* is the personality of the individual, which separates from the other components of the soul at death. Its equivalent in Vedic is the mental/emotional body. See also *ba*.

ketoacidosis: Like hypoglycaemia, this condition affects diabetics but also those who actively fast for long periods. It is caused by the breakdown of muscle and fatty tissue resulting in the release of ketones (proteins) into the circulatory system. This is often accompanied by a noticeable "pear drop" smell. It is a pathological condition that can affect the pH value of the blood and, like hypoglycaemia, can cause confusion and dysphoria.

mambo: Haitian Vodoun term for a priestess. Female equivalent of a houngan.

medium: A medium is someone who interacts with spirits through a psychic ability (e.g., clairaudience, clairvoyance, or automatic writing—the unconscious ability to write while guided by a spirit). The major difference between a medium and someone who has other psychic skills is that a medium interacts directly with the spirit world, as opposed to a psychic who just uses their own gifts. For example, while a medium and a clairvoyant may appear to have the same psychic faculty, the medium is seeing what is given to them by the spirit world, while the clairvoyant is seeing directly. Being a medium requires some psychic ability, a necessity to communicate with the spirit world. But not all psychics are mediums; they may not automatically have the ability to interact with spirits. It is also important to note that a medium is not necessarily the same as someone who "channels." Spiritualist mediums are quick to point out that they do not 'channel,' but rather act as a medium, a vessel for the spirit world (normally the spirit of a deceased person). By definition this implies that they are filled with the spirit that is communicating through them—an act of positive possession. In this respect, there is little difference between the modern medium and the oracular sibyl.

mediumship: The practise of relaying message from the spirits of the deceased while in a trance state.

oracle: Initially, the oracles were simple village people, prophesying for the tribe by communicating with the ancestors, the spirits of the dead, and with the many spirits of nature. As the belief in the classical gods and goddesses developed, the oracles began to communicate with these "greater spirits" and convey their messages and their will to the people. The prophets passed their techniques down to their students, and news spread of their abilities far and wide. Soon they were not just divining for their people, but also for visitors and foreign dignitaries. The time of the great oracles had been born, and what was once a simple village became a thriving temple of stone dedicated to the god or goddess of the oracle. The Oracle at Delphi remains one of the most famous and written about of the ten oracles in Greece and the ancient world.

pathworking: Guided meditation or visualisation exercises, such as the Underworld Descent Technique (see page 176).

possession: The idea that a spirit or deity can take control of our bodies and our minds. Historically, this was always done with express permission of the individual, and always had a positive effect on their well-being. The term 'possession' in its modern context is, therefore, a very misleading one, as there is, in fact, no ownership of the host's body, which remains their spiritual property. The spirit is only temporarily in control, and (except in extraordinary circumstances) possession only occurs with the express permission of the host. It is important to point out that the level of possession may also differ from individual to individual in any form of oracular or ecstatic spiritual work. Dependent, of course, on the level of their training and experience, it is quite common for aspects of a seer's personality to sometimes filter through into that of the deity if the seer's ego/persona is not fully repressed or if proper chakra alignments do not take place. Throughout history, people have been temporarily possessed by divine spirits who have not only entered their physical bodies but also have inspired them to commit great deeds.

prophecy (n): A prediction made by a spirit, seer, or oracle while in a trance or ecstatic state.

prophesy (v): "To utter by or as if by divine inspiration," "to speak as if divinely inspired," "to make a prediction" (*Merriam-Webster's Dictionary*).

qlipoth, qlipotic: A term found in Caballa. The meaning in Hebrew is "peels," "shells," or "husks." They represent the reverse or impure forces to those found on the Holy Sephirot.

ridden: The state of being possessed by one of the ancestral deity-spirits, or loa, as at a Vodoun ritual. *See also* horse.

seer: One who practices trance-prophecy, a role carried out by a person who is capable of bringing messages across from the divine, manifest as a spirit, a god or goddess, or even in the form of abstract images. They are literally the see–er. The sibyl, the pythoness, the vala, the high priestess, the medium, the channeller—these are different cultural terms for the same or similar role.

seership: The practice of trance-prophecy.

seidr: *Seidr* (Norse/Germanic) refers not just to trance but also to Northern European witchcraft, as well as sex magic, both being considered in the later patriarchal culture as being a form of negative magic. For this reason, modern practitioners distinguish between seidr as a whole and the trance-prophecy aspect, which they refer to as *spaework*, or *oracular seidh* [*seith*], which survived as the only accepted aspect of the seidr tradition well into the eleventh century. Seidr is done in community, with everyone around listening, thus making iterations subject to various interpretations.

seith: (Anglo-Saxon). *See* seidr.

trance: In simple terms, trance is a change in consciousness, where the individual's conscious self, or persona, is sublimated for a period of time, allowing direct access to the subconscious or unconscious mind. A sleep-like altered state of consciousness, usually characterised by detachment from one's physical surroundings.

Toronto Blessing: In 1994, a new minister introduced the concept of charismatic practise to the congregation of the Toronto Airport Vineyard Church, Ontario, Canada. The minister, Randy Clark, had been inspired by a preacher who was a proponent of the "Holy Laughter" revival phenomenon. Initially members of the congregation fell on to the floor, laughing and rolling around, but it rapidly developed into something much more. Crying, roaring like animals, and "crunching" (vomiting to release tension) also began to occur. They described it as an ecstatic experience, a "manifestation of the Spirit of God." The movement quickly spread, initially into the United States, and soon into England and as far as Albania and Cambodia. The experiences of the participants also changed: the ecstatic state was supplemented by individuals entering trance states, having visions of God, Christ, saints, and angels. While many criticised the movement as spiritually dangerous, this did not stop it from growing. Attendance at churches that were part of the movement tripled and in some cases quadrupled in size. By the late 1990s, the movement began to wane, although debate about its effect on the Charismatic evangelic church is still hotly debated.

One of the main criticisms of the Toronto Blessing was that it was by its very nature an occult practise, and was in the hands of people who didn't know that what they were doing was dangerous.* On this very rare occasion, we do find ourselves agreeing with the critics of this movement. Very clearly, there were trance practises being used, either consciously or unconsciously. The descriptions of participants entering into trance are no different from what is often described during or after an ecstatic or trance-prophecy ritual. Shaking, laughing, and crying can all occur in a trance state and in the presence of a deity or spirit form. The major difference is that most adherents of modern Pagan trance-prophecy and ecstatic techniques are well aware of the need to close down and ground chakras after such states have been experienced. This is the rare occasion when a Pagan can tell a Christian not to meddle in something they don't understand!

trance guide: One, often the priest, who guides the seer while she or he is in trance.

---

* M. M. Polona, "The Toronto Blessing," Stanley M. Burgess, ed., *The New International Dictionary of Pentecostal and Charismatic Movements* (Grand Rapids, Michigan, USA), 1149–1152.

trance-prophecy: a collection of methods found in many different traditions, ancient and contemporary, which embrace trance to connect to the divine in its many forms, the purpose of which is to communicate with divinity and ask for guidance. This can take the form of simple visualisation exercises, such as pathworkings, all the way to full possession by the deity's spirit. It can also include ecstatic states on a personal level and as a group experience brought on by trance and ecstatic ritual.

ultradian rhythm: This is a physiological cycle similar to circadian rhythms, but they cycle faster, between 90 to 120 minutes, and affect us both in a waking and sleeping state. A rest phase of 15 minutes transpires within this cycle, where the individual may enter into a relaxed state.

vibes watchers: (CAW and Reclaiming) ritual guardians appointed to monitor the participants in case they get into trouble during the trance-prophecy ritual.

žaltys: Translates from Lithuanian as "grass snake." In Lithuanian folklore, it is a household spirit that brings good luck and acts as a guardian to the home. It was sacred to the solar goddess Saulė. Grass snakes were often caught and kept as pets to invoke the good luck of the žaltys into the home.